Theorizing
CRIME &
DEVIANCE

The book is dedicated to Christine, Christopher and Alexandra

Theorizing
CRIME &
DEVIANCE

A NEW PERSPECTIVE

Steve Hall

Los Angeles | London | New Delhi
Singapore | Washington DC

First published 2012

SAGE Publications Ltd
1 Oliver's Yard
55 City Road
London EC1Y 1SP

SAGE Publications Inc.
2455 Teller Road
Thousand Oaks, California 91320

SAGE Publications India Pvt Ltd
B 1/I 1 Mohan Cooperative Industrial Area
Mathura Road, Post Bag 7
New Delhi 110 044

SAGE Publications Asia-Pacific Pte Ltd
3 Church Street
#10-04 Samsung Hub
Singapore 049483

Library of Congress Control Number: 2011933875

British Library Cataloguing in Publication data

A catalogue record for this book is available from the British Library

ISBN 978-1-84860-671-5
ISBN 978-1-84860-672-2 (pbk)

Typeset by C&M Digitals (P) Ltd, Chennai, India
Printed in India by Replika Press Pvt. Ltd
Printed on paper from sustainable resources

Every civilization which disavows its barbarian potential has already capitulated to barbarism.

Slavoj Žižek

There is a god of the marketplace, Eshu; he is a trickster, all mouth and balls.

(Yoruba saying)

CONTENTS

ABOUT THE AUTHOR

Steve Hall is Professor of Criminology at Teesside University. In the 1970s he was a nomadic musician, general labourer and avid reader of anything political or philosophical. In the 1980s he worked with young offenders in the deindustrializing north-east of England, and he was active politically during the steelworks and mine closures in County Durham. In 1988 he returned to university, and after graduating began teaching, researching and publishing. He has published widely in the fields of criminology, sociology, history and radical philosophy. His recent book *Criminal Identities and Consumer Culture* (with Simon Winlow and Craig Ancrum) has been described as 'an important landmark in criminology'.

ACKNOWLEDGEMENTS

I would like to thank academic colleagues too numerous to mention who have given me conversations and support during a time when ideas are being replaced by impacts and respect by citation statistics, especially Robert Reiner, Ronnie Lippens, Colin Webster, Colin Sumner, Steve Taylor and Pat Carlen. Thanks to Bob Lilly and Elliott Currie for support over the pond and to Jeff Ferrell for the transatlantic duel, which I think he might have won, but who am I to judge? Thanks also to John Lea for pointing out a potentially embarrassing statistical howler. Very special thanks must go to Mike Randall and Simon Winlow for their invaluable friendship and collaboration over the years, and to my MA and PhD students for so many stimulating conversations, especially Mark Horsley and Kate Burdis. Thanks, too, to all the Criminology staff at the School of Social Sciences and Law at Teesside University for offering me a port in a storm. Most of all, thanks to my family, Chrissie, Chris and Alex, for putting up with me.

INTRODUCTION

1

Since the 1980s criminological theory seems to have fallen into a condition of permanent crisis, unable to offer convincing explanations of the fundamental criminological question: why individuals or corporate bodies are willing to risk the infliction of harm on others in order to further their own instrumental or expressive interests. This book is an examination of that 'aetiological crisis' (Young, 1987), but from a perspective which raises the suspicion that the crisis was not a product of the discipline's entry into an entropic phase, but, on the contrary, to a large extent wilfully self-constructed. In this period Western criminological theory seemed to shift into its own customized mode of what Slavoj Žižek (2010a and *passim*) calls *fetishistic disavowal*, no longer wanting to know what creates the conditions in which rates of harmful crime increase to elicit the seemingly inevitable punitive reaction orchestrated by neoliberal governments. So resolute was the flight from aetiology that only a small number of approved explanations were allowed to remain in place as the foundations of non-conservative criminological thought.

These approved explanations will be examined as the book's argument unfolds. It will also investigate why, in this broad and enduring act of equivocation, various schools of criminological thought have systematically deselected specific theories and concepts that are, or could be, genuinely potent in their ability to explain criminogenic conditions and subjectivities and suggest specific anti-criminogenic forms of regulation or transformation at the deep level of economic and cultural practice. The result is that criminological theory is now largely anodyne, entropic, and politically ineffective. However, after recent events such as the financial crisis and the North African revolutions, it would appear that we are now entering a difficult phase of advanced capitalism where the restrictive intellectual current that has been dominant since the 1980s is running out of momentum. Many thinkers are now coming to the understanding that the visceral subject is far more than an effect of language and discourse, that history has not ended, that the economy is without doubt a major part of the bedrock of human existence, and that politics are far from dead. Crime might have undergone a recent statistical drop in Britain and the USA, but there is little doubt that illegal markets, criminal trafficking, violence and intimidation are now normalized aspects of socio-economic activity in a socially divided and politico-economically insecure world whose subjects are increasingly drawn towards the impoverished culture of consumerism.

In this climate Reiner (2007) suggests that criminology should return to the investigation of motivation, as do Gadd and Jefferson, who argue for a new psychosocial criminology that shows 'a willingness to move beyond the rhetoric of folk devils and moral panics ... to address the question of who these folk devils really are, what they have done and why and to try to make sense of their motives' (2007: 186). This book is an attempt to construct the beginnings of what could be called a 'new' theoretical perspective, but, of course, 'new' only in the sense that the ideas it imports are reconfigured and synthesized in a marginally different way. Whether such synthesis produces originality is left to the reader to decide, but the purpose of the book is not to produce novelty, nor indeed closure, but an initial theoretical framework with at least some degree of explanatory power.

Before this attempt can be made, however, some sort of working definition of criminological theory's principal objects must be established. At a very basic level, in the Western industrialized nations upon which this book will focus, crime and social deviance are concepts used in everyday life and the social sciences to represent all social actions or utterances that transgress socially accepted behavioural norms and ethical standards. Whilst 'crime' is restricted to actions or signs that exist beyond boundaries set by law, 'social deviance' incorporates crime but also includes any legal action or sign deemed unacceptable by the social group. Sociology and criminology share a long intellectual history of dealing with the concepts of crime and social deviance; a history that, roughly speaking, moved through the layered phases of classicism, positivism/integrationism, pluralism, radicalism and postmodernism.

Before these paradigms became established, the concept tended to be wrapped up with that of sin, and was thus largely the preserve of theologians, philosophers and legal theorists. The classical phase came into being when liberal Enlightenment thinking distinguished crime fully from the broader religious concept of sin. In the eighteenth and nineteenth centuries classical liberal thought developed from this historical watershed with a burgeoning faith in a rationalized legal system constituted by the new 'like minds' of universal reason. However, perhaps in too much of a hurry to leave behind the notion of sin, it tended to conflate deviance with the legal category of crime. Thus the cultural contexts in which deviance is named were absent from these early constitutional debates on law and punishment. Enthused by an ambitious transcendental conception of reason, liberalism also placed the autonomous rational and ethical individual at the centre of its discourse; thus crime and deviance were seen as the aetiological products of the individual's failure to exercise innate powers of will, reason and morality.

In Kant's intrinsicalist and deontological reasoning the deviant individual had failed to abide by the injunction of the categorical imperative (Kant, 1998). The refusal to conform to the demands of universal Reason as institutionalized in law was a wilful and punishable rejection of a gift from God. In the consequentialist logic of the British Utilitarians, crime and deviance were the products of the innately hedonistic individual's failure to act according to rational calculations of the harmful consequences of intended actions (Bentham, 1996). The line of demarcation between deviant acts that were to be criminalized and punished and those that should elicit mere disapproval and social censure was to be established by rational calculations of harm, but the tendency to think outside of socio-economic, political and cultural contexts meant that harm was conceptualized in individualistic terms and classified by a new bourgeois social elite, whose members tended to regard themselves, rather than the whole population, as the pioneers of transcendental Reason.

However, reducing disputes that might have had their origins in historical and structural conflicts between social groups to isolated conflicts between individuals did have a pacifying effect insofar as it atomized and therefore decreased the internal social and 'tribal' conflicts that had characterized pre-modern history, although by no means did it decrease the external 'tribal' conflicts between nation-states. In a way that to some extent echoed Freud (1979), Elias (1994) saw this as part of a broad Western 'civilizing process', the definitive aspect of modernity. However, the process itself has been characterized by a paradox. Within national territories social power relations remained distinctly unequal, yet extreme forms of violence diminished only to be somehow converted into a burgeoning assortment of less violent and largely acquisitive actions, some of which were criminalized more readily than others. At the same time, relations between nations were punctuated by increasingly destructive wars. This paradox and rather interesting conversion of 'criminal energy' casts doubt on the validity of the term 'civilizing', a question that will be addressed throughout this book.

Elias's theory, conceived and written just before the Second World War, emerged from a social-scientific movement that had been developing in Europe and the USA since the nineteenth century. During this early period the problems of philosophical and legal atomism and the disappearance of socio-cultural contextualization in legal thought and practice became apparent. As the social sciences moved into the twentieth century, a range of theories proliferated in the attempt to relocate ethical, legal and psychological conceptions of crime and deviance in their social contexts. Many noteworthy social scientists, such as Durkheim (1970) and Weber (2007), became very aware of the tension between modernity's civilizing/liberating momentum and its 'anomic' and 'disenchanting' tendencies. However, despite the rapid development of social thought, the metaphysics of liberal individualism still remained dominant, which created a fault line between individualist and social theories that still exists today. Another associated fault line can be said to run through the history of the sociology of crime and deviance; that which demarcates integrationism and pluralism. The integrationist definition of deviance, based on the assumption that a society is an integrated whole, is the appearance in everyday social life of actions or signs from beyond a society's boundaries, which can disrupt the collective sense of ethics, solidarity, normality, stability and predictability that glues it together. Crime can be reduced by integrating marginal individuals into the social body, its ethical codes and its economic opportunities. The pluralist definition revolves around the idea of actions or signs that transgress the behavioural norms or ethical standards of any one of a huge diversity of legitimate cultural groups that constitute the broader social body, which is never fixed or harmonious but in constant flux. Crime can be reduced by encouraging recognition, tolerance and the political and socio-economic inclusion of marginalized groups in a society that should be both multicultural and formally equal; basically, an attempt to integrate formally equal but diverse cultural groups into society, economy and politics without insisting on integration in the sense of cultural homogenization.

The presence of a monolithic capitalist political economy, however, exposes fundamental problems in both integrationist and pluralist thought. The continuation of socio-economic inequality and both ethnic and social conflict casts doubt on the possibility of social integration under the current politico-economic regime of liberal capitalism, whose principle of formal equality has not lived up to its promise in the concrete world of everyday socio-economic relations; it has turned out to be, as Badiou (2007) reminds us, all formal liberty and equality but very little actual fraternity. Although nation-bound societies contain many different cultures and individuals, there is usually only one economic system and one closely associated governmental and legal system, which, when it comes down to politics, law and economic participation and redistribution, must cater for all in the vital dimensions of material life-support and social justice.

Cultural groups and individuals can be nominally 'recognized' and 'tolerated' in all their supposed diversity whilst simultaneously being marginalized in socio-economic reality; compulsory recognition and tolerance does not guarantee equitable economic participation and just outcomes, nor the presence of an uplifting and truthful hegemonic culture. In other words, there are inevitable clashes between the principle of cultural plurality and the unavoidable integrationist imperatives of law, political economy and hegemonic culture, especially where the politico-legal system and the mass media disproportionately represent the interests of the structural socio-economic elite. Whether the elite should be classified in class, gender or ethnic terms, and how these structural categories might intersect, is a central issue in the social sciences. The complexity of these intersections will be examined later, but for the moment suffice it to say that the legal system is in the unenviable position of arbitrating between conflicting interest-groups; in the absence of cultural consensus and socio-economic equality a society's lawmakers face extreme difficulty in reconciling individual and sociocultural conflicts in ways that satisfy everyone.

As Downes and Rock (2007) quite rightly remind us, when criminologists approach any criminological concept they immediately confront the Tower of Babel, a dizzying array of contradictory visions of individuals and the social order, with correspondingly varied definitions of crime and deviance. To many of today's social scientists, who regard integrationism as obsolete and assume a genuine pluralist democracy to be the bedrock of society and unequal social power relations to be its currently unacceptable structural condition, social deviance is regarded as an ineluctably 'contested' category. However, as we shall see in more detail later, the 'criminological question' forces a concession from pluralists. Most liberals and postmodernists agree that a core of consensual criminalized harms does exist (Henry & Milovanovic, 1996), but the demarcation line between the consensual core and the contested periphery is not drawn in a democratic manner. The powerful elite has the ability to protect its ethically questionable or harmful actions by preventing them from being shifted from the periphery to the core, or, where its sophistic arguments in the past have failed to prevent this shift, using its formidable power and influence to shield itself from the full force of the law.

A revived universalistic argument such as this is heavily dependent on broad agreement over a concept of harm as the unifying ontological category that underpins crime and deviance. The simple ethical corollary is that what is harmful to human beings and their multi-layered life-supporting environments should be criminalized. Where harm is considered to be less serious on a consensual scale, it should be subjected to initially condemnatory yet eventually restorative social pressure, or, where it is very slight, possibly ignored. Current legal systems operate on a similar scale, but their categories of harm are heavily biased, and thus any such attempt to move towards a socially reconfigured universal and scalar conception of harm opens a rather large political can of worms. From conservatism's viewpoint the fundamental category of harm can be defined in a rather straightforward manner; actions or signs that offend the individual's person and property and also the universal values of a social order led by an inspiring and beneficent elite drawn from the upper echelons of business, politics and culture, whose status in the unfolding organic hierarchy is the 'natural' product of their successful application of those values to their everyday lives. The obvious flaws in this group-narcissistic 'wonderfulness of us' model have been exposed too often to repeat here, but the intention of this book is to move on from the standard critique of conservatism to criticize left-liberalism's claim that its alternative pluralistic and individualistic model presents on a plate the only progressive move out of this ideological straightjacket towards a future realm of justice and freedom. As we shall see, liberalism's struggle for progress and social justice has been less successful than it once promised to be.

This work will claim that although some concessions to situational relativism must always be made in the practice of criminal justice, the ethical naming of crime and deviance and the establishment of the line between 'core' and 'periphery' should once more become universal ontological issues, which should be at the heart of a broad left project that has no choice but to pull itself out of the quagmire of liberal-postmodernist relativism with the intentions of forging an alternative ideology and re-inventing itself as a genuine opposition to neoliberal capitalism. Such a return to universalistic ideology must be made in the light shed by an understanding of what stands in its way over and above the traditional opposition of conservatism. At the moment the most pressing problem for the broad left is that over the past fifty years or so its intellectual discourses have been colonized and paralysed by an accumulation of left-liberalism's compromises, products of a hangover from an immediate post-war period during which the possibility of the return of brutal totalitarian states was humanity's greatest concern. The 'New Left' constituted itself negatively and guiltily in its flight from totalitarianism, subsequently losing its ability to envision a positive sense of direction and falling in with liberalism's negative 'anywhere but that' political meandering.

The sclerosis of left-liberal criminology and the degeneracy of its research programmes (D'Amico, 1989; Lakatos, 1978), which now join conservatism in the position of being no longer capable of producing useful aetiological explanations of crime that reflect the times, is part of a broader intellectual and political problem that pervades liberalism in general. Another main theme in this book is the extent to which liberalism's intellectual culture is languishing in the midst of its own reactive and pervasive 'politics of fear', which is replete with symbols of 'absolute evil' (Badiou, 2002), inversions of the pathological individual or menacing ethnic group once ideologically constructed by the racist-nationalist forces who used the authority of the state and the means of modern technology and organization to commit the industrialized genocide of specific individuals and cultural groups (Bauman, 1991). We are all aware that a complex configuration of ethnic purism, racial hatred, nationalism and extreme collective fear, generated in the midst of economic collapse or post-revolutionary tumult and paranoia, was used to construct potent ideological justifications for the Holocaust and the Gulag, probably history's greatest crimes. In a 'state of exception' created as the political solution to a perceived national emergency (Agamben, 2005), the industrialized genocide of 'impure' ethnic groups, political dissidents and the 'class enemy' was decriminalized. More Promethean violence was to follow in the Cultural Revolution in China and the 'killing fields' in Cambodia. However, the fear that racist-nationalist forces or vengeful representatives of the former subjugated class will one day return to plunge politics into an abyss of violence and terror haunts the liberal imagination to the extent that the slightest whiff of condemnation or intolerance, unless directed solely at the state or any vestigial racist-nationalist group, is vigilantly outlawed from a debate that has moved firmly in the direction of a post-political ethics of pure negativity and escapism. As Eagleton argues:

> What one might loosely call post-structuralist or postmodern ethics reflects among other things a massive failure of political nerve on the part of a European intelligentsia confronted not only with the formidable power of global corporate capitalism, but still languishing guiltily in the long shadow of the Gulag and the gas chambers. (2009: 233)

The reader will certainly not find an argument here that the broad left should become complacent about the possibility of such a return, but simply that the overextension of liberal-postmodernism's inverted politics of fear has become an intellectually repressive and corrosive ethico-political panacea. In politics it all but destroyed the left's economic bargaining position and reduced the pressure for social-democratic regulations and reforms. In intellectual life it overwhelmed all other concerns and incapacitated any possible move towards a universal ethics of the Real that could reconstitute the left in a unifying political condemnation of an uninhibited transnational elite, which continues to operate in loose association with corrupt corporate-state officials and 'glocalized' forms of criminal enterprise emerging from a global outcast class and a former industrial working class in political disarray. In the midst of these relations of corruption have arisen global networks of entrepreneurial crime that pervade the social structure and straddle the boundary between legality and illegality. Many individuals who enter criminal markets rather reluctantly – in a desperate search for income, status and identity as their socio-economic infrastructures are broken by market forces and neoliberal economic restructuring – commit only minor crimes and eschew violence. However, as this work unfolds we will see that many harmful and violent crimes are the products of a concentrated form of criminality that has become established in various crucial nodes of illegal markets, and which is energized by what we will come to understand later as capitalism's 'disavowed obscene Real' and the individual's demand for *special liberty*.

The liberal-dominated left's failure of nerve and its subsequent ideological policing could be construed as extreme short-termism. When it destroyed itself in the post-war period in a convulsion of guilt, trepidation and fragmentation it created a vacuum in which a revitalized classical-liberal right was given so much free play that it crushed traditional one-nation conservatism, socialism and social democracy alike to establish neoliberalism as the dominant force in global political economy and culture (Harvey, 2007; Žižek, 2010). Now, with minimal protection, everything possible is governed by the unforgiving cyclical logic of the capitalist market. The likelihood of a return to politically institutionalized nationalist-racism is far greater in the conditions of socio-economic collapse that can follow the worst of the capitalist market's cyclical downturns. Stabilizing measures, built into the financial system after the Second World War, have so far prevented a collapse quite as profound as that of the 1930s. However, recently there have been a couple of close calls, and whatever downturns we face in the near future will be compounded by permanent structural phenomena – jobless growth, unemployment, the global economic marginalization of youth, spatially differentiated overproduction and underproduction, the global shift of economic power towards the East, ethnic tensions and declining natural resources – looming on a horizon that appears to be moving closer every year. In other words what was once cyclical is now becoming permanent and socio-structurally bifurcated as capitalism moves towards a series of potential downturns that are not recoverable in ways that can increase the security of the vast majority of the world's population. However, the transnational business elite and their technical/administrative functionaries might, perversely, benefit and grow significantly richer and more powerful, hardening and widening already polarized social divisions. The West's inability to summon up the political energy for a significant change of course after the financial crash in 2008 was palpable. It teaches us that liberal-postmodernism's prevention of a move towards a politics energized by the universal ethical condemnation of the obscene forces that drive capitalism, and mobilized by the resolute attempt to construct an alternative ideology and subjectivity based on a different way of organizing economies, might well, in a long-term that now does not appear to be too far away, backfire badly should we encounter an abrupt worsening of underlying economic conditions. Nationalist racism thrives under the economic protectionism that the majority in many nations can come to regard with minimal persuasion as the sole available solution to extreme structural socio-economic problems.

Under such stringent short-term ideological policing, which originated in the influential exporter disciplines of philosophy and politics and eventually filtered through the wholesale outlet of sociology, the weaker importer discipline of criminology has suffered more relativization than most other social-scientific disciplines, simply because it exists at the forefront of the mechanics of ethical condemnation. Relativism does have its weak and strong variants, but some branches that have influenced criminology do incline quite sharply towards the strong version; ethno-methodologists and subculturalists would claim that meaning is purely a local achievement, and some postmodernists, including Foucauldians, would argue that the social world is little more than a loose network of discourses, which classify the world in various ways to produce diverse and conflicting 'regimes' of truth, knowledge and subjectivities. Beyond a very small core of violent harms, all these discourses produce their own shifting categories of crime and deviance; according to the relativists it's better to let these discursive subjects get on with it and adjust – and possibly fragment and localize – the criminal justice system's practices according to their diverse requests (T. Young, 1999).

As we shall see later, in the midst of this celebratory fragmentation the very principles of universal ethics and symbolic efficiency have become the villains; for Derrida there can be no enduring universal Good without the continuous inventive dissidence that will allow no order of signs to establish itself as a tradition to stabilize meaning, ethics and politics; only the constant transgression and destruction of authority is Good (Eagleton, 2009). For the new breed of liberal-postmodernist there can be no abhorrent form of marginality or transgression, and by extension the decriminalization of all such forms apart from those characterized by extreme brutality is the way simultaneously to reduce crime and challenge institutional power. However, will it do to condemn universalism, affirm relativism and then conjure up a universal category when it suits, as Henry and Milovanovic (1996) do when they dismiss the search for the 'causes of crime' as 'futile' and in almost the same breath posit a single cause of 'domination'? Is there not a vast grey area between decriminalizable transgressions and extreme brutality, and how extreme does brutality have to be before it is criminalized as a real harm? Would the guaranteed statistical drop in crime that would follow further decriminalization be accompanied by a reduction of real harm, providing of course that liberal-postmodernists could agree on what it means? Would further decriminalization reduce the continuous stream of largely unacknowledged harms inflicted by corporate institutions or individuals on their victims, who are drawn largely from the working classes?

The ontological uncertainty that is the inevitable consequence of the decline of symbolic efficiency dumps every ethical decision that exists outside the nebulous core of 'extreme brutality' at the door of the individual, who now runs the risk of stumbling into the extreme condition of solipsism, where the pressure to construct some sort of coherent self and personal ethical code in the midst of radical indeterminacy permits the individual to see itself as the almost deified centre of the universe, in command of the construction of all moral categories and actions. Here, what the cultural critic Stanley Fish (2010) calls the 'dark side of liberalism' rears its head. Self-imposed isolation causes the individual to subscribe to a stubborn independence of mind that eschews all compromise and ethical guidance, but what seems like a noble existential 'inner directedness' can, in all but the most conspicuously harmful and incriminating cases, also exempt the individual from ethical injunctions to social, economic and physical responsibility for others and their life-sustaining environments.

In other words, do the direction and momentum of liberal-postmodernism, the 'official opposition' in criminological theory, play into the hands of right-wing libertarianism, which, as we shall see later, is the cultural hallucinogenic that acts as the seedbed for criminogenic subjectivity? Redirected like this, can neoliberalized versions of Deleuze and Guattari's (1987) rhizomatic 'lines of flight' lead anywhere but to Berlin's (1969) realm of 'negative liberty', where the individual can walk away guiltlessly from all social responsibility, a perversion of the 'positive liberty' to choose from the external social world of others that to which a compromise must be made? The extremity beyond even negative liberty is Agamben's (2005) 'state of exception', where the solipsistic individual can justify any harm that is required to clear the way for the gratification of their 'stupid pleasures', anxieties and prejudices (Žižek, 2008a), a realm of what we might call 'special liberty', where the obscene Real – the combined forces of envy, greed and so on that drive capitalism's subjectivity but remain unspoken in everyday discourse – is given the longest of leashes. If indeed we are headed towards this supra-social realm, with our libertarian pioneers in the lead, the formerly social categories of crime and deviance will be increasingly subjected to the whim of each individual, with potentially chaotic consequences, because, of course, these realms don't really exist, and those who imagine themselves to be the inhabitants still share a reality with those whose lives are affected by the consequences that follow the execution of these whims. This work will offer at least some evidence and argumentation that might help to inform decisions about whether such speculation is grounded in the reality of our times.

Partly in response to some of the excesses of postmodernist sociology, the concepts of consensus and progress, and therefore the possibility of working towards universal notions of deviance and crime grounded in an ontological conception of harm, have returned to the sociological agenda. Beck's (1992) solution to the problem of harm revolved around a concept of social risk calculation, by means of which the potentially deleterious effects of human actions in advanced capitalism can be foreseen, regulated and possibly avoided or minimized. This precautionary principle, emanating from the European social-democratic mainstream, has been taken on board quite seriously by contemporary criminologists and sociologists. For instance, individuals should be aware that their desire to pursue leisure activities at night might result in encounters with the well-known relationship between alcohol and violence, but at the same time businesses and policing organizations should also be aware that their own practices can help to minimize risk. Similarly, individuals should understand that the desire to drive an attractive open-top car might increase the risk of theft, but car manufacturers and police should also shoulder some of the responsibility. Thus risk is simultaneously individual and social, which slightly extends the minimized notion of social and governmental responsibility advocated by classical liberalism and libertarianism.

However, in the hands of those criminologists who have never quite managed to extract themselves from administrative pragmatism, this position has inspired theories and practices of risk management, which could be seen as rather defeatist because by default they accept crime and deviance as inevitable risks to be managed rather than universal emergent problems to be reduced by diminishing or transforming their motivations and generative contexts. In other words, we must ask the question of whether risk theory distracts us from the deeper issue of motivations and the underlying conditions that foster them. Combined with crude anti-aetiological 'moral panic' theories and the onward march of predictable Foucauldian theories that posit most crimes as categories discursively constructed as mythical objects to justify new forms of 'governmentality', the adoption of risk theory also helps to avert our intellectual curiosity from the obscene Real.

However, the concept of risk is underpinned by the accompanying concept of harm, which, as we flounder in liberal-postmodernism's sea of relativism, at least throws us a flimsy lifeline insofar as it is more ontologically grounded than 'crime' or 'deviance', but still a broad and rather nebulous term that could cover any event ranging from a minor individual inconvenience to an illegal military invasion or a large-scale environmental catastrophe with the potential to jeopardize the lives of millions. To guide us in the consideration of our potentially harmful actions, and to prevent brutal conflict erupting in the real world between seemingly irreconcilable differences, liberal philosophers such as Levinas (1999) suggest a default ethical universalism that avoids strong relativism and solipsism by tethering ethical diversity to the injunction to construct the self in empathy with the suffering of the Other, which of course has obvious connotations for criminology. However, hidden underneath transcendental idealism's deontological angst is a tacit presupposition that in the reality of competitive socio-economic relations and practices, and under the everyday pressure of dealing with market imperatives, which either tempt or compel even the most beautiful soul to overstep its self-imposed limits, the individual should perform some sort of utilitarian harm-calculation of the other's potential suffering before any act is committed. In the hurly-burly of everyday life in the ubiquitous capitalist marketplace, where, should important things not get done, the individual or indeed the whole nation can fall through a hole in the bottom into relative poverty and insignificance, strict deontological and empathetic ambitions regularly collapse into evasive and compromised felicific calculations.

In the everyday reality of uncompromising comparative advantage, *realpolitik* and structurally imbalanced power relations, where concepts of crime and deviance are constituted and reproduced, and where perpetrators are regularly caught and punished, legitimate definitions of 'harm' are not wholly constructed by an ethics of universal empathy, but, where it really matters, by the interests of the neoliberal elite (Hillyard et al., 2004). The elite certainly sanction the suspension of empathy towards those whose harms threaten their property and the flow of their entrepreneurial activities. Wherever possible, the elite, because they believe that we are all dependent on the success of their enterprises, insist that sympathy should be extended to those amongst their own kind who perpetrate what are often officially portrayed as unintentional harms in the course of maximizing profitability; thus these 'special harms', committed by those who have granted themselves the 'special liberty' to commit them, are rarely dragged into the inner core of criminalization and punishment. The influence of the elite does seem to have a profound effect on both legal and cultural definitions of crime and deviance and their modes of punishment, and the empathetic injunction, although still active in the criminalization of traditional interpersonal harms, seems to be no match for such concentrated power in the complex realm of social harm. Punishment is also a major harm, and the authority to punish those lower down the pecking order whose interpersonal harms are often the products of abject desperation, or who lack the means and ideological capacity to shield their ruthless activities from public condemnation, provides the neoliberal elite with a circus of scapegoats to distract the public's attention.

If the neoliberal elite thrive in an environment evacuated of traditional class politics, it could be argued that Levinas contributes to this evacuation with his reintroduction of the ethical as a safe and ultimately undemanding substitute for the political (Dews, 2008; Eagleton, 2009). The same can be said for Derrida, Foucault and most other liberal-postmodernist thinkers (Žižek, 2000; 2003). In his later work Foucault (1988) provided a spiced-up alternative to Levinas's perpetually but indiscriminately bleeding heart in his more hedonistic form of the 'care of the self', but the same distaste for the political is there for all to see. One has to try very hard not to see how this flight from the political has created a space for the free operation of neoliberalism's exploitative exchange relation and socially destructive economic dynamism, which create the fractious and unstable underlying conditions under which harms ranging from chronic structural unemployment to fraud and violence are more likely to occur, whether they are criminalized or not. It also expands opportunities for the 'special liberty' of the narcissistic subjectivity at neoliberalism's helm, which operates in different forms throughout the social structure (Hall et al., 2008). Neither liberal-postmodernism nor risk theory can deal with the ontology or the politics of social harm. Thus, it is unsurprising that in today's volatile economic climate where objective fears and harms multiply we should see the rejection of liberal-postmodernism, a growing critique of risk theory and the return of critical theory at the cutting edge of philosophy and politics (Douzinas & Žižek, 2010).

After the infamous Sokal affair, which demonstrated the fraudulence and vacuity at the heart of postmodernist thinking (Sokal & Bricmont, 1998), the term postmodernism has almost dropped out of circulation. After the Credit Crunch, the hope that major risks could be regulated and social harms avoided within the parameters of current political arrangements took a thumping body-blow. Over the past twenty years or so selected ideas from classical thinkers such as Hegel, Marx, Adorno and Lacan have been returning. In the hybridized classical thought of the Frankfurt School, human freedom is not a product of will, choice, rights, rational calculation or the unrelenting theatre of minor transgressions, but possible only in a social totality that nurtures it. History is not taking us to the realm of freedom with its own forward movement of the Hegelian Spirit. It is a struggle, as Marx and Freud claimed, for the difficult combination of self-realization and community against the forces of domination and narcissism. This leaves us with a fundamental problem. Are the forces of domination and narcissism inscribed and reproduced in systemic social institutions, social relations and cultural currents, or, at bottom, are they the products of the agency of ruthless individuals? When Hume (1967) complained about the state, the problem was, in a sense that presaged Agamben (2005) and Žižek (2000), the extent of its ability to act as a collection of institutions that allowed privileged individuals to maintain themselves in a position of unrestrained freedom; of interests, thought, choice, action, passion, prejudice and hate. The modern state has acted as a vehicle for the 'special liberty' of the bourgeois elite since its wellspring in Renaissance Italy (Hall & Winlow, 2003); nobody had more executive freedom than the Feudal aristocracy before them, or the Nazi or Soviet political elite, but it was secured by deception and the subjugation and exploitation of others (Žižek, 2008a). This 'special liberty' is beyond even the social irresponsibility of Berlin's 'negative liberty' to what we might call multi-dimensional executive hedonism, the free play of drive and desire in a supra-social realm established by exploitation, reproduced by money-power and protected by the bourgeois state and the secret codes of the international banking system. Whether the liberal left like it or not, this is a realm of *criminal sovereignty*, what the dream of freedom has come to mean for a large number of aspiring individuals recruited from all locations in the social structure by neoliberalism's libertarian ideology and mass-mediated culture. In reality few achieve it, but it energizes many.

Poised in opposition to this is the idea that ultimate freedom is not to be attained by way of existential choice, self-construction and permanent dissidence – which after a while becomes compulsory, predictable and therefore incorporable and capable of being pre-emptively manufactured (Frank, 1997; Hall et al., 2008) – but the ability to move beyond Berlin's preferred 'positive liberty' of choosing one's own ethical master, but away from negative liberty and special liberty in the opposite direction to rediscover a politicized landscape on which an informed, unaffected and democratically organized majority bestow upon themselves the authority to change the coordinates and conditions of existence in which they live. The main intention of this book is, following recent developments in Continental philosophy, to persuade the reader that we cannot separate today's forms of aspirant subjective freedom from the socio-economic totality, its relations of domination, its perverted variant of liberty and the willingness of prominent subjects to do harm to others to further their own interests. Following this philosophical revival, the principle of universalist ethics and politics should find its way into criminological theory, which, whilst avoiding a return to obsolete forms of integrationism, can make way for these intellectual developments with a firm rejection of liberal-postmodernism and risk theory.

However, if the argument that follows in support of this claim is to make any sense we must settle on a clear definition of harm. The new movement of zemiology aspires to displace legal conceptions of crime and cultural conceptions of deviance with the overarching concept of harm (Hillyard et al., 2004). The meaning of this term relates directly, through exploitation and irresponsibility towards the fate of others and their environments, to practices of domination in social, economic, cultural and technological practices, all of which leave some others in conditions worse than those in which they are found. Harm can be physical, social, psychological or environmental, and examples can include everything from street-crime and domestic violence to irresponsibly sold endowment mortgages and the negligent practices that allow deaths at work to occur or hospital super-bugs to thrive (ibid.). On this ontological basis, zemiology's ambition is to move away from narrow legalistic definitions of 'crime' because the diverse harms experienced by individuals across their life-courses are unevenly and ideologically criminalized. The legal system to which administrative criminology is a servitor brackets off many harms whilst criminalizing those that offend the prevailing ideology and cultural values, which are prone to giving maximum leeway to both corporate and individual entrepreneurs.

Zemiology's broad concept of harm was subjected to a predictable critique from the liberal left. Ericson (2006), for instance, argued that the inclusion of more 'harms' in the legal remit would simply expand the role of the criminal justice system and the scope of 'governmentality' rather than bring the pressure of social movements to bear on underlying political, moral, social and economic structures. Is this a valid concern, or is it simply the liberal left's mistrust of collective authority and restored symbolic efficiency knee-jerking into action? The continuing power of neoliberalism and its transnational corporations, and indeed the hapless stumble into the recent financial crisis, military interventions and austerity cuts that will further disrupt the already broken communities of the politically disunited working class, tend to suggest that, so far at least, the sum total of the pressure that social movements have brought to bear on deep political and socio-economic processes, and the concentrated power that presides over them, doesn't amount to much. Pressure groups such as 38 Degrees can cause British governments to think twice about peripheral policies, but such civil protest did not prevent Murdoch's monopolistic takeover of satellite TV – in fact it took a national scandal, a public inquiry, legal action and a share buyback to put even a dent in his transnational corporate juggernaut – or the austerity cuts, and nothing can touch the City of London and its power to make vitally important decisions about the global distribution of investment capital. These exercises of politico-economic power have caused and will continue to cause a multitude of harms in various dimensions. Perhaps the embrace of harm might allow criminology to shift its gaze onto more appropriate targets, restore some of the ontological cohesion around 'core harms' that has been skewed and twisted out of shape by conservatism and all but dissolved to a miniscule kernel by liberal-postmodernism, and even provide a modest contribution to the restoration of collective politics with the legislative authority to actually have some real effects on the system's remorseless 'deep logic'.

The redefinition of harm that should be addressed by the criminal justice system and, more importantly, by the political forces of change, is quite an exciting prospect, which would certainly prevent zemiology from collapsing into the standard utilitarian harm-prevention discourse that underpins risk theory and risk-management. The achievement of a workable degree of ontological and ethical cohesion from the diverse harms that can occur in the physical, financial/economic, socio-cultural, emotional and psychological realms requires persistent, inclusive, transparent and reflexive discussion, but it also needs some sort of initial grounding as a platform on which the discussions can take place. For Yar (2012), the current harms delineated by zemiologists remain heterogeneous and rather disconnected because the specificity of a founding ethical concept has not been achieved. He suggests that we ground harm in Axel Honneth's (1996) revival of Hegelian recognition, immanent in Hegel's famous theory of the master-slave relation; subjects and their identities are not entirely autonomous but always socially interdependent, thus the dominant are always reliant on the recognition of the subjugated, which compromises the master's autonomy and dominance. This ineluctable need for recognition is that which prevents the master, or what the master represents, from achieving 'special liberty' by means of the total subjugation of the slaves. The protection of social recognition is therefore essential as an initial step in exploiting the weakness of the dominant and making the subjugated aware of this weakness as their strength, thus providing initial impetus to the political project of *structurally* emancipating the subjugated. As Yar puts it:

> The theory of recognition can ground a theory of social harms, firstly, because it seeks to establish at a fundamental anthropological level the 'basic needs' that comprise the conditions of human integrity and well-being (what Aristotelians call 'flourishing'). The theory, as already noted, identifies a differentiated order of such needs through the categories of 'love', 'rights' and 'esteem' (Honneth, 1996: 131–9) … [A]ctions such as inter-personal physical, sexual and emotional violence within the family acquire their specifically *harmful* character because they violate the necessary conditions for a person to establish basic self-confidence through the experience of love. Public (including state sanctioned) practices of torture and abuse, theft and appropriation, amounts to a denial of those rights that meet the need for dignity and equality amongst others as citizens. Practices such as market discrimination or symbolic denigration on the basis of gender, ethnicity, sexual orientation and suchlike are properly harms in that they deny those subject to them the experience of self-esteem or recognition of the distinctive worth of their identities and ways of life. Thus for each of the many forms of harm that may be adduced as social problems, we find a corresponding basis in the refusal of that recognition which is the basis of human self-realisation. (Yar, 2012)

So far so good; the central problem is the refusal of social recognition in the denial of love, rights and esteem, which clears a huge space for the practice and justification of the full spectrum of harms. Will the restoration of recognition, as Honneth suggests, translate into social solidarity and progressive political change after its mediation through legal rights? Doubtless it would, but Honneth's theory, perhaps too faithful to a Hegelian conception of social relations put forward in a superseded era, ignores the severed social class relation in neoliberal capitalism. In an economically grounded social relation the master needed his slaves, but today's capitalists, benefiting from advanced technology, the mobility of capital and the precedence of finance capital, no longer need labour – at least not in the numbers and the grounded communities it once did – and the assumption that a democracy that retains political links between the classes still exists in anything other than a tokenistic form is an overestimation of the social functionality of the current democratic form. In the advanced capitalist era the major obstacle to the restoration of recognition is the masters' ability to extract themselves from any social relation and reject entirely the slave's judgement, replacing it with narcissistic self-affirmation. The masters have escaped responsibility to the extent that they have reached a position beyond even their traditional need to coerce the slaves into respecting them, which Kojève (1969) saw in Hegelian thought as the root of the master's tragedy and the slaves' resentment and latent power. Self-affirmation becomes one amongst the neoliberal elite's 'special liberties' – more powerful than most because it can be justified by performative market logic – and thus they elevate themselves in a historically unprecedented position where they alone have the right to grant recognition, which severs the social relation and suspends dialectical movement.

Until the business class can be moved to a position where they are forced to seek legitimizing rights from the majority before they embark on their potentially disruptive and harmful socio-economic undertakings, and the majority are restored to a position where what they say must be acknowledged by the elite, the mutual recognition that Honneth and Yar seek cannot be realized. Both thinkers prematurely assume an extant democracy and socio-economic interdependency in a neoliberal world that is rapidly assuming the shape of a global plutocracy, whose plutocrats are far less dependent on labour – and thus also less dependent on their legitimizing recognition – than they used to be in the era of high industrialism. Making even a first move towards mutuality requires a pre-emptive political move that shifts power and authority to an ideologically unaffected and fully informed majority who can grant conditional rights and legitimation on their own terms. It is only one step beyond this to a position where the majority can refuse to grant all rights and legitimation, a structural refusal that Žižek (2008a) suggests is the first step towards systemic social change.

The current return in radical philosophy to politics, ideology and subjectivity is an attempt to envision a way to construct deep democratic freedom and equality, a workable form of which Honneth seems to think already exists. Criminological theory must work towards an ontological conception of harm, but one that acknowledges not the ideal but the current real condition of ethics, socio-economic relations, ideology and subjectivity. In all such fields, neoliberalism won a resounding victory in the 1980s, which means that we have very little to work with and everything to work towards. The elite's position is not impregnable – it is never impregnable – but it has elevated itself to a protected realm of special liberty, of vast global power and influence so well insulated from responsibility to any specific territorial population that it no longer requires the affirmation of the subjugated. This situation, as we shall see, is cultivating types of dominant and domineering subjectivity throughout the social order, which are hostile to Honneth's desire for systemically active forms of mutual recognition, rights, esteem and love. It is the nature of this harmful subjectivity and its constitutive and reproductive contexts that criminological theory must drag itself out of its fearful shell to investigate; a subject motivated to inflict various degrees and forms of harm on others whenever it is deemed necessary to further the interests of the self.

This book covers a lot of ground, but a lot of ground needs to be covered to draw from a variety of fields in an effort to make a first step in this direction. It is organized as follows. Chapters 2 and 3 will explore the major patterns of practicing harm and its criminalization across the history of capitalism in England as they have evolved and diffused across the globe in the current neoliberal era, a shift from the *somewhere* of violent brigandage and the acquisition of land and treasure, through the *elsewhere* of sublimated social competition in the global economy to the *nowhere* of new criminal markets and money-hoarding in the orbital financial economy. On the way, we will ask why important dualistic theorists have been rejected as useful providers of explanations for these criminological patterns. Chapters 4, 5 and 6 will explore the liberal narrative that has filtered through sociology to dominate the approved canon of non-conservative criminological theories, and assess what appears to be the aetiological failure of this canon and the drift into degenerate research programmes. Chapters 7, 8 and 9 present the beginnings of a newly synthesized theoretical approach to crime and harm, using a combination of revised dialectical theory, transcendental materialist philosophy and a dualistic theory of historical process called *pseudo-pacification*. The Conclusion will simply sum up the argument and emphasize the vital need for new theories and political renewal in a neoliberal age creating unprecedented forms of social division and anti-social subjectivity.

HISTORICAL PATTERNS OF CRIME IN ENGLAND 2

If the motivation to misrecognize and do harm to others in the interests of the self is to be established as a basic ontological principle at the root of a criminological metatheory, it's essential to have at least a rough idea of how human beings have practiced this type of harm across time and space. A cross-cultural world history of harm in all its practical and symbolic variants is far beyond the scope of any single book, but because one of the vital principles behind the perspective this work presents is *diffusion*, it's important to pinpoint a specific shift in the practice of harm that occurred early in the modern history of England, which was to become the world's first fully industrialized capitalist nation and later export its business practices and mentalities worldwide. The purpose of this chapter is simply to provide some details and initial analyses, which together will constitute some sort of empirical backbone for the theory that follows.

After the Norman Conquest, righteousness and justice were established by might; victory in war and the ability to maintain some semblance of security were the main legitimizing factors. Throughout the twelfth and thirteenth centuries, a period in which the violent governance of the Norman rulers had failed to restore order, gangs of brigands periodically exercised control over whole towns and rural areas, a practice that continued in remote northern areas well into the sixteenth century. Gang rule was not simply about power and domination but also practical economic concerns, such as monopolizing import and export nodes, confiscating gold and silver and counterfeiting money. Kidnapping for large ransoms was common, along with violence and torture. These early brigands concentrated on the control of precious metals, money and trade, and had very little interest in politics, culture or agricultural and craft production. Under the misgovernment of Henry III, which allowed instability and civil war to blight the nation, violent gangs proliferated and enjoyed significant economic success, running all major trade in the port of Bristol, for instance, for a number of years and even managing to break into the Royal Treasury at Westminster. In an effort to restore law and order, Edward I, crowned in 1274 and advised by Italian and English lawyers, reorganized the whole criminal justice system (Hibbert, 2003). In 1283 the Statute of Winchester bolstered the traditional system of policing to deal with the violence and intimidation that had reduced confidence in government, property, wealth creation, trade and money and had become the principal impediment to the development of commerce. Lax control over law and order created an overall climate of fear and insecurity, where most of the population felt safer remaining in the defensive units of family and local community. A more efficient and effective criminal justice system allowed property rights to be protected and trade arteries to be opened up and maintained, and its inception coincided with the proliferation of market towns and commerce in general. The systematic reduction of criminal violence was a vital prerequisite for the diffusion of social and economic interaction and the early development of the market economy (Hall, 2000; 2007); it was not reduced because the sensibilities and ethics of the age demanded it.

In order to increase the success of the criminal justice system crime control was formalized in communities, which became the arms of the criminal justice system with practices such as 'hue and cry' and 'watch and ward'. By royal decree country roads were enlarged and roadsides were severely coppiced to reduce hiding places for robbers (Hibbert, 2003). Cohen's (1985) claim that justice and social control were at the time decentralized and informal is dubious; this was a period of formal reconstruction of previously informal local and regional control systems that had been disrupted in the violent aftermath of the Norman invasion. The Norman aristocrats were notably incompetent in estate management and governance (Dyer, 2000), and the formalization that followed was vital to the pacification of a country that had approached violent chaos in the years following the Civil War of Henry III's reign. At the epicentre of Edward's reforms was born the principle that every man – and it was indeed every man in such unashamedly patriarchal times – should be a policeman in the service of the Crown. What Cohen (ibid.) posited as the modern form of 'net-widening' was in fact the founding principle of the original change in the criminal justice system, made to secure royal governance and facilitate the development of a socio-economically interactive population in a nascent market system. What was different was the relative lack of efficiency; the mind was willing but the flesh was weak. Cohen is also rather mistaken about the lack of differentiation and classification; in the proto-utilitarian tariff offences, fines and punishments in fact were highly differentiated and classified. Neither was it a historically 'alien' system, as Foucault attempted to argue (1970; 1991); in the classification of crimes and the numerous crime/punishment analogues it was very similar to today's system and to other classificatory systems of the time. Closing times for taverns and curfews were common, and regulation of the dinner hours of labourers was encouraged. The reticular 'disciplinary society' was being born, as a gradual process outside of monasteries and military organizations accompanying the development of production and trade. It was not an abrupt change, as Foucault (1991) argued, at least not in England; sovereignty, discipline and control were concomitant and complementary practices from the beginning, not increments in an interrupted linear historical process.

The new criminal justice system's formalization and professionalization process was forced to change as production and trade developed. Busy merchants, artisans and labourers could not simply abandon their activities to take part in hue and cry and other formal citizens' duties. Consequently constables began to pay proxies to perform their duties, the beginnings of a rather ramshackle reticular state-run police force and town watch that was to last until the exasperated bourgeoisie of the eighteenth century resorted to private means to reduce the property crime that burgeoned during difficult yet opportunistic economic periods. Although the pre-modern system was hampered by corruption, incompetence and brutality, it still functioned well enough to facilitate the initial development of markets and opportunities for social mobility. When the initial bout of Plague subsided in the late fourteenth and early fifteenth centuries, when fields lay fallow and production and trade suffered, economic expansion became vital. Workers took advantage of higher wages, and began to dress in more expensive and stylish clothes, which, when it was seen by the elite to be 'getting out of hand', brought the reaction of the sumptuary laws (Sassatelli, 2008). This demonstrated that in the early proto-capitalist market system there was another side to discipline and oppression. If tacitly allowed or encouraged – which was certainly the case when economic expansion was vital – the seductive attraction of consumer culture and the symbols of status and social distinction could very quickly energize economic activity throughout the social body, but this was also seen as a socio-cultural problem because overly spectacular displays of opulence signified power and thus posed a threat to the elite's rule.

This fear of the disruption of the social order also resulted in higher taxes levied on workers, and it is no coincidence that the Peasant's Revolt took place when the opportunity for social mobility presented itself and the monarchical state reacted with forms of cultural and economic repression. Just as the state could facilitate, it could also suppress opportunities for economically-driven social mobility amongst a population that, as Macfarlane (1978) argues, contained many peasants and artisans who were already highly individualized, opportunistic and commercially minded, the energetic atoms that constituted a proto-bourgeoisie. This gives the Peasant's Revolt the ring of the Taxpayers' Alliance rather than the Socialist Workers Party, of classical liberalism rather than Bolshevism. Was this a struggle for emancipation and justice? Possibly, but for many it was also seen as a struggle to take opportunities in a developing competitive-individualistic culture for the accumulation of wealth and social mobility. This was a time when the need for enthusiastic and rewarding individual participation in economic expansion found itself in profound tension with the need to maintain social order and elite rule.

There are further problems with Cohen's (1985) analysis of the so-called 'master patterns' of criminal justice. From the reign of Edward I state involvement was not weak, decentralized and arbitrary but, even though inefficient, on the move towards centralization. The classification of crime and deviance – especially those categories connected to fines – was not poorly developed but highly developed along proto-utilitarian lines as a set of analogous economic metaphors. The hegemony of law and criminal justice was well established at the centre of the nascent socio-political reticulation, professional dominance was in the throes of being established at important administrative points in the system and the object of intervention was not exclusively the body but – under the auspices of Christian dualism and a firm grasp of economic necessity and opportunity in the minds of Royal Governors and the proto-bourgeoisie alike – also the mind and its attitudes to work and living habits. Moreover, theories of punishment were not only moralistic but also contained the concepts of just deserts and the analogous categories that constitute modern classical liberalism's deterrence system, and the mode of control was often exclusive and stigmatizing as well as inclusive.

Ridding ourselves of the discontinuous view of history proposed by Foucault (1970) and Cohen (ibid.) – for Foucault, abrupt discontinuity based on the rapid closure and reconstitution of systems of thought – allows us to investigate continuities with more confidence, and it reminds us that the problems of harmful crime, its perception and its control are very old, and, like the opposing forms of solidarity, justice and freedom, representable in universal terms (Žižek, 2000). Of course we should historicize the problem's forms and its underlying aetiological conditions, but – as we go deeper into its psychosocial and economic processes and structures – continuities, isomorphs and even transhistorical archetypes come into sharper relief. From the fourteenth century in England what we can see quite clearly is a broadly networked and formalized reticular system of criminalization and criminal justice that evolved to aid an economic project that needed concurrently to stimulate and pacify a volatile population and facilitate geo-social interaction, production, trade and governance (Hall, 2007). This is the context for the birth of a continuous dynamic reproductive process to be explored later as pseudo-pacification.

If the main problem of serious crime in the later Middle Ages was the nexus of violent brigandage and economic monopolization, Early Modern England from the mid-sixteenth to the mid-eighteenth centuries was characterized by a decline in most forms of homicide – apart from infanticide – and serious violence. It is generally accepted by historians that this decline was accompanied by an increase in economic crimes, although, as with all historical studies, this is difficult to prove (Sharpe, 1996). However, from the Tudor period court statistics were at least slightly more reliable, and it seems that in the long period between the sixteenth and eighteenth centuries, despite temporary undulations such as a notable drop in all crime between the early seventeenth and early eighteenth centuries (ibid.), the master trend seems to be a steady decline in rates of homicide and serious violence accompanied by a general rise in rates of economic crimes. Some historians (Gurr, 1981) trace the long-term decline of homicide in England back to the late fourteenth century. Petty property crime was more heavily prosecuted after the Tudor regime and during the rise of Protestantism; nevertheless, the 'increase in governance' and the development and institutionalization of Protestant moral codes seemed to stabilize or slow rather than reduce the rise in rates of property crime. We cannot simply attribute the rise in property crime to the expansion of criminalization; property crime already seemed to be rising from the early fifteenth century, when detection and prosecution rates were relatively low, and the sudden rise that such a profound change in symbolic practice would be expected to cause simply did not occur. All criminologists are aware that in historical studies statistics are inherently unreliable and the more sophisticated and penetrative qualitative research methods are simply unavailable; as E.P. Thompson reminded us, we can't interview tombstones (Marshall, 1982). However, on the back of sophisticated and painstaking empirical work, Sharpe (ibid.) concludes that, at least in this period of history, the predominance of long-term continuities and processes makes it difficult to argue that the types of abrupt social, political or economic disruption that populations encountered were the sole aetiological conditions for fluctuations in crime rates. Extrapolating from that claim, we might agree with Elias (1994) and his followers that some sort of long-term civilizing process was in train, but the concomitant rise in property crime, the maintenance of brutal forms of punishment and the consolidation of exploitative social relations despite increasing social mobility, suggests something related but in vital dimensions entirely different.

There were also earlier signs of a shift from violence to economic crime; in the fourteenth century criminal gangs still indulged in consummate banditry, but criminal prosecutions suggest that the more 'modern' form of theft was the most prominent offence (Sharpe, 1996). One of Elias's many followers – extending his argument to the whole of Europe where homicide rates, beginning slightly later in the sixteenth century, also declined (Eisner, 2001) – argued that the decline of homicide and violence was the product of the 'spiritualization' of traditional male honour, which was for most of pre-capitalist history a bodily form established and defended by violence (Spierenburg, 2008). This makes little sense when placed alongside the long-term empirical trends. Why would a more 'spiritual' population indulge in an increasing number of economic crimes ranging from petty theft to major fraud? The category 'crime' could be augmented further were we to shift to one of 'harm' that would include all the warmongering, bullying, dispossession, exploitation, lying, cheating and so on that accompanied the development of liberal capitalism (Seymour, 2008). Honour represented and enacted by bodily violence was not 'spiritualized' but sublimated and externalized into the system of symbolic objects that, through the valuation and social organization of symbolic, cultural capital and competitive struggles, connected the social world to an increasingly competitive and volatile market economy (Hall et al., 2008).

To put it plainly, as we became less violent and bloodthirsty we became richer and more pacified but possibly less honourable and, in the social body of the popular classes, certainly less egalitarian; violence looks to have been sublimated into symbolic and toned-down practical forms rather than dispersed into the transcendental realm of spirituality. What we seem to be looking at is a process of social diffusion and ethical evacuation wherein honour was relocated to the external symbolic economy to make room for motivations and practices that were by the standards of the day dishonourable vices, yet which were vital for the expansion of the capitalist economy. This required a partial relocation of central motivational values into a restrictive normative order associated with the concomitant pacification of honour and tolerance of dishonour. Whilst practices such as usury, exploitation, mendacity, deception and so on became tolerated and either legalized or punished less harshly to lubricate their social diffusion and augment their economic functionality, discretionary and occasionally brutal bodily practices of maintaining honour, centred around the family and assigned to patriarchs, were gradually prohibited. Traditional modes of honour encapsulated the values and norms associated with both motivation and prohibition, but the early stages of capitalism were characterized by a vital process of splitting, where motivational codes became dominated by controlled dishonour and transferred to political economy, and general prohibitive codes that operated throughout political economy, culture and the social were transferred to the cultural mode of asceticism, administered famously by Protestantism. Honour was split, sublimated and metamorphosed, its obscene double harnessed to political economy and its diluted prohibitive form deployed as the pseudo-pacifying practices of culture and law.

This was not entirely an elite affair. By the seventeenth century richer peasants were active in administrating the new Protestant moral codes in villages, creating amongst the new village oligarchs an inroad into the ethico-social hierarchy and, through jury service, the criminal justice system (Raftis, 1966). The 'embourgeoisement' process was well under way and the connection between economic wealth and institutionalized social influence was expanding the bourgeois socio-political reticulation. At the same time the ethics and practices of competitive economic privatism and political governance penetrated the heart of peasant culture. Even in its outlying areas English society in the late Mediaeval and early modern periods was not especially brutal even by today's standards (Macfarlane, 1981), but on the other hand the homicide rate in the late fourteenth century was at least thirteen times higher than that in the twentieth century, so perhaps Sharpe and Macfarlane are exaggerating the similarity as much as others exaggerate the difference. Nevertheless, there is little doubt that the early development of the pseudo-pacification process was somehow sublimating violence and dragging England out of a Dark Age that was, contrary to revisionist accounts that posit it as a time of peaceful transformation amidst the collapsing Western Roman Empire, every bit as violent and insecure as traditional accounts claim (Ward-Perkins, 2005).

However, the diffusionary and assimilatory nature of this tense stimulating-pacifying process and the slow recovery of the economy towards the prosperity of the Roman era do not negate the fundamental social class relation and economic exchange relation at the heart of the nascent capitalist economy. There is no doubt that the poor, gradually dispossessed of land and traditional subsistence rights, were disproportionately criminalized. Whereas minor acts of property appropriation committed by the poor were increasingly criminalized the 'crimes of the powerful' enjoyed an entirely different status. Until the nineteenth century forgery was regarded as a misdemeanour, and we must assume that a voluminous and powerful undercurrent of white-collar crimes simply did not figure in the criminal justice system's statistics. The gradual decline of local 'shaming punishments', the refusal to criminalize bourgeois harm and its subsequent absence from the statistical record kept representations of the economic crime rates artificially low and skewed disproportionately to the labouring classes. We might suspect that the wish to avoid social sanctions and shame was one motivation for the bourgeoisie to distance itself in social and geographical space from the broader community. The developing capitalist system seemed to be establishing an early and enduring distinction between *functional* and *dysfunctional* criminality, a prime example of ethics and ontology flying at dusk like the Owl of Minerva to justify the consequences of an extant socio-economic process. Dysfunctional criminals, those who threatened property or economic progress, were to be punished or, where possible, corrected, whilst functional criminals were to be reprimanded yet tacitly admired for displaying the sort of harnessable self-interest, iconoclasm and ruthlessly exploitative economic innovation on which the system's development depended.

Disproportionate criminalization was also accompanied by a decline in brutal punishment and a growing ideological belief in rehabilitation. From the sixteenth century onwards the shifts to the House of Correction, the fine, transportation and the prison showed that in the capitalist era the functional requirement for labour, production and order was replacing the traditions of righteous violence and analogous revenge and satisfaction (Rusche & Kirchheimer, 1939). Individual reform and the inculcation of conscience and discipline gradually became the first resort in the fields of governance and punishment; in England there was no abrupt change in the eighteenth century of the sort that Foucault (1991) claimed to have occurred in France. Undeniable class repression seemed to be operating hand-in-hand with the attempted ideological and practical inclusion of workers and the encouragement and stimulation of entrepreneurial desires in all individuals who showed early inclinations towards business. The alternative liberal/Whiggish view is that developing elite sensibilities gradually eschewed brutality and embraced a humanitarian, prelectorial and inclusive approach to governance, class relations and 'correctional' practices. What is missing in this and the standard functionalist and Marxist narratives is the concomitant stimulation of the individual's drives for wealth, conspicuous consumption and social distinction, which burgeoned and diffused throughout the social body in the period (Sassatelli, 2008; Sombart, 1967; Veblen, 1994). Whilst the poor were dispossessed, disproportionately criminalized, brutally punished and corrected in the most patronizing manner, it also seemed to be the case that the attitudes and practices of the ruling elite were softening. However, at the same time, basal drives for conspicuous luxury consumption and social distinction were gradually diffusing outwards from numerous nodal points where the desire for entrepreneurialism, economic success and social mobility was appearing amongst the lower and middling classes. Where early stirrings of potential class struggle had to be fully repressed, nascent bourgeois desires had to be both stimulated and partially repressed in order to be sublimated and controlled. If we use Lacan's (1992) distinction between drive and desire (Žižek, 2008), the drive exists in profound tension with the idealistic desire of *ascesis* – the ascetic life – that Protestants were trying to rework from its Christian roots into a secular control mechanism, whose function was to reorient drives and reconstitute desires in forms conducive to economic growth and social pacification. Mutating criminal motivations and practices as well as the criminalization process were embroiled in this historical shift.

The survival of increasingly reliable records from the mid-sixteenth century, concerned mainly with felony (which includes serious offences such as homicide, burglary, theft, rape and arson), allows us to bring our initial adumbration of criminality and the criminalization process into clearer relief. There were regional differences, but, in the main, prosecution of these offences peaked in the late 1590s during a period of bad harvests, and the 1620s, a period of severe social and economic problems. When criminal courts resumed after the Civil War the prosecution of felonies decreased, and remained low until the mid-eighteenth century, when the resumption of population growth and the economic dislocation that attended the run-up to the industrial revolution created the conditions for notable rises (Sharpe, 1996). Beattie (1986) shows us that between 1660 and 1800 banditry and codes of honour had almost disappeared. Many acquisitive and violent crimes were committed by young 'unruly apprentices' (Pearson, 1992), not members of a submerged underclass. The boundary between legitimate and illegitimate activities was porous, and individuals crossed over as market conditions changed. Brutal sensibilities were becoming more refined, and indifference to violence and death was receding. However, the shift in punishment from violence to imprisonment and transportation was perhaps not entirely driven by developing humane sensibilities – Beattie was probably wrong to suggest that it was, as Macfarlane (1986) argues – but also by fear of public disorder and, with growing affluence and taxation allowing the expansion of prisons and the advent of American colonies allowing transportation, an increase in the ability to incapacitate the perpetrators of dysfunctional crime or exploit their labour in colonies abroad (Rusche & Kirchheimer, 1939).

The political violence that pervaded the seventeenth century was replaced by relative calm and order in the eighteenth century. However, as the eighteenth century wore on and bourgeois rule established itself after the Glorious Revolution, the sublimatory dynamic returned and property crime rates increased in various periods of economic downturn, rising food prices and post-war unemployment; the rise accelerated further during the demographic shifts in the urbanization process. The increase in capital statutes in the eighteenth century – exemplified most notably by the Waltham Black Acts from 1723, which initially placed fifty new capital offences on the statute book, mainly derived from formerly customary practices of free appropriation (Thompson, 1975) – was accompanied by a reduction in the likelihood that they would be applied (Hay, 1975). Deterrence, pacification and order were now more important than violence, bloodlust and revenge in a socio-economic milieu that was becoming reliant on the seduction of individual entrepreneurs and workers who were willing to apply desire and effort to entrepreneurial activities. Sensibilities against brutality were developing alongside gradually diffusing ambitions for social mobility that had to be achieved in an exploitative yet creative and rule-bound manner. John Sheppard, the infamous former apprentice turned burglar and city dandy (Rawlings, 1999), was hanged chiefly because his rise through the social ranks was too spectacular and based on aggravated dysfunctional crimes; the ambivalence shown by onlookers at his hanging, a mixture of admiration and fear, suggested that to them his rise from rags to riches and celebrity had been driven by the approved spirit applied in a disapproved way, which had short-circuited the socio-economic functionality required by the system. The petit bourgeoisie took pity on him during his execution because he was *very nearly but not quite* one of them.

Early in its developmental trajectory the industrial-urban capitalist project, despite its capacity for wealth creation and the socially incremental diffusion of individual opportunities and rights, showed its tendency to crash and cause enormous social disruption and hardship. Between 1780 and 1830, an examination of court records showed an increase in crime of over 540 per cent in London (Rusche & Kirchheimer, 1939) as working class poverty increased alongside rapid urbanization, proletarianization and disruption to cultural reproductive mechanisms. The rise was exacerbated after 1815 as soldiers returned home from the Napoleonic wars to face recession and unemployment in the midst of expanding displays of consumption. This tends to suggest that Sharpe's claim, that economic and social disruption did not create the underlying conditions for rises in crime rates in the sixteenth and seventeenth centuries, might not apply to the eighteenth and nineteenth centuries, when life for a money-dependent population separated further from the land became increasingly reliant on the performance of the market economy and the availability of waged labour. It must be noted, however, that in this short period the sudden drop in prosperity and economic security for wage-dependent working classes was of a high magnitude, certainly high enough to raise concerns amongst the ruling elite of a revolution (Reiner, 2010), French-style in its practical form but drawing its spirit from lower in the social ranks. The dark side – indeed the disavowed reality – of the standard liberal-leftist formulation is that at the time the individualized and politically disorganized English popular classes lacked solidarity and an alternative ideology, and the ideological incorporation of many into the entrepreneurial and competitive-individualist spirit was at an advanced stage. In this period prosecutions rose, and the state, facing failure and gross inefficiency in private systems that had burgeoned from the mid-eighteenth century, began to take over the tasks of policing and punishment (Reiner, ibid.). It was during this period that criminology was first established as a statistical discipline and the elite began to develop a fearful and prejudicial concept of the troubled and petty crime-prone sections of the urban mass as a dysfunctional 'dangerous class', a concept that was not restricted to Britain but pan-European (Chevalier, 1973). However, in England and Wales property crime began to decrease again after 1850 – falling back into line with continuing decreases in homicide and serious violence – as policing improved and the institutionalization of social conflict evolved alongside the development of the labour movement in the broad context of a 'solidarity project' made possible by the stabilization and consolidation of industrial economy and society (Garland, 2001: 199).

However, court records show us more about class perceptions and criminalization than the extent of real crime or 'social crime', a term that attempts to conceptualize crime as a misguided proto-political act that in some way challenges a society's normative and political order (Hobsbawm, 1972). E.P. Thompson was at pains to point out that social crime was not 'nice' as opposed to 'nasty' real crime (Emsley, 2010), and the inability of the English working class to form effective political organizations until the mid-nineteenth century tends to suggest that if political motivations did lie behind some crimes they were sporadic and ephemeral. However, the nineteenth century reminded us yet again that the willingness to risk inflicting direct or indirect forms of harm on others in the process of furthering the self's interests is not confined to the popular classes. White-collar crime was rife in the late Hanoverian and Victorian eras, especially fraud and embezzlement (ibid.). Employers also regularly cut corners to reduce costs in production and distribution process, endangering their workers. The current 'crisis of enforcement', analysed by Tombs and Whyte (2003) as a characteristic of current forms of neoliberal political economy, is very much a continuation of the classical liberal norm. Despite compulsory auditing after 1830, powerful individuals and business organizations continued to commit a multitude of 'invisible crimes'. Regulation was 'light-touch' in the beginning; for instance, the 1844 Company Act did not insist that auditors should be trained accountants, and, even if it had done so, accountants are themselves in private business and only indirect representatives of the law. The business class could remain at a distance from the effects of their crimes and unethical actions, allowing continuity, and, being by and large better educated, could cheat the poor in a more effective manner, eschewing violence and intimidation whilst practicing the art of pacified exploitation with consummate ease. To elaborate on Thompson's point, neither is there anything 'nice' or 'victimless' about this sort of white-collar crime; there is simply a lack of direct violence and a longer causal chain of events that puts distance between the perpetrator and the harm suffered by the victims. White-collar crime is applied pseudo-pacification *par excellence*, the furthering of combined corporate and individual interests by indirectly causing immense amounts of violent and non-violent harms to multiple victims whilst maintaining a civilized image.

The nineteenth-century urban milieu presents us with an interesting stage of accelerated mutation in social forms of acquisitive crime. In rural areas, semi-professional poachers and poaching gangs were active in complex networks of entrepreneurial and social crime, selling their catches to innkeepers and individuals from the middle and upper classes. On the periphery of towns highwaymen, a vestige of the Mediaeval brigand, continued to rob the unprotected as they had done since early Tudor times (Hallsworth, 2006), but, as cheap, powerful weapons such as the blunderbuss became available for travellers, the practice died out in the early decades of the century (Matthews, 2002). As highwaymen had escaped capture by seeking sanctuary in rural areas inaccessible to the state authorities, urban criminals did the same in the ungovernable areas or 'rookeries' that were developing in sprawling commercial and industrial cities. As McIntosh (1975) explained, since at least the sixteenth century communities of thieves operated in both urban and rural areas, developing highly skilled routines for taking small amounts of goods and money from a large number of victims.

A rapid four-fold mutation occurred in nineteenth-century urban areas, where traditional picaresque and craft groups were displaced by modern project and business organizations. The picaresque organization, typical of pirates and brigands, was a fairly permanent hierarchal yet communal gang under one man's leadership, sometimes with a few supporting officers, and profits were shared among members according to rank. The craft organization was skilled but small-scale, focusing on thefts and confidence tricks, with a small but fairly permanent team, usually of two or three men, each with specific roles to play in specialist thefts; profits were shared equally at the end of each day. The project organization was a temporary informal contract arrangement between specialist criminals – burglars, robbers, smugglers or fraudsters – with a view to committing a

single crime or a short series of large-scale crimes, using complex techniques and advance planning. This was an ad hoc team of specialists mus-
tered, sometimes by an entrepreneur, for a specific job in hand, and profits
were shared on a basis worked out beforehand. The business organization
represented a final move from variations of the early communal warrior-
predator form to the bourgeois-capitalist form. Here, capitalist class relations and older predator-victim relations combined as extortionists or
suppliers of illegal goods and services, either preying on unwitting victims
or expropriating the 'produce' of 'worker-criminals' who took by far the
larger risk for smaller rewards, established some degree of immunity from
legal control by forging relations with corrupt political and legal officials.
This was an advanced social class relation of criminality in which functional
criminals formed an elite business class to expropriate the money and
labour-power of everyday victims and lowly dysfunctional criminals alike.
In the nineteenth century these monopolistic business organizations were
the largest in scale and the most enduring. However, by the late twentieth
century even these professional organizations were being replaced by loose
networks. Mutations in forms of acquisitive criminality to some extent
seem to shadow corresponding changes in legal capitalist business activity,
markets and social relations; in sociological terms, the central issue seems
to be that the violent collective acquisition, solidarity and egalitarianism
that characterized early groups were eventually swept away entirely in the
processes of deterritorialization, competitive individualism, contractualism
and shadow class formation.

How do we begin to theorize these basic trends? The historical evidence
does not point to a general 'civilizing process', a Whiggish concept that is
past its sell-by date (Wieviorka, 2009), but a complex psychosocial process
in which direct and unashamed violence and intimidation were gradually
sublimated into a multitude of criminalized and legalized forms of exploitation, deception and appropriation, which ran alongside and in tension with
what can only be described as a sort of insulating sleeve of ethico-legal
restraints, like the thick but flexible insulation around an electrical wire
carrying a powerful current. This points to a duality; not the benign
enabling agency–structure dualism of late twentieth century constitutional
theorists such as Giddens (1984) and Beck (1992) but a tense, volatile dualistic tension that produces a dynamic force driving the development of
capitalism/modernity. Rojek's (1995) conception of a dual modernity
structured by parallel forces of chaos and order in some ways echoes
Thorstein Veblen's conception of a 'simple dualism of barbaric versus non-
barbaric and communal cultural forces' (Mestrovic, 2003: 9). Excess and
wastefulness become signifiers of status, a notion later taken up by Bourdieu

(1986), but, in the pursuit of *jouissance*, the individual becomes ruthlessly narcissistic yet feels injured and in need of attention and affection. Lasch (1991) saw narcissism as a driver for people in upwardly mobile consumer societies such as the US and UK, but for Veblen (ibid.) it existed not only in consumer culture but in all institutions, including science and higher education. He depicted these cultural forces as 'social atmospheres' or 'out-looks' on the world. Thus, the barbaric part of the split narcissist is basically competitive, warlike, wasteful and orientated towards personal rather than communal achievements. His or her nemesis is the peaceful, cooperative, frugal and communal social type engaged in the 'instinct for workmanship', wanting to produce quality for its own sake, not for the sake of honour, status, and pecuniary reward (see also Sennett, 1998).

Like Freud and many other thinkers, Veblen was aware of the importance of unconscious drives and habits. He was also aware of the splitting and dissociation of the self in a schizoid culture that oscillated between barbarism and altruism. Things and people are idealized yet at the same time devalued, which allows sentimentalism to exist in tension with barbarism and replace any real civilizational development (see also Eagleton, 2009). What we call our civilization exists in the space between this barbarism and sentimentalism. Envy, self-absorption and consciousness of status are rampant, and empathy and altruism are in short supply. Veblen was aware of these cultural 'splitting' forces (Mestrovic, 2003) and the dynamic relationship between them, but in a vein reminiscent of the later Adorno (1967; 1973) he saw narcissism prevailing over the altruistic communal traits that characterized traditional working communities.

In contrast, most 'constitutional' social theorists such as Giddens and Beck work with a duality of structure in which the dual forces themselves are commensurable, flexible, interactive and largely benign; in true Kantian fashion the self-reflexive individual agent can choose between alternative ends and means, which, when institutionalized, can be continually altered – and, one assumes, the institutional structure itself continually reformed and improved – by the pressure placed upon them by groups of individuals in civil society. Beck's (1992) concept of risk was essentially a rationalized technique for mediating between individual desire/agency and institutional rules and norms. It's easy to see why short-term pessimistic figures such as Freud, Veblen and Adorno have been ignored, and whenever they rear their heads, quickly dismissed and pushed back into obscurity by what are by now almost autonomic defensive forces in the dominant liberal constitutionalist paradigm. Where liberal humanists see an integrated, autonomous and reflexive subject who acts as a moral agent in a dualistic social system – and most postmodernists see a discursive subject orientated to resistance as an automatic response to power – Freud, Veblen and Adorno saw certain human tendencies as the main part of the problem. Human beings are active agents and capable of benign desires and actions, but, without the most careful and humane nurturing in a social body orientated to that cause, also the most dangerous and potentially barbaric creatures on earth (Ehrenreich, 1997; Mestrovic, 1993). Perhaps that thought is far too restrictive and maternalistic for the unbound freedom-seekers of the broad liberal project.

Rojek (1995) also sees this tense and incommensurable psychological duality mirrored in the broad social forms and processes of modernity itself. One side produces order and the other chaos. However, as the historical evidence suggests, modernity's pacification process seems to have truncated both categories as it reconstituted and harnessed them in a dynamic process of 'orderly disorder' (Hall et al., 2008); we must remember that dynamism is the product of incommensurable forces pushed together in an unholy and potentially explosive relation, and what energy and forms we experience exist in a third space beyond the duality itself (Johnston, 2008). Just as the altruism that might have characterized life before the agricultural settlement did not remain in its ancient form, as capitalism developed the barbarism that can so often flourish in a state of chaos did not remain in the traditional form of the violent defence of honour and socio-economic promotion of the self and family group. Our potted historical evidence above suggests that, as altruism declined into sentimentalism, physical aggression was gradually sublimated into social competition and success was increasingly signified by the display of expensive consumer goods (Hall at al., 2008).

The diffusion of the ancient cult of luxury was not confined to England, but, in combination with the nation's notably atomized, anxious and socially competitive form of individualism, it was a uniquely powerful attractor and stimulator. Sombart (1967) revealed capitalism's powerful consumer motor in the spread throughout Europe of markets in luxury goods. As courtiers and courtesans increased their spending in a fierce social competition for status and honour, the capital cities became lucrative markets for these goods from the sixteenth century onwards. Whole industries developed to produce, supply and distribute them, providing the initial economic impetus for industrial capitalism, colonialism and slavery. Sumptuary laws were annulled in the seventeenth and eighteenth centuries to aid the social diffusion of a process in which luxury was recognized as a vice but necessary for the stimulation of industry and general wealth creation, an early version of the 'trickle-down' theory. Capitalism and its principal agents reacted to the knowledge that it thrived on excess, and excess carried high social status.

Ascetic restraint was unevenly distributed, and even though the upper classes were portrayed as a necessary evil, the implantation in the minds of the population of the idea that anyone with entrepreneurial talent could join them performed a vital economic function. It was offset by the notion of predestination (Marshall, 1982), but this was a relatively weak restraining force. Moral philosophers from Smith to Hume and commentators from Mandeville to Defoe condemned luxury yet recognized its economic function. Fielding condemned the dream of unrestrained 'luxury amongst the vulgar' as a fundamental cause of vice and crime, whilst acknowledging that the thirst for luxury amongst those able to control their drives, desires and ostentatious displays was a vital economic driver.

Since the expansion of the banking industry in the sixteenth century, wealth had been transferred from the aristocracy to the nascent bourgeoisie by means of moneylending and indebtedness. In their efforts to outdo each other, the bourgeoisie mimicked and restored the former glory of the aristocracy, and this *aristophilia* (Hall et al., 2008) increased the exchange value and the rapidity of circulation of luxury commodities. Local markets, rather than export markets, were initially of primary importance, and the existence of luxury consumption in close proximity to relatively extreme poverty in the urban area, now recognized as a principal criminogenic force (Taylor, 1999), was the normal state of affairs in European cities. As production was industrialized in the nineteenth century, there was a movement from speciality selling in the luxury market to bulk selling in the everyday markets, but the symbolism of status did not disappear in the developing mass markets, it was passed down and distributed as 'affordable luxury'. The symbolic status of mass-manufactured goods was maintained by advertising, where products could be associated with socially valuable images and the static relational value of rarity was displaced by the similar but linear-dynamic relational value of novelty.

Trading in articles of luxury was behind the rise of the early bourgeoisie across Europe, so it appears likely that the expansion of the trade in articles of luxury and the diffusion of the ability to afford these luxuries were principal forces behind the development of capitalism. Everyday goods, whose production and distribution were catered for quite adequately by pre-capitalist economic means, were relatively unimportant. The potent force of modern consumer desire is a compound of novel technological function, luxury status and exchange-value expressed as price. The exotic textiles, dyes, perfumes, spices, precious metals, precious stones, medicines, ornaments and so on sought by the rich suited the worldly, cosmopolitan entrepreneur because exotic materials had to be sourced from abroad, a norm established in the eleventh-century silk trade. Production processes were expensive, and again favoured those with capital, mainly because the inability of some of the 'rich' to pay meant that manufacturers and traders frequently had to absorb losses. The whims of the rich and their translation into symbols of social distinction to be desired by the aspiring members of the population fuelled production and provided markets with a constant renewable source of consumer desire. These new production processes and ever-changing fashions were detrimental to the guilds and local craftsmen; because volume production and sales did not occur until much later, luxury industries were the first choice for capital investment. It is easy to see how disruptive this process is on the psychosocial, cultural and economic levels, in England fuelling the anxiety of atomized individuals as well as increasing opportunities for the more ruthless and entrepreneurial, those who had no concern for figurations of interdependencies grounded in economic relations or the moral codes that restrained and pacified the quest for social distinction.

Sombart (1998) did not subscribe to any theory of dualism; he saw capitalism in declinist terms, as morally exhausted, unable to give dialectical birth to its successor, bearing no guarantee of the Marxist evolution into a higher form. Perhaps consumer-driven capitalism holds within it a dark, negative dialectic, as Adorno (1973) argued. This anti-Enlightenment view can be politically dangerous, fuelling fake reproductions of earlier cultures when the current situation appears impossible and the road ahead appears bleak. Sombart, in a far firmer and deeper way than Veblen, who glorified labour, brought seduction and consumption into the foreground in a way that complemented Marx's pre-psychoanalytical concept of fetishism as overidentification with commodified symbolic objects (Harvey, 2011) and presaged the otherwise incommensurate figures of Lacan, Mauss, Adorno, Lasch, Baudrillard, Debord and Bourdieu, who all linked the consumption of luxury items to the pursuit of social status, as opposed to Braudel's notion of it as anathema to the culture of the *ancien régime* (de Grazia, 1996; Mukerji, 1993).

Where Weber posited Calvinist Puritanism as the ethos of capitalism, Sombart saw it as an irksome pacifying restraint too easily brushed aside in a system that depended upon increasing luxury and decadence as its economic motor on the demand side. This presaged the neoclassical view that demand and its reflection in prices is subjective, but Sombart, as did Veblen, saw demand as socially constituted and reproduced rather than a product of the free choices of the 'sovereign individual'. Neither theorist, however, saw the relationship as one of functional dynamic tension, the generator of momentum. Protestant asceticism was not the 'spirit' of capitalism, the energizing force in its cultural and psychosocial forms, but, as advocated by

Adam Smith (1984), a vital brake, speedometer and steering mechanism needed to restrain and guide a compound economic, cultural and psycho-social force that was already under way.

Weber (2002) argued that capitalism was different to money-speculation, more 'ethically' driven, productive and socially responsible. He attacked classical Smithian economics, profit-maximization and the rational economic actor as an abstract and ahistorical doctrine. History was instead influenced by historically variable ethical factors (Marshall, 1982), a doctrine that still retains a strong presence in liberal thought. For Weber, 'world-views' are not ideological, unconscious, economic or derived from ahistorical economic orientations of the individual, yet he made his interesting distinction between the ethical businessman and the unethical speculator by resorting to the notion that responsible, ethical businessmen had a clearer conception of mutual economic interests. However, one only has to look at the permeability of the barrier between the two and the recent revelations of unethical business practice in today's tumultuous economic times (Shaxson, 2011; Tombs & Whyte, 2003) to refute that claim. This is the core problem with the Weberian liberal world-view; it sees capitalism as ethically-driven rather than driven by greed, envy, cynicism and the quest for special liberty but normatively restrained by relocated ethics (see Hall et al., 2008). Weberianism's penchant for restraint in its critique of bourgeois ethics and the obscene drives that underlie them – at times resembling little more than a loquacious hagiography – could be the main reason for its continued position at the top of the liberal-dominated sociological canon.

However, as the unethical and irresponsible practices that led to the credit-crunch came to light, it seems that Sombart and Simmel might have been nearer the mark. Simmel (1978) argued that money was the primary example of a means becoming an end, an enclosed and absolute psychologically-inculcated purpose. Mediaeval economic ethics revolved around the fairness of the distribution and consumption of material goods. Money was an evil, necessary only to overcome the practical problems of bartering and trading over longer distances, but as bourgeois culture developed from the marginal merchant and lower-middling peasant ranks of Mediaeval society the acquisition of money as profit and credit became vital for marginal groups who wished to infiltrate the system and prosper. Simmel's 'nurseries of cynicism' are:

> [T]hose places with huge turnovers, exemplified in stock exchange dealings, where money is available in huge quantities and changes owners easily. The more money becomes the sole

centre of interest, the more one discovers that honour and
conviction, talent and virtue, beauty and salvation of the soul,
are exchanged against money and so the more mocking and
frivolous attitude will develop in relation to these higher values
that are for sale for the same kind of value as groceries, and that
also command a 'market price'. (1978: 256)

Not that Sombart was unaware of the role of money in capitalism. Despite
the obvious political tyranny of the warlords, in the everyday economic life
of pre-capitalist systems balance was sought between expenditure and
income; the degree to which humans could consume above basic needs
depended on income, and expenditure was tailored to suit 'income'
expressed as the number of commodities produced (Sombart, 1998).
Money was not shared equally, but there was in the Middle Ages the
Aquinian notion of 'sufficient livelihood', which was seen as a moral good
in an unequal but participatory economy. Weighing and measuring amongst
the producing and small trading classes was very rough and ready; quality
was more important than quantity, and in the culture of the day there was
very little expression of a love for business and trade. Affection was focused
on production and the quality of the product, and products were often seen
as social symbols, means of structuring sentimental affection into relations
of reciprocal social obligation, a hangover from traditional gift economies.
There was a restfulness and contentment in good times, which seems to be
entirely absent today. How capitalism changed this restrained cultural climate to one of permanent psychosocial restlessness and economic dynamism lies at the heart of criminological theory.

    Whereas manual producers were driven by the ethos of producing what
was necessary, the aristocracy – and the clergy in the seigniorial systems –
were driven by the desire, as Alberti noted in fourteenth-century Florence,
'to surpass all others in splendour and ostentation' (Sombart, 1998: 4).
However, as the function of gold and other precious metals moved from
adornment to currency, the cultural emphasis shifted correspondingly from
aesthetics and sentimentalism to economic exchange, and greed for gold
shifted to love of money. This was diffused through European populations
from the thirteenth century onwards, starting with Italy and Spain, and the
Lutheran movement relaid the foundations of Christianity by transferring
the love of money from heresy to the epicentre of economic and social relations. Money was sought by extra-economic measures; violence, intimidation, scheming and magic, and the invention of money-making schemes
became known as 'projecting' or 'undertaking'. This produced a spectrum of
ideas that ranged from sound economic sense to childishness and frivolity

and unadulterated swindling: beauty lotions, elixirs of life, tonics, remedies and so on. The deregulation of trading activity and the reproduction of ignorance and credulity amongst the consuming population were important. The famous Cagliostro exploited female anxiety, vanity and narcissism, which also grew in the male cultures of the elite as they became the targets of this early marketing. It was an arena for the gamester's energy and passion, the playground of the Odyssean trickster (Adorno & Horkheimer, 1992). The problem at the inception of early capitalism was not just the *criminalization* of peasant customs associated with subsistence and common ownership but the *decriminalization* and tacit glorification of the roguish tricksterism of usurers, speculators, projectors and *undertakers*.

The glorified functional immoralities of the undertakers were separated from crimes by insisting that the former were not the products of sudden instinctive actions. If they were well planned, economically functional and used persuasion rather than the abrupt practices of transparent deception, intimidation or violence, they were allowed to cross the ethical line that separated criminality from acceptable business practice. The entrepreneur had to be a conqueror, a risk-taker, a crude psychologist, a gambler, an organizer and a trader all rolled into one. Narcissism met transcendence as it broke through all pre-existing symbolic prohibitions, and entrepreneurs constructed an image of themselves – which they also had the power to disseminate as they became involved in sponsoring arts and advancing communication technologies – as pioneers standing head and shoulders above the repressed, indolent and bovine mass. The Symbolic Law that governed pre-capitalist European ethical and socio-economic practices was a fetter to be removed, along with all 'feudal, patriarchal and idyllic relations' (Marx & Engels, 1972: 82).

In the early city states and later nation-states royal leaders sought communion with business leaders as they began to run their states like adventurous undertakings, which suggests that the state in its current form is a continuation of what has been since the Renaissance, or even the Statute of Winchester in the English case; essentially a bourgeois state (Hall & Winlow, 2003). In the shape of the Medicis, we saw for the first time in European history a family of bankers make the transition to ruling princes, such was the expectation, awe and power that the accumulation of money could command. Royalty, civil servants, bankers, speculators, landlords, freebooters, pirates, and everyday traders were captivated by the unfolding opportunities in the new economic order, and combined forces as they entered into its spirit and practices. Banking was the pinnacle of 'undertaking', a product of the huge amounts of money that could be made by lending out other people's money on the 'magical' principle of fractional reserve lending

(Mellor, 2010; Rowbotham, 1998; Shaxson, 2011). Only the independent criminal from the lower orders who refused to sublimate and transpose his acquisitive practices into 'undertakings' was excluded, only to be re-included later as a retrospective romantic figure in literature and revisionist history once his real threat had passed. For instance, the piracy and highway robbery that numbered amongst the first capitalist undertakings were glorified and romanticized because of the role they played in the expansion of state power and capitalist markets; this was undertaking, whereas independent criminality was simply crime. In the summer of 1563 no less than four hundred privateers were reported to have roamed the English Channel, and by 1717 no less than fifteen hundred were said to be operating off the shores of Carolina, exempt from practical legal restraint or moral disapprobation from their country of origin (Sombart, 1998). Privateers were known for greed, brutality, organizational capacity, superstition and childishness. Much early trading was freebooting, plain and simple, and natives from conquered territories were the principle targets of deception and thinly disguised theft (Harvey, 2010).

Simmel's (1978) more metaphysical, psychologistic and transhistorical concept of the mentality that thrived in capitalist societies was historicized and explained in more generative detail by Sombart (1998), for whom the capitalist undertaker was a mixture of ruthlessness, calculation and extreme childishness in desires and tastes, especially those orientated to novelty. All these drives were to be held in check by the cultural commands of asceticism and a legal system adjusted to the deregulatory needs of capitalist development, the protection of private property and the maintenance of social order in a climate of extreme individual restlessness and ambition. The socialization process became schizoid, as families were expected to instil in children extreme competitive and acquisitive urges at the same time as restrained, civilized means of practicing and satisfying them. We cannot see Protestantism as the progenitor of the spirit of capitalist adventuring; the capitalist market and its early undertakers can be traced back to the tenth century, and the early merchant adventurers – the Raleighs, the Cavendishes, the Drakes, the Fuggers – also pre-dated the Protestant era. We must suspect that Protestantism was a hastily assembled insulation and control mechanism for a very powerful force whose socio-cultural destructiveness and economic dynamism had been recognized. However, rather like Durkheim (1970), who relied on the transhistorical Aristotelian notion of the 'malady of infinite aspirations' – a crude, unelaborated guess at a reductionist bio-psychological impulse – and Merton (1938), who relied on 'culture'. Sombart could not explain the basis of the desire for unlimited acquisition. To gain initial insights into this problem we had to wait for

Veblen, Freud, Lacan and the Frankfurt School. However, what we should note here is that all these 'depth thinkers', as well as others such as Bourdieu and Baudrillard, have been largely dismissed or marginalized during the development of twentieth-century Anglo-American criminological thought.

In contrast to this highly critical depth thinking, the Whiggish view of modernity focuses on the benign, choosing individual as the great achievement of civilization, whilst acknowledging in Weberian fashion the difficulties encountered when confronting the need to make free choices in relative isolation. For instance, Thomas (2009), basing his analysis on the period 1530–1780, from the Reformation to the American War of Independence, reflects on the difficult task of deciding on how the individual should live. The ideal of personal autonomy became a motif of Enlightenment liberalism, a celebration of the ability to choose one's own objectives and fulfil one's own desires. Individual becoming and fulfilment were seen as the great rewards of the liberal victory over the preceding Dark Age of tyrannical social and religious conventions. The liberal philosopher Martha Nussbaum echoes the preciousness with which the guarantee of non-interference in 'certain choices that are especially personal or definitive of selfhood' (in Thomas, 2009: 11) is regarded. It shows how strongly liberals believe that we all will and choose ourselves into being.

Here, the absolute objectivity of Plato and Aristotle's *eudaimonia*, obtained by the realization of the life in the highest forms of philosophical contemplation and backed up by activity in political and cultural life, was dissolved into an impossibly complex concatenation of individual life-choices. There is no room for ideology, the unconscious and the Real, and society and history become, like neoliberalism's ideology of the market, an aggregate of free choices. De-emphasized is the fact that freedom was to be structured under the harsh logic of the market; the traditional rigid form of authority was replaced by a form that was more flexible yet no less severe, and freedom was won at the expense of security. If one failed to show ambition, drive and independence of spirit, one deserved one's lot as a wage-slave in a servile occupation. If we descend for a moment back into the reality underneath Nussbaum's ideal world of privatized imagination and free will, it seems likely that all choices concerned with one's material position or with the general moral and political coordinates of society itself were dependent on access to money, power and influence.

Thomas and Nussbaum exemplify a liberalism that overstates the achievements of its historical development as a free space for the creative individual whilst disavowing its obscene underbelly of violence, exploitation, appropriation and corruption (Davis, 2002; Seymour, 2008). Capitalism, liberalism's underlying economic system, is a community founded upon the master signifier of money. Primitive accumulation, the initial struggle over the means of accumulating money as capital, was – and, as we shall see later, in some forms still is – every bit as violent and predatory as the feudal appropriation of land:

> The original accumulation of capital during late medieval times in Europe entailed violence, predation, thievery, fraud and robbery. Through these extra-legal means, pirates, priests and merchants, supplemented by the usurers, assembled enough initial 'money power' to begin to circulate money systematically as capital. The Spanish robbery of Inca gold was the paradigmatic example. In the early stages, however, capital did not circulate directly through production. It took a variety of other forms, such as agrarian, merchant, landed and sometimes state mercantilist capital. These forms were not adequate to absorb the vast inflows of gold. Too much gold pursued too few goods. The result was the 'grand inflation' of the sixteenth century in Europe. It was only when capitalists learned to circulate capital through production employing wage labour that compound growth could begin after 1750 or so. (Harvey, 2010: 49)

Technically speaking, the expansion of capitalism's production-enhanced money economy should have rendered violent, criminal accumulation redundant. But 'primitive accumulation' by dispossession continues to play a role in capitalist development, providing alternative markets for the absorption of largely debt-free capital and the production of profit. Violent and fraudulent predatory practices, straddling the boundaries between legal markets such as sub-prime mortgage lending and illegal markets such as drugs and body parts, still feature today. Emile Zola (2007) observed speculation and gambling at the heart of the enterprise, and Keynes (1935) was fully aware that the practices of putting capital into circulation, if not necessarily the actual choices of goods, are driven by the beliefs, desires and anticipations that he termed 'animal spirits', an aggregative form independent of the free conscious choices of individuals but directly connected to disavowed unconscious drives operating as libidinal energy sources. Most of the great minds in literature and economics have been aware of 'animal spirits', but it is an aspect of the human condition that has been systematically avoided by most liberal philosophers and social scientists. In its acquisitive forms criminality is simply an alternative method of speculation, gambling and primitive accumulation (Hall & Winlow, 2007); low investment, high return, and, in the economic sense, low-risk, which is traded in for a high risk in the legal sense. Even many of its expressive forms, such as violence against women in the domestic sphere and bullying in the workplace, reflect the ability to avoid productive labour and dominate in a way that can cause direct harm but also reduce the other to the status of a serf.

Whenever serious criminals embark on a project, the objective is usually money, and, broadly speaking, the motivational forces are to be found in variants of 'animal spirits', a concept hatched by Keynes (1935) as he was writing his *General Theory* in the midst of the Great Depression. Champions of the neoliberal revolution such as Hayek (1948) and Friedman (2002) consigned it to the historical dustbin as they revived the utilitarian notion of the human being as an intrinsic rational calculator and the neoclassical notion of the market as a transparent information system matching supply with demand. However, now that the Credit Crunch and its aftermath have once again shown us why neoclassicism was discredited in the first place, a new wave of economists such as Akerlof and Shiller (2009) see capitalism as a creative and dynamic system populated by largely benign beings, but with a soft underbelly that derives from the system's need to call upon irrational and intractable 'animal spirits'. Social scientists of the past knew that animal spirits run deep in culture and the human psyche, but today they have eschewed that investigation and focused on the surface forms of language and discourse. However, that the capitalist economy stimulates and harnesses irrational human fears, drives and desires is simply accepted by the better economists.

One of the more interesting animal spirits is 'money illusion'. In strict economic terms it is the failure to see money as a form relative to prices and the tendency to see it instead as a nominal form that is an absolute and reliable storehouse of value and unit of exchange. Both businesses and workers are prone to money illusion as they consistently fail to factor in to their decisions the inflationary tendencies in price and wage rises that will eventually negate the value of both profits and wages. It assumes particular importance in the financial dimensions of savings and securities, where inflationary tendencies and money illusion feed into corruption, bad faith and the spread of the sort of irresponsible speculation that has seen many financial companies fail.

However, perhaps economists, with their tendency to see such problems as avoidable systemic aberrations and 'moral hazards', omit the probability that money illusion is an unavoidable and primal psychosocial product of life in the capitalist system. After the historical break with land and family as the primary foundations of security and the subsequent shift to the commercial market economy, the need to attribute some degree of stability to money as a storehouse of economic value and a symbol of social standing must have been extremely pressing. Some substitute for the lost objects of security and solidarity had to be found; even though the traditional forms were neither reliable nor progressive they were better than nothing in a post-imperial Dark Age permeated by brigandage, famine and myriad forms of insecurity. However, in an unstable and disruptive period where trust in the social world and individual behaviour is in decline, the social function of money as a simple technical means of exchange (see Mellor, 2010) is an unattractive proposition. Insecure individuals seek money in excess of its basic technical function as a *substitute* for an unstable socio-economic world, not just a representation of it and a means of trading within it; as such, faith must be placed in money as a reliable storehouse of value over a lifetime. Money comes to be imagined as a form of reliable private property in an unstable commercial system where the former stable storehouses of value – land, labour, buildings and loyal family and community members – are disrupted, atomized, commodified and increasingly susceptible to market forces. The orientation here is towards what Marx (1954) famously described as compulsive money-hoarding. It does not take a great leap of the imagination to suspect that a greater feeling of security of rightful place in families, communities and the broader social processes of production could reduce the individual's psychosomatic dependence on money.

Along with Marx (1954), Veblen (1994) also saw the financial institutionalization and domination of the credit/debt nexus as a means of creating a dominant layer of fictionalized money that broke social bonds and subjugated the whole productive/communal dimension of the social into a position of total control and dependency on capitalism's financial institutions. According to Mellor (2010), the history of capitalism is also the history of a developing 'financialized society' where value is expressed predominantly in terms of money. Solidarity and security are no longer seen in terms of the public or the collective but in terms of the individual protecting property rights and achieving a sense of security through the accumulation of money as a storehouse of value. However, security in money is an illusion, and there is no hiding place in property; where money is susceptible to inflation and irresponsible lending practices, property is susceptible to deflationary spirals where the owner is left with something worth less than its initial purchase price, seen regularly in today's housing market as 'negative equity'. In the world of capitalist commerce, nothing is stable as a storehouse of value. Stories still exist of what life is like in a hyper-inflationary economy where land, labour and family have been substituted for money, yet *money itself* has also collapsed as a storehouse of value and a medium of exchange. The citizen is tempted to short-cut the whole affair and simply try to attain as much property *and* money as possible, in whatever proportion; property, it is hoped, will offset inflation whilst money offsets deflation.

The privatized capitalist money-form has replaced our dreams of solidarity and cultural enrichment because the limitlessness of its vision fills the whole horizon. As Harvey (2011) reminds us, we cannot own billions of material objects; the reality of doing so would be impossible and worthless, and the dream absurd, a true psychotic state of being. But the dream of owning billions of dollars is normal, in fact celebrated and reproduced by the institutions of popular mass-mediated culture. Money has also colonized the valorization mechanisms of high culture, even though it has not secured a complete victory. It could be said that the deep critique of consumption as the destroyer of organic forms of life parallels the critique of money as the corroder and eventual destroyer of politics and social relations; it is not that money and consumer culture take advantage of destructive atomizing forces, but that they themselves number amongst the most potent of these forces (Jameson, 2010). With the accumulation of money comes an accumulation of social power in a paradoxically devalued social body. Money and the means of physical protection and enforcement still go hand in hand with status, and crime – most notably fraud, corruption, illegal trafficking, robbery and banditry – is an efficient means for the successful practitioner to achieve the social position and accumulate the social power that money confers upon the individual, but all this is done at the expense of corroding the social itself.

The accumulation of pockets of money can be imagined by individuals to secure them against an unpredictable future (Langley, 2006), and as such it has displaced, demoted and brought under its control violence, production, institutions of social obligation, honour and all the other forces that once constituted the social matrix as the bedrock of prosperity and security. Successful criminality is an efficient way of avoiding debt and tax whilst elevating the individual up the ranks of security and post-social status. In many well-heeled urban streets, successful criminals are the only people who can afford to move in alongside the usual bankers, consultant surgeons, lawyers, celebrities and business owners. We must move away from the romantic notion that criminals try to set up alternative systems of honour and trust (Linebaugh, 1991) to the more realistic notion that they operate in an alternative debt-free money economy and post-social hierarchy. According to many criminals, everyday lives plagued by debt, moderate incomes, low social status, sacrifice and responsibility are for 'mugs' (Hall at al., 2005). Wider systems of trust and exchange reduced to money also enhance social and geographical mobility; the current phase of accelerated globalization allows global criminal markets in money and goods to operate in the slipstream of legitimate global markets (Nordstrom, 2007). These debt-free and tax-free criminal markets, where trust is organized organically, are in the pure economic sense, if not the cultural and interpersonal senses, more stable, especially when on the demand side of their economic equation they deal in the baser and thus more reliable human drives and desires. At the local level these markets are also more easily monopolized and defended by criminal networks, which have displaced traditional 'family firms' operating in their 'manors' and now constitute themselves by means of more complex and volatile relations of trust (Von Lampe & Johansen, 2004). Operating a local protectionist policy in a more untrustworthy cultural climate might cause intermittent turf wars, but it will not crash the criminal economy.

The most fundamental service successful acquisitive crime provides is the expansion and reproduction of alternative markets whose traders and consumers are kept from sinking so low into the economic quagmire that their only way out would be an unwanted outbreak of political solidarity. It also helps to solve capitalism's fundamental problem, what Harvey (2010) calls 'surplus capital absorption'. At this socio-economic depth the demarcation between functional and dysfunctional crime becomes truly blurred. During such times in which legitimate investment opportunities decline, criminal markets absorb and circulate capital that is largely debt-free, provided either by welfare payments, wages or profits accrued in the myriad complex transactions of crime itself. The 'profit on alienation' principle (see Wood, 2002) aligns crime with early forms of merchant capitalism and, as Karl Marx demonstrated in *The Grundrisse* (1973), crime adds an additional level of material activity that helps capitalism to break through the limits of its investment capabilities set by the economic conditions that exist at any given time, especially during periods of recession and capital retraction. As global crime proliferates and mutates it helps to absorb and circulate capital and produce profits, which eventually filter back into the system as criminals who achieve varying levels of success become more active in various consumer markets. At the same time as it creates supplementary international markets, the criminal economy in its 'glocal' form (see Hobbs, 1998) re-energizes local and regional supply networks and replaces opportunities for economic activity that have been lost in the wake of deindustrialization. Criminal markets can actually reintroduce lost stability and opportunity into local areas, avoid dependence on the decisions of the financial industry and avoid the trap of debt slavery; all at the same time as corroding the local community's social relations and quality of life.

Historical patterns of crime are complex, and those who are interested are advised to read the voluminous literature. However, underneath the complexity the basic shift in the pattern of criminal motivations and practices across the modernist-capitalist era has been two-fold. Firstly, a move from violent to relatively less violent means of controlling sectors of production and trade and dominating others; the traditional means of violence was monopolized by the nation-state. Secondly, a shift in the balance from collective forms of grounded honour and security provided by the social institutions of the family and community and the material forms of land, tangible goods and precious metals to the imagined honour and security provided in an atomized post-social world by money and the ability to display consumer novelties as symbols of success in the competitive market economy. These shifts seem to have occurred as important interactive aspects – functional, consequential and expressive – of the broad development of the capitalist market economy. We must remember, however, that these shifting criminal motivations also ran alongside 'social crime', a product of the anger, resentment and senses of absolute and relative deprivation felt by those economically dispossessed and socially marginalized by the capitalist system. However, denied the hope that can be provided by functioning collectivist identities and politics, many criminals embraced bourgeois ambitions and took advantage of opportunities in an expanding consumer-driven economy. From the brigands who monopolized land and early commerce in the insecure times of thirteenth-century England to the criminal networks that today attempt to corner sectors of markets in legal and illegal goods, successful criminals represent the extremity of a cultural form forged in competitive and systematically fragmented economic activity. All over the word we must suspect that forms of criminality exist at points between pre-modern territorial brigandage and late-modern deterritorialized business networks, and at points between social and entrepreneurial crime. Whilst unsuccessful criminals hang on as atomized and exploited casual labour in criminal markets or sink back into welfare dependency, the ruthless undertakers, the movers and shakers who are 'gifted with ferocity' (Veblen, 1994: 145) in both their warrior and entrepreneurial guises, driven by anxiety and attracted by seductive visions of self-aggrandizement (Hall et al., 2008), continue to remind us what the obscene Real underneath our way of life is all about.

CRIME TRENDS IN THE NEOLIBERAL AGE

3

Although the previous chapter constructed a rough adumbration of historical crime trends in England, we must not get the impression of crime rising and falling *en masse* like a Mexican wave in a football ground. The category 'crime' itself is hotly contested and of course socially constructed, so the fine details of the general trend are inordinately complex, and of course 'crime trends' are not synonymous with 'harm trends'. Crudely demarcating the social body into groups serves us badly; throughout this historical period a hugely diverse range of harmful and minor crimes have been committed by individuals and institutional groups throughout the social order, and there is no such thing as the 'criminal culture', the 'criminal gender', the 'criminal class' or the 'criminal underclass'. Minor delinquency might have been quite common amongst young people (Pearson, 1992), but the various types of serious harmful crimes we have seen across the history of the capitalist/modernist project are minority activities, 'undertakings' that for various reasons in various situations are committed by individuals willing to risk the infliction of serious harm on others in the process of furthering the interests of the self, whether those interests be material, social, pleasurable or cathartic. Difficult economic conditions produced opportunities and alternative markets in which specific individuals chose to indulge in crime as an alternative to political solidarity, and as a personal undertaking, an illegal enterprise to either acquire material goods or achieve positions of domination and status, or mollify some deep desire for pleasure; late-modern consumer culture has become expert in combining these urges in a single potent form harnessed to economic growth (Hall et al., 2005).

However, as we have seen in the previous chapter we can risk a tentative adumbration of the general historical trend in England, and later Europe and the USA in their specific time-frames (Hall & McLean, 2009), as a definite decline in murder and serious violence in the public sphere accompanied by a probable increase in property crimes. In the nineteenth century violence was still a problem in many spheres, but in general the homicide rate continued to decline (Eisner, 2001) and street violence became less common despite spates of robbery and occasional gang fights (Hallsworth, 2006). Instrumental and acquisitive crimes were committed by those with the drive and the nerve required to do so, an inclination expressed by various vernacular terms, most commonly 'the bottle'. The active criminal is an individual whose domineering, acquisitive and thymotic status-seeking drives are just sufficiently stimulated – and whose pacifying sensibilities are just sufficiently underdeveloped – to allow high levels of risk-taking. From Edward Teach, Jack Sheppard and Dick Turpin onwards, the spectacularly successful criminal does not upturn the social order, as Rawlings (1999) argues, but, in Lacanian terms, conforms to the vulgar competitive Real and the narcissistic Imaginary with too much enthusiasm whilst contravening the normative insulation expressed by the fundamental injunction that the individual should achieve success in a way that is as ruthlessly competitive as necessary, yet pacified and within the boundaries marked by the selective negativity of the law (Hall et al., 2008). Too much stimulation of obscene drives and/or too much recession of pacified sensibilities will produce the reckless and largely unsuccessful impulsive opportunist, or the 'jumpy jack' in north-east English criminal vernacular. This individual thrives in conditions characterized by the relative absence of the ethico-political desires that create the active social subject. Active political subjects increase and criminal subjects decrease under conditions of healthy institutionalized social conflict (Wieviorka, 2009), not so much homeostatic stability as a dynamic equilibrium that provides identity, hope and purpose, what we will come to understand later in the argument as the resumption of the social dialectic. The most indicative examples are the 'solidarity projects' in mid-nineteenth-century Britain, New Deal USA and post-war social-democratic Europe (Currie, 2010; Garland, 2001; Lea, 2002; Reiner, 2007). In fact, in Britain we could regard the gradual consolidation of industrial society, the awakening of class consciousness, the institutionalization of class conflict and the resumption of dialectical momentum as the most anti-criminogenic period in British history, as John Lea's (2006) well-known graph demonstrates (Figure 3.1).

In the abstract and individualist terms that liberalism prefers, this period in history was not more socially 'equal' or 'free' than it is today. Throughout the twentieth century significant rights and freedoms have been won on behalf of individuals, especially those belonging to minority groups. What did exist in this earlier period, however, was gathering socio-political solidarity and dialectical momentum in which a vital sense of mutual interests and common fate could grow amongst diverse individuals and cultural groups. Many eyes were fixed on a future horizon of mutual prosperity,

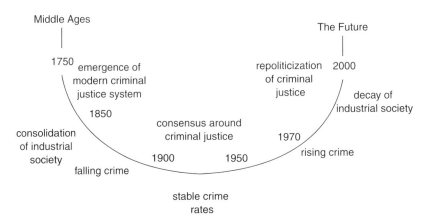

Figure 3.1   John Lea's (2006) graph comparing crime rates with social change, 1750 to the present

peace and solidarity, and it is quite possible that this constitutes the vital underlying condition for reductions in harmful crime from the real motivational perspective, rather than simply from the social constructionist, discursive and crime-control perspectives, which, when all the decorations are stripped away, are little more than games of language and social administration. However, the solidarity project was a fragile process, always under intense pressure from powerful conservative and classical-liberal counter-ideologies, internal dissenters and precarious, undulating economic circumstances. Perhaps the more powerful – and certainly the most seductive – amongst the counter-forces was not conservative repression but the 'modern' classical-liberal ethical doctrine that life is an open competition and successful individuals should take all opportunities for prosperity and freedom and keep all the rewards achieved by their efforts. In *La Belle Époque* this counter-force was at its height amongst the elite strata as successful entrepreneurs made vast fortunes on the back of working-class masses in industrialized nations whose intense imperialistic competition made economic life precarious and political life volatile. This trajectory culminated in social polarization, irresponsible financial speculation, economic depression and two world wars; Western industrialized nations that had been characterized by internal pacification processes experienced social strain and rising crime, and periodically exploded into catastrophic bouts of inter-state violence instigated by plutocratic elites who exercised assiduous control over the state and mass media apparatuses.

The fragility of the English solidarity project was reflected in rising crime rates, which, after six decades of decline, began to rise again slowly in 1921 (Reiner, 2012). Every first-year student should know that we must never

underestimate the effects of changing criminal justice practices when ana-
lysing crime statistics, but, if we do that, in this case the final analysis is not
the one that the liberal left would prefer. Crime rates rose immediately
after a decarceration process and a period where discretionary police practice was becoming more lenient (Reiner, 2010). Had the police continued
to arrest individuals for very minor offences, the statistical rise would have
been significantly more abrupt. Crime rates rose steadily in proportion to
population expansion throughout the 1930s and 1940s, to some extent
casting doubt on the myth of the communal spirit of the Depression and
War years, and through to the mid-1970s, eventually exploding in the
1980s. This rise occurred at a time when police strength and the prison
population were both rising, which suggests either that the statistical 'crime
rise' was a product of changes in government policy and police practice that
produced more arrests and recordings, or that a real rise in harmful crime
created a discernible public need for a rise in policing, arrests and impris-
onments. Police statistics are of course epistemological representations of
police actions taken, not of some ontological reality 'out there', and are
thus notoriously unreliable. Therefore representational estimates of the existence of 'harm' in the real world are the results of police perceptions and
practices, government policies and, therefore, as Emsley (2010) reminds us,
in a society in which government tends to represent ruling-class interests,
class perceptions. This argument can be countered by the claim that because
governments rely on legitimation by the public, and criminal law is not representative entirely of bourgeois interests (Cole, 2001; Thompson, 1975),
public perceptions generated by real public experiences and needs are more
important. Then again, of course, public perceptions can be manipulated by
the mass media on behalf of and prevailing hegemonic ideologies, but these
perceptions also change as sensibilities develop (Young, 2007); it might well
be the case that, in a historical period in which the majority of individuals
have become accustomed to a relative lack of real threats in everyday life, they
are more fearful and less tolerant of minor violations of their negative rights.
In other words our relatively irenic times might have produced individuals
who are more sensitive and easily scared by minor threats and mass mediated
images. The obvious logical extension of Young's argument, which has only a
feint presence in the left-liberal canon, is that in a climate of increased threats
these sensibilities will diminish (Winlow & Hall, 2006; 2009b).

There is probably a kernel of truth in these phenomenological arguments based on shifting perceptions and sensibilities, but it is very difficult
to accept that shifts in government policies, police practices and public
perceptions and sensibilities are the sole causes of the gargantuan rise in
recorded crime in late twentieth-century Britain, and the rise in violence

and the far more statistically reliable category of homicide since the 1950s (Reiner, 2007). As Young (2004) reminds us, to accept statistical constructions and their accompanying ideological biases without serious criticism is indeed to fall under the spell of 'voodoo criminology'. On the other hand, to deny the existence of harms that in everyday reality range from the localized and the interpersonal to the global and the structural is to fall under the spell of voodoo phenomenology. Strictly speaking, none of this has anything to do with social science, theory or philosophy; it is a political argument between pragmatic social managers, pessimistic declinists and optimistic progressivists, or, on another slightly offset axis, disciplinarians, humanitarians and self-appointed arbiters. However, we should not accept without criticism the current orthodox view that these triangular polarities represent true ideologically opposed arguments, because of course a genuinely alternative ideology was never a serious possibility in the West's social-democratic era of 'compromise politics'. The struggle took place, as we shall investigate in more detail later, between two anxious anti-dialectical progressive liberal and declinist conservative 'steering groups' whose diametrically opposing fears were the products of their respective visions of either *the barbarism of order* or *the barbarism of disorder* (Oakeshott, 1996), overseen by a third liberal-pragmatic umpire trying to strike a risk-assessed balance between them; alternative ideology and political praxis exist in a third space beyond this managed undialectical struggle.

Can current criminological data and knowledge help us to move beyond progressivist and declinist ideologies and construct more reliable pictures of harmful crime in the broader global context? If we take a brief comparative look we can see that England and Wales have the second highest rate of recorded crime out of 37 European countries, and since the 1980s we have weighed in with roughly twice the western European average. Counting rules for police-recorded crime changed in 1998/9 and 2002/3, which has exaggerated both decreases and increases in the overall rate in the following period. This supports neither the declinist nor progressivist side. In the latter half of the century, from 1950 to 1992, the era in which mass consumption and consumer culture pervaded Britain and severe economic disruption irrevocably changed British life, recorded crime in England and Wales increased twelve-fold from 461,000 to 5,592,000; it's difficult to believe that there were corresponding shifts of anywhere near the same magnitude in public sensibilities and perceptions, government policies, police practices and imprisonment rates. By 1998/9 the crime rate had fallen back to 4,482,000, still 10 times the rate in 1950, but the 2008/9 figure of 4,704,000 is higher, showing that to a small extent the decline began to go into reverse. The declinists' sleight-of-hand is to blame crime rises on cultural disintegration caused by immigration and the permissive sixties, whilst ignoring profound economic disruption, widening socio-economic inequality and the fact that immigration and permissiveness did not create such crime explosions or punitive reactions in the more economically stable western Europe (Hall & McLean, 2009; Reiner, 2007). The progressivists' sleight-of-hand is to locate the crime drop in a short period of time; a 40 per cent drop in this period translates into far smaller proportional declines should we take the medium-term view since 1950 or the long-term view since 1900.

Overall, the police statistics for the post-war era in which social democracy mutated into consumer culture and neoliberal political economy show a 1,200 per cent increase up to the mid-1990s and then a 40 per cent decrease between the mid-1990s and 2008/9. A long-term movement of twelve steps up, two steps down in a comparative context in which Britain is the second-worst in Europe is, in the vernacular, not much to write home about. It's uncontroversial to say that the USA has experienced the highest homicide rates – and the USA and Britain have amongst the highest rates of crime – in the industrialized West, along with the highest rates of most other negative social indicators (Wilkinson & Pickett, 2009). These crime rates have been exceeded in some developing nations and post-communist nations, in which the reasons for what is more likely to be a greater proportion of 'social crime' compared to predatory crime are certainly more understandable; enforced economic restructuring and politico-cultural disruption, extreme poverty sometimes approaching the absolute, extreme social inequality and in many cases corrupt failed states or neoliberal puppet states that can neither exercise control nor provide welfare. In Britain and the USA, however, such excuses are relatively thin on the ground. Indeed, if we look at a rise in the rate of indictable crimes known to the police in England and Wales from 2.4 per 1,000 of the population in 1900 to almost 120 per 1,000 in the early 1990s – a 4,800 per cent rise during a century when the population rose only about 60 per cent, the number of police officers rose about 300 per cent and police practice became more lenient – we must be looking at an underlying real rise in offences of a notable magnitude. The rate did fall back to 116 per 1,000 in 2008, and many offences could be represented as quite minor, so what proportion of that total is constituted by a rise in the willingness of individuals to do serious harm to others in the interests of the self is of course another question.

In order to negotiate a path beyond what we have come to know as the rather sterile argument between positivism and phenomenology since 1979 – when early victimization studies knocked the purist form of left idealism off its ideological throne and paved the way for more penetrative analyses

by feminists investigating privatized and gendered interpersonal violence
and left realists investigating intra-class crimes and harms – we need to
build a more realistic picture. There is little doubt that there has been both
a long-term rise in recorded crime in England and Wales throughout the
twentieth century and a dramatic rise in recorded crime since the 1950s:

> Between the 1850s and the 1920s crime remained on a plateau.
> During the 1930s there was a period of substantial and sustained
> increase, continuing through the early years of the Second World
> War. In the decade following the war there were several short
> cycles of rising and falling rates, but no clear trend. But from
> 1955 recorded crime began a massive and sustained long-term
> growth. (Reiner, 2007: 63)

Of course, the police statistics are misleading national averages that take
into account neither victim knowledge nor local and regional differences,
nor the dark figure of crime. The existence of the dark figure of unreported
and unrecorded incidents of possible criminalizable harms is often estimated at about 70 to 80 per cent of the total. The British Crime Survey
statistics are of course more representative of 'reality', but still not reliable;
researchers have begun to interview individuals under the age of 16 only
recently, and of course data is constructed from the unverifiable perceptions and knowledges of interviewees selected by researchers and responding to their potentially leading questions. That crime is a socially constructed
category belies the notion that somewhere out there is a concrete reality
that can be revealed by sophisticated statistical work; the reality we are
investigating is not 'crime' but a bubbling processual magma of individual
harms existing across many axes; constant/sporadic, individual/institu-
tional, intentional/unintentional and so on. Many of these harms – especially those committed by the powerful – are either not criminalized or not
thoroughly investigated or prosecuted. Such positivist data is always unreliable, but, on the other hand, if we approach the issue through the lenses of
phenomenology, language and discourse we simply end up with a will-o'-
the-wisp, a swirling mist of sense impressions and linguistic categories, a
realm of impenetrable Kantian noumena to which we have no true access
even with our most sophisticated systems of research techniques and symbols. Yet, the magma of harms rumbles along underneath us on its implac-
able course, often ruining the real lives of real individuals and groups alike
in ways over which we seem to have little control other than measures of
situational prevention and *post hoc* justice that seem to satisfy very few victims, especially those who live in the more troubled locales and suffer the

constant 'background static' of petty crime and aggression (Horne & Hall, 1995). If we settle on the belief that all we can ever achieve is a hazy, adumbrated phenomenological snapshot of this vast magma then we might as well give up on criminological theory, or at least aetiological macro-theory. There are voices amongst us who would advocate such a position (Cohen, 1988), and were it to be taken, the discipline will have moved fully across the spectrum from crude positivism to its opposite, pure phenomenology and discourse analysis, from facts and numbers to words and pictures, from a position that seeks to know and control reality and the Real, often with oppressive or exploitative intentions and catastrophic consequences, to a position where we run away from both like scared rabbits and leave the medium-term future as a hostage to social managerialism and the long-term future as a hostage to neoliberal markets. This catastrophism and fear will be investigated later, but in the meantime, we must find a way out of the ideological mists of both positivism and phenomenology/discourse. Despite the multitude of problems, it's still possible to distil something useful from the diachronic statistical picture:

> [I]t seems that the broad pattern of change over the last half-century is clear. The overwhelming, most dramatic change is the huge increase in recorded crime. Probably a significant (but ultimately unascertainable) proportion of this was due to reporting and recording changes up to about 1980, so the statistics exaggerate the increase in crime. After 1981, with the advent of the BCS, it is possible to be more certain, especially about the 1980s when the two statistical series went in the same direction. Although a small fraction (about a fifth) of the recorded doubling of crime was attributable to more reporting by victims, there can be no doubt about the crime explosion that took place. After 1992 the two series diverge, and interpretation becomes vexed and controversial. Nonetheless, it seems more likely that there has been a diminution of overall crime, especially property crime, as the BCS indicates. (Reiner, 2007: 75)

To look at it in a little more detail with findings from the British Crime Survey:

> Long-term trends show that BCS crime rose steadily from 1981 through to the early 1990s, peaking in 1995. Crime then fell, making 1995 a significant turning point. The fall was substantial

until 2004/05. Since then, BCS crime has shown little overall
change with the exception of a statistically significant reduction
of 10 per cent in 2007/08 (the lowest ever level since the first
results in 1981). The apparent increase of five per cent in BCS
crime this year is not statistically significant. Trends in BCS
violence, vehicle-related theft and burglary broadly reflect the
trend in all BCS crime … The 2008/09 BCS found that the risk
of being a victim of any household crime was higher in the most
deprived areas compared with the least deprived areas in
England. Trends in household crime in the most and least
deprived areas in England have been broadly similar between
2001/02 and 2008/09, with the exception of trends in burglary.
Burglary has decreased in the most deprived areas since 2001/02
while it has remained stable in the least deprived areas … Fifty-
nine per cent of robberies in England and Wales were recorded
by just three forces, the Metropolitan Police, Greater Manchester
and the West Midlands, that represent 24 per cent of the
population. (Walker et al., 2009)

If we add to that Dorling's (2004) finding that the murder rate in deprived
areas is six times higher than the national average, the upshot is that we are
looking at a real explosion of both minor and serious harmful crimes that
occurred disproportionately in the areas of permanent recession created by
the Thatcherite deindustrialization process. Parker (2008), working in the
USA, which also experienced crime explosions in the early 1980s and
1990s, also used statistical analysis to reveal that the crime decline was as
unequal as the crime explosion, with serious harmful crimes declining far
less rapidly in socially distressed deindustrialized areas with high unemployment and racial tensions. Would such a survey in Britain produce similar results? According to Webster (2002), the picture is indeed similar.

   With the vital caveat that longitudinal statistics can only ever provide a
very rough initial adumbration of the underlying magma in which practical
reality and the ideological Real co-exist, there is a possibility that the distinction between violent and non-violent crime might add just another
notch of clarity to the picture and create a tentative connection to reality.
Reiner's (2007) perspicuous analysis of post-war statistics in Britain
pointed towards an 80/20 split between property crime and violent crime
rates in both the police and BCS statistics in 2005/6. Property crime has
always been in preponderance, but in 1976 the split was about 95/5, and
in the 1990s about 90/10. The upshot is that the noughties have seen a

proportionate rise in the rate of violent crime when most other crime rates had stabilized after the initial decline in the mid-1990s. What we can say is well put by Reiner:

> Within the decline in overall crime, the most worrying serious violent crimes have continued to rise. Insofar as the decline in crime overall is due to more successful adoption of protective equipment and prevention routines by crime-conscious citizens, rather than any reduction in the root causes of offending, the burden falls on potential victims above all. While prevention tactics, burdensome as the may be, are preferable to victimization, they are a product of insecurity, and indeed may reinforce rather than reduce fear. What is required is not reassurance about crime but about the causes of crime. However, this cannot be provided so long as neoliberalism, the fundamental source of increasing criminality, and of the accentuation of insecurity and law and order solutions by media and political discourse, remains triumphant. (2007: 162)

We must frame the decline in non-violent crime in the context of a significant increase in the prison population and surveillance, control, security and risk management. There is little doubt that crime declined in Britain and the USA in the 1990s and stabilized in the noughties. We cannot deny that prison incapacitates many habitual offenders, alongside those who should not be imprisoned and those who should be in receipt of treatment for mental health problems and drug addiction (Roberts, 2003). Technological crime prevention and security has also been partially effective. This was allied to socio-economic changes; a more buoyant labour market in the credit-funded service economies, a demographic decline in age-groups normally associated with high rates of crime and changes in drug markets and their policing (Reiner, 2007). However, we also need to look at the mutation of crime, violence and 'harm', and local/regional differentials in the 'unequal crime decline' (Parker, 2008), changes in reporting and recording trends that inform police statistics and victim surveys, and the normalization of actions over time that are slowly being decriminalized as sensibilities and expectations change (Young, 2007).

The 'decline' of crime is simultaneously a real and perceptual phenomenon, and it is tied in with the disappearance of the Real and its actors as they are absorbed in the derealized and therefore anti-democratic symbolic realms of the 'telecracy' (Stiegler, 2010a). In simpler criminological terms, some marginalized individuals simply get what they want in the virtual world of Facebook, eBay, pirated music downloads, games, movies and pornography, and, aided by the tranquilizing effects of cheap smuggled drugs and tobacco (Antonopoulos, 2008), disappear into it, off the streets and largely out of trouble (Treadwell, 2011). Recent research has revealed the partial 'disappearance' of British urban drug gangs from the street into cyberspace, where more efficient distributive networks can be organized (Aldridge et al., 2010). The exception is alcohol, which in large doses and conducive circumstances can disinhibit psycho-cultural restraints and bring underlying aggression to the surface (Winlow & Hall, 2006). Nevertheless, individuals cannot remain in a state of indoor tranquility all day and every day, and petty property crime, violence, intimidation and anti-social behaviour continue to be serious problems in specific locales; under-reported, under-recorded and poorly understood and controlled by the agencies of the social management apparatus (Hall et al., 2008). The picture is unclear, and the relative paucity of criminological research, whose themes and programmes are restricted by dominant social-conservative and social-liberal agendas, which tend to explain away most anti-social activity as either the real product of faulty socialization in a declining culture or the ideological-conspiratorial product of a general 'moral panic' industry organized by the state and the mass media, is not doing much by way of illumination.

The upshot is that positivist accounts of the extent and distribution of crime are conceptually narrow and socially skewed, but they are almost certainly not 'exaggerated'; throughout the social structure, from the organized violence of the corporate state to the petty intimidation and anti-social behaviour in the dilapidated community, rates of harmful crime are far more likely to be underestimated. Broadening both the category and the research's social parameters would produce far higher figures than those we glean from either the police or the BCS. We must understand that the mainstream social research management/funding structure and agenda are the children of paternalistic Victorian philanthropy in Britain (Bushaway, 2003) and the slightly more hip philanthropy that characterizes the liberal progressivist movement in the USA (Melossi, 2008). The fundamental principles of both – the improvement of social justice, well-being and prosperity by modifying government policies without criticizing or disturbing the extant socio-economic system or its fundamental obscene exchange relation and subjective drives – belong to social liberalism; any other discourse is seen as an unwelcome intruder. With research agendas and findings restricted by these rigorously enforced principles, precisely how much harm is being caused by individuals and institutions to others out there in everyday life is at the moment impossible to estimate with any precision, even with the addition of the British Crime Survey, the Scottish Crime and Justice Survey and the USA's National Crime Victimization Survey, none of which follow up superficial survey data with penetrative ethnographic methods or theorization.

Nevertheless, we can use comparative longitudinal and spatial data to build a very rough picture of movement and mutation, if not ontological reality in its diachronic and synchronic forms. If we attempt a brief breakdown of crime, starting with volume crime in England and Wales, we can estimate that domestic burglary rates doubled after 1980 and then halved back to their original level (Kent, 2007), and contemporary forms include significant innovations and mutations, including distraction burglaries, car key burglaries and specific item burglaries. Many drug addicts are involved in burglary, so it is not necessarily a 'rational choice' crime. Car crime underwent a similar pattern without the increase, with innovations allowed by sophisticated export networks; methods of theft have tried to keep up with increasingly sophisticated technology (Brown et al., 2004). Shoplifting has undergone a sustained increase, following fashion trends that promote changes in stolen goods markets (Sutton, 2009) and the increasing desire for the 'shopping experience' (Hall et al., 2008).

Street crime, despite causing concern and fear disproportionate to its incidence as 2 per cent of all crime, is one of only a few crimes that rose continuously throughout the 1990s and early 2000s (Hallsworth, 2006), and it feeds a thriving illegal market in stolen electronic goods such as mobile phones, MP3 players and laptop computers. Because the BCS researchers have not until very recently interviewed individuals under the age of sixteen, the large number of victims and perpetrators in this age-range has not been represented in the statistics, and thus criminologists are reliant on police data. Although young people, as we shall see in more detail later, tend not to specialize too much in the contemporary criminal world, a diverse range of tactics have developed as street robbery has proved lucrative in the age of valuable miniaturized electronic goods; depending on the situational environment and the nature of the victim, the 'blitz', the 'confrontation', the 'con' and the 'snatch' are the most popular and effective (ibid.). Interpersonal violence in the burgeoning night-time economy has also risen exponentially since the 1980s, an environment in which over 90 per cent of incidents remain unreported and unrecorded (Winlow & Hall, 2006), although this has quite possibly decreased after more effective policing strategies were introduced and the recession that followed the Credit Crunch in 2008 reduced the size of this sector of the leisure economy. In this period police and criminologists have become more aware of a rise in alcohol and drug smuggling, a market in which illegal and legal sectors have increasingly merged.

Of all the everyday volume crimes, however, drug distribution remains the most ubiquitous and lucrative (Ghodse, 2009), part of a global industry and market. Less restricted by the pragmatic social-liberal agenda, theorization of the global crime scene is also less squeamish and more revealing to criminological theorists, even though reliable data are perhaps even sparser. In the globalized 'fraud and fake' dimension of criminality, only a small proportion is dealt with by the criminal justice system. It is also grossly under-researched, so the data from all sources are unreliable. From the small amount of data we have we can see that criminal practices in this dimension have become more sophisticated and accelerated by the prevalence of the internet (Yar, 2006). Practices range from payment card frauds at the low end of the spectrum to reckless lending at the top (Levi, 2008). In official circles these crimes are often regarded as 'victimless' despite the inconvenience and distress experienced by the actual victim – which in some cases involves protracted difficulties with credit rating agencies – and costs that are passed on to the consumer and the taxpayer, which indicates the privileged position that business crime seems to enjoy in the criminal justice system's hierarchy of harms. Scams, worth £3.5 billion in 2006, are on the increase in the wake of rapid advances in communications and computer technology (OFT, 2006).

One of the main problems criminologists face is that in the legal sense these crimes exist in the grey area between criminality, civil wrong and immorality, often dealt with by civil law and consumer protection legislation as well as criminal law (Passas, 2005). In other words, most dimensions of crime and harm are so poorly researched and reliant on the broad and partial strokes of police or survey data that, despite the existence of more sophisticated and revealing research methods, we are largely working in a realm of empirical darkness, which of course turns crime and harm into the most potent political and ideological footballs. We seem to spend an inordinate amount of time poring over data that we know is partial and using it to support pragmatic, utopian, dystopian or conspiratorial claims that usually turn out to be absurd or useless. The only reliable data we have – homicide rates and imprisonment rates – are, with notable exceptions (Currie, 2010; Dorling, 2004; Matthews, 2005), underused in the construction of mainstream theories and tend to be discussed more often in criminological subdisciplines or human rights discourses.

Since the Ancient World globalization has been a vision of conquerors and traders alike (Braudel, 1995), and of course every expansionary phase of commerce brought with it increased opportunities for trafficking, piracy and the expansion of illegal distributional markets, along with technical advances in criminal organization and practices. In pure trading terms the development of the globalization process was more rapid in *La Belle Époque*, but since the 1980s technological developments, the transnational diffusion of production centres and trade arteries and the intensification of market dependency have qualitatively transformed the process. We now confront a globalizing economy in which time-space compression, the spread of neo-liberal ideology, neoliberal economic restructuring programmes and attempted cultural homogenization in the direction of Western competitive individualism and consumerism are having profound effects on the lives of most of the word's populations. In some ways these changes have been developmental, but in others regressive (Lechner, 2009). We now witness the return, in modern technologically-enhanced guise, of the traditional practices of merchant capitalism; the renewed dominance of 'profit on alienation' as goods are transferred from cheap markets to expensive mar-kets, and neomediaevalization as private entities become the dominant politico-economic actors, disturbing and suspending the struggle for sub-stantive democracy and threatening the legitimacy of nation-states. Advances in communications technologies have accelerated the develop-ment of global criminal networks and operations, which have been further enhanced by the expansion of transport, especially shipping, where the illegal distribution of tangible commodities can be buried under the huge volume of ships unloading at large port complexes. This makes inspection very difficult and the bulk of illegal trafficking almost impossible to detect and regulate. For capitalism, efficiency in trade is defined by the uninter-rupted circulation of goods, and slowing up shipping and dock work for the sake of frequent regulatory checks would disable the global economy (Nordstrom, 2007). Criminal traffickers duly take advantage of this relent-less imperative.

Capitalist globalization has polarized the world into regions of extreme wealth and poverty. In an economic climate of unforgiving market competi-tion and gridlocked interdependency, in which the fate of the individual and the whole nation hangs in the balance, crime and terrorism become mega-risks that have to be taken by those in desperate situations (ibid.), or which appear as opportunities to those in advantageous positions; desperation meets temptation in a complex dynamic process. At the very epicentre of global capitalism the advent of global markets, financial institutions and transnational corporations, amidst the diffusion of deterritorialized net-works and the decline of state-centred social democracy, has placed the speculative financial industry in an almost unassailable position of domi-nance over the power of workers to further their interests by means of tra-ditional nation-bound labour politics. In this post-political environment of economic deregulation the acceleration of the global movement of financial and productive capital has in its wake increased the global movement of commodities and people, breaking down and atomizing collective political and ethical traditions. Unless we have faith in the optimistic liberal concepts of third-way politics, methodological individualism as reflexive modernity, and the arrival of a new cosmopolitan cultural togetherness as *bona fide* theoretical frameworks (see Boyne, 2001, for a discussion), it's possible to see the upshot of this economic change as a three-track global social structure of exploiters, exploited and outcasts (George, 1999), a split that is now unfortunately mirrored in the post-solidarity working class itself (Žižek, 2010a). For a struggling actor anywhere near the periphery of this structure it is now almost a privilege to achieve and retain a position as an exploited wage-earner. There is little doubt that the combination of desperation and temptation experienced by individuals able to connect in trafficking networks, where legal and illegal sectors are merging to include both the marginalized subproletariat and the corrupt middle and elite strata, has accelerated the migration into criminality of individuals who have rejected solidarity and become attracted to the opportunities provided by the shadow-economy for profit and special liberty.

The bulk of the migrants into the bottom end of criminal markets are young people, especially males. The broad context of global youth unemployment is quite daunting. The International Labour Organization recently issued a report (2010) documenting the severe impact of the global economic crisis on employment prospects for the world's youth. The report presents detailed statistics on the growing number of those in the age-range fifteen to twenty who find themselves out of work. The most striking findings are those showing the rapid rise of youth unemployment from the eruption of the financial crisis in 2008 onwards. At the end of 2009, according to the report's introduction, global youth unemployment stood at 81 million, a rise from 11.9 per cent to 13 per cent during this period, an increase described as 'sharper than ever before'. In 2009 alone, the number of young people out of work globally rose by 6.6 million. Most significantly, it stated that although the unemployment rate would drop slightly from 2011, there would be no return to the lower jobless levels of the pre-crisis period. Youth joblessness has put the term 'a lost generation' on the lips of pundits too numerous to mention. The number of NEETs in Britain – those not in employment, education or training – has risen to 1.082 million, or 18 per cent of the youth population. There simply aren't enough jobs. More than 100,000 of young unemployed people have degrees, a fact that is driving the underqualified into the low-paid, insecure casual sector, which, in the absence of a strong, politicized collective identity, increases the temptation to move into the more lucrative – even in some cases more dependable – shadow economy. The unemployment rate among young people varies according to economic class, ethnicity and locale; without qualifications 38 per cent; black 30 per cent; Asian 26 per cent; or living in the West Midlands 32 per cent. The length of time young remain unemployed is also on the rise; almost 200,000 under the age of 25 have been unemployed for a year or more. Youngsters without skills or qualifications are especially at risk, and unsuccessful transitions from school to work or education can leave deep scars on the psyche and increase the 'drift' into criminal practices and markets at a vulnerable, impressionable age (MacDonald & Marsh, 2005; Pitts, 2008).

The global drift into criminality is rarely denied outright, but the statistics representing this migration are very sparse and elliptical indeed. Yet, despite this pervasive ignorance, empirically unfounded criminological arguments between pessimists and optimists about the rate and the nature of the drift continue unhindered. Hil (2000), for instance, embodies the left-liberal umpire's position as he criticizes Martin and Schumann's (1997) 'pessimistic' claim that crime is increasing rapidly in conjunction with the changes brought about by globalization. Hil complains that the authors 'provide no critical analysis of the way criminal statistics are collected' (2000: 373). This is true enough, but if we can't produce adequate local and national statistics there's very little chance of producing adequate global statistics; it takes ethnographic researchers years to produce detailed knowledge of unreported crimes and harms in small residential areas (see Bourgois, 2003; Hobbs, 1995; McAuley, 2007; Winlow, 2001). The empirical darkness suits the optimists and the pessimists equally well. For the optimists, if statistics show decline they are valid, but if they show increases they are invalid and vice versa for the pessimists. The criminological literature is littered with umpire's adjudications such as Hil's, which offer no data, no analysis and no theory. This confines such criminologists to a role analogous to the music critic; they inflict critical observations on others' musical performances yet compose no tunes of their own. In contrast, Reiner's (2007) penetrative longitudinal analysis, along with Dorling's (2004) spatial comparisons of murder rates and Currie's (2010) investigations of inner cities number amongst alternative modes of investigation that actually offer data, analysis, theory and a political context to move us beyond this sterile argument.

However, what we *do* know is interesting. According to Soothill et al. (2008), in Britain:

> [P]atterns of offending have been shifting among the 16–20 age group from more specialist activity to more versatile criminal behaviour … we can estimate that the proportion of the young adult

male population who are involved in highly versatile offending ...
has dramatically changed. This proportion has doubled from around
one in 50 of the male 16–20 population in the early 1970s to one in
25 in the late 1990s. For the female 16–20 age group, we observe
an even more spectacular increase in versatile offending, from one
in 2,000 in the early 1970s to one in 300 in the late 1990s – nearly
seven times the original proportion. (2008: 91)

They continue:

The number of young people coming before the courts (i.e. the
participation rate) has declined. The problem is that higher
proportions of those young people who come before the courts in
recent years exhibit greater versatility and more violence. (2008:
93; original italics)

These researchers also note an increase in violence amongst a higher proportion of versatile young criminals. The gender gap still remains significant, but we see a partial androgenization combining with a step on the
road from the specialist criminal to the all-purpose opportunist. What
seems to be occurring is that despite the demographic and administrative
factors lowering overall criminal statistics discussed above, there has been
a mutation in which crime is being committed by marginalized young people in more versatile and more intense and harmful forms.
   McAuley's (2007) ethnographic study suggests that, in the wake of failing regeneration programmes, unemployment, high crime and deteriorating infrastructure continue to be the defining characteristics of the former
heavy industrial locale featured in his study. In the new urban ghetto what
young people call 'the life' has evolved into 'a chaotic and violent social
world overshadowed by crime, drug abuse and desperation' (2007: 5).
Criminal self-employment, the illegal form of 'undertaking', is a way of
escaping the workfare merry-go-round that produces no palpable results.
Respect and self-respect together constitute a protection against the dispar-
agement rained down upon them in a consumer society, and the anhedonic
nihilism recognized by Fisher (2009) amongst marginally more advantaged
FE students has in this context driven a discernible migration into criminality. Many young people were involved in real crime, intimidation and violence, most of it unreported and unrecorded (Hall et al., 2008; McAuley,
2007), in a climate of entropy and decay where the reality is approaching
the media image (see Žižek, 2010a).

Researching in a different but equally impoverished inner-city environment in London, which of course has a longer and more firmly established tradition of organized criminal activity than McAuley's industrial heartlands (Hobbs, 1989; McIntosh, 1975), Pitts (2008) argues that youth crime is a serious and widespread phenomenon that cannot be dismissed, and in its gang form it is loosely structured yet tightly connected to the global criminal economy. The structural gang hierarchy consists of 'elders' at the top and 'shotters' at the bottom, and many of these are truly 'glocal' in the sense that they are connected to international gangsters through more stable and sometimes family-based intermediary groups. Motivations such as rational choice, status frustration and seduction are accompanied by 'involuntary affiliation'; in other words joining what you can't beat for protection and then getting inextricably tied up in the culture and its practices. It looks as though both external and internal ranking systems are hierarchal and structured by intimidating yet status-enhancing leadership exercised by oligarchic undertakers whose overt ruthlessness sets the bar for the rest. The structural shape of Pitts' youth gang tends to confirm the notion that serious acquisitive crime backed up by intimidation and violence is orchestrated by minority undertakers, yet it absorbs and assimilates a larger number of young people in the process of migration into criminality. When Karl Marx (1954) argued that dominance and exploitation are simply manifestations of the underlying principle of competition in the capitalist system, and thus the characters of those who occupy proactive positions in the system were irrelevant, he made one of his biggest errors. As we shall see later, the active presence of ruthless competitors in key positions furnishes the system with its subjective energies in the dimensions of appropriation, exploitation, production, management and consumption; without such fuel the reproductive system would lose momentum and enter a phase of entropic shutdown.

Whether there are oppositional subjectivities, cultures or institutional traditions with any political potential amongst the global outcasts is too great a diversion for this book, but there is little doubt that, broadly speaking, this global structure of opportunity, inequality and marginality has, alongside the concomitant diffusion of consumer culture and its ideological symbols of identity and distinction, accelerated the drift into criminality (Aas, 2007). The current replication of the urbanization process first encountered in the industrialized Western nations between the eighteenth and early twentieth centuries has created a 'planet of slums', replete with poverty, economic insecurity, insanitary conditions, poor housing and, in the worst locales, sheer desperation (Davis, 2006). Urban slum-dwellers live close to the most opulent megalopolises yet seen in the history of capitalism, and if this proximity to spectacular displays of wealth, status and pleasure does not create some basic Mertonian 'social strain' amongst the more depoliticized and media savvy individuals it's difficult to suggest what will. In this socio-economic climate – the most advanced and ubiquitous form of unregulated economic dynamism yet seen, constituting and reproducing social relations polarized by extremes of opportunity and desperation – widespread corruption and criminal networking also appear in their most advanced forms. Older forms of static, geographically-bound organized crime – the old urban 'manors' run by criminal families and gangs – have been to some extent displaced by loose networks of local and global criminals who use locales as 'glocal' nodes in vast global trading systems based on illegal or illegally transported goods (Aas, 2007). The late twentieth century has also witnessed friendlier relations between formerly hostile national organized crime gangs such as the Sicilian and Russian mafiosi, the Triads and the Yakuza. The expansion of trafficking in illegal goods such as drugs and weapons, combined with the illegal trafficking of legal goods such as people, alcohol, cigarettes and money – together with a huge range of everyday commodities and stolen goods traded on black markets – has provided immensely rich pickings. This has created illegal markets large enough for all undertakers, ranging from traditional organized crime groups to opportunistic part-time individuals, and made collaboration rational and more profitable.

Drug markets are still the big money-earner, together the largest 'illicit market' in terms of turnover and the number of individuals involved, a number that includes the richest criminal entrepreneurs in history, such as the legendary Colombian, Pablo Escobar. The overall market turnover is currently estimated at over $2 trillion, and the most prominent consumer market is the USA, from where distribution networks have expanded since the 1960s. It is interesting to note that these illegal markets did not expand from 1933 when some drugs were made illegal, which, even if we acknowledge that the war on drugs has been a counter-productive failure, makes the claim that the criminalization of drugs expands illegal markets and increases violence seem rather hollow, even though that might be a more convincing argument for the consequences of the prohibition of alcohol in the USA. The real issue is not the relationship between drugs and the criminal justice system but demand, its drivers and its interactive relationship with a supply side that can use the addictive properties of drugs to maintain it at a high level. It is interesting to note that despite economic instability drug use declined in western Europe from the 1920s to the 1950s (Paoli et al., 2010), in times of militant working-class politics and a greater degree of ethico-social cohesion, which managed to maintain momentum during the early post-war period of mass immigration, a fact that negates the arguments of those who try to blame immigrants for increased crime. Drug use in the UK expanded in the wake of the spurt that occurred in the globalization of the economy in the 1970s. The 1960s and 1970s were characterized by the Vietnam War, mass consumption and the emergence of youth 'subcultures' based on a fake, manufactured form of rebellion that was little more than depoliticized disobedience and hedonism (Frank, 1997; Hall et al., 2008; Heath & Potter, 2006); drug use became yet another assimilated mark of distinction. The drug market's production and distribution systems also provide precarious and dangerous yet potentially lucrative opportunities for business and employment for those whose official qualifications and cultural capital are considered to fall below the standards required by the mainstream.

The drift into criminal markets was exacerbated in the 1980s and 1990s as the decline in manual jobs ushered in the 'accredited society' (Taylor, 1999), in which even the most menial jobs required formal qualifications that in the main had become mere tokens of selection rather than awards signifying skill or knowledge. It was poorly educated and poorly qualified young men who suffered most and drifted into criminal markets, but, following Escobar, middle-class adventurers such as Howard Marks (1997) also got in on the act; a sort of rough class hierarchy emerged to structure the business. Global networks form 'glocal' connections with young people whose local knowledge and cultural capital can help to attract customers, boost sales and distribute drugs in clandestine networks that combine socio-cultural relations with economic transactions. At first it was mostly cannabis and amphetamines, but as purer forms of heroin became available from south-east Asia a rapid expansion of the number of regular heroin users became apparent in the 1980s (Paoli et al., 2009). Crack cocaine became popular in the late 1980s and drug use diversified and expanded year after year throughout the 1990s (McSweeney et al., 2008). Drug use declined between 1995 and 2008, but there was a corresponding decline in the demographic age group usually associated with it. Drug use itself does not contribute significantly to violent crime amongst drug users, but it can add to the disruption of community cohesion, family life and youth transitions, and high levels of intimidation and violence can be experienced by members of criminal networks involved in trafficking. Although the personal use of softer drugs is perhaps not as harmful as we are led to believe, the drug industry is not benign: it corrodes institutions and processes of social reproduction in communities, it brings corruption, violence and instability to regions of production and transit, and it opens up routes and creates criminal networks conducive to other forms of crime, including human trafficking and smuggling (Paoli et al., 2010).

Decriminalizing drugs would certainly reduce statistical crime rates – but of course decriminalizing any criminal activity will reduce statistical crime rates – and it might also reduce levels of real harm in production and distribution networks. However, the potential zemiological effect on psychosocial life in everyday reality is unknown, and some researchers insist that decriminalization would increase levels of everyday use and addiction (MacCoun & Reuter, 2001). Will governments of any political colour take the risk that a fully decriminalized drug market will be benign? Probably not, and, again, the rather tedious bi-partisan argument that dominates the drugs/crime issue has tended to distract criminology from the main issue, which of course is the psychosocial genesis of drive and subjective desire; why do the demand for drugs and the willingness to risk harm to others for personal profit or pleasure vary in different social time/space locations? The discussion of subjectivity later in the book might furnish us with the beginnings of a theoretical platform on which we can approach this question.

Moving up the social scale, it has become almost a criminological truism that corporate financial crimes present a greater threat to the economic and cultural fabric of society than everyday volume crimes (Minkes & Minkes, 2008). This broad family of crimes, which includes price fixing, inflation of share prices and market value, false accounting and misuse of corporate funds, straddles the legally constituted boundary between crime and deviance. Snider (1993) estimated that the cost of US street crime, at $4 billion per annum, was at the time only about 5 per cent of the cost of corporate crime. Despite its zemiological magnitude in terms of the degree and range of harms it can cause – bankruptcy, insolvency, insecurity, unemployment, repossession and so on – in principle it suffers from the same 'crisis of enforcement' that Tombs and Whyte (2003) have revealed in the field of health and safety regulation. So far the current major investigation by the FBI into the banking practices that led to the financial crisis in 2008 has failed to throw up anything of note; it is probably not overly cynical to suspect that it might indeed be cosmetic. In Western law we can prosecute individuals, and we can prosecute institutions in a roundabout and wholly inadequate way that has to deal with the legally instituted cult of methodological-individualist intentionality (see Harding, 2007; Punch, 2008), but, no matter how much harm is caused, we cannot prosecute the capitalist system or the players who play within its extant rules. Tombs and Whyte (ibid.) are unerringly correct that in the neoliberal era the powerful have further augmented their ability to protect themselves from critical scrutiny, but, because even powerful individuals and groups are disposable and can be sacrificed, and large corporate institutions are split into distinct companies and departments, it must be said that in the long-run an increased ability to prosecute powerful individuals and institutions might be yet another example of counter-productive reformism. On the other hand, it could save lives; this Sophie's choice between saving lives and livelihoods in the short term whilst allowing the system to survive and cause more harm in the future is how the system has an asphyxiating grip on its ethico-political opposition, a contract agreeing to painfully slow and contested short-term concessionary reform in return for the continuation of systemic economic restructuring that will cause widespread, long-term harm. We are forced to trade with little particles of the present for the whole of the future.

Corruption and barbarism, it has often been said, go all the way to the top. Alongside corporate crime in the elite stratum, gross harms, the abuse of human rights and civil liberties, torture, exploitation, corruption and environmental destruction are regularly inflicted on populations by states, often in collusion with big business interests (Cohen, 2000; Green & Ward, 2004). Disruptive structural adjustment programmes demanded by transnational corporations and financial institutions, and often obsequiously facilitated by corrupt governments, cause profound social harms (Cain & Birju, 1992), and at the very top of the scale in harmful government collusion with neoliberalism's global programmes, are offensive instrumental wars are dressed up as defensive humanitarian interventions. The Westphalian nation-state legitimizes its monopoly on physical force by protecting its citizens from internal or external threats, and it forefends possible charges of crime and harm on a massive scale with correspondingly grandiose claims of righteousness and the protection of its own citizens; brutal means are justified by what is usually, except in times of genuine threat, a fantasized end administered by cynical *realpolitik*. No state – democratic or authoritarian – has entirely clean hands.

However, if state crime manifests the *barbarism of order*, which has at times assumed terrifying proportions, one does not have to look too hard into the deregulated paraspaces of the global economy to find manifestations of the opposite, the *barbarism of disorder*. Global capitalism's vast money-generating trading system, which connects new customers to new production centres and distribution circuits worldwide, has generated a dark side of violence and corruption that straddles the legal and the illegal. In the virtual world of cybercrime, illegal or unlicensed activities such as sex trafficking, gambling, hard-core pornography, money and investment scams, illegal intellectual property distribution, data and identity theft, malicious leaks, smear campaigns, extortion and sabotage have all been facilitated by the growth of communications technology and the interconnected global market. It could well be a lot more; Naim (2005) estimates illegal money-laundering at about $5.9 trillion, or about 10 per cent of global GDP. Such huge financial power

wielded by individuals such as Warren Buffet and George Soros, as well as the
networked institutions of the global banking/finance complex, can shape
markets, configure patterns of major capital investment and control weak
governments. In this rarefied politico-economic stratum power is transferred
from states to immensely powerful individuals and small groups, and thus the
individual–state relation is precisely the reverse of that posited in Garland's
(2001) 'culture of control', and the issues of human rights, freedom and
democracy it throws up are every bit as profound. Offshore banking is justified as a manifestation of the special liberty to exploit labour-power, accumulate assets, trade and grow wealthy – since Locke, the Manchester free-trade
movement and the repeal of the Corn Laws this particular economic liberty
has been established by liberalism as a fundamental and inalienable human
right – which deprives producers of fair rewards just as it deprives nation-
states of the ability to exert political control over their economic fortunes and
gather the tax revenues needed to fund public infrastructures. Corporate- and
bank-friendly governments, such as the current Coalition in Britain, can aid
the process by subtly and quietly altering tax laws and ideologically delinking
harm from crime to facilitate the growth of tax havens as domicile sites for
companies and individual capitalists. These sites currently hold something in
the region of ten trillion dollars' worth of 'taxable assets' (Monbiot, 2011),
or in Marxist parlance financialized 'surplus value' generated by the expropri-
ated labour power of an increasingly marginalized and insecure global working class operating under the harsh logic of both legal and illegal markets.
Over 30 per cent of these assets are generated by global crime (Shaxson,
2011); in this estimate – which, because of the banking industry's codes of
secrecy, might well, as Naim's (ibid.) higher estimate suggests, be a conservative one – we are looking at a global criminal market generating profits of
over $3.5 trillion per annum. The violent acquisition and defence of the *some-
where* of land and its material produce prized by the Mediaeval brigand or
warlord has been replaced by the generation of profits by exploitation in
imbalanced exchange relations in glocal markets, and the transfer of money
through the portal of an offshore banking industry, whose secretive and laby-
rinthine practices have evolved over centuries in the very task of avoiding
regulation and progressive taxation, to *nowhere*, the orbital financial economy.
If there is a master pattern here, it is that modes of successful criminality followed, and in some cases innovated, the relentless historical marketization,
individualization, abstraction, financialization and pseudo-pacification of
socio-economic activity as capitalism diffused across the world following its
origin in England.

  After a brief period of respite in the era of industrial consolidation and
socio-political solidarity from the late nineteenth to the mid-twentieth

centuries in the USA and Europe, crime and imprisonment rates exploded in the USA and Britain in the 1980s as these nations shifted abruptly to a deregulated neoliberal political economy, whilst they remained lower in western Europe as its states stuck closer to the social-democratic model (Currie, 2010; Hall & McLean, 2009). As neoliberal restructuring programmes disrupted traditional or industrialized national economies and societies across the globe, from post-communist Russia and eastern Europe to Africa and Latin America, crime rates also soared. Only the more authoritarian politico-cultural systems of East Asia maintained low crime rates by repressive means as neoliberal economic logic and culture flooded into their territories. In neoliberalism's diffusing cultural environment, grounded in a collective obscene Real that seeks to negate all pre-existing socio-economic exchange relations to maximize exploitation and returns on investment, legal and illegal markets, and individual, state and corporate criminality have not simply become epistemologically blurred but ontologically co-evolutionary and functional. Despite the existence of cultural variations that can insulate themselves with varying degrees of success (Gray, 2002), it seems that the fundamental psychosocial conditions constituted and reproduced by neoliberal capitalism are inexorably criminogenic insofar as they tend to generate a cluster of illegal entrepreneurial forms that has shifted the norm far beyond the social crime traditionally motivated by a sense of social injustice.

SOCIAL THEORY AND CRIMINOLOGY: THE UNDERLYING LIBERAL NARRATIVE

How do we begin to theorize the vast and complex diffusionary process roughly sketched out in the two previous chapters? The better student textbooks present the development of criminological theories not simply as a self-contained process driven by its own internal momentum but as a process embedded in shifting historical, political and philosophical contexts. Valier's (2002) point that theories of crime do not come from 'nowhere' but relate to changing social orders is true enough, but it tells us little about the actual power struggles within social orders, which theories dominate and why, and whose interests they serve. Earlier theories cannot be regarded as obsolete and casually discarded (ibid.) and we cannot assume that criminology follows some evolutionary logic, that new theories replace old ones because they are improvements in a linear incremental process; the development of criminological theory is not like that of washing powder, car engines or mobile phones. In the currently dominant liberal-pluralist way of seeing things, older theories are welcome to take their place in the plurality of epistemological positions on offer, but there is no single lofty position of authority from which all others can be judged. If criminologists accept this fundamental liberal-pluralist limit, then we must also accept the modest role of the under-labourer (Loader & Sparks, 2010), the Lockean classifier and facilitator of discursive interactions between theories and subdisciplinary interest-groups.

Loader and Sparks's rather benign characterization of the broad criminological community as a sort of Sunday School teacher celebrating her young charges' imaginations and arranging polite discussions between creative minds, is a neat description of the discipline's current structure and its place in the broader social research community. However, it tends to underplay the extent to which the more radical and broad-thinking

participants are also warned not to take their new-fangled ideas too seriously, and the extent to which they will lose credibility if they do. On one
hand, the power that judges the credibility of theories could well be democratic and contingent, a restless and constantly mutating body of opinions
shifting through intersecting phases of conflict and consensus based on perpetual immanent critique and empirical testing, an affirmative decision on
pluralism that has been reached by the organic plurality itself. On the other
hand, however, the declaration that the social and intellectual worlds must
be plural rather than founded on ontologically grounded universal values,
practices and experiences could be nothing more than a dominant current
in modernity's intellectual history, a command from a hegemonic power
that appears as a legitimate authority because it has used its power to convince the majority that all such commands are the products of democratic
agreements or compromises made in the past. History is always written by
winners, often in ways that lead us to believe that the winners did not really
win. As such, we could be looking at what by now is a traditional liberal-
modernist authority that *does* in fact occupy a lofty authoritative position
from which it naturalizes and thus conceals by means of externalization and
mystification its fundamentally ideological position; in other words it's a
power that has the power to pretend it's not a power, but a legitimate consensual authority. The liberal under-labourer could be in fact a stern over-
seer whose authority in a structured criminological hierarchy is legitimized
by some unwritten agreement allegedly made in the past, now counter-
feited innumerable times in a retrospective imaginary by historians and
philosophers devoted to the reproduction of its Mosaic Law.

This fetishistically disavowed structural hierarchy in criminology is a
reflection of liberalism's general socio-political order. Telling everyone that
they're all partly right whilst staging spectacular but alas never completely
successful attempts to redistribute and equalize power, wealth and civil
liberties in a tolerant and melioristic democracy is indeed a very effective
way of maintaining what appears to be a legitimate authority over a relatively long period of time. However, the course of true liberal capitalism
never runs smooth; its history has been punctuated by tumultuous socio-
economic crises and eruptions of dissatisfaction, hatred and violence, and
plagued by the constant drip of petty crime and corruption. Whatever it is
that liberal pluralism is intent on suppressing seems to lie quite close to the
surface and periodically tends to erupt in our midst. In the light of these
failings, will we ever be satisfied by resigning ourselves to the fundamental
axiom of the timeless plurality of human societies and accepting the edicts
that theories can be nothing more than epistemological frameworks that
represent phenomenological or discursive positions constructed by society's

various interest groups to explain perspectives of an unknowable totality? As a dominant hegemonic power moves into old age, an increasingly larger proportion of it sinks into history and is therefore able to be historicized. As critical analyses assembled from experiential observations of increasingly frequent eruptions of its hidden contradictions gather strength, the hegemonic power must fight back by denying the critique of its ontological validity and stressing its epistemological plurality and reflexivity, and, where that fails, resort to the cruder tactic of invoking the symbols of absolute evil to issue grim warnings that any attempt to put the critique into action and replace the system will inevitably result in tyranny, death and destruction. However, because these frequent eruptions just keep on occurring, how long can we avert our eyes from what might be behind this epistemological plurality, Kant's noumenal realm of the unknown universal – in more fittingly dramatic terms Hegel's 'night of the world' or Lacan's 'Real' – and its manifest effects when the history of thought tells us that it is our curiosity and not our fear and conventionality that constantly gets the better of us? The implications of liberal pluralism's self-appointment as an authoritative agent to arbitrate and order criminology and sociology's positive intellectual freedom will be discussed later in the chapter, but for the moment let's take a brief look at the stuff that makes up the plurality, the major political positions that underpin the Western intellectual scene.

Some years ago Jock Young (1990) outlined the major political-philosophical positions that underlie the main criminological theories. Although Badiou (2006) denies the right of 'political philosophy' to call itself a *bona fide* philosophical form – philosophy should not be concerned with 'what is' but moving from 'what is to what is not' – and in doing so shows the inherent conservatism in liberal pluralism itself, it is certainly useful for revealing the ontological categories on which today's entrenched theoretical positions are founded. From a criminological perspective, Young's chapter outlines the main Western conceptions of subjectivity and links them to their political roots. We have to accept that politics and philosophy pre-date social sciences by millennia, and therefore during their development the social sciences have had little choice but to import basic concepts from these older intellectual traditions. In some cases social science reworks the concepts, but in many cases the 'reworking' is little more than cake-decorating and the fundamental ontological principles tend to remain much as they are. In very basic terms the political positions and their related ontological forms look like those presented in Table 4.1.

Criminology's various theoretical paradigms import basic categories from the exporter disciplines of politics and philosophy, but, despite the range of choices on offer, in the everyday reality of intellectual and political

Table 4.1 Orthodox Western political philosophies and their conceptions of subjectivity

Paradigm	Ontological conception of subjectivity
Conservatism/theocracy/tradition	Free-willed, wicked; in need of discipline and traditional wisdom/bonds
Classical liberalism/rationalism	Free-willed, hedonistic, calculative, but capable of benevolence/sentiment
Social liberalism/social democracy	Benign, charitable, affable, sociable, creative; in need of care to prevent 'damage'
Scientific positivism/determinism	Determined by internal and external forces
Radical liberalism/libertarianism/ anarchism	Benign, sociable, flexible and creative; damaged by oppressive authority
Marxism/socialism	Dialectical; a product of ideological struggle in unequal and contradictory social relations
Postmodernism/ post-structuralism	Playful, sceptical, ironic, malleable; largely benign but can be cynical
Feminisms	Gendered; oppressive traditional masculinities, benign creative femininities/ new masculinities

life in the West these choices are arranged in a loose hierarchy, where a combination of conservatism and classical liberalism in a dominant position struggles with a combination of social liberalism, radical liberalism, feminism and, latterly, postmodernism in a subdominant position, with scientific positivism usually denying its roots in conservatism and social liberalism to present itself as a neutral means of data generation, causal analysis and prescriptive policy making. In short, the basic structure of criminology, social science and social policy is one in which a general conservative-classicist paradigm stands in opposition to a general liberal-progressivist paradigm. Marxism, Hegelian dialectics and psychodynamics have been proclaimed dead, but if criminology wishes to remain relevant it will eventually be forced to deal with the fact that since the consolidation of Latin American socialism at the turn of the millennium, the financial crisis of 2008, the austerity cuts in the West and the revolutionary stirrings in the Middle East in 2011, these positions have, in reconstituted forms, made something of a comeback in intellectual life at the expense of liberal progressivism (Douzinas & Žižek, 2010).

Criminology's aetiological crisis (Young, 1987) – a period from the 1980s when many of the ontological and causal assumptions of the liberal-progressivist paradigm evaporated in the heat of rising crime rates and declining political solidarity – is a signal for a thorough revision of the discipline's theoretical canon right down to its philosophical roots. In order to do so we have to be brave enough to express our dissatisfaction with the dominant ontological assumptions of subjectivity itself. We will look at subjectivity in detail later (Chapter 8), but the first question is 'how did we get where we are now'? The simple answer is that we were carried here by a liberal-progressivist current that constituted itself in opposition to the conservative-classicist paradigm that dominated Western life up to the mid-nineteenth century and restored itself to that position of dominance in the 1980s.

However, liberal-progressivist social theory and criminological theory did not fall down to earth in a shower of rain one day in 1850. Along with liberal intellectual life in general, it has deep roots in the beginnings of modernity, when the Manichean struggle between good and evil that structured Christianity was abandoned as a purely theological issue. As economic competition and unruly populations appeared in Europe's capitalist nation-building phase, the art of governing internal and external relations became a secular politico-cultural priority. The relationship between the state and the individual is thus at the root of liberal criminology, and discussions of crime and its control often begin with Machiavelli and his famous dictum that for the ruler fear rather than love is the more effective instrument of control (Valier, 2002). However, this is a crude view of Machiavelli. His other major work, *The Discourses* (2003), shows him to be far more idealistic, whereas *The Prince* (1961) shows him in his eventual state of disillusionment and cynical pragmatism, and this philosophical position was consolidated further as post-Hobbesian conservative pragmatism toned down and naturalized the fundamental concept of 'evil'. With the aid of Protestantism's relocation of the struggle from the heavens to the individual psyche, 'evil' was reformulated as the latent and tractable product of anxiety and unruliness (Hobbes did not use the term 'wickedness' in his major formulations) and shifted attention to its rational and socio-political control. Crime was separated from sin, and its official ontology was monopolized by the nascent bourgeois state to further legitimize and expand the control practices that in England and Wales had been developing, as we have seen, since the late thirteenth century. For Hobbes, *Leviathan* (1996) was indeed a set of institutions designed to protect humanity from its own tendency to descend into a 'war of all against all'. This ontological certitude of humanity as naturally anxious, hostile and unruly justified the continuation of the Platonic strategy of the 'noble lie', the ruling elite's entitlement to withhold the full spectrum of their knowledge from the public; in the vernacular 'to tell them only what they need to know', which in its modernist

variant runs from Machiavelli to Leo Strauss. Nevertheless, Hobbes'
expectation was that individuals would see the sense in ceding a portion
of rational sovereignty – the 'knowing ego' that was posited by Descartes
as the innate capability of each individual – to a central governmental
authority.

This current was carried forward in the eighteenth century by Locke
(1997), whose theory of the self as a creature 'concerned for itself' also
brought into play naturalistic notions of liberty and autonomy. However,
liberty and autonomy do not mean libertinism and, despite Bentham's
(1996) placement of hedonism – the seeking of pleasure and the avoidance
of pain – as a blind drive at the centre of pre-subjective human psychology,
for Mill (2006) the actions of individuals towards others need some
restraint if all concerned are to have an acceptable quality of life. In classical
liberalism's minimal-state philosophy the power of *Leviathan* was to be
reduced to a minimum, but this is still a vague and arbitrary limit set by
those who hold superior socio-economic power, political authority and
cultural influence. Bentham prioritized happiness over autonomy, a principle that justified the state's role as a protectionist organizing mechanism
acting on behalf of individuals, and even Weber (1978), although a supporter of the independence of law and regarded by many as the quintessential liberal social theorist and critic of overbearing bureaucracy, agreed
that the state should have a legitimate monopoly on violence (1978). The
state's electorally-mandated right to restrain individuals, who have inalienable rights and liberties, and how in practical and ethical terms it goes
about its business, became the issues at liberalism's epicentre. This was the
domain of legal philosophy, and post-war British criminology, growing as
it did in law schools, has from its beginnings been focused on the legal-
philosophical issue of the dualistic tension between state control and
individual freedom. The core of the discipline is immersed in and bounded
by this legal-normative discourse, and the individual–state relation, along
with the issues of social inequalities and well-being, are also at the epicentre
of liberal-progressivist social science in general.

Classical liberalism preferred individualized forms of punishment and
deterrence made to measure for the ideal-type human being, who, according to this doctrine, should be self-interested, competitive, innovative,
entrepreneurial and self-motivated, yet simultaneously self-restrained, law
abiding, civic minded and concerned that no harm should be inflicted on
others by himself or anyone else. The interesting point about all liberal
philosophical and social thought is that systematic inquiry into the motivations behind selfishness, competitiveness and the willingness to risk harm
to the self and others is not a necessary component in the construction of

fully-functioning social theories of risk, harm, crime and deviance; this is just stuff that happens when people go about their business, unfortunate aberrations that occur as individuals err in an otherwise economically prosperous, morally healthy and socially progressive way of life. Mainstream inquiries into criminal motivations tended to be left to the more conservative and positivist schools of philosophy and psychology, whose explanations are usually based on the principles of hard-wired biological traits, inherited personality types and faulty socialization. Radical Marxist and socialist thinkers, in a rather tense alliance with some of the more Romantic conservatives, tended to focus on the competition and moral decay brought about by liberal capitalism. Neither school pleases anybody on the progressivist side of the fence.

However, classical liberalism, despite its emphasis on rational choice and personal responsibility, was not without its underlying principles; it just preferred to keep relatively quiet about them, and therefore they feature only rarely in its narrative. Its ontological imposture was to reconceptualize the Hobbesian concept of latent anxiety with the potential of hostility in chaotic circumstances as the positivist drive of manifest hedonistic selfishness posited by the Utilitarians; put simply, a dangerous drive that could be triggered in specific circumstances and therefore should be repressed was replaced by a natural drive that was permanently activated no matter what the circumstances and therefore should be accepted as natural and controlled by harnessing it to the capitalist economy. Even Kant (1999), a noted anti-utilitarian, understood the 'sensuous impulses' as potentially dangerous forms of unreason from which only duty can divert us and reason can set us free. Conversely, a philosophical current running from Spinoza to Hutcheson and Hume posited the drives as dominant and in need of cultivation to create the moral sensibilities vital for peaceful interaction. This ontological transposition of the primary human drive allowed classical liberalism to accelerate the process – which, as we have seen, began in the Late Mediaeval economy – of dismantling and reconstituting many of the traditional cultural codes and disciplinary institutions that were holding back the economic, political and cultural liberties of the individual and replace them with individualized systems of punishment whose costs were to be mentally internalized as deterrents by each individual. This dismantling of prohibitionist codes was rather attractive to individuals seeking freedom from constraints for all sorts of motives, and as such is one of the main reasons why classical liberalism triumphed over conservatism, idealism and socialism in the West's economic powerhouses and set the parameters within which progressive social liberalism – the restraining force that evolved reflexively from a growing awareness of classical liberalism's failings – was forced to work.

Despite the major ontological distinction between free will and determinism, classical liberalism was not 'opposed' in any political sense by the
scientific positivists who rose to prominence in nineteenth-century Europe,
with their mixture of biological, psychological and social determinism.
Garland (1985) misled us when he labelled criminology's biologically based
positivistic strand the 'Lombrosan project'. Very soon after the initial
Lombrosan proposition that criminality was the product of genetic atavism
achieved temporary credibility, scientific positivism embraced environmental factors in a movement that marginalized pure genetic determinism.
The orientation in positivism's search for the determining causes of human
behaviour was imbalanced towards the 'malfunction' in child development
and socialization, and, as such, it was well suited to an active decision-
making role in classical liberalism's ever more intricately ranked and classified criminalization processes and social liberalism's investigations into the
complex causes of crime. Positivism produced the dark side of eugenics but
also what was at the time considered to be the progressive anti-punitive
side of social welfarism.

In social liberalism's hybrid philosophy, which was behind the welfarism
that was to be institutionalized in Britain in the early twentieth century,
scientific positivism enjoyed a tense but complementary partnership with
classical liberalism, specializing in the correction and bureaucratic micro-
management of individuals whose crime-prone lives were seen to be the
products of various combinations of faulty neurobiological wiring, psychological development in childhood or socialization in difficult familial or
communal environments. The concept of the difficult communal environment created by relative poverty, unemployment, poor education systems
and so on was as near as scientific positivism got to the formulation of a
political or social-structural stance that challenged liberalism's dominant
individualistic positions of free will and soft bio-environmental determinism. However, following the deontological interventions of T.H. Green,
who declared that each individual is bound by a duty to promote the common good and build a fitting reproductive environment for the future
socialization of good citizens (see Brink, 2003), the basic positivist tenet of
environmental soft determinism was absorbed and reformulated by liberalism through an individualistic-agentic lens as the backbone of the influential
empirically informed social policy strand that still dominates mainstream
social sciences today. The environment might in some way affect our behaviour, but it does not create our core rational and moral constructivist being
through whose agency, if we do our moral duty, we create our environment. Marx's observation that we inherit most of our politico-economic,
cultural and social environment from the past was given the standard liberal

treatment; acknowledged, absorbed and reformulated as an issue already being dealt with by democratic piecemeal reform.

Liberalism's basic enduring difficulty is the Hobbesian problem of order; if the individual is to be freed from the *Ancien Régime* and its political tyrannies, yet inherit a social environment free from hostile threats posed by other individuals, she must voluntarily enter into a social contract in which a minimum degree of rights and freedom must be given over to a governing body. In return for this sacrifice of positive rights, the individual is given a set of new negative rights administered by law. If the Mediaeval monarchical state was a protection racket imposed on the population by violent warlords (Tilly, 1985), the modern state is a protection mechanism entered into voluntarily by its citizens. Ideally, this state should be accountable and the law should be a relatively independent body, but it does not take a long search through the critical literature to cast into doubt both the openness and accountability of government and the independence of law in the modern 'security state' (Wilson & Lindsey, 2009) and the capitalist economy and class society it administers (Bourdieu, 1987). Liberalism's politico-philosophical debate over the balance of individual rights and social and governmental needs, which has culminated in a tripartite stand-off between Rawlsian redistributivists, Nozickian libertarians and communitarians such as Walzer and Sandel, is long, complex and beyond the scope of this book. The essential polar opposition, however, is between, on the one hand, libertarians and classical liberals who insist that involuntary taxation is theft and that anything other than an assiduously minimized government is an ineluctable threat to freedom and, on the other, social liberals who understand that a more even balance must be struck between individual rights and social needs, a category that requires both a moral obligation towards the good society and democratic political governance to put the ideal into practice.

In both camps, capitalism and its dominant subjectivities are let off the critical hook. Consequently, absent almost entirely from this debate are the issues of subjectivity, ideology and the constitution of the subject's desires and thoughts, which, in the pure Cartesian view, are nothing other than the products of the autonomous reflections and choices of the individual. What was in the pre-modern world everybody's business – including God, the Church and the state – is in the modern world nobody's business but the individual concerned (see Thomas, 2009). No serious doubts about the delicious teleological promise of individual freedom and market-driven prosperity and progress were tolerated. Romantic and radical critiques emerging in philosophy, the humanities and social/political theory, such as those of Rousseau or Blake, who saw bourgeois individualism, capitalism, industrialism and urbanization wreaking destruction on nature, culture and the moral sensibilities of the human subject (Clayre, 1977), were roundly dismissed. However, some of the more progressive thinkers on both sides of the tense but functional *quid pro quo* relationship that developed between classical liberalism and scientific positivism saw the importance of social and environmental factors. For instance, Mill (2006) acknowledged the limits to liberty defined by harm and the vital need of sociability, and the socialistic positivist Ferri (2009) recognized the importance of environment on the behaviour of the human organism. In an era where unsociability and aggression were naturalized and individualized – and where Mandeville's (1970) notion, still controversial to pious conservatives and social liberals alike, that harnessed vices are more useful than virtues as drivers towards mutual prosperity was gaining purchase amongst economic liberals – deeply critical ethical or macro-sociological explanations for our tendency to do harm to others were thin on the ground.

The political implications of the early criminological statisticians' work on the link between economic recessions and crime rates were played down. The philosophical principle that harmful crime was a problem caused by the failure of personal morality and reason, a deontological deficit that in the last instance can be addressed only by the individual, remained in a dominant position over the soft determinism of social liberalism. The vital issue of the formation of subjectivities related to material and ideological environments laid down in the process of capitalist development was avoided in the liberal debate, hived off to positivist psychologists and psychiatrists in the depoliticized medical, educational and child development professions. In the wrong hands simplified and distorted theories drawn from biological positivism justified the eugenics movement in Europe and the USA, which assumed terrifying proportions in the Nazi regime. However, although the softer schools of psychological and social positivism can still be accused of justifying some abuses of human rights such as indeterminate sentencing, and proving counter-productive in the processes of social classification, labelling and deviancy amplification, under the watchful eye of liberalism they became domesticated technologies of social management in the welfare states established throughout Europe and the 'New Deal' USA in the twentieth century. In return, scientific positivism offered liberalism increased functionality and credibility in an economically unstable age where science and the idea of scientific control had become extremely valuable currency.

The development of progressive liberalism in the womb of classical liberalism and conservatism in the *post bellum* USA followed a different course over a different time-scale after it had fended off a powerful nascent socialist movement that rose to prominence in the early twentieth century. However, it's fairly safe to say that classical liberalism, social liberalism and a rather unwelcome but tolerated scientific positivism formed a tense yet functional ruling politico-cultural triumvirate in the successful capitalist nations of the late nineteenth and twentieth centuries, a triumvirate that is still dominant in the mainstream today. Apart from the quixotic movements of Romanticism – which throughout the course of modernity had been sublimated from political reality and confined to the realms of art and literature – and a waning traditional conservatism that met its final demise in the Thatcherite/Reaganite era, the only genuine opposition to dualistic liberalism and its tamed Rottweiler of scientific positivism came from the Marxist and socialist movements. The Marxist thinker Friedrich Engels (1987) and the Dutch socialist criminologist Willem Bonger (1916) numbered amongst the small few who saw connections between the basic ethico-social framework of capitalism, the formation of the demoralized monadic subject and criminology's potential explanations for the harmful crime and deviance being committed throughout the social structure. In an effort to redress the imbalance of power in capitalist social relations, the critical criminologists who superseded these early theorists focused on the crimes of the powerful. However, what also disturbed radical thinkers such as Engels and Bonger, for whom the whole system was the perfect crime, was the tendency for some amongst the impoverished working classes to commit intra-class crime, an issue brought back into play rather controversially in the Thatcherite era by left realist criminologists (Lea & Young, 1993).

The willingness to harm and deprive others in the interests of the self was a daunting indication that sociability, political solidarity and class consciousness were neither natural tendencies nor the easiest of things to encourage, even in liberalism's brave new world. Marx and Engels (1972) saw petty criminals as part of a *lumpenproletariat*, a subclass whose unethical, anti-social beliefs and practices bore some affinity to bourgeois exploitation, and as such were detrimental to the class solidarity project that in his teleological forecast was to lead to communist revolution. Marx's lack of sympathy for all criminals including petty criminals – in fact it could be said that he judged them harshly – was, alongside liberalism's outright rejection of revolutionary politics, one of the principle reasons why only distinctly humanistic variants of Marxism were politely if rather unenthusiastically welcomed as guests in the essentially liberal project of criminology. It must be said that by the time he wrote his final work *Das Kapital* (1954; see also Harvey, 2011), he had arrived at the conclusion that the dialectical dynamics and logical requirements of the system had completely superseded the ethics of the individual and class fraction as capitalism's dominant force. He argued that in a system based on the exploitation of labour power the differential morality of individual capitalists was largely irrelevant, but that early harsh judgement remains as a stain on the lens through which social liberalism views Marx and Marxism. A brief perusal of the right-wing press, however, would suggest that many of today's classical liberals, in their neoliberal guise, would probably agree with it.

Despite liberalism's multiplicity, its core principle is that, after some basic socialization during childhood, freedom is paramount amongst the human virtues, the greatest benefit that any way of life can bring. As a historical project, did this actually work? If liberalism is the only road to a better future, why do the quintessential liberal nations of the USA and Britain, both characterized by a balance of classical (neo)liberalism and social liberalism, experience more violent crime and seem to need a far more intrusive punishment and surveillance system than 'old' western Europe with its residual collectivist traditions (Currie, 2010; Hall & McLean, 2009)? Is it simply that since the Thatcherite/Reaganite restoration period the USA and Britain have become imbalanced towards the classical liberal side and allowed their social liberal welfare institutions and their organic civic traditions to run down whilst unjustly applying punitive principles? If so, as Tonry (2004) argues, they simply require a better democratic government to revive social liberalism. This is the standard answer, but to admit that, however, is to deny liberalism's basic promise of individual freedom in a civilized society without the significant presence of the 'big state' of regulation and welfare interventions and the 'big society' of conservative traditions. In this scenario Slavoj Žižek (2000) seems to have a point when he describes today's dominant political discourse as 'liberal conservatism'. Is the persistent problem of crime simply the price of freedom that we have little choice but to pay, or is there something so fundamentally wrong with liberalism's grand historical project that it has no choice but to reconstruct and rely upon late-modern versions of the statist and conservative-cultural institutions from whose tyranny it initially sought its freedom?

We could begin to answer this question by questioning the nature of freedom itself. We have already seen the tendency of positive liberty to be easily perverted and assume the form of negative liberty, and, beyond that, special liberty. From this perspective it appears that liberalism offers not a universal form of freedom, but a historicized form unique to itself, whose bearers tend to be anxious, solipsistic, hyper-competitive and in need of a significant amount of monitoring and restraint. If this bears any resemblance to the truth, the radical liberal and anarchist dreams of ultimate freedom in a beautifully disordered yet benign society are for the foreseeable future quite dangerous fantasies. It was for its own volatile and opportunistic subjects that classical liberalism reluctantly but dutifully entered into partnership with social liberalism to construct the 'tough love' society of monitoring, care and nurturing juxtaposed with economic independence and legal deterrence. In this way, this advanced form of what we will come to know as the *pseudo-pacification process*, the hope was that the potent mix of libidinal and aggressive energy at the psychic core of each individual could be simultaneously stimulated, harnessed and anodized at the same time, fuelling economic growth with endless quasi-social competition whilst guaranteeing civilized and non-violent social interactions. Can civility grow and reproduce itself indefinitely in a socio-economic environment characterized by ruthless interpersonal competition and systematized exploitation? Liberalism has no choice but to believe that it can. The whole social liberal research community is geared up to the task of sustaining this faith and finding ways of putting it into practice without disturbing the subjectifying socio-cultural structures and processes required to reproduce anodized competitive individualism and sustain economic growth. No need, then, for fancy psychosocial theories that might erode the faith that sustains the whole liberal-capitalist project.

Lacking a direct relationship with philosophy, politics and economics, and rather tentative and highly selective in its relationship with psychology, criminology has relied largely on sociology for the 'fancy theories' it has chosen to import in the past. Sociology has been proclaimed dead on numerous occasions, but after the debate on modernity and postmodernity ground to a halt there were calls for new thinking, a return to theory and method (Mouzelis, 1995; Turner & Rojek, 2001). This is not a crisis but a condition of paradigmatic entropy that shouts out for a re-energizing shot that can be provided solely by interdisciplinary synthesis and a more honest approach to theory, supported by empirical excursions into reality and the Real, the 'thingish' internal neurobiological world, the external world of objects, events, relations and systems and the ways in which they irrupt upon each other to create the realms of perception, consciousness, desire and social dynamics. However, this cause will not be helped by restrictive research funding practices and injunctions on thought. In a recent brochure from the Academy of Social Sciences (2010), criminology is now no longer sociological but filed under 'well-being' and defined exclusively as 'scanning for crime' and 'situational crime prevention', the only mode in which criminological research can have 'impact'.

As if the recategorization and tight restriction of research programmes is not bad enough, sociological thought is also restricted by current trends in social theory and the philosophy of social sciences, the 'wholesale outlet' from which criminology imports most of its ideas. For instance, the sociologist

Roger Sibeon (2004) fills a whole book outlining a prohibitive code that prevents a lot of thinking and inspires little. His self-penned Mosaic Law is based on a liberal version of Manicheanism imported into the discipline. Here the battle rages between Evil, expressed as the 'four cardinal sins' of reductionism, essentialism, reification and functional teleology, and Good, expressed as agency, social action, dualism (the benign agency–structure version), ontological flexibility and so on. Liberal social theory goes about its business in a way that mimics classical liberal philosophy, by setting its universal limits on plural positive freedoms (in this case ideas/theories) with a cluster of negations and prohibitions; you can think any way you want *but not like this*. Liberal sociology's hypocrisy is quite stunning; it draws the negative rules that order its system from the four cardinal sins above – anti-reductionism, anti-essentialism, anti-reification and anti-teleology – but in the same breath it reduces the subject to an essentially autonomous, rational benign agent caught up in the quasi-reified abstraction of reflexive modernity towards the functionally civilized teleological terminus in history, i.e. liberal democracy. The liberal right go one stage further to tell us that no alternative economic system is possible, thus the end of history has already been reached and this is as good as it gets. The 'positive edicts' such as reflexivity and agency are merely rules and methods by which the individual should negotiate the space of positive freedom without contravening its negatively defined limits; they do not suggest what we should be reflexive about, or suggest reflexivity's cause or direction, and they do not suggest what sort of agents we are or what cause we should be involved in other than the equally vague and negative cause of 'emancipation', which is an amorphous flight from a tyrannical past to an unclear future.

This sort of position adds weight to Slavoj Žižek's (2000) claim that intelligent liberals don't actually believe in their own principles, or in the claim that they can be put into practice in any convincing or enduring way beyond the position already attained during liberalism's time-limited progressive phase, which culminated in the post-war civil rights movements and their socio-legal achievements. Yet, chronic economic instability, profound social divisions and cynical exploitation still exist, and the true extent of this – along with liberalism's inability to deal with it at its roots – is what the liberal establishment is happy for us to pretend that we don't know even though we know that we do know. The liberal establishment cannot flatly deny these phenomena, but it can present them in differentiated, tractable forms that can be managed as single issues. True to this principle, Sibeon goes on to insist we avoid the idea that 'government and public policy can be reduced to a single substantive principle of explanation' (2004: 2). On the one hand this proliferates the targets of social research and government and public policy intervention (or non-intervention), but on the other it is a decree that social thought and political action should avoid big issues and critical assaults on concentrated power.

How, for instance, would we apply anti-essentialist, anti-reductionist 'ontological flexibility' to the recent financial crisis? Would it be wrong to reduce the problem to the current historical stage of advanced capitalism's systemic logic, which seems to provide ample justification for the irresponsible and faith-bound activities of free-marketers and bankers? Of course capitalism is a multi-dimensional system and a co-evolutionary process and there is always more than one prime mover (Harvey, 2010), but the various dimensions or 'activity spheres' – technological-organizational, social-relational, institutional-administrative, productive, ecological, reproductive-cultural and mental-subjective – do seem to circulate around a fulcrum of primary principles, forms and dynamics. It's always complex, but, at its core, is it always *that* complex? Because government and public policy have always been strictly reformist, and usually light-touch, they have had no choice but to identify and deal with the complex peripheral manifestations caused, directly or indirectly, by primary systemic forces, or at least made very likely in the conditions they lay down.

For Harvey (ibid.), the primary systemic force in operation in advanced global capitalism is the imperative of *surplus capital absorption*, the need to invest mobile capital in profit-making activities, no matter how risky they are or where in the world they take place, and ensure a return of about 3 per cent or over. Higher returns attract more capital and therefore more economic development, and therefore this very simple yet immensely potent principle determines patterns of industrialization, deindustrialization, population movement, viable livelihoods and cultural homogenization all over the world. Many of the primary and secondary effects of its application seem to be relatively independent of the will. Crime did not *have* to rise sharply in the nineteen-eighties as the social fabric was ripped apart by rapid deindustrialization in many British and North American locales, but, as whatever substantive values still existed in the cultural fabric were corroded by insecurity, rampant consumerism and atomized competitive individualism, it was likely that it would, and, sure enough, it did. The Credit Crunch did not *have* to happen in the wake of the irresponsible but non-criminalized lending practices of exploitative financiers, lubricated by the 'light-touch' regulation of nervous neoliberal politicians as the systemic pressure to use rising values in the housing market as a substitute for relatively declining industrial wages to satisfy expectant consumers rose to bursting point, but, again, it did. Would the reflexive agency of a better social liberal government and a more informed public have prevented the

capitalist system tipping over into a crisis and producing a deleterious aftermath, or would it have merely delayed the inevitable? The precise forms and
timings of such crises are unpredictable, but that does not detract from
their inevitability at some point down the road. Had we rejected the liberal
edict proposed by Sibeon and so many others and based the regulation of
the economy on a single – if rather complex and multi-faceted – explanatory
principle, we might have stood a chance of either averting the crisis or
generating enough public support for serious systemic change.

To avoid this and maintain course, liberalism and liberal social science
place stringent restrictions on social thought. For Althusser (1969), in his
analysis of Marxism as a theoretical paradigm, social thought is split into
three realms (see also Mouzelis, 1995). Generalities I are extant theories
whose concepts can be criticized, synthesized and used in the constitution
of useful ideas in the realm of Generalities II, the basic formal conceptual
tools, which in turn can be used in the realm of Generalities III, a fully
developed substantive theory of processes, drivers and laws of motion.
Together, these interconnected levels of abstraction form a platform of
constructs on which social thought itself can take place. A similar process
takes place in all paradigms; Weberian, Foucauldian and so on. What the
principle liberal edict in social theory does is to restrict the passage of
approved thought from I and II into III, which discourages or discredits
substantive theory formation at the deepest and broadest level. For the
liberal only two things can exist in this deep realm; the choices and agentic
constitutional practices of the autonomous reflexive agent and the linguistic
discourses with which the subject constitutes itself. The ontological and
processual core of the world is radically indeterminate, therefore the only
substantive theories that can exist in Generalities III are those concerned
with reflexive agency, subjectivity, the state/individual relation and social
movements, the substitute for allegedly dead universalistic politics.
Theories grounded on good data and concepts from Generalities I and constructed in the arenas of Generalities II and Generalities III could suggest,
for instance, that the market-driven economy is not self-regulating but –
driven by the 'animal spirits' posited by Keynes (1935) and the processual
and systemic logic demonstrated by Marx (1954) – prone to cycles of
expansion, stability, instability and crash. There is nothing indeterminate
about this at all. Light regulation is not enough; either deep and substantial
regulation or systemic change is required. It would seem that the universal
idea of democratic control of the vital financial core and its investment
practices would be a good one (see Mellor, 2010, for further discussion).

Underneath the edict that either blocks the passage to Generalities III or
restricts creative intellectual activity within it is the social-liberal reformist's

fear of large scale political intervention in fundamental social institutions, relations and dynamic processes. Whereas crass and hasty reductionism, essentialism, reification and functional teleology oversimplify life's complexities, the fearful dilution of big politico-economic and socio-cultural issues in the name of pluralism and ontological flexibility atomizes, domesticates and neutralizes our conceptions of the issues and the required political action, which in some cases might need to be governmental 'public policy' action but at other times action from the realm of true politics. In the political dimension, these liberal edicts, themselves based on the *a priori* assumption of fundamental pluralism and temporal and spatial variability in which concentrated power and systemic imperatives simply occupy unexceptional places in the plurality, are intellectually and politically restrictive. Here one could invoke Simmel's (1955) formalism; diverse cultural manifestations do not belie the existence of central systemic functions and formal institutions. It is perhaps better to think in terms of reticulations and isomorphs, of diverse cultural forms tethered around central systemic institutions and forces. In universities we find diverse forms of managerialism and entrepreneurialism, for instance, but it would be foolish *not* to reduce them to essential economic and ideological imperatives – profitability, consumer choice and so on – whose power appears reified because it is *actual* as long as it remains unopposed, and which appears to function as if it is driving us towards some teleological nirvana of peace, progress and prosperity. Neoliberalism's managerialist edifice is of course the Lacanian Big Other, a formal power that does not really exist but *does* exist as an actual force as long as we fail to oppose and replace it, and continue to *act* as though it does (Žižek, 2008). In the field of social thought the most effective and enduring way to continue to act in this way is to follow Sibeon (ibid.) and believe that it doesn't, whilst in everyday life continuing to follow its edicts and organize a procession of pseudo-activities to intervene lightly in its symptomatic effects.

Thus, as long as agents continue to work on its behalf, Touraine (1995) is correct to break the anti-reductionist, anti-essentialist and anti-reification rules to posit existing society, in effect, as an actor, in the same way that Bhaskar (1997) is correct to ascribe effective actuality to the capitalist system's underlying structures and dynamic processes. However, in Žižek's (2010a) formulation these things are not causes but intermediary effects of our disavowal and inaction, which appear as actualities as they enact the obscenities of the even more stringently disavowed Real. We can work with a non-reified conception of the social actor as a being with the capacity to make decisions and act upon them, but we cannot assume the absence of disavowed ideology, economic compulsion or hegemonic cultural influence.

Sibeon's pluralistic light-touch reformism – redolent of what Perry Anderson (2011) recently described, without putting too fine a point on it, as the 'guff' of the Third Way – performs an important ideological function in depicting the system as a product of decisions and actions, which is the thinking behind a new breed of sophisticated social-liberal apparatchik. His claim that empirical enquiry should lay the groundwork alongside a minimal, open ontology with no ontological or meta-theoretical closure ignores the way in which empirical data can be selected and manipulated, the fact that events in the social world are often fleeting *ignii fatui* that fail to show on the empiricist's radar, and, because empiricists cannot be everywhere at once, complete data can never be gathered. Empirical research is expensive, and the focus of research is controlled by corporate and governmental bodies and trust funds, which, although they vary in their themes, were usually set up by social liberal philanthropists. Behind Sibeon's (ibid.) 'open social ontology' is the Popperian (2006) 'open society', behind that is a tightly closed liberal metatheory and philosophy, and behind that are liberal meta-politics. Behind liberal metapolitics is liberal capitalism, the most successful of history's violently and ideologically closed socio-economic forms, and behind that is the deep fear of necessary and wholesale change. These edicts operate on behalf of badly concealed liberal ideology, in the name of which Sibeon seeks to baptize us in the waters of reflexive modernity to cleanse us of our sins.

The sociologist Charles Turner (2010) gives liberalism's ideological screw another few turns. He attempts to synthesize disparate thinkers to argue for a 'theoretical liberalism'. He follows Isaiah Berlin's (1969) edict that any attempt to organize society in a way that might realize universal ideals will end in tyranny; again, the liberal mind is opened only after closing it to the outlawed possibility of the re-enaction of the very universal values that initially inspired liberalism to oppose feudal and religious power and bore fruit in the post-war civil rights victories. We could argue that the potential outcome of the situation is more dangerous without the universal values that liberalism condemns, yet which are simply more potent collectivized variants – modified in the light of the failings of liberalism – of the original values upon which its own historical break with the past was founded. For Turner, who seems unaware of Berlin's (ibid.) alternative concept of negative liberty as the dark side of liberal subjectivity, all this is far too deep, and to go too deep is to go beyond the limits of social inquiry. Turner seeks to elevate the culturalist paradigm to a dominant position where the self's contrived 'art of living' is the only real problem on which we should act, whilst retaining a few selected ideas from classical thinkers as our guide. The argument is transparently normative; this is what we should do, and to do anything else is both ineffective and dangerous. Where Sibeon simply places before us a set of methodological and conceptual obstacles, Turner seeks to slap an outright ban on depth and universalism.

Turner, talking about the cultural significance of the ideal type in modern constitutional theory, argues that reality is 'shaped by human action into institutions' (2010: 76). The reciprocal shaping of human action, and the emotions and thought behind it, by the ideological and practical politico-economic power of extant institutions, and their unified role in what is an historical and globally expanding capitalist system, are largely ignored at the beginning of his analysis and brought in mid-way, but only as illustrations of a specific form of cynicism employed in social theory. This cynicism is associated with depth. Following Simmel (1978) and Sloterdijk (1987), he admits that the capitalist money economy sustains base motivations that can colonize our systems of value, which gives other products of depth-thinking such as racism or patriarchy their fundamental metaphor. He casts the obscene Real outside the subject and its social relations into the economic system. Where the system is guilty the subject is innocent, and in an attempt to clarify the distinction he contrasts cynicism with scepticism, which is the tragic recognition of our inability to realize and practice our highest values. In a way reminiscent of the Romantic tragederian, all the tormented individual can do is valiantly attempt to construct the self as a work of art in the midst of the inevitable failure of the broader social system.

Liberal criminologists employ the same tactic, portraying the criminal as the temporary failure who can be rehabilitated to keep on getting up off the ground to try and try again in the Herculean task of being a Good person in the midst of Evil. The liberal subject is absolved of any blame, and plays no part in the system's constitution and reproduction. Is this not liberalism in its characteristic posture of denying the Real and avoiding any confrontation with its systematized practices and its active subjects? Is the one who Turner calls the cynic not the true reporter of the Real as the obscene and relentlessly active underside of liberal capitalism and its dominant subjectivity, a realist who throws back the ideological curtain that conceals the brutal practical imperatives and barbaric desires on which the system's reproduction depends? Turner shoots the messenger as he fails to differentiate between the cynic and the reporter who reveals a neoliberal world driven by institutionalized cynicism, envy and exploitation. If it is so difficult to be a Good person amidst of Evil circumstances, would it not be easier if those circumstances were to be changed and made more conducive to the task?

After berating Bourdieu (1986) for connecting cultural activity in a functional sense to social class, Turner then turns his ire on ideology critique, which purports to unmask deeper structural forces. Sloterdijk (1987) made the rather uncharacteristically thoughtless remark that the one who is explaining the other's ideology won't let his own ideology be explained, but this is countered by Žižek (2008b) who quite rightly posits the social struggle as always unavoidably and unashamedly ideological; we need ideology and efficient symbolic structures to make any sense of the world and construct tolerable ways of living. One must admit to being a social democrat, socialist, communist and so on and having powerful ideological commitments, but ideologies are not static and we must reinvent the left's underlying ideology after first admitting that the current ideology is in disarray. Only establishment liberals and empiricists are afraid to reveal their ideological commitments, because they are not supposed to have any. They prefer to believe that social institutions and practices are constituted by methodological individualists in creative, contingent and therefore entirely flexible and unpredictable ways as they constitute themselves and the world around them in circumstances of their own choosing, and, thus, we must assume, inherited from the past only in the most pliable and renewable forms.

Here Turner (2010) is appealing to obsolete forms of agency and culture that have been roundly rejected by many of today's most prominent cultural theorists (see for instance Stiegler, 2010b). We need not entirely disagree with liberal theorists that agency, culture and discourse are important phenomena, but we must not posit nature, desire, technology, labour processes, organizational forms, administrative structures, socio-cultural institutions and the incessant logic of the capitalist economy as components of an inert and ultimately pliable background. We must, in other words, look to co-foundationalism rather than anti-foundationalism (Harvey, 2010) and to the compulsory formative demands the system places on all those whose livelihoods, status and identities are dependent on them. However, if we are to reject liberalism's Kantian notion of the subject as a moral constructivist voluntarily obeying a set of a priori categories amenable to reason, we must also question the Marxist notion that the morality of the individual is irrelevant to the reproduction of the system (Marx, 1954; see also Harvey, 2011, for a discussion). We are all pressured into performing functions in one or more of these dimensions, despite the ideals and intentions we might harbour, and it is unwise to dismiss the possibility that some individuals, in return for rewards offered in a Faustian deal, embrace this cynicism and internalize it as a driver and a justification; this is, after all, an effective way to integrate the self and prosper in a cynical, exploitative and unforgiving system. The trigger for such adoption and internalization is the subject's acceptance of the capitalist system's compulsive logical needs and performativity, a system whose energy is generated by the conversion of vices and 'animal spirits' into economic dynamism. The criminological questions we must ask here are whether to varying degrees individual subjects collude willingly in the system's cynical logic, and to what extent that collusion is internalized in the Real, the hidden ideological supplement – that which incites us to action but remains unspoken in public – at the core of subjectivity.

Turner's (2010) attack on Bourdieu (1986) is a denial of the class inter-ests behind the cultural forms that constitute the judgement of taste, yet the latter sections of his book are full of haughty judgements of those who he regards as inferior beings because of their determination to ground cul-tural forms ontologically and aetiologically in underlying functions, imper-atives and interests. Unger's (1987) parallel charge that 'deep structure social theory' disorientates political change and plans of programmatic action is correct only in the sense that it disorientates those programmes in the realms of identity politics – more, it pours scorn on them – that embody fetishistic disavowal and sustain the illusion of progressive trans-formation (Dean, 2009). The main cause of the Credit Crunch in 2008 was the result of congealed labour power converted by exploitation to produce surplus value in the form of money, and, to obviate the perennial problem of surplus capital absorption, lending that money irresponsibly and passing off toxic debts and related layers of insurance premiums as assets by con-cealing them in falsely rated packages alongside good ones. Whatever we did in the past by way of 'political change and programmatic action' got nowhere near the inner sanctum of this process and the undertaking behind this major event, which momentarily revealed in stark relief the submerged obscene Real. In this case the undertaking was to deceive investors by irre-sponsibly lending to borrowers in precarious economic circumstances who could not pay back, a manifestation of the obscene Real that generates the agentic energy in the financial hub of our economic system.

Two years after this ethical, intellectual and economic disaster at the financial core of the system was rather bad timing for the publication of a thesis denying depth. Turner's (2010) demeanour as a writer, displayed throughout the book in a prissy, affected style replete with cheap insults and dismissals of those who seek depth as 'crude', 'cynical', 'lacking in intellectual ability', 'lesser thinkers', 'apparently sophisticated', 'boring' and so on, which contrasts starkly with the obsequious elevation of his favoured liberal theorists as 'geniuses', reveals his Bourdieusian struggle for cultural, symbolic and economic capital in the liberal cultural studies field in which he operates. He also identifies the postmodernist-liberal-culturalist position with the 'tradition of thought about the art of living that begins with Socrates and ends with Foucault' (2010: 169), which shows ignorance of the fact that Socrates was himself a depth thinker well aware of the obscenity of the Hyde-like Real that lay underneath his ability to conquer it and create a fragile ethical self that threatened the Athenian structural power elite, who thrived in the conditions created by unashamed, violent class exploitation. There is only a very tenuous link between Socrates, the great thinker who proclaimed the birth of the subject, and Foucault, the lesser thinker who proclaimed its death, and any stronger link is bound to elevate Foucault beyond his station. Even Berkeley's idealists, Locke's liberals, Blake's romantics and Husserl's phenomenologists – even the Emperor of dandies himself, Oscar Wilde, in *The Picture of Dorian Gray* – had advanced conceptions of this underlying obscenity in both its systemic and subjective forms. To posit utopia as a twinkle in the eye of a smug liberal dandy preening his personal ethics in front of the nearest mirror whilst the world's vital infrastructural support systems fall apart, high murder rates plague inner cities and the imprisonment rate in the USA reaches Gulag proportions is the true act of cynicism. Depth theorists do not reduce ideals and values to the base obscenities that structure and reproduce oppressive socio-economic systems, but seek to recover the ideals and values that have been relocated or cast aside, to strengthen them and apply them politically in ways that can drive out the obscene supplement or at least reduce the grip it has on our lives. Turner's position embodies liberal postmodernism's *fetishistic disavowal*, the injunction that one must never attempt to symbolize the Real in public, so we can continue not wanting to know what we already know and therefore continue to live and act as if we don't know. To deny depth and reduce values to a surface role, allowing the obscene Real to continue to impoverish the lives of the vulnerable is beyond cynicism; it is political and intellectual cowardice.

All this sneering smacks of a desperate cover-up. If the Real is the kernel of ideology that resides in the fetishistically-disavowed desire of the subject, Turner's critique is simply a long-winded exercise in the fetishistic disavowal of an ideology of political catastrophism, and it is the motif of a liberal narrative in decline. Ideology-critique reached a peak with Althusser (1969), but since the 1980s the whole world of ideology, subjectivity and desire has been largely absent in mainstream liberal sociology, which suggests that the descent into 'decorative sociology' during the cultural turn (Rojek & Turner, 2000) has deeper roots than the flight from social-structural relations. Not only do we lack a macro-sociological analysis of British decline, as Bryan Turner (2006) rightly argues, we also lack such an analysis of Britain's systemic and ideological development, which, since it was the first truly industrial-capitalist nation, has ramifications for our current global situation as we enter yet another systemic crisis of the industrial-capitalist form itself.

Moreover, decades of liberal dominance, controlling research programmes and selecting and deselecting theoretical frameworks, has denied us any insight into the vital ontological category of the subject of ideology. Thus, referring to the list at the beginning of the chapter, in criminological theory we are compelled to work in an ontological straightjacket, restricted to the radical liberal and social liberal conceptions of the subject as the only alternatives to the wicked hedonistic calculator preferred by today's dominant ideologies of neoconservatism and neoliberalism. However, ideology and subjectivity have reappeared rather spectacularly on the intellectual agenda (see Badiou, 2006; Žižek, 2000). Sociology and criminology are ideally placed to make major contributions to this debate as well as advances to the understanding of criminal/harmful subjects and institutions if, as we shall see as this argument unfolds, they can import some of these ideas and look beyond the undialectical ethico-social relation between the individual and the state.

TWENTIETH-CENTURY CRIMINOLOGICAL THEORY: FROM AETIOLOGY TO CONTROLOLOGY

5

As faithful reflectors and disseminators of approved ideas, most socio-logically based criminological theory textbooks – sometimes after a quick trawl through nineteenth-century statistical work and early psycho-logical schools – tend to avoid early Marxist, socialist and Freudian thought, which, as we can see clearly in the work of Engels (1987), Bonger (1916), Aichhorn (1931), Lacan (2006), Fromm (2000) and others, harboured strong post-positivist aetiological commitments to the examination of the motivations behind human behaviours such as criminality in their social, economic and cultural contexts. They also tend to avoid the work of the unique dualistic thinkers from the early twentieth century, such as Veblen and Simmel, with whom we had a brief encounter earlier.

Many commence with the Chicago School, where the aetiological com-mitment was still apparent, but in the shape of Durkheimian functionalism, which dominated the School's early period in the 1920s and 1930s. However, although the advocates of the early Durkheimian current shared his faith in the ethical individual and the ethical institution as the functional centre of the social, they did not attempt to avoid the problematic criminlogical trends that were conspicuous in the expanding cities, especially the 'transitional zone' (Park et al., 1925). The high incidence of criminality, prostitution, suicide, mental disorders, disease and poverty were classified as the pathological products of social disorganization, in turn a product of the moral dissensus and harsh economic competition experienced by incoming populations in this zone of instability and transience. Harsh eco-nomic competition also created the conditions in which ethnic closure and mutually hostile territorial subcultures were more likely to establish them-selves and, in a general anomic climate, indulge in crime and violence. This was a classic Durkheimian formulation; rapid socio-economic change threatens social cohesion, there is a breakdown of meaning and practice as the authority of central social institutions declines and there is an anomic and therefore criminogenic 'time-lag' as values and norms fail to adapt to abrupt change. However, Durkheim and his followers were also optimistic modernists who regarded the move from mechanical to organic solidarity as positive and inevitable; consequently they were inclined to see these localized ethico-social lapses as temporary intervals in a progressive project. With such faith in ethical individuals and the ability of socio-cultural institutions to mutate and repair themselves like biological organisms, the Durkheimians felt no need to indulge in critical depth thinking; wounds such as social disorganization and anomie could heal themselves while the overall social organism kept running for its prize.

For Durkheim (1982), a small amount of crime is normal because it performs the functions of establishing moral boundaries and communicating the nature of prohibitions to the community; a 'society of saints' would not last long. To this communicative end justice and punishment stage a vital 'morality play' around the theme of crime (Sparks, 1992) and together constitute a functional institution; without some idea of what is profane the nature of the sacred cannot be established (Durkheim, 2001; Girard, 1977). Crime cannot be appreciated or eliminated but only visibly condemned and regulated to prevent its expansion beyond its normal, functional volume. Too much crime and punishment is pathological, a sign of a dysfunctional anomic society that is failing to maintain its moral centre as it drifts into a condition of 'normlessness'. The central problem was the failure of moral forces and institutions to evolve and adapt, and to regulate a society in a phase of rapid change. Durkheim did not see change, differentiation and increasing complexity as bad things in themselves, and Melossi (2008) reminds us that he was anything but a collectivist. He was an optimistic individualist and, contrary to many of the pessimistic critics who saw individualism and contractualism as corrosive to reproductive systems of collective morality, he saw morality living on in the 'non-contractual elements' of interpersonal contracts made between individuals. He was, however, worried about unbridled, amoral individualism, which means that he placed subjectivity and its tendency to be overpowered by the timeless Aristotelian 'malady of infinite aspirations' at the centre of the problem. Yet, despite his affirmation of individualism, he was also suspicious of the abstract methodological individualism and its independent powers of interpretation at the heart of the liberal discourse. He recognized the social reality into which we are 'thrown'; society and its institutions exist before us and outside of us, and its functional, harmonizing ethics and prohibitions must be communicated and diffused amongst all individuals.

The very idea that the ethical individual was merely a cog in the Marxian capitalist system or a wretched creature driven by Freudian unconscious drives and desires was anathema to Durkheim, probably to the extent that it was to Weber. He saw class struggle as simply another form of social rupture, a source of collective anomie and a threat to cohesion. However, Simmel questioned the notion that social conflict is dysfunctional (Coser, 1964; Wieviorka, 2009). His work was well-regarded in Europe, but in US social and political thought myriad superficial 'detail reformers' had taken over from 'depth reformers' such as Veblen, who had endured hostility from conservatives and progressive liberals alike, and Simmel was similarly marginalized. As the Soviet system degenerated into Stalinism, Marxism and Marxist-Leninism were cast out even further on the margins, but in doing so the liberal–conservative alliance missed out on the interesting notion that conflict is not a pathology but a principal force of integrative cohesion, although cohesion must be seen as a temporary, fluid form; as Weber (1949) said, peace was a change in the form of conflict. For Simmel (1955), conflict was a form of socialization; following Freud he saw it as an essential part of ego and identity development for the individual and the group. Whilst Durkheim saw conflict as primarily disruptive, for Simmel it could re-establish unity on a higher ethical level. The suppression of conflict and its modes of expression will cause disunity and dis-identification, a sure way of promoting the dissolution of the group. In a similar vein Wieviorka (2009) views the current change in European social conflict from its insti-tutionalized post-war form – disruptive in the short term but constructive in the long term – to its deinstitutionalized neoliberal form as permanently atomizing and disruptive, perhaps placing society in danger of total long-term dissolution.

The wish to avoid conflict and transformative dialectical change was shared by conservatives, classical liberals and progressive social liberals alike. This was pure intellectual pragmatism, a way of dealing with the *fait accompli* of capitalism's increasing individualism and social disruption. Durkheim saw intervention in the 'natural order' of talent and reward as the only way forward in an inexorably re-ordering world (Melossi, 2008), beginning with a critique of inherited wealth, the spectre of accumulation and transmission that would rise again to expose Nozick's (1974) libertari-anism as untenable. Here Durkheim was moving towards an early version of social-liberal 'equal opportunities' thinking. However, what we must bear in mind at this stage is that this pragmatism created a restrictive intel-lectual environment in which conflict, struggle and forms of subjectivity whose harmful actions could not be rectified within the existing structural coordinates of liberal capitalism were to have no place in theories of social integration, social change or criminogenesis. Engels, Bonger, Veblen, Simmel, the Freudians and all other 'depth thinkers' were to be given short shrift, a tradition that, as we have seen in the work of Turner (2010), today's liberals wish to continue.

The American sociologist Robert Merton was a major integrationist thinker. He picked up on Durkheim's concept of 'anomie' in his explanation of crime, deviance and other reactions to social difficulties. He was aware of the high crime rates in the 1920s and 1930s before the second-wave New Deal, and noticed that the growth of the American economy was disrupting the nation's core institutions, morals and norms. What Roosevelt had coined as the 'American Dream' was having a profound effect on social integration. Merton (1938) argued famously that the cultural pressure placed by the Dream on Americans to succeed in terms of wealth and status was creating strain as it clashed with an unequal structure of opportunities. This strain was splintering society into various reactive paths to subjectivity, and some individuals fell into modes of withdrawal and detached them-selves from the collective and its vital limits and boundaries. Some remained within boundaries as they inclined to conformity and ritualism, but others pushed at the boundaries as they sought innovation, retreatism and rebellion. The degrees of disadvantage suffered by individuals will tend to influence the paths taken, and innovation and rebellion in locations of extreme disadvantage and social disorganization can be criminogenic.

The standard criticisms of strain theory are that it assumes a society with consensual values, goals and norms and it ignores the possibility that closed meaning-systems in a social plurality can establish and reproduce their own unique values, goals and norms. It also assumes universal pragmatism, the principle that individuals are forced to solve problems in determined struc-tural situations, which is too rationalistic and deterministic, and it is also essentialist and universal; are we not driven by diverse alternative goals? The criticism that it cannot explain hate-crime and violence is harsh because detachment from the social could quite easily foster resentment towards proximate competitors and the mainstream alike, thus provoking violence. The criticisms that there is little mention of gender and race, and that the theory overpredicts criminality hold true, but the complaint that strain cannot explain the crimes of the powerful probably does not; if the malady of infinite aspirations is what it says – infinite – then the ability to imagine incremental degrees of success is also infinite, which means that strain can occur at any point in the social hierarchy where ambition is strong, moral boundaries are weak and opportunities are blocked. This relates to what could be the main problem with Durkheim and Merton; Durkheim conceptualized the malady of infinite aspirations as natural and permanently active rather than constructed and latent, and although Merton avoided naturalism and saw it as the product of a culture that glorified material success, he did not investigate this cultural process, what might lie underneath it or what forces and energies the American Dream could draw upon in a any great detail, preferring instead to focus on secondary modes of adaption and the structure of opportunities. We will address this problem later (Chapter 8) when we look at transcendental materialism.

At no juncture were fundamental underlying desires and values explored or questioned by Durkheim, Parsons or Merton as materialized constructions; they were assumed to be either natural or culturally adaptive, an insistent or reactive unruliness that can be contained quite easily if social institutions perform their functional and ethical tasks and socialise individuals with reasonable efficiency in a social structure that provides equal opportunities for competitive individuals. To deal with Hobbesian conflict and attempt a theory of subjectivity, Parsons (1964) proposed a diluted and one-dimensional variant of Freudianism, the internalization of the social contract in the ego, facilitated by appropriate socialization in families. This was bolstered by the popularity of ego psychology, an Americanized branch of psychoanalysis that had taken root in the 1930s and marginalized the idea of the super-ego as a psychodynamic force independent of the ego. That most European Freudians commentating on crime dealt with the super-ego did not impress the Durkheimians, possibly because the concept had one foot in the unconscious and thus challenged optimistic liberal conceptions of individualism, choice and freedom. Melossi (2008) argues that Merton's work parallels that of Karen Horney, whose 'acquisition anxiety' was part of a deep Freudian critique of American culture that was emerging at the time, but the connection is rather tenuous. Merton saw deviance as 'normal', part of the process of 'creative destruction' that is often attributed to Schumpeter but in fact can be seen earlier in the work of Marx and the anarchists in the nineteenth century. In Merton's work there was no real critique of the destructive aspect of the process, nor of primary motivations or the culture that generates them. Instead, he aimed his critique at the dissolution of moral boundaries and the unequal availability of opportunities for disadvantaged individuals. Horney (1937; 1950), on the other hand, was part of a neo-Freudian psychoanalytical movement that included Erich Fromm (1974) and Alfred Adler (1999), which explored the anti-social matrix of anxiety, inferiority, narcissism, aggression and acquisitiveness. This contained the intellectual germs of what were to become searing critiques of the pathogenic psychodynamic drivers behind industrial and consumer capitalism. By ignoring this 'front-end' tension, Melossi misrepresents the connections between the intellectual currents that were influential in the mid-twentieth-century period; the neo-Freudians criticized the purposes for which drives and desires were being stimulated and shaped, and their lack of internalized moral restraints, whilst Merton bemoaned the absence of opportunities to fulfil them in socially acceptable ways signified by external boundaries. Merton entirely lacked a psychosocial 'depth critique'.

The eventual shift in the Chicago School from Durkheimian organicism, with its critical notions of social disorganization and anomie, to appreciative liberal pluralism was fundamental, indeed seismic in the development of twentieth-century criminological theory. Its advocates rejected the notions of demoralization and egoism emphasized by the Marxists, socialists and the critical Freudians, along with Simmel's depth critique of modern urban life. Put very simply, in the early to mid-twentieth century there were major shifts from Romantic-conservative and Marxist-socialist critiques telling us there was something inherently wrong with capitalist societies through social liberal critiques telling us things could go temporarily wrong with their ethical institutions to liberal appreciative studies telling us that there was no such thing as a 'capitalist society' and things can only go wrong in the way we, as autonomous interpretive individuals, regard and treat each other. We would do well not to underestimate the importance and profundity of this shift. For the latter the very bedrock of the social was a shifting magma of plural cultures and individual interpreters and actors of life; beneath this there was nothing at all but an inert and flexible infrastructure that can only be constituted and energized by individual agents. If the basic problem is that we lack care, empathy and tolerance in our real and symbolic relations with others, there must be a compulsory transformation of the principle that underpins criminological theory from criticism to appreciation; to argue otherwise would be judgmental and hypocritical. Relations, however, are essentially symbolic, and precisely how appreciation in symbolic relations can be transposed into appreciation in real (material-socio-economic-political) relations without upsetting the capitalist apple cart is an issue, as we shall see, that proved to be a thorn in liberalism's side. There is no doubt, however, that in sociological and criminological theory as well as politics and culture, this was the beginning of the headlong flight from depth critique to a *zeitgeist* entirely dominated by various shades of liberalism. The most telling intellectual action was in the USA's 'Progressive Movement', a loose concatenation of social-liberal activist groups in the popular and academic communities offering an alternative to the declining labour militancy and socialist movements that had risen to a threatening prominence in the late nineteenth and early twentieth centuries. Giddens' 'third way' (1998) was little more than a slogan pasted on a well-established tradition in an abortive attempt to revive its fortunes in a markedly changed world in the grip of neoliberalism.

The injunction of 'appreciate' appeared to be ethical, but in an important way it was expectantly functional, an attempt to exhort new forms of life to produce plural mores of civility and citizenship amongst the individuals who belonged to them. Melossi (2008) argues that the European solution of strengthening the state cut against the grain of the American tradition. However, he also tends to romanticize this tradition and underestimate the extent to which the labour movement grew as a means of creating political solidarity out of pluralist chaos. The US murder rate in the nineteenth century was underestimated right up to 1900. Textbooks tend to estimate it at about 1 per 100,000 in that year, but only the states that were characterized by industry, labour militancy, political solidarity and functional administrations were returning this low rate; other states – some of which were genuine minimally-governed parastates – were not returning their data, but Eckberg's (1995) demographic work suggests that their murder rates were significantly higher, and had this data been returned the national rate would have been nearer 6 per 100,000. In areas of political solidarity state administrations grew as organizing and regulating mechanisms, but in areas of hostile 'pluralism' states grew as means of legitimizing and performing the drastic measures that, since America's recognition of itself as a chaotic, violent society in the 1830s, were requested by the people themselves to counteract the fear that had rational roots in a nation that had since 1780 become increasingly violent (van Creveld, 1999). Ideology and old memories of persecution taught the people that they *should not* want the state, yet experience in the hostility caused by a minimally-governed competitive capitalist society taught them that they *did* want it.

In essence, politics was marginalized in favour of culture, voluntarism and the rule of law in the 'progressive period'; that is until the system broke down and the state had to clean up the mess under Roosevelt in the 1930s. One does not have to be an ideologically bound supporter of the state to accept the fact that it was a necessary regulator of the chaos and violent criminality that tended to characterize minimally regulated capitalism. From 1900 to 1933 the homicide rate had climbed from 6 to 10 per 100,000, and Prohibition, even though it did not help matters, cannot be the principal cause because the homicide rate had been climbing for nineteen years before its inception. The main problem was more complex than liberalism's usual suspect, the 'reactionary-punitive state'; in the period from the good showing of Eugene Debs's Socialist Party of America in the 1904 elections to Roosevelt's regulatory clampdown in 1933 the rapid decline in the short-lived American solidarity project seemed to coincide with an equally rapid deterioration of culture, state administration and the relation between them. As the ethos of politically aroused solidarity was replaced by that of individualism and cultural pluralism, powerful criminal organizations prospered and established mutually beneficent relationships with corrupt state officials. Horkheimer (1982) famously compared the ruling class of every era to racketeers, but one of liberalism's problems is that it tends to draw a line between the dominant and the rest whilst dismissing the ethical and politico-economic demarcation between the exploiting and exploited social classes, thus missing the homology between those who *are dominant* and those amongst the plurality of individuals and cultures who wish to abandon their class *to become dominant*; to join the exploiters as the quickest way to avoid exploitation. Protection of interests and violent domination are mutually supportive. Each constitutes and legitimizes the other, and together, with the promise of protection justifying domination, and domination guaranteeing an enduring monopoly on protection, pave the way to structural racketeering, blurring the boundaries between the illegal and the legal as well as the state and civil society. In other words, the barbarism of order and the barbarism of disorder seem to be two sides of the same coin.

It is easy to rail against the indigenous elite's labelling of the immigrant workers in Chicago as 'dangerous', but the real situation was complex; the immigrants were entering a brutally competitive society, and the absence of political solidarity, state support and an organized guarantee of economic participation or redistribution left them with little choice but to compete. The immigrants who saw militant collectivist politics as the solution were quickly deterred by the tacit liberal–conservative alliance. The successful entrepreneur had the highest status in the Gilded Age, so for many entering this hegemonic climate individual economic enterprise was quickly accepted as the preferred choice, the 'way things are done'. However, entrepreneurialism at the bottom of a brutally competitive society can be a robust affair for those undertakers determined to succeed rapidly from a position of weakness and exploitation. Until the New Deal arrived as a diluted social-democratic substitute for rejected socialism and achieved some stability, not just the immigrants but the whole culture was precariously placed and potentially dangerous. Some immigrants had backgrounds in brigandage (Melossi, 2008), and as such they were unlikely to take lying down either threats from the industrialists' hired thugs acting as state agents or the prospect of a life of poverty or dull, unrewarding manual labour. The likelihood that many would seek various degrees of involvement in criminal undertakings was high.

What was behind the Chicago School's switch from a critical stance to an appreciative stance? It served a dual purpose insofar as liberal ideology sought to appreciate the individual's struggle against an unjust system and also protect offenders from harsh punishment, whilst somehow disconnecting the unjust system itself from the nature and will of individuals. For the School's founder Robert Park, the inherently pluralistic crowd was to become the general 'public', their sentiments were to become 'public opinion' and their interests were to become the 'public interest'; no need for the political and mythological class unity that Karl Marx (1972), George Sorel (1972) or even the far less confrontational James Keir Hardie (Benn, 1992) had been preaching in Europe. In the larger movement that Park represented, were we witnessing the most ambitious and concerted of all depoliticization strategies? Park offered to domesticate and tame the crowd without repressing its libidinal energies, to turn it into an energetic yet tame 'public' on behalf of the elite. Groups such as the Socialist Party of America and the Wobblies (Industrial Workers of the World) had been organizing strikes and threatening to spread European notions of socialism and Bolshevism amongst the disorganized and volatile immigrant groups (Zinn, 1980). To counteract this, American Progressives, mirroring the Fabian movement in Britain, offered to help the lower orders to organize themselves into ambitious consumers, compliant workers and active but pacified citizens in a nation that regarded itself as the most democratic in history. The more politically orientated amongst the immigrant workers seemed to accept the right to free speech and free organization as an alternative to mounting a political struggle for the state's central organizing power.

The ideology behind the Progressive Movement came straight from the heart of European liberalism. Weber's (1978) sociology was based on the ethico-rational individual; society is a product of individuals acting together and little more. Even Durkheim – often placed in opposition to Weber because he saw economic change propelled by its own dynamic momentum and social phenomena as external, objective forces constraining the individual – identified the individual as the prime mover in the ethical maintenance or transformation of society's institutions and norms. This is based on the fundamental assumption that human beings are self-conscious and possess the ability to construct and reconstruct themselves and their social worlds in the realm of reflective thought, language, meaning and systems of communication, to which the modern term 'reflexivity' is now ascribed. Collective social and political entities have only limited power to impose ideas and action on individuals. Liberal social theory in the USA imported ideas from the European philosophical school of Phenomenology, which is based on the principle that individuals consciously impose meanings on the world. Where Schutz (1967) and Garfinkel (1967) compressed the whole process of meaning-generation through rule-making games into consciousness, Berger and

Luckmann (1966) compressed the whole of reality through socially structured intersubjectivity into consciousness. This is not to say that phenomenologists and social constructionists deny the existence of real things with
distinct emergent properties, but that the social meanings of these things are
constructed consciously by individuals in systems of communicative interaction. However, in these theories of social noise, there is very little room for
the social silences, the disavowed, unspoken drives and desires that float
between the unconscious and conscious realms, constructing tacit meanings
and energizing actions. For liberal thought the process that ties together who
we are, what the world is, and how we act in it is the preserve of conscious
thoughts and intentions informed by 'reasoned' value systems.

The American tradition of progressive liberalism, which has had the
most profound influence on Western criminological thought, is also a child
of phenomenology, but in a practical context. The roots of symbolic interactionism lie in the pragmatism of James (1981), Pierce (1887–8) and
Dewey (1998). For Pierce, our knowledge of objects lies in our practical
relationships to them, so knowledge will change only as our practical relationships change. Not only does this have a tendency to epistemological and
ontological relativism, but it also equates truth, and by extension value and
beauty, with function; what is correct, good and beautiful is what works for
us in the context in which we find ourselves. It fits with Weber's notion that
if we think there is a society because it is useful to us, then we will act as if
there is a society, and if we do this at least we will see the members of that
society as valuable like ourselves. We will see later that this essentially liberal pragmatic-constitutional formulation is morality and subjectivity in
reverse, the basis of the *fetishistic disavowal* that aids ideology in its task of
maintaining the obscene Real at the front of the process and sociability at
the back as a fragile aftermath.

If Rock (1979) is right that pragmatism developed through an American
interpretation of Hegel, it looks like Hegelianism in an unholy alliance with
Utilitarianism, where the *World Spirit* moves forward to consolidate our
sociability only if the costs are not too high and the benefits practical. The
basis of value in meaning is calculated function and adaptability, the foundation of the 'social interaction' that Mead (1934) and Blumer (1969) placed
at the centre of their analyses. The rule that the social scientist cannot
'know' anything over and above the meanings of the actors being studied is
axiomatic, grounded in Mead's theory of the construction of the subject in
conversation between two internal entities – the 'I' and the 'Me' – and
external significant others. We create our identities around a running com-
mentary as we go about achieving ends in our everyday practical lives. For
Goffman (1959), we manage our impressions in order to achieve pragmatic

social or economic purposes. How Turner (2010) cannot detect the onto-logical crudity and the cynical pragmatism in the 'genius' Goffman is some-thing of a mystery, but then again love is blind. There is an unexamined pan-instrumentalism in American liberal thought that would interest any impression-management business guru; it's quite possible that it already has. It is quite remarkable that this thinking has contributed so strongly to what we now know as 'radical' liberalism. If we know nothing more sub-stantial than the thoughts of others, and if egocentric instrumentalism is passed off as pragmatism and tacitly accepted as the ethical foundation of our lives, what is there to be radical about?

Joas (1998) argues persuasively that Mead's hope for identity-formation by democratic inclusion ignores the capacity of violence and exclusion to stabilize an identity already constituted in hostile environments in interac-tion with hostile others, which therefore seeks to retain narcissistic closure (see also Winlow & Hall, 2009b). Symbolic interactionism's major weak-ness is in its non-dialectical dualism; in the I/Me duality the running com-mentary is performed by the 'I' as self-conception and targeted at the 'Me' as self-perception. The Symbolic, influenced by significant others, simply defines the Imaginary, with no place for the Real and its unconscious, tumultuous presence in the neurological circuits of the material body and its ability to receive and interpret in proto-symbolic form the irruptions of external reality (Hall et al., 2008; Johnston, 2008). The accompanying notion that 'causes' are impossible because they are always interpreted before action takes place reckons without the fetishistic disavowal of the Real, the vulgar injunctions and prejudices we follow and the desires we seek to realize but dare not speak or, in many cases, even think, which allows them to grow in a dark cellar of unreflexivity.

In an attempt to move beyond both strain theory and pragmatism to a richer conception of culture as a site for social learning, Sutherland (1947) argued that criminal traditions can be established by differential association as young people become immersed in criminal subcultures, which are reproduced as 'folkways', often in the entire absence of historical circum-stances, conscious pragmatic motives or aetiological conditions. Sutherland claimed that although it's often difficult to shift such learned behaviour, what is learned can be unlearned. Thus criminal habits have nothing to do with poverty, psychopathology or any other structural/processual conse-quence. However, in *The Professional Thief* (1937), he noted that everyday professional criminals liked to associate with politicians and corporate executives because they shared a common liking for forms and techniques of *predatory control*; only the scale of operation was different. In a cultural theory supposedly based on the absence or amnesia of instrumental motives, all of a sudden one appears in a central position. Did he not wonder why predatory control permeated the social structure and became a rendezvous for the criminal undertakers from all social classes, or what the aetiological genesis of such a ubiquitous, compelling and seemingly attractive practice might be? Differential association theory was a theory of transmission or reproduction, not of genesis or cause, and we were further from a 'depth critique' of liberal capitalism and an explanation of the aetiology of harm than we had ever been.

Albert Cohen (1955), a former student of Merton and Sutherland, retained strong links with strain theory and argued that subcultures under social strain and status frustration will find new ways of achieving status whilst simultaneously hitting back at the system. Thus delinquent acts are often not acquisitive and instrumental but done for 'kicks'; they can be malicious, negative, versatile, hedonistic, non-utilitarian and autonomous. However, this formulation misrecognized the standard philosophical connection between hedonism and rational calculation; in fact in classical liberal philosophy – and in the work of its critics such as Veblen (1994) – the gratification of hedonistic desire in the realm of special liberty is seen as the *principal benefit and the ultimate aim* in the pursuit of which costs will be risked in instrumental strategies. Pointless hedonistic leisure represents the pinnacle of the status system in capitalist societies as it did in most hierarchal pre-capitalist societies, the 'stupid pleasures' that for Žižek (2008) number amongst the prizes in Agamben's (2005) 'state of exception', where dominant power suspends social codes and laws.

Wolfgang and Ferracuti (1967) argued that subcultures of violence are expressive and based on honour, excitement and the acquisition of territory, and in a similar vein Miller (1958) argued that subcultural norms and values are distinguishable from the mainstream insofar as they represent trouble, toughness, smartness, excitement, fatalism and autonomy. The same critique applies, but here we also encounter the most spectacular conflation of norms and values and fetishistic disavowal of the existence of the core values that are the wellspring of these expressions at the heart of capitalist culture and political economy. Leisure was the mark of social distinction for the barbarian warlord and the successful bourgeois alike (Sombart, 1998; Veblen, 1994), and violence and appropriation were the extra-economic political and social powers active at the beginning of the capitalist project, now disavowed and sublimated but still active. Indeed, Downes (1966) later realized that the real relationship is an instrumental-hedonistic one between delinquency and leisure. This later insight moved us away from the false assumption that the values at the heart of delinquent subcultures are qualitatively different from those of the mainstream. The theoretical problem here is the conflation of values and norms (Hall et al., 2008). The ultimate values and goals are indeed very similar; the achievement of status by dominating others to achieve territorial control, material comfort and personal autonomy by exploiting, intimidating, gambling or using any means other than everyday mental or manual labour, followed by the celebration of these achievements with spectacular and victorious displays of hedonistic pleasure. However, as we shall see later when we discuss the stimulation/pacification nexus (Chapter 9), the accompanying norms and rules are very different in that they deal with sublimation and restriction.

Matza's (1964) subsequent theory of the tendency of young males to drift in and out of delinquency suffered from the same inappropriate conflation. Mainstream values and goals have remained constant through the bourgeois epoch as the generators of desire amongst a politically significant majority, which includes delinquents, who are not 'rebels' but hyper-conformists (Hall et al., 2008; Heath & Potter, 2006) seeking a short cut to the realm of special liberty where 'stupid pleasures' can be enjoyed with impunity. Individuals who inhabit socio-economic locations that make their desires difficult to gratify in ways acceptable to the mainstream drift in and out of normative-practical strategies, but not necessarily values and beliefs. In fact shifts in values and beliefs are quite rare without a profound conversion of the individual's psyche (Maruna, 2001) or a social revolution (Badiou, 2006). Techniques of neutralization and the justificatory rhetoric that expresses and operationalizes them are not the products of embarking on a 'moral holiday' but of underestimating the importance of normative restraints whilst expressing naïve faith in values and goals; it is a temporary lapse of fidelity to the vital fetishistic disavowal on which the whole system survives, exposing the Real, the obscene underlying drives whose energy propels the system forwards. What for Matza (ibid.) was an automatic if rather delayed maturity and reflexivity is simply the individual's growing understanding of the importance of socially acceptable normative-practical strategies as he enters the socio-economic mainstream that structures the transitions from youth to the responsibilities of adulthood.

However, just as capitalism's barbaric underlying Real was consolidating itself as the great homogenizing and energizing force in post-war consumer capitalism, pluralism cranked up the pressure on the strain theory orthodoxy. The Californian School of phenomenology had argued that deviance is only understandable via the 'sociology of everyday life'. Sociologists must look at the 'rules' that apply in subcultural nooks and crannies in the appreciative way established by the later Chicago School. Although it was never made clear, the assumption here was that different rules must evolve from the practical application of corresponding generative values and goals, and the whole process can be thought of as a 'meaning system' that connects all the parts to each other. Here the important concepts of social conflict and dialectical tension were absent, but the New York School of phenomenologists assimilated conflict theory and admitted that some meaning systems can become more established than others in the social structure, constituting a dominant macro-system. The deviant might offer a different and interesting perspective on life to the criminologist, but to the dominant culture he is a threat to the fragile order of meaning into which most people have subscribed. Here there is tension, but it is an intercultural tension between dominant and subordinate meaning-systems within the overall society that can be relieved by democratic negotiation and the equalizing of symbolic power, not a dialectical politico-economic tension between class interests or a psychodynamic tension between the passion of the Real and the meaning of the Symbolic that cannot be relieved without moving the whole society to a superior ethical level.

Symbolic interactionism picked up on the insights of the structural wing of American phenomenology and posited the social reaction to deviance as the most important factor in the constitution of criminal identities. In the 1960s Lemert (1967) and others reasserted the liberal-pluralist axiom that societies were not organized around common goals, norms and values, again inappropriately conflating norms and values and simply and uncritically assuming pluralism right down to society's bedrock. The cultures and subcultures constituted by reflexive individuals intentionally practicing their values, he went on to argue, are not adaptive splinters but the fundamental constitutive elements of society. Following the New York School's intersection of cultural pluralism with social-structural power, Lemert (1974) argued for a move towards the placement of symbolic interactionism on a broader social-structural scale and the application of labelling theory to the processes of social reaction and identity construction. In a move based on the complete dismissal of ideology, hegemony, desire and capitalism's core logic, the structural wing of symbolic interactionism posited identity as the product of a struggle between the dualistic self and the labelling power of the institutionalized authority of the elite as 'significant other'.

For the symbolic interactionists, individuals lack sure knowledge of who they are, and therefore they accept meanings from outside. The standard process is that an act of primary deviance, which is usually quite petty, provokes an overzealous social reaction, and the criminal label attached by the dominant authority is reinforced in the individual's psyche as he is dragged into the criminal justice system amongst others who have been similarly labelled. Secondary deviance is more likely to occur after the identity is established, the much-vaunted 'self-fulfilling prophecy'. In England, Cohen

(1972) and Young (1971) claimed that the process causes increasing alienation and spirals of deviancy amplification. Tannenbaum's (1938) earlier notion that Western culture is absorbed by a 'dramatization of evil' with the working-class criminal as the 'folk-devil' was supported by C. Wright-Mills and other Weberian cultural leftists and eventually embraced by British academics (Cohen, ibid.; Hall et al., 1978; Taylor et al., 1973). The initial rises in crime rates that occurred in the late 1960s could therefore be explained as the product of a 'demonizing' social reaction and a 'demonized' socially constructed identity. The underlying socio-economic realities and cultural currents that seemed to be criminogenic in different forms throughout the social structure were acknowledged as the 'real problem' in terms of ongoing inequality and oppression, but rarely in the criminological sense as sites for the formation of subjectivity. Primary deviant acts were all too often dismissed as merely the initial stage of the deviancy amplification process.

The theory was a perfect fit with liberalism's doctrine of minimal state intervention, which in turn struck a chord with the view of the European New Left, which had established itself in the late 1950s after Nikita Khrushchev had revealed the true horrors of the Stalinist purges in the Soviet Union. This whole paradigm of social thought had nothing to do with the social-scientific and philosophical investigation into why individuals are willing to do harm to others in the interests of the self; it was the direct product of the anti-revolutionary resolve of the social liberal and liberal progressivist movements, consolidated by the political catastrophism and anti-statism that pervaded the intellectual atmosphere of the immediate post-war world. Given the scale of the Stalinist horror this reactionary anti-theory was entirely understandable, but it emerged at precisely the wrong time in the evolution of post-war political economy; the beginning of the long-term economic crisis that was to culminate in deindustrialization, social disruption and financial crash. It severely weakened the left's resolve to construct an alternative ideology and thus gave unwitting yet vital support to the libertarian anti-collectivist core of neoliberal capitalism, which was to be triumphant in the coming decades.

Did the critical criminology that emerged in Britain and the USA in the 1970s fare any better? Generally, there are three major themes in critical criminology: 1) criminologists should focus on why some people and not others are labelled as criminals rather than focusing on the characteristics that distinguish criminals from non-criminals; 2) moral panics about street crime are engineered to justify harsh and authoritarian laws; 3) the criminal justice system is a tool used for the purpose of maintaining the status quo and serves the interests only of the powerful members of society. We can see quite clearly from the first principle that critical criminology demands yet another rejection of ontology. It was a hybrid that grew to prominence when conflict theory, labelling theory and subcultural theory crossed the Atlantic to combine with European humanistic Marxism and democratic socialism. The principal demand was that criminology and the criminal justice system should focus on the crimes of the powerful and the unfair labelling of the powerless. For the New Criminologists (Taylor et al., 1973) the 'deviant' was energized by a proto-revolutionary sense that something was 'wrong' with mainstream society, its institutions and its values. Where the powerless caused little harm and were disproportionately criminalized, the powerful caused far more harm and were criminalized far too little. Criminal behaviour amongst the working classes was largely the product of criminalization, lack of welfare and reactionary social control.

British socialists and humanistic Marxists added the ingredients of class and social structure, which had been either marginalized in American plural-ist accounts of social conflict or conceptualized in terms of unequal oppor-tunities rather than unequal structural positions, outcomes and politico-economic power. Where structural power was taken into account, for instance by Mills (1956) and the New York School, it was conceptualized as a Weberian elite rather than a Marxist ruling class whose material interests were in direct conflict with those of workers. Although Gouldner (1973) dismissed the subculturalists, phenomenologists and symbolic interactionists – with their stockpile of amusing but politically useless ethnographies – as 'zookeepers', he still placed his faith in reflexively generated resistance framed in a one-dimensional and undialectical anarchistic view of the good individual pitted against the evil collectivist state. British theorists detected too much emphasis by American theorists on pluralism, creativity and innovation – which tended to ignore tradition, conformity, ideology and class struggle – and brought class conflict firmly back into the picture in an era of working-class institutional militancy, highlighting the class nature of property crime and the structural focus of state law and punishment.

As we have seen, the British criminologist David Downes (1966) rejected both strain and subcultural pluralism. The tough values to which working-class boys conformed as a solution to structural problems, he argued, were also influenced by mainstream values. Here we have an early insight that could have been developed into a critique of the formative sub-jectivizing power of dominant ideology, but it did not receive the attention it deserved and remained undeveloped (Hall et al., 2008). Despite the political failure of the French rebellion in 1968, which prompted philoso-phers such as Althusser (1969) to look deep into the power of ideology, and the continuation of working-class Toryism in England (Parkin, 1967), the formation of working-class values was instead viewed through the lens of conflict and resistance. Following in the wake of the first National Deviancy Conference (NDC) in 1971, Taylor et al. (1973) criticized positivism's collusion with the establishment's definition of the deviant as the underperforming, immature hedonist who was a slave to impulse. However, if we discard the standard Home Office/Cambridge Institute conception of this as an *abnormality* rather than an *orchestrated normalized psychosocial form* that under certain conditions leaks past its restraining normative insulation, we have, as we shall see later when we discuss transcendental materialism and pseudo-pacification, a portal into a far deeper criminological critique of modernity and capitalism.

However, in the wake of the NDC a number of researchers, ignoring Althusser's more pessimistic structuralist and neo-Lacanian examinations, pressed home the class-resistance nexus. Phil Cohen (1972) explained xenophobic skinhead cultures as the products of a clash between working-class Puritanism and emergent consumer hedonism, where the subculture provides imaginary ways of constructing a 'magical' resistance to authority. McVicar (1974) and Willis (1977) also explained the hard machismo values in working-class youth, who regarded schooling as a massive irrelevancy, as the product of authentic resistance to a dominant culture. However, Willis's more circumspect approach produced the important further insight that this sort of ill-thought rebellion inevitably led to further conformity and assimilation in a subordinate position. However, yet again, this vital caveat, like Downes's earlier insight, was largely ignored as a basis of further research and theorization. Cohen, Hall and others associated with the Birmingham School of Cultural Studies (see Hall & Jefferson, 1976) continued to posit subcultures' 'imaginary relations' with structure, state and media as forms of misguided proto-political resistance. A little later, following early work by Cohen (1972), Hall et al. (1978) combined the notions of moral panics and authoritarian populism with the Gramscian notion of hegemony as components of an ideological mechanism for restoring order in the midst of the instability caused by the first major structural economic crisis in the post-war era. The concepts of hegemony, the authoritarian state, moral panics and subcultural resistance were combined with an increased sociological awareness of racist attitudes to black British citizens (Gilroy, 1987). Racist sentiments were manipulated by right-wing politicians and mass media to create public alarm over law and order and manufacture consent over an authoritarian populist agenda that suited the ruling class as it recognized the need to fend off labour militancy and restore a purer and financially efficient form of capitalism.

However, all of this was in the political sense overstated. Racism was of course a very real problem, and the law-and-order card was indeed played

to moderate effect, but it was the Thatcherites' campaign against the
Labour Party's alleged mismanagement of the economy that did the real
damage. The salutary lesson for the left is that outside the traditional institutions of unions and militant parties there was no politically harvestable
resistance; the majority of the working class failed to rebel as the
Thatcherites dismembered their very mode of existence in front of their
eyes. As we shall see later, the liberal left's 'failure of nerve' meant that it
offered little effective support at a crucial point in history. The culturalist
and liberal-individualist influence, which posited society's main conflict in
terms of cultural tension and the individual versus the state rather than class
struggle, shifted the left's critical trajectory in multiculturalist, anti-statist
and pro-individualist directions, dismissing all forms of determinism and
downplaying the restrictive effects of ideology and underlying material
conditions, which only some sort of institutionalized collective authority
has the power to alleviate or transform.

The right's next ideological step, made far easier by the liberal left as it
cleared the way with its constant downplaying of the subjectifying power of
ideology and experience and its mistrust of collective politics, was to claim
that if the capitalist-corporate state is bad for the individual the social-
democratic or socialist state will be even worse. The parlous condition of
actually-existing socialism in Eastern Europe and elsewhere seemed to suggest that the very idea itself lay dying on its terminal beach. This potent
combination of negative circumstances paved the way for the entry of neoliberalism, with its populist anti-state and anti-taxation 'solution' to the
decline of Keynesian economics. However, intense mass-mediated ideological pressure depicted the economic crisis as much worse than it actually
was; in 1978 Britain's trade surplus was over £350 million and North Sea
oil was coming online, the proceeds of which could have refurbished British
industry. The end result was an epochal political triumph in the 1980s, leaving the left with the politically weak residues of social movements, identity
politics, political correctness and appeals to a constitutional agency, which
seem powerless to constitute anything other than a reconfiguration of
unequal abstract rights in the capitalist socio-economic system as it stands
(Dean, 2009).

The abject failure of the post-social-democratic liberal left to restrain
neoliberal economic restructuring and prevent the recent economic crash
leaves us with little choice but to reassess and perhaps take issue with the
sociological and criminological theory associated with it. The rather
thoughtless declaration that the counter-cultural radicals 'were still right'
(Cohen, 2009: 6) despite this failure condemns us to the fate of endlessly
repeating the same mistakes, of turning, as Marx (1963) observed, the

initial tragedy into a series of farces. The main problem seems to have been a one-dimensional view of the relationship between the state and the individual, and at the highest level of abstraction between authority and freedom. Hall (1988) described the politics of neoliberalism as 'authoritarian populism', Foucault (1991) saw a vast array of disciplinary technologies and discourses creating regimes of knowledge that bear down with their normalizing and subjectifying power on the hapless individual, and Cohen (2000) identified the main ethico-political problem as the individual's tendency to conform to authority. Taking the argument further, Garland (2001) imagined fearful and authoritarian currents amongst the public placing pressure on the state to 'do something' about crime, which has resulted in a punitive 'culture of control' that justifies today's high imprisonment rates and intensified surveillance and correctional measures in Britain and the USA.

However, the psycho-politics of fear cuts both ways; where the right imagine monstrous criminals, the liberal left imagine monstrous publics and panoptic-punitive states. The whole liberal-left paradigm misreads neoliberal capitalism, which is highly seductive as well as repressive, reliant on a complex undialectical tension between orchestrated forms of conformity and rebellion (Hall et al., 2008), 'undialectical' in the sense that it generates a huge amount of energy, yet this energy is static and the system does not in the socio-historical and ethical senses move forward. No socio-economic system over-reliant on authoritarianism, discipline and control and obsessed with punishment could generate the human energy required to grow so rapidly and survive as long as capitalism has done. Indeed, the crucial role played by the banking industry and its irresponsible investment and lending practices in the deindustrialization of large sectors of Britain and the USA in the 1980s and the recent Credit Crunch would suggest that, where it matters, we have far too little control. Many on the liberal left might even agree with this, but the point is that the possible retrieval of political control of vital economic institutions and processes has been thoroughly marginalized to make way for the discourses of culture, identity politics and permanent Derridean dissent, subversion and 'transgression'. We will explore this in more detail later.

Despite the accretion of one intellectual and political failure after another since the 1980s, the positive outcomes of the radical left-liberal turn in sociological and criminology were the research agendas on human rights, racism, sexism and homophobia, which lent weight to lobbying against the discrimination experienced by these groups throughout all social institutions, and the further headway that was made in research on hate crimes (Ray, 2011) and the crimes of the powerful (Burdis & Tombs, 2012).

The hegemonic cultural glorification and political protection of the needs of business have allowed the elite to tarnish any critique of corporate crime as 'politically motivated', the advocate of potentially dangerous interventions in the business cycle that produces wealth and, at the end of the day, materially sustains us all. For the elite and all who approve of their ideology, 'bending the rules' in business is just a natural part of the game, a necessary evil forced upon those who need to cut corners and bypass various ethical prohibitions in order to ensure continuing profitability, in fact usually more necessary than it is reprehensible. For Murphy and Robinson (2008) this constitutes a sixth mode of Mertonian adaptation, the 'maximizer', a combination of conformity and innovation. Critical criminologists know, however, that government, corporate and white collar crime is most certainly not just 'bending the rules'; it actually kills, maims and steals as much as everyday volume crime whilst costing on average about four times more (Levi, 1987), which makes Murphy and Robinson's (ibid.) 'conformity and innovation' appear rather euphemistic, if, as we shall see later, analytically useful. As we have seen, current research exposes the continuing power of this hegemony and the reluctance of the state to regulate practices in the workplace that are dangerous and potentially deadly to workers (Tombs & Whyte, 2003). The conundrum for the left is that if the state's role is dualistic, in the sense of being simultaneously repressive and protective, then some forces of repression, exploitation, violence, intimidation and so on also exist outside the state, in the shape of specific individuals and private groups, a problem that is not easily addressed by a discourse that sought to abandon the distinction between criminality and non-criminality in civil society and turn the aetiological investigation into criminality into a critique of state-centred social reaction.

Radical left-liberal thinking regarded itself as an incremental improvement of the old radical thinking, even though, as we shall see later, that 'old' thinking is in many important ways superior and returning with gusto in the new radical Continental philosophy (Douzinas & Žižek, 2010) arising in the wake of the liberal left's complete failure to stem the tide of the neoliberal restoration and prevent its global diffusion. At the time of its inception the NDC's mission was to forge a new sociological criminology in the space created after an attack on positivism and its core notion of individual pathology, and to seek vocabularies of motive in the sense of the meaning of crime and deviance to the actor. The individual and the freely constituted intersubjective group were authentic and truly political, the state was repressive (Gouldner, 1973), and the voices of the former should be the focus of appreciation rather than mere objects in the state's statistical and actuarial calculations (Young, 2004). Radical 'socialist diversity' was the path to liberation, releasing unlimited human potential (Carrington & Hogg, 2002). How private individuals and organizations who refuse to embrace this joyous new world – or, in some cases, are ruthlessly active in the politics and everyday practices that systematically prevent it from ever getting off the ground – and continue with their exploitation and intimidation are to be dealt with was rarely discussed; perhaps, in the warmth of the new community, they would just melt into air.

Despite the noises this left-liberal project made for radical transformation, it continued to rely for its political application and funding on the regulatory and redistributive ability of the underlying social-democratic framework that managed the capitalist economy. In other words it remained dependent on a significantly imbalanced compromise with the state-capitalist partnership it criticized and sought to transform. However, although, it must be said, the social-democratic compromise produced some results (Reiner, 2012) it was to be rudely interrupted with a force whose disruptive energy was at the time beyond the imagination of many on the social-democratic and liberal left. Classical liberal thinking returned in the 1970s during the gathering crisis of Keynesian capitalism in the old industrial nations of Europe and the USA, which had descended into a stagflationary spiral in the heat of competition from developing economies in the Far East and a substantial rise in oil prices. The liberal right had already engineered an initial political breakthrough in 1971, when Nixon's abandonment of the Bretton Woods agreement made the first move towards the release of the capital controls that had been the lynchpin of Keynesian economic policy. This allowed productive capital to flood out of the old industrial West into low-wage, low-tax developing economies abroad. During the same period productivity was rising rapidly throughout the capitalist system, largely because of the introduction of the PC and advanced communications technologies into the workplace, which meant that where growth was occurring it tended not to be labour-intensive. Consequently, in Britain and the USA, deindustrialization, unemployment, inflation and a surfeit of inactive surplus capital all rose together to threaten the social order, profitability and the value of money, all close to the heart of the dominant bourgeois class. Whilst western Europe continued to deploy deeper-reaching social-democratic strategies, growing unemployment and relatively declining wages entered into a tectonic conflict with the intensification of consumer desire and the increased availability of personal credit to place immense Mertonian strain on British and American populations. Rising expectations combined with the decline of political solidarity and the rise of a consumerist cult of hedonistic individualism to clash with a sudden retraction of opportunities, and crime rates entered a period of escalation that was to culminate in the crime explosion in the 1980s (Reiner, 2007; 2012). This added more weight to the defeatism ideologically inculcated into the public's view of the social-democratic welfare and rehabilitation system (Melossi, 2008).

The subsequent raft of social and economic problems befalling the Keynesian project presented the liberal right with the perfect opportunity to press home the advantage and make a major breach in the wall of the social-democratic dam; it was 'sink or swim' as everything that had floated on the still waters of social democracy's reservoir was swept into the flood-waters of unregulated capitalist dynamism. The epochal movement towards the global diffusion of neoliberal political economy and the subsequent rises in crime, terrorism and reactionary politics in destabilized paraspaces all over the world could have been prevented had the powerful nations of the industrialized West taken a different route and kept faith with social democracy, further strengthened democratic control of capital movement, assisted sustainable growth in the developing world and moved towards globally networked democratic socialism. Many on the liberal left, however, were still operating in the shadow of the Gulag and saw the state as a more serious threat to individual liberty than the return of both wings of the traditional right as they muscled their way back into politics to grasp the helm of neoliberalism's global project. To this day the very idea of insti-tutionalized working-class opposition to bourgeois politics and culture is regarded as anathema by some on the anarchist and libertarian left (see for instance Ferrell, 2007). Instead, we now have Beck's 'cosmopolis' (see Boyne, 2001) or Hardt & Negri's (2001) 'multitude'. We await with baited breath their political assault on the global capitalist class, who, despite the multitude's fulmination after the Credit Crunch, still seem able to wield concentrated power and influence whilst accumulating assets and circulat-ing them around a global network of tax havens with ease and impunity. The liberal left's strategy was to focus through a regulatory lens on the crimes of the powerful and play down the harm caused by street crime in the 1970s, but this tactic backfired and inadvertently aided the neoclassical right's strategy of downplaying the criminogenic destruction wrought upon communities and institutions by its 'structural readjustment' of the US and British economies in the 1980s (Currie, 2010; Hall et al., 2008), something it is now attempting to replicate worldwide (Harvey, 2007).

On the other side of the fence, the neoliberal and neoconservative right took advantage of rising crime rates in the 1970s and 1980s to intensify its ideological attack on progressive politics, rehabilitation and the optimistic liberal view of human nature that had risen to ascendancy during the social-democratic era. After what can only be described as a rare historical blip of socio-economic stability in the capitalist project, the pessimistic view of human nature returned as the dominant public ideology. In a line that follows from Aristotle through Hobbes and Durkheim, selfish exploitative action is not regarded as the product of just necessity but of the 'malady of infinite aspirations', the 'beast within' that must be domesticated by the disciplines of culture and law. The gratification desired by human beings is almost unlimited, and the utilitarianism at the ontological heart of economic liberalism posited hedonism as the driving force of human nature. For both conservatives and neoliberals the question is not 'why do we commit crime?' but 'why don't we commit crime'? The motivation is always present, a universal and timeless aspect of the human condition, and the process of controlling it has no terminus. Conformity is good for us; the curtailing of the hedonistic urges of the individual benefits the collective by maintaining the social order, which, without obedience to vital disciplinary rules and their reproductive institutions, would collapse into a Hobbesian 'warre of all against all'.

For conservative control theorists, delinquency occurs when the individuals' bonds to society – attachment, involvement, commitment and belief – are broken and the affective-disciplinary juxtaposition at the heart of the social contract breaks down (Gottfredson & Hirschi, 1990). On the other hand, neoliberals invoke the utilitarian deterrence principle to argue that if rationally calculating individuals seeking to maximize hedonistic gratification are made aware of the certain costs represented by the presence of an efficient criminal justice system, the majority will be deterred and cause no harm to others (Wilson, 1975). Despite the ostensive ideological differences, in political reality neoconservatives are working alongside neoliberals (Žižek, 2010a) to maintain the population's affective bonding to society's vital institutions, which helps to sustain both the myth of voluntarism and the legitimate authority of these institutions. If reasonably successful, this allows neoliberals to foster the negative-hedonistic variant of freedom amongst the population and use the socio-legal system to maintain boundaries and keep most of it in check. It's rather like watching Edmund Burke working in partnership with Bernard Mandeville, where organic traditionalism, moral sentimentalism and institutional loyalty can soften the vices summoned from the individual's hedonistic core and turn them via rational calculation into socio-economic virtues that function to maintain social order yet simultaneously release the egoism, interpersonal competition and measured exploitation that fuel capitalist economic growth.

This ability to stimulate and diffuse desire, structure individual prospects and maintain a fragile sublimatory control over the anarchic energy produced by the process is, as we have seen, currently lost on the liberal left, but it is also lost on the conservative and neoliberal wings of the right. Murray, for instance, in his theory of the criminogenic 'underclass' (1994), picked up on the notion of the autonomous subculture and its threat to mainstream norms and values. This was almost a pessimistic and condemnatory mirror-image of some of the liberal left's ideas that we have briefly explored so far; the autonomous individual and the subculture assiduously reproduce their values and norms and intentionally act in ways that are influenced by them. Crime is not committed by the poor, but by individuals with a poor attitude towards life that prevents them becoming useful citizens, workers and members of communities. Reviving the traditional Protestant distinction between the 'honest and deserving' poor and the 'dishonest and undeserving' poor, Murray classified the former as unfortunate and the latter as feckless, lazy, selfish, stupid, hedonistic, immoral, usually drunk and therefore unemployable. To link crime with poverty insults the honest poor. The USA 'reached the future first' and saw their hardworking communities falling apart in a carousel of drugs, crime, illegitimacy, school drop-out and casual violence, the growth of which social-liberal welfare measures failed to stop; worse, welfare simply increased the culture of dependency that dispirits naturally independent individuals. Liberal-left intellectuals are part of a 'cognitive elite' that is totally out of touch with the reality of everyday life and unaware of this grave cultural crisis, which cannot be solved by full employment or increased benefits; indeed the latter will simply foster even more dependency and exacerbate the problem.

Murray blamed a 'permissive' left-liberal value system that is completely out of kilter with the mainstream, although he admits that some of the worst values are shared and are being transmitted to future generations throughout the social structure. What for Murray was merely a brief aside is in fact a portal into a wholly different social analysis that contradicts his basic claim that the fundamental values of the 'underclass' are qualitatively different from those of the mainstream, especially the 'top' echelon. As it stands, Murray's discourse is an example of extreme cultural reductionism and voluntarism, which proceeds in complete ignorance of the ubiquitous influence of ideology, structural inequalities of power and the dispiriting material conditions of existence that are inherited by the losers in the competitive capitalist socio-economic system. The state welfare system came into being to prevent the poor that exist as a functional part of the system (Lea, 2002) sinking into the sort of despair that can cause either rebellion or the total cultural disintegration that Murray (1994) seems to view as the product of some sort of subcultural voluntarism, in itself a confused and untenable concept because of course the obscene Real operates throughout the social structure. Who, other than those whose complete disvaluation by capitalist ideology and its practical economic functions is slowly dawning upon them, would wilfully wreak destruction on their own selves and their own culture?

It didn't take too long to witness the reality that underpins the liberal left's fear: works such as Wilson and Herrnstein's (1985) *Crime and Human Nature* and Herrnstein and Murray's (1994) *The Bell Curve* removed the mask of subculture and voluntarism to reveal rather guilelessly their under-lying Real, an obscene prejudicial discourse based on the notion of genetic traits anchored in inherent class and racial inferiority and reproduced by 'underclass' culture. The upshot is that the poor and the wealthy deserve their respective social positions because they are the products of merito-cratically organized, hierarchically ranked and genetically transmitted dif-ferential abilities; here we find the primary force behind the process of social disvaluation, and it is firmly rooted in capitalist ideology, Protestant culture and their attendant pseudo-sciences. One cannot overestimate the intellectual error and the political danger that such eugenicist discourses represent; that Murray was invited to a debate by Labour Home Secretary Jack Straw in 2000 leaves us wondering what might lie beneath neoliberal politics; if not fascism then perhaps the sort of populist desperation that inevitably appears in the latter stages of serial incompetence.

The publication of works such as these momentarily justified the liberal left's great fear, but, despite the persistence of this marginal eugenicist undercurrent, in the reality of everyday politics the more pragmatic ideas that constituted neoliberalism's classicist-utilitarian strand had the most telling effects on criminal justice policy in Britain and the USA. As crime rose in the 1970s, Wilson (1975) recognized that America already had high prison populations and the death penalty, thus the deterrent effect of increased punitiveness would be minimal, so he concentrated instead on the certainty of punishment. Criminals must live with at best the certainty or at least the probability of arrest and conviction. He made the concession with conservatism and liberal democracy that severe punishment might foster an increased sense of injustice and damage legitimacy, so he opted for fixed sentences as the better option. Incapacitation was still important for serious criminals, but Zimring and Hawkins (1997) concurred with Wilson's Benthamite principle that punishment must be swift and certain but not necessarily severe; severity was always the hallmark of ineffective justice systems, and we had learnt from history that the more severe the punishment, the less likely it is to be applied (Hay, 1975). Nevertheless, when it came to aetiology, Wilson's rejection of progressive thinking was almost complete. Crime is simply evil done by evil-doers, and why they are

evil does not matter as far as public safety is concerned; the costs of offending and the benefits of conforming must be adjusted. He stressed that most
predatory crime was intra-class and had nothing to do with the fight against
inequality or some putative 'class-struggle'. Individuals are rational benefit
maximizers, and it makes more sense to steal cars than to wash them in a
declining economy where jobs are becoming scarce. Wilson's thinking
fuelled the rise of a raft of contemporary deterrence and routine activities
theories, out of which grew policy strategies such as increased surveillance,
situational crime prevention, target hardening, securitization, responsibili-
zation, community policing and so on. These measures, in conjunction with
tougher sentencing policies and increased prison populations, now constitute the general 'risk-management' approach to crime prevention. The
principle and practice of 'zero tolerance' also announced its presence on
the stage of right-wing policy, based on Wilson and Kelling's (1982) 'broken
windows' thesis, which claimed that minor misdemeanours lower the
tone of a neighbourhood and encourage more serious crimes. The whole
ambition – decisive and partially effective during the solidarity project – of
reducing the motivations to do harm to others at their socio-economic,
cultural and psychological roots, was cast aside more completely than it
was by the liberal left, who, despite their catastrophism and loss of nerve,
still campaigned in measured ways for social equality and justice.

Even though these strategies were short-term, post-political, atheoretical and anti-intellectual, they were seen as pragmatic, and they functioned
to serve the neoliberal politics of the day by offering concrete advice to law
enforcement agencies. On the practical-empirical level the overriding
problem is that they didn't work; crime continued to rise in Britain and the
USA throughout the 1980s as working-class communities and their political
institutions were decimated to clear the way for deindustrialization and the
shift of capital investment abroad. It was reduced only by increasing prison
populations, expanding the correctional and surveillance networks and
creating a large number of fragile jobs in the 1990s. Many of these were
casual and low-paid 'McJobs' (Ritzer, 1993) in a finance-service economy
that was boosted by encouraging the advertising industry to intensify
demand, using a rising housing market as a guarantor to extend unprecedented amounts of credit to everyday people in difficult circumstances and
turning Britain's City of London and the USA's State of Delaware into two
of the world's premier tax-havens to attract the global finance capital
required for increased lending. On the theoretical level, critiques of conservative and neoliberal theories are now well-established, but, although
most of the demolitions were convincing, the demolishers had to make a
number of concessions; crimes of the powerless are usually intra-class and

can be seriously harmful and corrosive; social constructionism must be challenged and the ontological reality of crime and its harmful effects has to be reinvestigated; egoism as a consequence of contemporary socialization must once again be taken seriously; the liberal left's shibboleths of social inequality and relative deprivation are inadequate as total explanations of the crimes of the powerless.

At the turn of the 1980s the liberal-left-idealist continuum that had held sway in criminology's radical circles since the early schism in the Chicago School was to be rudely interrupted, not just by neoliberalism but by dissenting forces growing in its own paradigm. In 1982, following in the wake of the national victimization studies in the USA, the first British Crime Survey was conducted, and in 1985 the Islington Crime Survey took a finely detailed look at the experience of victims of crime at the local level. The results were salutary because the surveys' methodology produced pictures more realistic than the police statistics. The survey data were poor in many respects, such as on repeat victimization, domestic violence, homicide, crimes committed against victims under 16, and the supposedly 'victimless' crimes of the powerful, which of course require a very different methodological and intellectual approach to break through the codes of secrecy that the powerful are able to maintain. However, the surveys' ability to at least partially illuminate the 'dark figure' of crime revealed an abundance of intra-class crime that was causing actual harm and psychological stress to vulnerable victims. Many of these victims inhabited run-down areas of permanent recession that were being thrown up by the capitalist economic crisis (Currie, 2010; Dorling, 2004; Taylor, 1999). The aggressive, egoistic and anti-social values that the right realists emphasized and the left-idealists downplayed seemed to be 'actualities'; this caused a seachange in leftist criminological thinking.

Although men were the usual victims of street crime and street violence, many victims of petty crime and intimidation, and most victims of domestic violence, were women (Ray, 2011). If early radical sociological and criminological thought ignored the issue of racism it had also ignored the other vital issue of gender. Women figured lowly as perpetrators but in many cases highly as victims. This was not part of a historical continuum; women participated in the food riots of eighteenth- and nineteenth-century England, and between the seventeenth and nineteenth centuries up to 45 per cent of Old Bailey defendants were women, but they constituted only 17 per cent of conviction rates, mostly for drunkenness, larceny and assault (Feeley & Little, 1991). The rates declined by the end of the nineteenth century, a product of the general repression of women's role in most human activities apart from reproduction and domestic labour (ibid.), but, also, as we have seen, as part of a general decline of crime during the solidarity project. However, earlier second-wave feminists had argued that women had some 'natural' inclination to sociability, nurturing and non-aggression; crime and violence were therefore masculine traits. Others followed up the gender role theory by arguing that women were socially constructed by male power as 'irrational' and 'untrustworthy', and forced into roles of passivity, domesticity and conformity. However, modern studies emphasize how rational and purposeful much female crime is (Davies, 2003), mainly concerned with the amelioration of poverty and family provision. What they don't emphasize, however, is that in neoliberalism's late modern continuum most women appear to be no more likely than men to embrace political solidarity and reject individualistic strategies of either coping with extreme relative poverty, or, in an increasing number of cases, keeping pace with consumer trends. Recent research for the retail industry has shown that one of the most significant increases in female crime across the social classes has been shoplifting for designer goods (Centre for Retail Research, 2009).

Criminology's negligence of women as victims and perpetrators of crime prompted Smart (1976) to argue that feminism should abandon criminology, whilst others, such as Carlen (1988), sought to reform criminology and integrate gender with class and race to forge a more complete analysis of socioeconomic marginalization and crime. Criminological theory has been the target of reform from a number of feminist perspectives, whose influences on the discipline have been too diverse for the scope of this work (see Renzetti, 2007, for a digest). However, if most of them have one ontological claim in common it's that there is some connection between crime, domination and the masculine gender form; violence against women, especially, is an expression of patriarchal male power. Although early feminism's essentialist notion of biologically determined masculine aggression has largely been discarded, it has been replaced by the claim that the use of violence in the patriarchal institutions of the state and the family is supported by patriarchal culture. Men have the material and symbolic power to define the world in their terms, and where it is not purely misogynistic the instrumental objective behind male violence against women is to prevent women challenging that power. However, Gadd (2002) and Jefferson (2002) argued that violence against women and privatized aggression in general are not advocated by modernity's masculine cultures, and Ray (2011) points towards recent research that shows intimate partner violence to be the product of psychological, social, economic and cultural circumstances that together constitute a picture that is too complex to be explained by 'patriarchal culture'.

This recent recognition of complexity also casts doubt on the orthodox liberal-feminist claim (see for instance Gilligan, 1982) that women would bring more caring and civilized attitudes into positions of power, which would be a force for progressive transformation. It is becoming more apparent that the recent movement of more women into positions of power is not changing the world – in the past 30 years capitalism has certainly not become more stable or civilized – but, as we have seen, it seems to be changing the behaviour of those women, or in some cases attracting women whose characters are already well suited to domination. If the stringent demand to 'get things done' that accompanies the occupation of powerful positions in the capitalist system is currently changing women, we are permitted to suspect that in our robust past this demand was also active in the formation and reproduction of both crude and subtle forms of aggression amongst men.

The idea that the worst aspects of capitalism are expressions of a domineering form of masculinity is liberal constitutional theory in its purest form, without even the caveat of unintended consequences; the intentionally applied values of the powerful and influential make the reality of the world, and the world will be changed by abandoning traditional masculinity and equalizing the balance of power in the gender order. In her concept of 'hegemonic masculinity', Connell (1995) argued that patriarchy is reproduced by the hegemony of a domineering destructive masculinity, which, backed up by the threat of violence, reproduces the subjugation of subordinate masculinities. For Messerschmidt (1993), violent crime is a product of males 'doing gender' in the traditional way, an enacted, lived out expression of this cultural form as it reproduces itself and the social order in which it dominates, or the expression of a protest masculinity that reworks the themes of domineering hegemonic masculinity in the margins.

This position has also recently been exposed to searching critiques. We have already seen the statistical sleight-of-hand behind the argument that crime and aggression are expressions of masculine culture, but looking at this argument in a social structure differentiated by class exposes further weaknesses. The fact that the incidence of interpersonal physical violence is higher in class fractions – where there also might well be a substantial dark figure of unreported female violence – at the very lowest point in the hierarchy of wealth and power suggests that in the wider socio-economic order 'hegemonic masculinity' is an unsuccessful dominance strategy. Hegemony is the non-violent cultural means by which the *successful* socio-economic elite, in order to naturalize and reproduce its power, manufactures consent amongst the subordinate classes; neither violence nor unsuccessful masculine forms can be associated with hegemony. By using contrived and ambiguous concepts such as 'reworking' and 'the patriarchal dividend' to make it fit the context where the gender order intersects with the social order, the term 'hegemony' has been twisted out of shape to the extent that it has been rendered meaningless. The elite rule by non-violent hegemonic and legally institutionalized means, backed up by measures of organized violence that have been legitimized by a hegemonically reproduced majority that includes males and females. Thus the physical violence that permeates the margins cannot simply be a 'reworking' of something that is so formally distinct. In terms of achieving or protecting wealth and power the 'patriarchal dividend' has proved to be worthless in marginal locations, where attempts to use violence to maintain power that does not exist results in pointless interpersonal hostility, the breakdown of relationships, imprisonment and the collapse into further immiseration and hostility, which can end in death (Hall, 2002; Ray, 2011).

Ray (2011) appears to be right that disorganized, interpersonal physical violence is largely a product of the socio-economic marginalization that has disproportionately affected working-class males, who together with marginalized women now constitute the global 'precariat' (Standing, 2011). However, alongside this exclusion we have seen the development of a cultural injunction to include the self as a symbolic competitor in the atomized, emasculated world of consumer capitalism. What have been disrupted in this 'bulimic' late modern process, which juxtaposes cultural inclusion with economic exclusion (J. Young, 1999), are the working-class cultural and political institutions and codes that had achieved a notable amount of success in fostering and reproducing masculine and feminine subjectivities that were conducive to solidarity and averse to interpersonal hostility, yet remained tough enough to participate in collective opposition to the ruling class. This afforded a sense of security to males at the bottom of the socio-economic order, which reduced interpersonal violence and allowed socio-political conflict to be played out in an institutional structure in the relative absence of physical violence (Wieviorka, 2009). Of course thuggish males still existed in the domestic sphere and the street, as did thuggish females who administered severe physical punishment to children in the domestic sphere (Stein, 2007), but the general trend was an inversely proportional relationship between interpersonal violence and socio-political solidarity (Hall and Winlow, 2003; Reiner, 2007). However, later work by Connell and Wood (2005) examined the notion of 'transnational business masculinity', an insecure managerialist subjectivity that manages personal life rather like an enterprise. Again, when women can be seen to adopt this form of subjectivity quite readily, the notion that it is yet another expression of 'masculinity' has to be questioned, but, as we shall see later, the idea itself, if relocated from the gender order to a more complex aetiological field of psychosocial forms and relations, resonates with Sombart's conception of the undertaker, and thus could play a part in explaining the willingness to risk harm to others.

Nevertheless, despite the inadequacies of some of the standard feminist and profeminist theories, victimology became established as a discipline (Goodey, 2004). The evidence produced by early victimological studies demolished the left idealist notion that the intra-class crime and harm perpetrated by the relatively powerless was manufactured, from a small presence in reality, as a grossly exaggerated idea in people's heads by the state and the media to justify authoritarian populism. If such reactionary politics could be justified by a stark reality that lay at the kernel of right-wing ideology, perhaps the liberal left should have been prompted to reassess the gravity of the situation that the decay of industrial capitalism was causing and offer alternative explanations. However, still driven by political catastrophism and a tacit faith in liberalism's ability to maintain a progressive course, it chose to avert its eyes and speak of underlying politico-economic, psychosocial and cultural causes almost as an aside, a *fait accompli* about which little could be done. left realism rose amidst a declining left idealism to accuse the latter of neglect of real harmful crime and insensitivity to its victims (Lea & Young, 1993); crime had been romanticized and the victim neglected. Even though the financial cost of white-collar crimes significantly outweighed that of the crimes of the powerless, harm cannot be measured in economic terms, and much of the latter was predatory, intimidatory and intra-class, corroding communities from the inside and creating fear, suspicion and unhappiness amongst their inhabitants. The proletariat were victimizing the proletariat, the Robin Hood idea of crime had to be challenged, and intra-class crime was not a means of political protest or wealth redistribution.

Left realism moved through a number of developmental stages (Lea, 2002; Matthews & Young, 1992), but its founding principle held strong, expressed succinctly by Elliot Currie:

> [T]here can be no enduring solution to the prison problem unless we simultaneously address the crime problem – in particular, by creating strategies that can reliably shut down the 'pipeline' that shunts people with distressing predictability from our most devastated communities into the criminal justice system. I argue that as long as we continue to tolerate (or foster) the social conditions that continue to produce stunningly high levels of violence and victimization in the United States, we will remain stuck in a crime/prison cycle from which no amount of tinkering with sentencing for nonviolent offenders, or with the conditions of parole, will really free us. (2010: 1)

As a category crime is a socio-legal construction, but the harm it causes is real. The localized conditions of economic hardship and social dissolution have been neglected by the forces and discourses of liberalism, whose advocates are reluctant to admit, except as an occasional aside, that these conditions are highly criminogenic. Most street crime is not just intra-class, but also intra-ethnic and intra-gender. Left idealism's sustained attack on the criminal justice system is one-sided; many working class communities in economic trouble were lobbying for more police protection from intimidation by criminal entrepreneurs and harassment by anti-social individuals. Left idealism was sinking under the weight of its own absurdities, such as the notion that crime in America was the product of a 'moral panic' when the number of murders in the city of Los Angeles was greater than that in most European countries. As we shall see in the following chapter, it was the absurdity of the moral panic argument as a sign of political abandonment, rather than a moral panic itself, that was helping to generate insecurity, reinforce authoritarian populism, supply legitimacy to the right and destroy faith in the left.

Left realism offered an astringent force to purge the excesses of Left idealism, which was losing credibility amongst working-class people who were persistent victims of crime in disintegrating, economically impoverished communities. There was a strong Mertonian strand in left realism; individuals are socialized to accept the desirability of material success, and non-economic values and roles are given little cultural or financial support. The American Dream tends to universalize and homogenize values and roles, creating a tendency for an anomic and therefore criminogenic culture that has expanded from its source in the market economy to penetrate and pervade the institutional structure of American society (Messner & Rosenfeld, 1997). This strand was taken up by a group of British thinkers who perhaps could be called 'late modern' criminological theorists, whose work investigates the complex tension between cultural inclusion and socio-structural exclusion. It moves beyond the Mertonian paradigm to incorporate contemporary work on consumer culture, psychosocial being and late-modern modes of exclusion, thus constructing a more thorough understanding of subjectivity and the dynamic tension between psychosocial motivations and socio-economic conditions and constraints (Hall et al., 2008; Hallsworth, 2006; Reiner, 2007; J. Young, 1999). This is the platform from which the new perspective to be found later in this book will be launched.

However, many liberal criminologists found the European post-structuralist and postmodernist movements more attractive. These movements grew out of disillusionment with modernity and the myths of science, reason, progress and universal truth that were thought to have inflicted untold suffering on millions of peasants and proletarians. The Holocaust, the Gulag and the genocidal wars that had punctuated Hobsbawm's 'age of extremes' were all products of modernism's totalitarian inclination, which had marginalized alternative discourses and subjectivities. Saussure (2006) had argued that we are spoken by our language as much as we speak it. Our knowledge of the world is neither objective nor subjective but conventional because the relationship between the sign and the referent (external object) is entirely arbitrary. The meaning of a sign lies in its relationship to other signs, not in the sign itself, and there is no fixed relationship between the sign and the natural, aesthetic or ethical properties of the object. Post-structuralists took this further and argued that the internal relationship between the signifier and the signified is arbitrary and capable of constructing meaning, at which point we lose contact with the objective and structured social world altogether and enter a realm where the relationship between the word 'criminal' and the individual doing something some of us might regard as wrong is neither natural, timeless nor even social/conventional, but a contingent product of floating signifiers and contested discourses and subject-positions; multiple, historical and temporary. There is nothing objective about crime; it is a result of the exclusion and criminalization of otherness by a dominant discursive formation. Criminology has merely been granted a privileged position by modernity and its dominant discourses, and thus has no real extra-discursive authority (Foucault, 1991). We have reached the end of moral certainty, we must resist essentialist notions of criminality and, despite the stark patterns in crime rates that we saw in previous chapters, there is simply no point in continuing the attempt to construct a grand criminological theory that will explain all crime. For Derrida (1967), we must relentlessly deconstruct old truths and new ones as they come online, exposing the politics and interests that lie behind their 'metaphysics of presence'.

The principle to emerge from postmodernist criminology was to decriminalize where possible (T. Young, 1999), but, after all the intellectual gymnastics and spilt ink, all that does is to recycle the fundamental problem thrown up by the establishment as a socio-legal norm of Mill's (2006) concept of liberty. Who decides what harm is and, in a legal system forced to boil down the complexity of everyday life to a simple binary decision between guilt and innocence (Luhmann, 1986), where punishment is differentiated by tariffs only after guilt has been established, how do we decide where the harmlessness stops and harm begins? The problems of relativism, culturalism and nihilism that afflicted postmodernist social science seemed to be even graver in law and criminology; with both the protection of the public and the integrity and freedom of the individual perpetrator or victim at stake, this is an area that really cannot afford to get things too wrong. Criminology and law — and indeed any branch of sociology that was associated with crime, deviance and harm — was forced to backslide. Affirmative postmodernism came into being to address such problems, and its advocates argued that we should deconstruct facts to reveal the values, interest and politics behind them, then defy Derrida and reconstruct the findings into some sort of consensual decision on where freedom stops and harm begins.

Henry and Milovanovic (1996) suggest that we distinguish between core and peripheral crimes, but, of course, yet again that propels us right back to Mill and other first-wave liberal thinkers. Postmodernism, it seems, was a regressive movement that wished to move back to the primary unsolved liberal question of radical indeterminacy simply by airbrushing out of the intellectual picture all the problems that have accumulated since the Enlightenment declared individual freedom. By wiping the slate clean, starting again and replacing the autonomous subject with the discursive subject, postmodernists sought to replace the will to power, and the structured social power that arose from the accumulated victories of politico-cultural contests, and rewrite the rules of power in the hope that an endless, permanently sublimated and unwinnable set of contests could energize a pure reflexive dynamic and launch us into a future of pure contingency and creativity.

There was to be no fulfilment of the postmodernists' hopes for 'discursive closure' on modernity and a subsequent new dawn. Postmodernists dismissed or marginalized structural power relations, concentrated power, capital's relentless economic logic, the limitations of the essentially anxious individual and the obdurate need to establish some sort of clear consensus on where harm lay and prohibitions should come into play. This allowed advanced capitalism's structure and dynamic forces to consolidate themselves in spite of — in some cases, as we shall see later, because of — postmodernism's incessant ponderings and circumlocutions. After 1980 there was a quite massive transfer of wealth and political power from the bottom to the top, and the wealth/power gap was polarized to a degree not seen since *La Belle Époque* (Harvey, 2007). In criminological terms this meant an expansion of special liberty and opportunities for the elite class and the socially corrosive yet individually energizing amalgamation of augmented repression and seduction for those in the bottom strata who looked upon the elite with fear and envy. Postmodernism had no answer to the epochal re-gouging that occurred as social democracy's dam was sabotaged and shattered by neoliberalism, allowing capitalism's destructive/creative torrent to flow across the social landscape with its full force. The elite's perfect crime relocated itself at the epicentre of an increasingly deregulated and globalized political economy whilst the imperfect crimes of the powerless precariat exploded as their lifeworlds, twisted further out of shape by the contradictory tension of economic exclusion and consumer-cultural seduction, sustained multiple fractures. Such inescapable turmoil exposed the weakness of postmodernism and the structural allegory; no amount of playing around with culture, language and discourse seemed to be having the slightest effect on the gouging torrent. It is not difficult to understand that decriminalization can effect phenomenological and statistical reductions in crime, given that crime is a social-symbolic category, but whether it can reduce harm, which, especially in the zone of 'core crimes', has at least one foot in ontological reality, is an entirely different matter.

Postmodernism and criminological theory had never sat too happily together, and within the parameters set by the fearful rejection of institutionalized class conflict and the failure of postmodernism's flight into the far reaches of linguistic constructivism to bring back any worthwhile results, it's not surprising that the autonomous existential subject should return, with its principles of radical indeterminacy, creativity, choice and free will (see Lippens & Crewe, 2009). The new school of cultural criminology (see Ferrell et al., 2008) also contributed strongly to a revival of the traditional Anglo-American phenomenological and subcultural themes that grew out of the famous schism in the Chicago School. Thus 'edgeworkers', and others living on the margins, can create new alternative and positive ways of life out of their transgression of the old order (Lyng, 2005). This time round, though, there was more acknowledgement of the broader mass-mediated world of symbolic interaction, from which subcultures appropriate and rework meanings and styles by means of 'bricolage' (see Lévi-Strauss, 1970). Crime, the fear of crime and its control are all consumed by audiences as a set of identity-forming narratives with political connotations. Because we can't rely on the powerful group's definitions of the labelled groups, we must go inside them and discover the surprises of morality, meaning and practice; the ability of small intersubjective groups to resist dominant narratives and construct their own meanings should, where possible, be encouraged, not criminalized. Writers such as Katz (1988) and Presdee (2000) enriched the paradigm by including the pre-linguistic emotional drives to resistance and transgression in their analyses, whilst being very careful to avoid the neo-Freudian notion that it is the psychodynamic tension between resistance and repression that creates subjective, political and historical movement. For the cultural criminologists, champions of the American liberal edict that all progressive momentum requires is for individuals to be free, the resistors simply need to win and keep on winning. Where postmodernism rejected the authentic subject and posited resistance as an automatic phenomena occurring in the exteriority of language and discourse, on which new subjectivities needed to hitch a ride, the existential and cultural criminologists returned the authentic resistant subject to the table.

In this brief trawl through the development of sociologically-influenced criminological theory in the twentieth century, we can see clearly two major shifts away from aetiological depth theories, which attempted to construct contextualized explanations of human subjectivity and its criminal or delinquent motivations, to surface-theories that constructed the individual as a relatively deprived victim – sometimes defeated and sometimes irrepressibly resistant – of the forces of illegitimate authority, repression and discipline. We had moved from aetiology to what Jason Ditton (1979) dubbed 'controlology', the study of systems of control, and for the liberal left these systems defined criminality and therefore to a large extent created their own subjects and objects of control. Conservative-positivist and classical liberal theories trundled along their tracks with little development, remaining in place as the dualistic mainstay of the criminal justice system as they went in and out of fashion in academia. On the radical liberal side of the fence, the first vital shift was from social disorganization and anomie/strain to the more appreciative notion of cultural innovation in the Chicago School, and the second was, from the 1960s onwards, the importation and integration of symbolic interactionism and labelling theory into psychological, cultural and structural theories to construct the 'new criminology'. The source of motivations shifted from an otherwise harmoniously functional system's failure to integrate individuals, whose marginality was the product of disruptive phases, to the inherently unjust system's tendency to marginalize, economically impoverish, mistreat and unfairly label or 'subjectify' the delinquent, thus, in some cases, creating the hardened and less tractable criminal form. The alternative idea, first mooted by early socialists, Marxists, psychoanalysts and dualistic theorists – that criminality was the leakage beyond its insulation of an obscene force at the very heart of the liberal-capitalist system itself – was avoided as the narrative that posited liberalism as the undisputed force of freedom and progress became dominant.

LIVING WITH THE UNDEAD: THE FAILURE OF LIBERAL-LEFT THEORY

6

What stood in the way of the resistant individual, the natural transgressor? At the heart of the liberal left's analysis lies a standard form of rationalist ideology critique, where the rational individual's perceptions of reality are distorted by ideology, and these distortions are reproduced by a hegemonic cultural narrative that serves the political status quo by demonizing the dangerous classes and naturalizing the elite's state-centred social power. As we saw earlier in the work of Murray, this 'dangerous' and 'non-deserving' section of the poor is represented as a threat in order to convince the majority of the need for protection (Reiman, 1979), which is offered in the form of the authoritarian neoliberal state and its heavy-handed criminal justice system. Reiman does admit that the failure to address the real material and social causes of crime is an issue, but the crucial issue is that the system's symbolic order reproduces a disturbing image of a dangerous criminal class, which exaggerates the real harm they cause to others and turns the public against them rather than the ruling elite. In his theory of 'Pyrrhic defeat' crime is cultivated and accepted to justify the continued need for protection (see also Christie, 1994); the state continues to act like a Mediaeval protection racketeer (Tilly, 1985), constructing a demonic image of the 'dangerous classes' that stretches back into Early Modern Europe and reached a peak in the eighteenth and nineteenth centuries. Garland (2001) has given this standard line of thought a late-modern update by arguing that the current wellspring of this enduring symbolic power is the power-elite's 'culture of control', a late-modern form of 'crime-consciousness' cultivated by the state and the mass media on the back of the high crime rates suffered in Britain and the USA since the 1970s. By using 'crime consciousness' to propagate sentiments of risk and insecurity amongst the governed, the state has justified its further expansion of what Foucault (1988) called 'disciplinary technologies' and Cohen (1985) called 'net-widening' activities in the form of new surveillance and risk management strategies, which have displaced welfarism as the normal complement to imprisonment.

More about Foucault later, but from the basic anatomy of this idea it's not difficult to discern that at root it's yet another variation on liberalism's standard 'politics of fear' theme, which was refitted for criminology in the form of the 'moral panic' thesis. In a recent speech at an awards ceremony, Stanley Cohen (2009), the thesis's main publicity agent, cited novelist Saul Bellow's dismissal of the 'reality instructors', a warning never to trust those who report everyday reality; perhaps this category might include criminal justice practitioners, ethnographers or members of the public. In the same speech Cohen proceeded to dismiss climate change as yet another moral panic alongside crime; over my shoulder go two cares. If his sweep is broad enough to include both crime and global warming one could be forgiven for suspecting that he might see the representation of almost any human problem as a deliberate exaggeration designed to create fear and justify authority. On one hand we could give Cohen the benefit of the doubt by regarding his declaration that at the moment there's nothing happening out there worth getting too worried about as a valuable contribution to the struggle against the evils of authoritarianism, and to the protection of the demonized other and the building of solidarity amongst those whose internal divisions make them easier to rule. On the other, we could accuse him of contributing to a historical line of anti-Socratic cover-up politics that stretches from Plato through Machiavelli to Leo Strauss, who sought to repress *parrêsia* and keep the people in a state of blessed ignorance by telling them only what they need to know and strictly no more. Who are easier to rule, those who are agitated and divided or those who are ignorant and complacent? Thanks to sterling ideological work by its right and left wings, which covered both bases, it would seem that liberal-capitalism has an embarrassment of riches in this field. As we shall see shortly, the avoidance of too much agitation and the concomitant production of just enough complacency are the positive and negative sides of the left-liberal politics that have been imported into the social sciences.

The principle behind the liberal left's political catastrophism and intellectual repression is the obverse of that of conservatism. Whereas conservatism fears the *barbarism of disorder*, the liberal left fear the fear of the *barbarism of disorder* insofar as it might invoke a *barbarism of order* that is even worse. For instance, Todorov and Brown (2010) argue that the civilization/barbarism duality is a universal presence in human ethical discourses. We must overcome our fear of the 'other' because it can produce an evil worse than the initial evil that elicited our fear. Thus we must learn to live together in a tolerant plurality of cultures. This is the standard liberal argument, but really it tells us little about the context in which fear and hatred are generated and reproduced. How can we expect anything other than anxiety and fear in a relentlessly unstable market-driven socio-economic system, based on the pursuit of comparative advantage and structured by an obscenely corrupt exchange relation, an unforgiving interpersonal and international competition riddled with unequal outcomes, corruption and cynicism and prone to recession and periodic loss of livelihoods? If we could do something about the instability of the platform on which we struggle to lead fulfilling lives we might be able to attend to the problem of fear and hatred with more confidence and optimism.

Should public fear be criminology's principal object of analysis? Left realists argued that fear was rational in certain situations where crime was high, informal control weak and policing lax (Lea & Young, 1993). Recent research on the 'fear of crime' demonstrates that fear:

> functions to alert the individual to potential threat [and to] provide protection and reassurance and buffer the individual from the effects of crime fears… In treating individuals who take precautions and successfully manage perceived risk as experiencing a damaging form of worry about crime, research has risked exaggerating the extent of fear of crime as a social problem [and] assumed that any expression of worry contributes to the status of fear as a significant social problem. (Jackson & Gray, 2010)

This insight builds on past work (see Ditton & Innes, 2005; Warr, 2000). However, these corrective analyses swing the pendulum too far in the alternative rationalist direction. The fundamental problem is that both positions fail to distinguish between anxiety and fear, and nor do they examine the deep structural object of fear, which is an economic system that *really does* teeter on the brink of collapse and ensures that the individual who inhabits the 'precariat' *really does* live near the precipice of total economic, cultural and existential insignificance (Hall & Winlow, 2005). Each one of us is a potential victim of crimes of the powerful, of fraudulent activities that risk jobs and pensions, and of corrupt politicians and social managers who squander our taxes, and the lives of those whose lowly economic position forces them to live in run-down high-crime areas are also affected by more immediate fears of street crime and violence.

The absence of the crucial distinction between anxiety and fear is the philosophical problem at the root of the moral panic thesis, and it leads us into a dualistic analysis of something that is more complex than the exclusively

right-wing 'politics of fear' and 'politics of distraction'. In the 1990s some
sociologists proclaimed an age of anxiety (Bauman, 1997; Pahl, 1995); it is
perhaps ironic that Pahl's latter work was funded by currency speculator
George Soros, whose gambling on the international currency markets in the
early 1990s further destabilized an already unstable British economy whose
working population had suffered deindustrialization for over a decade. Soros
did more than most to promote further anxiety at the very economic bedrock of society. However, there is an even deeper psychosocial level that we
must briefly explore. For Wilkinson (1999), anxiety is not a distinctively
new phenomenon, and not necessarily attached to contemporary reasons.
Mills (1959) saw the root of anxiety in our ability to understand the structural and processual undercurrents of our lives, but in doing so he also failed
to mobilize the anxiety/fear distinction; if we did have some sort of understanding of these structures and processes as objects, or 'actualities' that have
profound effects on our lives (Bhaskar, 1997), anxiety might augment rather
than diminish, eventually metamorphosing into fear as the 'actuality'
becomes clearer. Wilkinson goes on to argue that we cannot explain
increases in anxiety simply by noting new ways of representing it. For Freud
(1979) the root of the trauma is not over-representation but our inability to
recognize the object of threat and danger, a principle followed up by Tillich
(1980) as he argued that anxiety is not the fear of a known object but an
obdurate disquieting suspicion of the unknown yet possible future implications of the negativity represented by the object. Turning anxiety into fear is
not one step worse but one step better, a lesson liberals should learn if we
can transcend the moral panic orthodoxy and seek political engagement. For
instance, if we had not been ignorant and vaguely anxious but genuinely and
rightly scared by a clear understanding of the inevitability of the crisis that
followed neoliberalism, with its social deinstitutionalization, deindustrialization and deregulated banking, a large majority would possibly have voted
against it. Perhaps they would have gone one better and voted for a clear
ideological alternative – either socialism or a proper social democracy with
capital controls, progressive taxation, abolition of tax havens and nationaliza-
tion of core financial systems and productive industries – rather than the
flimsy management system preferred by social liberalism. Capitalism reproduces itself not on the back of irrational fear but in the political vacuum
created by the absence of realistic fear.

Alas, left-liberals have already chosen on behalf of the non-conservative
section of the population, and it is a negative choice for the inevitable crises
of neoliberal capitalism as the lesser of two evils, influenced by their own
irrational fear of the inevitable human rights catastrophe that awaits us
should we choose to implement a clear alternative. Hence, left-liberalism

must attempt to strike a difficult balance between the anxiety-inducing condition of too much ignorance and the fear-inducing condition of too much knowledge. The orthodox liberal notion that the mass media cause or cultivate anxiety can be countered by the idea that they provide vehicles for its discharge and alleviation, preventing it turning into objective and politically generative fear; unlike horror stories, most crime stories and crime news items conclude not with an explanation but with a comforting resolution rather than an ongoing tragedy (Silverstone, 1994). We might not understand the causes of crime, but we know that others are there to manage it – nowadays with a bit of help from the 'community' and the 'big society' – thus we can continue in our normal condition of anxiety and complacency, and dependence on fragmented post-political authority and its pragmatic agencies. Fear of the known is replaced by the anxiety generated by the unknown consequences of unknown objects and actions embedded in unknown structures and process; we confront daily a magma of 'little evils', whose sources are largely unknown but whose manifestations are, we are told, easily managed by state authorities with a little help from the public; a 'little help' that must get bigger as the state's coffers are emptied in the act of bailing out a banking industry that teeters on the brink of insolvency as a result of its irresponsible lending.

The 'moral panic' orthodoxy, taught on every criminology course in Higher Education and still active as a major theme for research programmes, has been subjected to a number of critiques. Hunt (2003) argues that a shift has taken place in processes of moral regulation over the twentieth century. The boundary separating morality from immorality has been blurred and contemporary moralization is expressed in shifting, hybridized configurations of risk and harm. Ungar (2001) argues that today's risk society has normalized and conventionalized many of the harms whose over-representations might once have incited the exceptional anxieties required to whip up moral panics. Acknowledging the failure to find reliable indicators of moral panic, he dismisses the concept as too vague to capture the way today's multiple crises are represented (see also Hier, 2008), which to some extent chimes with Garland's notion of the normalization of 'crime consciousness'. Hall et al.'s (1978) use of the moral panic thesis in an inappropriate cultural context also exposed its weakness; the criminal or delinquent actions of young people in disadvantaged locales did not threaten mainstream values at all, which are of course competitive, individualist and entrepreneurial, only mainstream norms (Hall et al., 2008). Such weak concepts are the result of the failure to rectify the initial elementary error made by Cohen (1972) of labelling the Mods and Rockers as 'non-conformists', even though they were conforming to the master-signifiers of edgy coolness and youth tribalism constructed around consumer objects that had been propagated by the fashion industries since the late 1950s (Frank, 1997; Heath & Potter, 2006).

Fulmination and hyperbole in populist right-wing newspapers such as the *Daily Mail* create neither a moral tremor in society nor a panic that might have political effects. Cohen and his colleagues appear to be more frightened of the *Daily Mail* than either the *Daily Mail* or the population are frightened of crime and bouts of unruliness amongst young people. It's well-known that the *Daily Mail*'s former owner Lord Rothermere supported fascism in the 1930s, but in that decade the communist *Daily Herald* was the best-selling daily, indicating that the presence of 'authoritarian populism' does not erode popular support for a clear alternative ideology (Curran & Seaton, 2003). We can look further into the past; there have been eruptions of fulmination about 'crime waves' since the socio-economic dislocations of the eighteenth and nineteenth centuries periodically increased urban and rural crime rates (Rawlings, 1999). However, they had little effect on the abandonment of brutality, the gradual humanization of the criminal justice system, the emergence of radical dissent and political campaigning and the gradual inclusion of the lower classes in the parliamentary system. Nor did they prevent the emergence of the proletarian solidarity project from 1850 onwards, or the decarceration movement and the inception and development of the welfare state throughout the twentieth century. In most nations apart from the closed ideological enclave of Nazi Germany in the 1930s, alarmist bourgeois pamphleteering has had little effect on politics or culture; it could even be hypothesized that as more informed left-wing pamphleteering shifted the focus from the 'demonized other' to reveal the deleterious psychosocial and cultural effects of pre-regulatory capitalism it contributed towards the construction of a radical alternative ideology based on solidarity. Since the Second World War there have been few signs of a major shift in popular morality towards fascism or other forms of authoritarianism, and nor have the population 'panicked' to the extent that they would vote *en masse* for extreme nationalist parties or the return of brutal punishments. The old conservative bloc that was a strong voice in the 1950s, and which harboured some fascist tendencies in its margins, has passed into history, destroyed by neoliberal forces in its own ranks. Concern over the decline of social institutions such as church and family is secondary, conformity is now voluntary and there are no 'alternative lifestyles' that threaten the norm; today's approved alternative lifestyles are manufactured as economically vital grist to the mill of consumer capitalism. Youth groups are never 'outlawed', no matter how hard they try; many harbour libertarian and entrepreneurial inclinations yet still identify with social work- and psychiatrist-speak (Žižek, 2008a) in ways that express their total incorporation into the neoliberal world and its social-liberal administrative system (Hall et al., 2005).

However, the *Daily Mail* and the rest of the 'conservative' press do seem to be taking advantage of the resignation and exasperation felt by many of the more sensitive individuals throughout the social structure to the grinding selfishness and anti-social behaviour of numerous groups ranging from troublesome youths on sink estates, to spoilt and unruly sportspeople, over-paid celebrities, faceless bureaucrats and corporate executives, corrupt politicians, irresponsible bankers and financial traders and organized criminal traffickers. Jeremiads featuring these groups as villains appear regularly in their pages, but they have not produced 'moral panics'. In fact they have not produced anything at all; rather, the press has taken opportunities to sensationalize a low-intensity current of nebulous disgust and anxiety that – because the 'New Left' has failed spectacularly to produce a clear and inspiring alternative ideology since the 1950s when communism's degeneration into Stalinism was illuminated – has no cultural or political outlet other than the self-appointed moral guardians of the conservative press. Thus the vague yet potent feeling afflicting neoliberal nations is not 'panic' but the anxiety-without-an-object sustained by resignation to a dispiriting late-modern malaise of decline and degeneration punctuated by serial economic crises.

The degree of normalized anxiety varies from nation to nation, but it is stronger in the free-market nations of Britain and the USA, and weaker in the social-democratic and conservative corporatist nations of western Europe; but we must remember that global economic and ideological pressure is gradually forcing neoliberalism on these quintessentially collectivist nations. Cowling (2008) rejects 'moral panic' as a Marxist concept, and Jewkes (2004) exposes more of its weaknesses, but now we must go one step further and insist that it doesn't actually exist, other than as a commemoration of a fractional aetiology of past totalitarian horrors in the liberal imagination. What *does* exist is a constant, flowing magma of normalized anxiety that erupts into extreme concern during unstable periods, yet still stops short of the objective fear that would restart politics in the post-political world. Objective fear is far more difficult than vague anxiety to turn on inappropriate scapegoats.

However, claiming all scapegoats to be innocent will not work, because, in a competitive individualist society, nobody is innocent. During crises it becomes clear that, in the absence of solidarity, wherever there is competitive interaction everyone is to some extent a real threat – in today's jargon an 'existential threat' – to everyone else by doing little else but conforming to the system's competitive injunctions, the 'rules of the game'. It's almost as if the system's social and interpersonal relations have evolved to sustain anxiety yet prevent it from crossing the boundary into fear. Only gradations of the extent to which the individual's competitiveness and will-ingness to exploit others is sublimated can create a scale that can demarcate between directly or indirectly harmful competitive practices. Periods of stability are not characterized by peace but merely a truce made possible by the expansion of the number of winners, but even the truce is made on the platform of an agreement to remain within the normative boundaries set by sublimated modes of competition. The moralistic fulminations that are supposed to incite moral panics, but never do, are in fact manifestations of the standard and long-running Durkheimian morality tale that establishes the moral boundaries that mark the circumference of most societies (Sparks, 1992). However, they perform this task in an apolitical mode that fails to alert the population to the underlying social conflicts that could produce political dissent but instead, in a systematically atomized and dein-stitutionalized culture, produce deviance and outbreaks of interpersonal harm (Muncie, 2001). Muncie is, in the Lacanian sense, referring to the magma of social micro-conflicts that rage on the surface of the unsymbol-ized Real, the obscene exploitation, envy and enjoyment that lies at the core of capitalist culture and its socio-economic exchange relations. The political source of the reluctance to symbolize the Real is criminology's crucial unanswered question; unanswered because it is unasked, and pre-cisely why it is outlawed from the agenda in such a strict and vigilant man-ner is the most interesting aspect of the intellectual problem.

Moral panic theory has been applied uncritically since 1971 (Kidd-Hewitt & Osborne, 1995). This suggests an internally degenerate research programme (Lakatos, 1978), but in the Kuhnian (1962) sense it is a para-digm of thought that, despite its degeneracy, continues to be reproduced by external political influences. In an ill-judged response to mounting criticism, Goode and Ben-Yehuda (2009) invoke flat-earth populism by arguing that if lots of researchers and theorists in criminology use the concept in their research programmes it must be good, which of course ignores the principle of reflexive critique and displays ignorance of the political forces behind the durability of social-scientific paradigms. If the relatively powerless public are gullible in the face of manufactured fears, could we not suspect that relatively powerless researchers are gullible in the face of the fears manufactured by the dominant paradigm in left-liberal criminology, a mirror-image of the dominant paradigm in mainstream positivist-correctional criminology? The latter fear is entirely objective, of course; without research funding and publications their careers are in jeopardy.

Goode and Ben-Yehuda (ibid.) have extreme difficulty in pinpointing the source of moral panics; do they originate from the conspiratorial elite, or from morally enterprising interest-groups, or from individuals in the life-world? The first two look like aspects of grand conspiracy theory and the final one looks like the gross patronization of unenlightened and less rational everyday people. In fact street robbery *was* increasing in the 1970s. There was a rational and real basis for public concern, especially in disadvantaged areas. Young black people were involved because their oppression was so much worse, their family structures and communities were breaking down under economic pressure and they were forced to the bottom of the labour market. Most of the people rightly concerned were themselves black, members of communities under duress (Hall & Winlow, 2003). Of course racists and racist politicians moved in and old prejudices reared their ugly heads, but racism and panic over law and order were not the causes of the electoral success of neoliberalism; the problem was the liberal left's fragmentation and failure of nerve at a crucial point in time when the neoliberal press manufactured myths about the broad left's inability to deal with economic difficulties. Goode and Ben-Yehuda (ibid.) also argue that the public tends to find sensationalist and stereotypical accounts of reality more interesting than 'empirically true' ones. This, as we shall see in the following chapter, constructs a true/false dichotomy that denies the dialectic and allows dominant research groups with superior resources to keep on extracting factoids from the empirical world that can allegedly 'prove' their case. This constant appeal to abstracted empiricism distracts attention from the fact that we are not dealing here with a conflict between truth and reality but a conflict between the ideologies of the neoliberal-neoconservative right and the liberal left, neither of which seek truth or the construction of an alternative ideology and politico-economic project.

Social liberals might counter that since the mid 1990s their management acumen has reduced the crime whose underlying conditions neoliberalism caused. We have already seen some of the main criticisms of this new 'empirical fact', but we could add that the rewards of crime are now so cheap and easily available that it's barely worth the effort and the risk involved in committing crime oneself. It also seems that ever more young people are sinking into the sort of passive anhedonic nihilism that Fisher (2009) noticed amongst some British FE students; committing crime is simply too much effort, and apathy is the real driver of choice. This is an unusual position for a leftist to take; it was the outgoing traditional conservatives, now virtually extinct, who tended to be more honest about the Real. Bell (1978) spoke of the prodigal, promiscuous and irrational urges that were emerging in the shallow culture that attended late capitalism, whilst Lasch's (1991) famous Freudian treatise emphasized narcissism; both admitted that indeed this culture was a product of consumer-driven capitalism itself. Perhaps honesty is more likely when a group lets go of its faith in what is and its claims to efficacy in managing the system in which its faith is entwined.

A similar honesty is now emerging amongst the socialist left, in both its remnants and its renewing forms. For Fisher (2009) authoritarianism exists in a society that is nominally democratic. In today's plethora of dystopian movies it is easier to imagine the end of the world than the end of capitalism (Jameson, 2010; Žižek, 2010); dystopian dreams are no longer pretexts for imagining different ways of living, but for our world at its extreme, not in the process of its end times but at its 'undead' terminus, a permanent living social nightmare at the end of a cul-de-sac from which there is no escape. For Žižek, Alfonso Cuarón's *Children of Men* is a spectacular condensation of what those trapped in the most difficult locations are living through now, not some apocalyptic point in the future but the long, slow unravelling of capitalism's strands, an entropic process that we all have to live through. Belief and engagement have been replaced by aesthetics and spectatorship, a veil that is thrown over belief to protect us from the totalitarian consequences of believing. We look with Kantian aesthetic disinterestedness on our conditions of existence as if they were exhibits in a museum. It is the rule of money; sterile, repulsive, and profoundly inegalitarian, but presented to us as not the best but the least worst of all possible worlds. Capitalist realism (Fisher, 2009), sustained by the undialectical spat between the liberal–conservative right and left, is the product of the 'least-worst' thinking that has deflated our ethics and our ideals and lowered our expectations to a level so far below their threshold that we can no longer see beyond it.

Amongst the political catastrophists of the 'new left' none were more active than Michel Foucault in lowering expectations and atomizing opposition. In his treatise on punishment, Garland (1990) did not dig deep enough into the paradigms of thought represented by the major thinkers he discussed, and he missed an important distinction on which a number of subsequent thinkers converged, namely the dynamic separation and tension between *proactive domination* and *reactive control*. Foucault's (1998) modern life, managed and normalized by the technologies of biopower, must be contrasted with Baudrillard's (1994) modern life of seduction in the simulacra of the hyper-real. Deleuze (1988) had questioned Foucault's 'miniaturization of the state' in his immanent concept of power, and Baudrillard (2007) developed this critique to argue that in the realm of micro-power where Foucault saw power at its most potent it is actually dead. Foucault's theory of power belonged to a bygone age, it was obsolete; he saw the shift from the despotic to the disciplinary to the microcellular, but did not make the final move to its disappearance in simulacra. Whether class struggle disappeared is another question, but, that aside, this final move coincides with a major shift in crime and deviance, where the ostensible reduction in actual crimes is a sign of their disappearance into simulated modes of exchange where, in a Western world saturated by media and inundated by imports of cheap commodities from the developing world, production and acquisition become less problematic and exchange – of pornography, drugs, smuggled and counterfeit goods, pirated media productions and so on – propels crime and criminals into the hyper-real. Criminal forms are 'normalizing' and 'subjectifying' themselves on an ontological plane detached from the tentacles of the state and its statistical records.

Foucault's intellectual project is collapsing under the weight of further sustained critique. For Foucault, if the social world's ontological 'objects' are produced as mere classifications by normative discourses that shift over time, often quite abruptly, neither subjectivity nor objectivity can anchor epistemology. Classifications are neither fixed and objective nor arbitrary and subjective, but governed by rules that temporarily structure 'discursive formations' that are constructed on the back of partial, time-limited objective knowledge. As Callewaert (2006) argues:

> Foucault has a tendency to put everything on the same plain level: science and knowledges, implicit and explicit, utterances, propositions and statements, discursive and non-discursive practices. Even when he makes analytical distinctions between these concepts, they all refer to entities that play on the same playground for the same stakes. He does not analyse so much how things work, he rather notices that they work in a certain way. He conflates agency and structure rather than account for their dialectics. That may be what he meant when he once said he wanted to be considered as a 'gay positivist': what counts is what is said as a plain fact, as just this way of saying it, and not all possible underlying meanings, uses, functions, origins of what is said. The question is to discover whether what Foucault says on this and many other issues we have touched upon is the same as Bourdieu, or rather the opposite. Both point to the same issue, both frame their solution in similar terms. But their point is sharply different. Bourdieu is comprehending both agent and structure, both discourse and action, respecting not only their different but their antagonistic logic, and therefore he is not, like

Foucault, exposed to the danger of promoting the devastating trend in the social sciences today, where the everlasting need to tone down science, positivism and behaviorism lead to the absurd idea that social practice is nothing but free construction of meaning.

Bourdieu and Wacquant (1992) argued that Foucault lacks the dispositional link between history's objective structures to the meanings and practices of agents, which for Bourdieu was of course *habitus*. But *habitus* itself is problematic, a description of an internalized effect of the embodiment of the guiding sign-values of cultural and symbolic capital in the actor's struggles through socio-economic fields rather than a product of the subject's ideal/material dialectic. The depiction of structures as 'objective' is nothing less than undialectical metaphysical realism of the sort that bedevils the British Realist movement. Nevertheless, Bourdieu's notion of the *habitus*-forming struggle through fields of power relations is more useful than Foucault's crude notion of biopower as discursive subjectivity and the training of bodies by disciplinary technologies, but the correspondence of *habitus* to field means that *habitus* still lacks the Lacanian 'third nature' that would give it dialectical clout; it is an energetic internalized guide and vehicle for the agent who works through a 'logic of practice' in structural fields (Bourdieu, 1990) rather than a constitutive force in itself. However, Foucault's 'biopower', an enclosed loop composed of state domination and automatic resistance, simply lacks an opposite and is therefore undialectical (Jameson, 2010). Power and resistance short-circuit the dialectic, an immediate impulse that requires no struggle of intellectual or political development to bring itself into symbolic being. At the root of this problem is Foucault's notion that the Enlightenment's forces of domination automatically produce resistance, which misses Adorno's (1973) double negative, where the narratives of Enlightenment and its paranoid opposition are both simultaneously correct and erroneous. Therefore, a criminological paradigm too much in hock to Foucault cannot see that the state and its putative resistance in civil society both contain the latencies of the *barbarism of order* and the *barbarism of disorder* at the same time as the *security of order* and the *security of disorder*. Each cancels out the other, which appears to the politically reticent liberal mind as a satisfactory balance in a secure position of stasis rather like a solved simultaneous equation, and thus no dialectical movement is possible, only piecemeal reforms of the system as it stands.

Such formulations underestimate the structural fragility and volatility of the real system that rumbles on underneath the comforting distractions of the simulacrum. For Baudrillard (2005), power and desire are infinitely reversible, and the reversibility of power can be epoch-changing, as Heraclitus and Vico knew well; the cycle of hubris, nemesis and enantio-dromia characterizes the rise and fall of all empires. But nobody really wants power, to hold it or exercise it; its secret has been lost, which means that today's budding Empires, such as the USA, cannot get off the ground. Only the pretence of management remains, the calculations of risks and the shifting of bodies from institution to institution, from task to task, from production to leisure. It's a nostalgic fad in the end time where power has disappeared into a series of management simulacra. As for Foucault, says Baudrillard (2007), if only people were resisting disciplinary biopower, and if only there were a disciplinary biopower to resist, then we might see some action. But simulated desire produces no such resistance, and it is certainly not apparent amongst young people who lead crime-prone lives (Hall et al., 2008).

From Baudrillard's critique we could extrapolate that Foucault was the most sophisticated representative of the liberal-left paradigm that warns us not to look up at concentrated power and not to look down at the real system as its Real-drive disrupts and shatters real socio-economic worlds to replace them with neoliberal markets, a liberal post-Marxism that is at once fearful and nervously triumphant. In the act of fixing our attention on gov-ernmentality and biopower Foucault distracts it from the Real quite beauti-fully, with a sumptuous rhetorical narrative that takes us all the way back to Classical Greece (Foucault, 1998), and thus he raises fewer suspicions than the clumsier liberals with their dour cautionary tales that warn us not to look up to the Real's stratosphere, the sovereignty and special liberty of the global elite and their concentrated money-power. In his rejection of the repressive hypothesis (Foucault, 1991), the rhetoric of discursive produc-tivity is equally effective as he tells us not to look down to the depths of the Real, the pre-symbolic drives and desires from which institutionalized envy, with its simulated social struggles, draws its libidinal energy. Thus the unattractive struggle for sovereign power that has been democratized, dif-fused and latterly simulated throughout the modernist epoch, and which has reached new heights of intensity as liberal-capitalist hegemony spreads across the globe, cannot be fully represented in intellectual culture, and neither can its underlying sources. Investigation of the realms of sover-eignty and depth are met with discouragement if not outright prohibition. This plays into the hands of right-wing classical liberalism and neoliberal-ism, for whom the separation and protection of the market economy, its libidinal energy-source and the image of its heroically successful entrepre-neurs from intellectual critique and political control was vital to the repro-duction of the elite's wealth, allure, legitimacy and concentrated power:

> [A] strategic displacement of the social and historical 'problematic' from the economic to the political level, from the determination 'in the last instance' of the economic to a new kind of determination in the last instance of the political which, in virtual Cold War terms, shifts the focus of discussion from capitalism to bureaucracy, and from the factory and the commodity form to the grid of power relationships in everyday life and the various forms of 'repression'. Max Weber's sociology is an early form of this essentially anti-Marxist displacement strategy, and Foucault's theories ... seem to serve much the same function today. (Jameson, 2010: 350–1)

What postmodernists had in common was their defence of the whole spectrum of challenges to received knowledge (see Matthewman & Hoey, 2006), allied to their denial of the Real of unspoken knowledge and desire. For Callinicos (1989) and Eagleton (1995), postmodernism was a reaction to the thumping political defeats of the 1980s. When the dust had settled, it was not the postmodernists who had anything useful to say about the objects they had uncovered: experience, emotion, sensuality, media, identification and subjectivity. Eschewing ontological foundations for pure epistemological relativism, postmodernism simply appeared, pointed to objects neglected by modernist discourses, and disappeared without saying anything particularly useful about any of them. After the Sokal affair everyone tried to disown postmodernism, but for Eagleton (2010) the ethical emptiness of postmodernism had already been presaged in literature:

> On the whole, postmodern cultures, despite their fascination with ghouls and vampires, have had little to say of evil. Perhaps this is because the postmodern man or woman – cool, provisional, laid-back and decentred – lacks the depth that true destructiveness requires. For postmodernism, there is nothing really to be redeemed. For high modernists such as Franz Kafka, Samuel Beckett, or the early T. S. Eliot, there is indeed something to be redeemed, but it has become impossible to say quite what. The desolate, devastated landscapes of Beckett have the look of a world crying out for salvation. But salvation presupposes sinfulness, and Beckett's wasted, eviscerated human figures are too sunk in apathy and inertia even to be mildly immoral. They cannot muster the strength to hang themselves, let alone set fire to a village of innocent civilians.

However, what is finally burying postmodernism is the spectacular return of socio-economic class relations in the public's line of vision, reappearing in stark and unmistakeable relief during the recent financial crisis and its subsequent austerity cuts, which are targeted principally at economically insecure workers and welfare recipients, even though some amongst the middle classes also stand to lose. Such an economically grounded notion of social relations and politics has, since the nineteenth century, been displaced in most forms of liberal thought, and as we have seen in previous chapters, most thinkers other than Marx – for instance Veblen and Simmel – who grounded social thought in the economy, have been marginalized. For Rojek and Turner (2000) the general 'cultural turn' produced an entertaining but quite useless decorative sociology. This found its way into those works of cultural criminology that refuse to make connections between structural and cultural forms except to portray the latter as potential means of transgression and escape.

As much as we might agree with Rojek and Turner's critique and their timely plea to restart serious scientific and philosophical investigations – which we will pick up later when we examine transcendental materialism – the onset and endurance of risk theory has temporarily thrown up another obstacle. When O'Malley argues that today 'a heightened emphasis on risk-taking is colliding with a heightened emphasis on risk-containment' (2010: 10) he is recognizing the cultivation of desire and the need for its containment, but again, along with Katz (1988), he assumes that the modes of risk-taking we see are driven by urges to dissension, subversion, transgression and, ultimately, freedom. A short conversation with a right-wing entrepreneur – or a brief read through Kipling's *If* – would reveal that a reputation for taking risks has even greater value as cultural capital in traditional bourgeois culture than the ability to display the rewards of the risky action. Risk has been from the beginning enshrined in this culture as a sacred *thing*, and, like any other genuinely powerful psychosocial motivator, it is a *torment* that comes into being when proximity to the sacred triggers an intractable anti-subjective drive that overwhelms symbolically tractable subjective desire. Put simply, the adherents to mainstream culture *love* risk in its individualized, transgressive, rule-breaking entrepreneurial form, but they have no idea why they love it. In contrast, collective political risk in its revolutionary form, where the subject risks all – his own life and the lives of others – in an effort to change the coordinates of his existence, occupies the position of the chief profanity.

Deleuze (1987), Foucault (1991) and many other radical left-libertarian thinkers have seen the explosion of desires, lifestyles and new modes of gratifying hedonistic urges as the progenitor of new modes of regulation and control. Somewhere, out there, are myriad and multiform struggles for freedom that require containment. New radical thinkers, drawing on the core ideas of Lacan and others, are hinting quite strongly that this is not the case, and indeed that Deleuze was the quintessential apologist for neoliberalism as the least-worst option and the potential portal to future freedom (Žižek, 2003). These struggles are in fact products of a far more powerful form of containment; manufactured drives have overwhelmed Ethical Realist desires, and the 'repressive state apparatus' is not just that but also a response to the explosion of real harms caused by individual and corporate activities. The idea of increased censorship is nonsense; there has never been less censorship, apart from that which censors the rebirth of the political. The new world is driven forward by the injunction to enjoy proliferating experiences, and the only thing that is censored is the ideological source of the injunction itself and the way it serves the system. O'Malley's (ibid.) point that the upper classes were encouraged to take economic risks for the good of the nation whilst the lower classes were condemned to hard work and prudence is quite right, but it ignores the desire and ambition that for centuries – as we saw in Chapter 2 and will pick up again later – have been gradually diffusing outwards throughout the social body to stimulate working-class entrepreneurialism, which was driven by seduction and deep admiration, not class hostility.

O'Malley is also right that the broadening of access to risk-taking is not so much a problem generated by increasing insecurity but a privilege that was once monopolized by the risk-taking 'adventurer'. It's not about escaping control but re-asserting control by deliberately placing the self in a testing situation, which has been denied to the lower classes for a long time. It's the social distribution of the ability to take risks and exert control that distinguishes post-war forms of thrill-seeking from their forebears. This is true, but it ignores the vital distinction between high-risk physical adventuring and capitalist adventuring, which was driven by the minimization of risk by monopolizing markets, and the shift of emphasis from physical adventuring with its existential rewards through capitalist adventuring with its economic rewards to consumerist adventuring. The latter is based on what Žižek (2008) calls the 'stupid pleasures' of consumption, the expensive, commodified adolescent risks that Lyng (2005) talks about; skydiving, base jumping and so on. It's appropriate to question why the otherwise very interesting sociological work of these 'edgework' theorists is brought into the criminological debate; on the whole these adolescent consumer adventurers are not criminals, and in many cases not even miscreants, and nor, on the whole, are they criminalized.

Citing the example of gambling, O'Malley (ibid.) argues that what were once expressions of resistance against imposed prudence are now standard commodified pleasures for sale in the market. Yet, gambling has existed at the core of the capitalist banking system throughout the course of its history, a system that now invests in the expansion of a 'prosumer' economy (Marazzi, 2010), where capital accumulation has shifted from the traditional Fordist production/consumption/profit nexus to an arrangement where consumers themselves act as producers and distributors, thus doing capitalism's work for it in a vast Amway-type pyramid scheme or an Ikea-like DIY supply chain. Perhaps Oedipus's disapproval of gambling would pose the greater threat to the system; was it worth killing him to end up as a hamster in a global capitalist wheel whose surplus value is handed over to the corporate gamblers of the financial markets in derivatives and securities? Probably not, especially when we consider that the principle of symbolic efficiency – the ability to construct an alternative ideology and move forward collectively – died with the King, and it is anathema to the doting, incestuous liberal Mother.

Perhaps the main problem to emerge from the decline of symbolic efficiency, as Dews (2008) notes, is that liberalism constantly fails to take evil seriously, which has ensured its decline as a political force and the gradual loss of its negotiating power in its pact with capitalism's obscene forces. In the mind of the liberal humanist, evil is simply a metaphor used to define and communicate a subjective moral experience, yet the frequent occurrence of extremely harmful actions in the real world would tend to suggest that this is a culture in denial. Thus in the criminogenic 1980s it was not Reaganism and Thatcherism as a joint politico-economic force in reality but punitive Reaganite and Thatcherite reaction that bore – and still bears – the brunt of liberal critique. In all previous politico-economic orders horrifying things have happened on both large and small scales, evils that have been perpetrated in the normal running of a system, which are so extreme that they appear to be aberrations, deviations from that norm. Today's liberals use the powerful mass media to construct an illusion in real time, which parallels that of the revisionist historians who portray the collapse of the Roman Empire as a process of struggle by ethnic groups from domination to a peaceful and tolerant co-existence; from imperial oppression to humanity's 'natural' and 'benign' condition of accommodating pluralism. Ward-Perkins (2005) presents the more likely reality in the decline of economic, social, political and cultural functionality and complexity and the path to a bloodthirsty Dark Age barbarism in which cultural sensibilities and material life descended to prehistoric levels. Criminal violence became the standard method of acquiring land and property, as well as establishing and maintaining order in brutally hierarchal communities. This pours cold water on the naive Foucauldian analyses of the era as one in which a kaleidoscope of new spiritual discourses and subjectivities replaced brutal Roman discipline. Ward-Perkins' (ibid.) riposte to the naive fantasies inspired by Foucault, Deleuze and others – which are linked to the post-human tendency in today's liberal social theories of communicative networks and the hyper-social as, once again, the site of new discourses and subjectivities – is that a brutal phase of history might repeat itself as capitalism disintegrates in the absence of an alternative system.

Liberalism cannot deal with such historical processes intellectually because the normative idealism at the heart of its thought understands acute forms of unjustifiable action only as a moral evil caused by a lapse of the volitional subject and a failure to live up to the cultural standards to which each individual is capable of being attuned (Nabert, 1955). This collapses normative idealism into its opponent, naturalism. The liberal imagination is haunted by the terror of naturalism, of the possibility of the autonomous individual being overrun by unconscious natural forces and causes independent of the will. As the barrier to the tumultuous processes of capitalism and modernity, liberalism simply opposes a lame injunction to aspire to the required moral heights, as Dews puts it rather pithily 'like a headmaster signing off the end-of-year report' (Dews, 2008: 11). Liberalism operates in a permanent 'cool' mode (see Loader & Sparks, 2010), but we must understand that this coolness is an attempt to counteract a system that has no choice but to maintain individual ambition and economic dynamism in a condition of high intensity, where they are in permanent danger of overheating.

Liberalism also ignores the fact that freedom can be established only in the denial of drive, where desire can be turned by will against drive. Virtue, as Schopenhauer (2008) argued, might be a stranger in a world where human beings pursue their interests with a cunning, egoism, solipsistic narcissism and malice that sometimes seems boundless. To posit good as foundational is deception, and it induces cynicism as individuals grow to see their teacher as their first deceiver. However, it is something else to suggest that the intensity with which the 'evil core' of the individual exerts pressure on desire and will is both variable and prone to crude forms of manipulation. It is not simply egoism, which can be civilized through empathy and *amour-de-soi*, but *drive* that places the individual firmly and inextricably at the centre of the world (Žižek, 2000), and here we have to add more depth to our earlier concept of the willingness to do harm to others in the interests of the self. If 'bad' is selfishness at the expense of others, 'evil' carries more weight because it is driven by the need to relieve the torment that is driving the will. Psychoanalysis draws on these Schopenhauerian insights, as Dews reminds us:

> Psychoanalysts, even from widely differing traditions, have
> concurred that evil is best understood as the attempt to inflict
> one's own experience of the evacuation of meaning on others. In
> his study of serial killers, for example, Christopher Bollas has
> suggested that such individuals seek to induce in others their own
> early experience of a total, traumatic breakdown of trust in the
> benignity of the adult world. (Dews, 2008: 133)

Later (Chapter 9) that 'breakdown of trust' will be located as a traumatic
and formative historical event in English bourgeois culture, but for the
moment we can see that evil is dependent on the power it can arbitrarily
exert on others, and it is this power that in its social form has been transferred into the abstract form of money. The corruption of the post-war
political class and their abandonment of the settlement on behalf of the
global financial elite constitute a traumatic breakdown of trust on a mass
cultural scale, more so because the municipal welfare technicians had
manoeuvred themselves into a position of *in loco parentis*. It did not produce
serial killers and child molesters, but it did send a heavy current of cynical
nihilism through the social body.

Perhaps only a counter-current of asceticism can negate the traumatized-
narcissistic will that seeks to impose suffering on others, an unwelcome
Puritan intervention in the age of freedom and sensuous expression.
Nietzsche was the high-priest of uninhibited expression, but his mistake
was to see the outward directed drives as spontaneous, and he fell back into
the naturalism he was trying to escape. Thus he could not see the aroused
will for what it was, a post-aristocratic high-intensity artifice created by the
voiding of community and the stimulation of anxiety, and the social process
of blocking aggression and inculcating guilt as the historical construction of
the super-ego, forcing aggression inwards to sublimate the will and convert
its aggression to symbolic forms, harnessed via its organization as a social
struggle for distinction into an economic driver (Hall et al., 2008). It was
thus a small step from Nietzsche to Ayn Rand, and far from moving into a
period of transcendence where the human being overcomes the struggle of
the ideal against the supposed natural impulse, we moved into a period
where the struggle was shifted to a far higher level of intensity yet, at the
same time, a far lower level of spontaneity and idealism. Manufactured
desires and drives tailored to economic expansion and ushered to the bor-
ders of *jouissance* struggled against a flexible and concessionary ethico-legal
means of managing them. This occurs in a condition where the eternal
return has cancelled the dualism of past and future, but in the *negative* sense,
where the solidity of the past and open possibility of the future are both

denied by the permanent present of market pragmatism. Deleuze's wish that within the confines of market pragmatism some sort of idealized Nietzschean affirmation will return to usher in a world of delightful difference and previously unknown happiness, along with Foucault's dream of discursive closure and renewal as the dynamic force for new forms of life as the disciplinary society is dismantled, have been shattered on the concrete ground of empirical reality as the same old prejudices, fears, struggles and tensions have yet again broken free from their shackles; resource scarcity, geopolitical wars, mass global unemployment, genocide, crime waves, corruption, torture and so on. Do we have to keep on suffering this, Dews asks, to satisfy the ideals of 'justifying life' in the 'eternal return'? There is much becoming as history restarts, but in the main it is neither novel, nor innocent, nor life-affirming. Many of the minions have had enough of this inscrutable and portentous idealism, and with cynical resignation busy themselves in the search for available entrepreneurial opportunities.

Adorno (2000) worked with a more plausible conception of the human subject. The human being has the ability to control and manipulate its drives in the interests of the organism's survival. Weak and vulnerable human beings have always been threatened by powerful natural forces. For Ehrenreich (1997), life-affirming joy can establish itself as a potent psycho-cultural form – that is, internalized in the psyche and reproduced by culture – in the moment we fend off these threats with violence, intelligence or trickery, and thus we live with the constant possibility that in hostile circumstances we will associate joy with triumph achieved by violent or fraudulent means. We dream of the permanent removal of threats, a fantasy driven by the demand of Spinoza's (1996) variation of the Stoical concept of *conatus* for homeostasis, and throughout human history we have been the subjects of this drive for negative freedom by means of control. Freedom, survival, control and domination are unified in our unconscious impulses and expressed in our dreams. The subject is no illusion, and neither is it simply a work of art and self-becoming; its latent but potentially energetic foundations are already present and inherited from our past. For Adorno we are prone to illusion only when we conceive ourselves as the meta-physical monad entirely separate from the natural (Dews, 2008). This illusion is present in Mead's (1934) symbolic interactionism and all other Cartesian and Kantian influenced theories of the self. Only the Freudian tradition accounts for the dynamic struggle between the natural, the conscious and the unconscious. The Lacanian 'split ego' connects subjectivity with desire, the conduit between the unconscious and the external world of objects and symbols, and thus we must not continue to regard external reality or our experiences of it as dependent on our acts of cognition and communication. Experience of reality and immersion in ideology are incul-cated in the unconscious as the disavowed Real, which influences our thoughts and actions from positions beyond conscious control; as we shall see later, in Hegel's words, 'the spirit is a bone' (see Johnston, 2008).

Where Hegel saw history as the unfolding of the good, Marx saw the historical predominance of blind, natural compulsion. For Adorno, in liberal-capitalist society the good exists only as the brake on sublimated and harnessed evil:

> Marx's 'false unity' is that of a social existence in which the satisfaction of material needs through socially determined forms of economic activity exerts constraint over the free development of human powers and capacities. For Adorno, however, it is the formation of a subjectivity opposed to nature *as such* that poses the problem. (Dews, 2008: 193; original italics)

Hence the dominance of 'identity thinking' and 'instrumental reason'; it is no coincidence that these energies are behind the two principal and most common forms of crime, those of *expressive domination* and *acquisition* achieved at the expense of others and their environments. The catastrophes of the capitalist world are the products of a 'radical evil' that has its roots in the core of universal human subjectivity. The active manifestation of this 'radical evil' is the mind perfectly adapted to the world that has been con-structed by the primitive survivalist core of human subjectivity; the greatest evil is our failure to oppose with Socratic reflexivity our bestial nature and assiduously and carefully ensure the establishment and reproduction of our opposition in our cultural and social institutions. Liberal capitalism renders this impossible because it denies the existence of *death drive*, our bestial nature as will, instead relying on dynamic economic progress and expressive freedom on a bed of ethico-cultural inertia. We cling anxiously to the prin-ciple of self-preservation when we have outgrown the conditions that posed so many threats (Adorno, 1973); this anxiety ensures continuing self-alienation, competition and the need for dominance and control by a plutocratic group who 'lead by example' in the name of social cohesion and productive efficiency. *Death drive* is Freud's term for Schopenhauer's malignant and sadistic will. It seeks for no reason other than obscene enjoyment to revolt against all restraint, meaning, value and rationality, it is the universal rebel without a cause. However, those who are driven to seek obscene enjoyment by constantly violating all laws and norms are bound more closely to these systems of rules because they are so fixated on violating them. Thus, just as evil is as ludicrous as a clown passing itself off as an emperor the fake transgressive struggle against misconceived evil is as ludicrous as a small boy passing himself off as a revolutionary.

Postmodernism was liberalism's final attempt to prevent awareness of underlying drives and processes and universal moral problems, replacing them with the fatalistic acceptance of permanent fragmentation, uncertainty and flux. But it was a movement that gained momentum when the destructive effects of neoliberalism had not reached full pitch, and it underestimated the defensive longing for regressive forms of solidarity that would emerge as competitive individualism, alienation, anomie and communal breakdown reached new heights. Left-wing thought has abandoned its thinking on these real problems and it no longer has the 'critical apparatus' to conceptualize them. It is necessary to refer to the traditional right, but to reject their solutions, which inevitably revolve around the restoration of traditional discipline and its organic institutions, which have already failed to restore order by repressive means (Stiegler, 2010a). For Simondon (1964), the real problem is that without a collective identity the individuation of a sociable subject is impossible. Collective individuation has been destroyed by marketing and the construction of the consumer as proletarian, the prosumer (see also Marazzi, 2010), and thus:

> The individual who can't manage to individuate himself suffers. And when he suffers, he needs an outlet, a pharmakon, a scapegoat. And so he turns necessarily on everything that will seem abnormal or less normal and hence produces exclusion. There is a real destruction of the superego. The theory of psychoanalysis, or rather, the practice of psychoanalysis, has consisted a great deal in arguing that the superego was something necessarily repressive and regressive. Not at all. The people who say this haven't read Freud. Freud never said that. For Freud, without a superego there is no psychic apparatus. And I argue that the superego is currently being destroyed. A psychoanalyst told me very recently, 'No, it isn't being destroyed, because there are cops everywhere.' But I replied, 'That isn't what the superego is; the superego isn't cops.' That's just control. Can we say, for example, that when the Nazis entirely militarized German society that it was a development of the superego? Not at all, it was a destruction of the superego. The superego always involves a sublimatory investment. If there isn't this, then there isn't any authority in the good sense of the term, because there are two senses of authority: authority in the sense of repression, which leads to authoritarianism, and the authority of

the author, the authority Antigone appeals to against Creon (Antigone says there is the authority of the divine law). And the superego is the combination of the two. A society without superego is a barbaric society. I think today we are developing a society without superego, which clearly gives rise, in reaction, to temptations to produce a repressive, barbaric order. (Stiegler, in Crogan, 2010: 164–5)

One of the issues raised by conservatives is attention, or the lack of attention span in so many of today's individuals raised on the mass media spectacle. This renders problematic what Marcuse, Deleuze, Foucault, Illich and so many other left-libertarian thinkers said about the repression of desire by discipline and schooling. For Wieviorka (2009), the delinquency and urban violence we see today are largely the results of the exhaustion of the institutionalized social conflict that characterized the era of industrial capitalism and, we could argue, were the bases of capitalism's two core collective identities in dialectical tension. Where O'Malley's (2010) optimistic and complacent left-liberalism celebrates an array of political opportunities, more sober and realistic analyses such as those of Martuccelli (2001) and Wieviorka (ibid.) see a fragmented world where forms of domination, inequality and conflict diversify and proliferate. We exist in the formally complex space between what Wieviorka (2009: 25) calls the 'different registers' of entirely institutionalized power, authority and conflict and entirely unbridled domination, criminality and violence. However, his suggestion that violence is a ludic outpouring of pure libido, beyond meaning and a reduction of the human being to its animalistic drives is hampered by his denial of Lacan, who offers the most convincing account of these cruel drives as the congealed ideology that cannot be symbolized as it draws upon the Real; it is simply beyond our quite systematically impoverished symbolic order's ability to symbolize the Real, yet what it represents is the extremity of an important aspect of the everyday ideology and subjectivity that *functions efficiently* in the capitalist economy. To open the way for today's hopeful agentic model, Wieviorka explicitly denies all the paraphernalia of the Real:

It will be noted that the notion of the subject we are adopting departs considerably from that proposed by psychoanalysis, and especially Lacanian psychoanalysis. For the latter, the 'pure' subject is, as Marcos Zafiropoulos says 'a subject without an ego … a mere function of the symbolic structure' (2003: 89). For Lacan 'The subject proceeds from his systematic subjection in the

field of the other' (1994[1973]: 188). The subject is assigned its
role by various influential determinisms: traumas, lack, family
complexes, the death drive and so on. (2009: 147)

What we can see clearly here is an attempt by liberal theorists to revive the
subject as an autonomous agent by presenting the constituents of the Real
as deterministic in some sort of old-fashioned positivistic way. In fact the
constitution of the healthy ego after the Oedipal phase is an essential aspect
of Lacan's conception of the maturing subject, and the subject's engagement with the Symbolic Order furnishes it with the vital ability to reflect
upon the Real and its irruptions in the Imaginary, to turn them from determining forces to that which should be the focus of scepticism and transgression. Wieviorka's essentially Kantian analysis based on the *a priori* category
of social justice as the sensate prime mover stands in stark contrast to Freud
and Adorno's recognition that the self-preservation instinct is activated
under conditions of distress and anxiety.

Wieviorka (2009:135) posits three dimensions of the anti-subject; functionality, delirium (or 'delirious rationality') and *jouissance*, but this attempt
to present such extreme disaffected cruelty as beyond our ability to symbolize it is an act of symbolic impoverishment, which feeds into the fundamental ideological process of denial as *fetishistic disavowal*. Put simply, we
must transcend the myth that these brutal, condensed occurrences of the
Real are incomprehensible events that simply erupt out of nowhere, or out
of some pathogenic zone beneath our humanity and culture; rather, they
represent the proximal extremities of the dynamic structural tendency of
cruel indifferent exploitation that has been systematically incited and harnessed. As we shall see later (Chapter 8) there is no *qualitative* difference
between the cruel indifference that dismantles the ethical barrier placed
around child molesting and that which allows child labour and fatal acci-
dents in workplaces; the difference is in their positions on a gradient from
the functional form of the *dispersed distal norm* to the dysfunctional form of
the *condensed proximal extreme*. The gradient is a product of capitalism's
imperfect attempt to produce and restrain the anti-subject in a manner that
allows it to co-exist in tension with the superficially civilized subject, a tension that retains the anti-subject as an active force in the lower register of
functionality. The violent anti-subject enters the dimensions of delirium
and *jouissance* whenever the barrier of civility is poorly constructed and
internalized or deliberately opened in the face of extreme threats or disruption to the subject's protective infrastructure. The rise of crime, violence
and fascism in times of social and economic disruption demonstrates quite
clearly that a reservoir of anxiety and obscene proto-symbolic drives is

already there in a latent condition waiting for a symbolic call to arms. The liberal-humanistic denial of the Real can indeed prevent the call to arms by replacing it with a call to negotiation and peace, but it also feeds into the denial of the Real's existence, effectively storing up trouble for the future.

Jodi Dean (2009) offers a more potent critique when she argues that our failure to take responsibility for, and offer a serious challenge to, the neo-liberalization of the world's economies has led us into the trap of celebrating the isolated imaginary freedoms of communicative capitalism. The celebration of consumption, identity and communicative networking on a landscape of post-collectivist freedom is a forlorn attempt to disavow our failure to support collective responses to political, social and economic problems; if we add Stiegler's (2010a) claim to the analysis, this also constitutes a failure of individuation. We didn't actually lose, says Dean, we quit, which is worse. However, it was probably even worse still; as we have seen in previous chapters, the liberals who took over intellectual leadership of the left were never really serious about constructing a collectivist politics in the first place. In fact liberalism has always seen the collective as the great Evil to be historically transcended.

Yet, to displace politics like this courts atomism, nihilism and unrest, and ushers in violence of a new sort, beyond the institutionalized conflict of the industrial era. The reduction of the politics of the Real to communicative acts has run parallel to the importation of forms of linguistic philosophy into the social sciences. Such has been the impact of this flood that both the Real and reality have been marginalized in discourse. It is considered embarrassing – even heretical – in some circles to suggest that one has discovered a bit of reality out there, which has its own ontological existence, structural location and actual dynamic force outside of language and other forms of representation. There is no bridge between phenomena and noumena that we can all construct and cross over with the whole sensory apparatus that we share, only multiple language games, negotiated meanings, discourses and regimes of truth. This reduces politics to an atomized spray of micro-communicative acts such as posting comments on blogs or pressing buttons on cyber petitions. The abrupt expansion of communications media also prevents adults from keeping secrets from children, and we lose all the innocence that allows the flourishing amongst the young of the subjectivities that dream that a better future is possible (Postman, 1982). At the same time it creates an environment that enhances criminal networks and allows new forms of crime; internet grooming flourishes as those whose innocence collapses before the appropriate transition to adulthood meet those who seek to exploit it. Technological fetishism fuels the retreat from the collective action and political institutions that constitute citizenship,

replacing them with a politically inert yet frantically communicative telecracy (Stiegler, 2010a), in turn fuelling the atomization of the population
and the emptying of communal space. As Dean observes, in the current
debate on the uses of the internet:

> Internet users appeared either as engaged citizens eager to participate
> in electronic town halls … or they appeared as Web-surfing waste-
> of-lives in dark, dirty rooms downloading porn, betting on obscure
> Internet stocks, or collecting evidence of the US government's
> work with extraterrestrials at Area 51. (2009: 43–4)

We have here an important factor that joins the others in the recent
decline and mutation of crime; do these keyboard-ridden 'waste of lives'
need to commit crime to obtain what they want, and if so, do they have
the skills and wherewithal that crime requires? Many individuals who live
isolated, marginal existences are satisfying their needs in ways that avoid
involvement in crime, whilst new markets for supplying cheap goods and
services have appeared in the criminal shadow-economy (Nordstrom,
2007). At the same time as some petty crime appears to decline, increased
demand in the shadow-market creates the climate for the expansion of
serious criminal trafficking and the new 'glocal' networks, which undertake to manage supply.

Criminology's role in the depoliticization process is its refusal to raise
the particularities that constitute its subject matter – the specific crimes
and anti-social actions that characterize late modernity – to the level of the
universal, as one of a series of interconnected problems created by the
system as a whole, and which confront it as potential threats. Those who
Dean (2009: 62) describes as overinvested, overidentified free marketers
appear to be delighted by risk and the thrill of the hunt that the market
provides, and she links Passavant's (2005) concept of the 'consumer/
criminal doublet' to what Žižek (2010a) names the decline of symbolic
efficiency. There is little doubt that, like classical industrial capitalism,
neoliberalism possesses the powers of compulsion and ideology required
to produce the subjects it requires. Just as the warrior-citizen and the
peasant of pre-capitalist societies mutated into the disciplined producer
and consumer of the industrial era, neoliberalism is in the midst of producing the fluid, imaginary identities 'that converge around the strange
attractors of the insatiable shopper (shopaholic) and incorrigible criminal'
(Dean, 2009: 63; see also Hall et al., 2008), the shadow-economy's variant
of Marazzi's (ibid.) 'prosumer'.

In the suspension of symbolic efficiency the new modes of 'governmentality' are not institutionalized concatenations of the technologies of biopower but means of cleaning up the spillages from the energy generation process; Foucault's mistake was to posit this insulation as the discursive constitutor of criminality and its control. As Dean and Passavant remind us, Lacan replaced his original idea of the symbolic order anchored around a master signifier to one loosely structured by contingent and fragile nodes of enjoyment that appear as quilting points of *jouissance*. Seen by poststructuralists as opportunities for freedom of identity in a loose and shifting plasma of language, it is rather a profusion and diversification of the means by which identity could be bred in captivity. For Žižek (2010a) the decline in symbolic efficiency means a decline in trust as the general storehouse of knowledge of 'what everybody knows' is 'deconstructed' out of existence with no replacement in sight. No questions can be answered and no doubts assuaged, there is only an endless procession of opinions and sceptical dismissals. Cultural and political life is now like a Derridean sentence with no final closure of meaning.

We came to follow Derrida, Foucault and the rest in their celebration of this chaotic and politically inert mess as a new site for potential freedom because the decline in symbolic efficiency was celebrated as the sign of the final escape from totalitarianism, the ultimate aim of the liberal catastrophist. Deep symbolic investment in catastrophism is the commonality around which the liberal left and the liberal right converge, and in comparison to which all their other differences are minor and easily subsumed. However, as Dean (ibid.) reminds us, the decline of symbolic efficiency also means that our language and other symbolic systems can no longer claim reliable connections to reality. Thus our institutions of nurturance and solidarity and pre-punitive authority and discipline – schools, families, parties, unions and so on – have also declined. In the absence of symbolic efficiency and the traditional institutions through which the subject can speak, and which speak through the subject, which are the subject's purpose and which give purpose to the subject, the anxious atomized individual has little choice but to work hard in isolation to experience all the hedonistic and symbolic enjoyment on offer in the mass media, marketing and institutionalized leisure industries (Rojek, 2010; Smart, 2010).

Where internal self-controls have weakened and sunk beneath a critical level, the individual is controlled by the forces of the state (Passavant, 2005); the 'culture of control' is therefore not principally proactive but reactive, a return with the technological means of greater efficiency to a project that emerged, as we have seen, in the chaos of Mediaeval Europe. We can see that conservative control theory is correct in that individuation and self-discipline require a citizen bonded to a social body, but the conservative social body and its institutional complex is simply an agency whose nurturance and discipline act on behalf of the external control mechanism, which in turn has evolved – despite initial resistance – to service the disruptive dynamism of the capitalist market economy. In the mainstream conservative criminological narrative still dominant in academic and governmental circles the criminal is seen as an aberration, an individual who deviates from socially acceptable 'behaviour' because of either faulty socialization into mainstream values and norms or efficient socialization into deviant values and norms. Criminals, we are constantly told, can be rehabilitated by reintroduction into mainstream culture (Bottoms, 2002) or diverted from criminality by early intervention in childhood (Farrington, 1996). However, this discourse unhelpfully conflates values and norms rather than viewing them in dynamic tension, and thus fails to recognize that there is no symbolic efficiency in the mainstream system of values and meanings underneath the fragile normative order. Relying on normative efficiency, in the sense of peak efficiency in the normative order's ability to construct restrained and strictly rule-bound individuals, yet again denies the potency of the Real and therefore relies exclusively on the fragile insulating normative order itself, which can so easily collapse at specific points where it lacks material and cultural resources and is not reproduced with the utmost efficiency (Hall et al., 2008).

For Dean (2009: 66), the imaginary identities that constitute themselves in the midst of this instability are 'extremely vulnerable'. Circuits of leisure, entertainment and consumption now insist that the subject enjoys the maximum number of sensations and experiences. No closure of satisfaction or contentment is possible, so the sense of freedom is accompanied by a nagging sense of anxiety over the failure to get the most out of everything on offer. Consumer capitalism sustains desire by constantly disappointing subjects as they experience objects of desire, which thus keeps alive the aim of desire, which is to stay alive; desire's desire is nothing less than eternal life. The more ultimately disappointing everything is, the more powerful consumer capitalism grows because there are so few confident subjects who can judge external experiences by the standards set by their own internal symbolically grounded judgments. The anxious, captivated individual is incorporated wholly in the new ideological formation; each new form of cultural subversion, itself born of the master signifier of the 'cool individual' that still holds its position at the centre of the otherwise fragmentary Imaginary/Real order, is prefabricated for incorporation, repackaging and selling manufactured symbolic objects back to those who think they are the 'originators' and to the crowd that has gathered around them as they are immediately ordained as such (Frank, 1997). To imagine oneself as 'excessive, extreme and unregulated' is to imagine oneself, as Dean (ibid.: 67) puts it, as 'a composite of the neoliberal market itself'.

For Dean and Passavant, the criminal represents the threat of loss, the monstrous figure that would deprive us of our enjoyment, and the fear generated by this threat mobilizes and justifies the expansion and intensification of the control, surveillance and punishment mechanisms of neoliberal governance. However, the analysis posits this sense of loss as more fundamental than the sense of envy and resentment that is institutionally cultivated as a drive and a subjectivizing force to energize the system (Žižek, 2010). Yes, the criminal arouses fear as he threatens to steal the law-abiding worker's *jouissance*, but far more fundamental to the arousal of the victim's ire is that the criminal has found a short-cut to the common goal of *jouissance*, one that does not demand the mundane labour that the victim must endure. Envy and resentment are aroused by the possibility of being cheated and therefore out-competed in the open competition in which everyone is a compulsory entrant; the criminal's boldness is a means of extracting himself from the victimhood we all share, our ignominious position of 'prosumers' forced to undergo systemic exploitation in return for morsels of *jouissance*. Underneath the image of the criminal as a threat that triggers fear of the loss of specific rewards, which both Dean and Passavant are right to point out, is the far more potent image of the general criminality that represents a systemic threat to our basic ability to earn the rewards and distinguish ourselves as 'winners' in socially acceptable ways. Passavant draws on Garland's (2001) 'culture of control' thesis, but this standard left-liberal dualism is an attempt to explain criminality and the complex emotions it arouses amongst the public in the terms of the discourse in which Garland is interested, the politics of fear and otherness, rather than the discourse that can provide the most explanatory power, that which revolves around the seduction, desire, competition, envy, resentment and *sameness* – after all, victim and criminal share the same goal of *jouissance* – that operate at a far more fundamental psychosocial level in the capitalist system. Otherness in the order of normative strategies is overridden by sameness in the deeper order of values, drives and desires (Hall et al., 2008). To put a Lacanian twist on this, it is not the 'fear of the other' as a monstrous figure but the anxiety of the fragmented, helpless self as it tries to attract the desire of the other and forge an identity as a competent performer amongst others; the subject does not fear the other as a monster but as a figure potentially more competent, more successful, more interesting, more attractive and thus *more human than the self*. Bound up in the same ideology of the disavowed Real, the criminal shoves his instant success and special liberty in the victim's face.

Criminality is not merely a discursive object constructed by state power, law and the criminalization process, a figment of the imagination that a fearful and stupid population are duped into believing. Crime produces universally discernible and distressing harms to all sorts of victims who had been concealed by the discourses of radical liberalism and left idealism in the 1960s and 1970s as much as they were exaggerated and projected onto the working class by the right realists. Paramount amongst the harms criminality produces is the general psychosocial harm that even the moderately successful criminal can inflict on all individuals who see themselves as relative failures in their attempts to succeed in an inherently competitive system by trading mundane labour for rationed rewards; and they must pay taxes, too. Like financial traders, celebrities, negligent bosses, offshore tax-avoiders and corrupt politicians, criminals remind everyday people that they are hapless 'mugs' ensnared in an exploitative system. This constant reminder, combined with some criminals' willingness to raise the bar of harm in the act of exploitation, is even more socially divisive and corrosive than the 'construction of the other' because it generates the underlying cynicism, resentment and hostility alongside which – in the absence of a universal language of systemic critique – 'othering' is simply a reactionary anthropomorphic means of symbolizing the underlying system of institutionalized envy and competitive individualism that generates and reproduces these emotions.

Foucault eschewed the Real of consumerist envy, class antagonism and exploitation hidden by ideology, and had no means of conceptualizing the generative core of the socio-symbolic order. His idea of discursive generation is weak, yet his conception of discourse has been the most popular term in Anglo-American academia for 30 years, and its 'ubiquity coincides with the belief, fostered by Foucault himself, that they provide compelling alternatives to the Marxist paradigm of ideology critique as well as to psychoanalytic accounts of subjectivation' (Vighi & Feldner, 2007: 141). Foucault saw reality simply as an object of classification and contemplation, and lacked a coherent conception of ideology or the subject. He ignored the Real at the heart of all symbolic fictions and attacked modernist – especially Marxist – conceptualizations of economism, repression, autonomous subjectivity and power maintained by ideological distortions. Everything that eludes consciousness he externalized in discourse, removing entirely the idea of unconscious drives and desires, placing them instead on the 'dark side' of external phenomena as they were discursively constituted.

For Foucault truth was the product of regimes of power and knowledge, which could alter perspectives and perceptions of phenomena. Even in his later writings the subject was a product of 'technologies of the self' that require no self-representation in the conscious or unconscious mind. He achieved a thorough historicization and relativization of systems of thought; perhaps too thorough as it left intact virtually no ontology and no trans historical truths, norms or values. The 'positive unconscious', as he called it (Foucault, 1970), was 'out there' in ever-changing systems of knowledge, 'regimes of truth'. The Freudian negative unconscious, the product of tormented drive and repressed symbolism, is replaced by a duality of the scientist's consciousness and the positive unconscious of science, symbolized by the knowledge-claims or 'discursive objects' of historically and culturally relative scientific discourses. Thus, through discourse and the objectifying, subjectifying and normalizing power of discursive 'technologies of the self', the biopower regime is productive rather than repressive. In one fell swoop, Foucault simply bypassed the Imaginary and evicted the Real as the repressed, unsymbolizable surplus of ideology in its powerful couplet with drive. He acknowledged the void in external discourse, and thus did not present knowledge as a totality, but the operation and effect of the void was never theorized; there's nothing like a negative void as a cause of major effects in the sort of positivist system that Foucault proposed. He avoided this problem in his archaeological works by denying causality and positing 'existence without predicate'. Epistemic paradigm change has no causes or conditions, and the implication is that there is some inherent transformative tendency, perhaps some natural life-cycle or other form of immanent positive causality, in discursive regimes of truth. The dialectical gap between the discursive void and the positive content is completely overlooked, 'a weakness that he shares with the tradition of anti-dialectical materialism from Newton to Luhmann' (Vighi & Feldner, 2007: 153).

In contrast, Žižek's (1989) model of ideology is a domain split between an outer layer of rationalized symbols and an inner core of unsymbolizable, disavowed enjoyment. For Foucault, the concept of ideology was passé because reality itself is a symbolic fiction constructed by discursive practices, and ideology critique would simply reaffirm that fact. All ontological questions are suspended, again in favour of discursive practices. Ideology is unnecessary because regimes of biopower operate disciplinary discursive practices that inscribe themselves directly into the body. However, what Foucault cast 'out there' was for Žižek firmly back 'in here', at least as far as subjectivity, politics and the social are concerned. Ideology does more than 'mask the truth', it organizes the dialectic between the two vital dimensions of the subject and the socio-political order. The demarcation and disavowal of the Real means that people follow official ideology cynically, only occasionally discerning glimpses of the Real in its presentation; harmful crime is such a 'presentation of the Real'. The more liberated we think we are the more we are ensnared in the superego command to 'enjoy', which binds us to the market; it is the individual's emotional estimation of her ability, compared to that of the other, to achieve enjoyment and a spell of special liberty that is threatened by criminality's short-cutting capacity, a threat that compounds the fear of the harm that, in the process, the criminal might be willing to inflict on the self.

Enjoyment inflames desire as it is constantly disavowed by the ideology of its practitioners. This moves Žižek beyond the traditional ideology critique employed by critical thinkers such as Chomsky (2003), which sees ideology simply as a mask concealing real truth, and beyond Foucault's notion of regimes of truth. Ideology does not simply distort reality, and neither is it an ever-changing milieu of discursive practices where the hegemonic struggle over power is about privileging some systems of knowledge and denying others. Where Foucault denied a world external to discourse, echoing Derrida's conception of textuality, for Žižek the world external to discourse is not reality 'out there' but the 'internal external', a hidden, disavowed, obscene interior layer, a non-discursive core of pure ideology energizing the subject, its desires and its practices; what is outside is inside, or 'extimate' in Lacan's (1992) term. Here is an undialectical tension between, on one side, a pre-symbolic barbarism energized and given shape by the pure, unrepresentable core of ideology demanding obscene enjoyment, and, on the other, whatever political civilization our collective superego and symbolic practices can muster. This is the basic psychosocial structure of the criminological process of pseudo-pacification, a dynamic drive in which each secret investment in obscene enjoyment is held in check by a prohibition, which allows the specific desire to be sublimated and symbolized as a commodity, thus energizing the marketplace through the practice of consumption. For the capitalist subject, ideology is only realized in *jouissance*, pure, senseless enjoyment as the prize at the end of the game.

Surely Harvey (1991), Jameson (1991) and Žižek (2000) are right that post-structuralism and postmodernism are *the* functional ideologies of advanced capitalism because they have performed the vital task of growing in the interstices of a guilty and malfunctioning left and *from the inside,* extinguishing it as opposition. On a scale that extended beyond traditional left-liberalism they were the ultimate catastrophist New Left reactions to the horrors that followed political intervention in the twentieth century. They picked up pace after the 1968 riots in France, which, to the left-liberals, looked like they were about to launch the nation into another bout of revolution, terror and totalitarian control; the principle architects of these functional ideologies were French and the take-up rate by intellectual aficionados and bootleggers in Britain and the USA was high. Rather than risk a repeat of the past, neoliberalism was ushered in past a frightened leftist ostrich that buried its head in the interior technical operation of language and image whilst the newly confident neoliberal right commandeered the Real, the Symbolic and the Imaginary with renewed control of political economy, mass media, consumer culture and the education system. We are witnessing the final colonization of the Higher Education system right now (Collini, 2010).

The postmodernist liberal left joined forces with the distinctly non-relativistic right to usher in the 'end of history', to the sound of a great collective sigh of relief. The structural and post-structural allegories, proscribing universal ethics and problematizing classification by mutual recognition of emergent properties, denied certainty or stability in the meaning-generating relations between referents, signs, signifiers and signi-fieds. This provided the liberal left with an anti-political, anti-philosophical justification for avoiding intervention in the internal Real and external real-ity, simply by denying that any reliable knowledge of their respective ontologies could be produced. Most of the harmful criminal practices we face today are the direct or indirect products of deep politico-economic and cultural interventions by the neoliberal right, interventions that proceeded in the absence of any serious challenge by a catastrophist left that had grown fearful in the shadow of its own past. Radical criminology, once a major supporter of political interventions in the social relations, hegemonic ethico-cultural meanings and material conditions that constituted and reproduced crime-prone locales, desires and identities, was ushered through the same decontamination chamber and cleansed of its political impurities. The first step in the establishment of a new perspective on crime and deviance is to disrupt the coordinates of the undialectical conservative-liberal hegemony in criminological theory.

THE RETURN OF THE DIALECTIC

7

Apart from a few notable exceptions (see for instance McAuley, 2007; Winlow, 2001), criminologists tend to disregard the working-class experience in its full diversity, from its incorporated crypto-proletarian majority – itself divided into culturally conservative and liberal factions – to its radical activist, outcast and opportunistic philo-bourgeois minorities. Liberal sociologists have often been lukewarm to working-class institutions such as unions, and dismissive of working-class culture except in a rather patronizing, tokenistic way (Selke et al., 2002); the measured panegyrics of Hoggart (1957), Williams (1971) and others now seem like a distant memory. In fact the middle-class monopoly of the social sciences has carved out a space in which liberal-postmodernists have been given free rein to declare the death of class as a valid sociological category. Unless they devote themselves fully to the task of representing the world through the liberal lens, working-class intellectuals are also marginalized in the academy (Dews & Law, 1995; Ryan & Sackey, 1984; Wilson, 2002), so the ability to pursue research interests and publish works that represent a phenomenology anchored in the ontological reality of everyday working-class experience is severely restricted. Sociologists and criminologists have examined the experiential core of gender and race, but, lately, class has been largely absent. Left realism brought it back into criminological theory, if rather vicariously and through a rationalist lens, and a dwindling band of advocates continue to publish valuable research (see for instance Currie, 2010; Lea, 2002), but the liberal mainstream has done its best to marginalize the discourse and its basic insights. Consequently, those working-class individuals who become enmeshed in crime are caught on the horns of a dual stereotype; the conservative media's portrayal of dangerous drug-addicted brutes or the liberal intelligentsia's portrayal of innocent victims of oppression. Being pathologized by hard-line conservatives and classical liberals or patronized and protected *in loco parentis* by social liberals only serves to intensify the hardened perceptions of those who experience daily the alienation, anxiety and resentment that is already an inherent characteristic of their position in advanced capitalism's atomized social world.

Debates about the identity and composition of the working class – whether it exists at all in today's atomized world, the extent to which it can still incorporate all wage-earners despite cultural and political differences and the way it intersects with race and gender relations – continue to rage (Skeggs, 2004). However, what tends to be obscured in the theoretical smog thrown up by all these debates about process, culture, reflexivity, symbolic exchange and so on is the certainty that in the pure economistic sense of a mass wage-earning unit of production the working class in general has lost much of its functional grip on the capitalist economic system. Even highly skilled technocrats, the new aristocracy of labour, can find themselves in relatively insecure positions in unstable markets, and for some time now sociologists have been aware that the proletarianization of the middle classes has jeopardized their economic security (Lea, 2002). It is perhaps rather odd that left-liberal sociologists have been emphasizing identity politics and class's cultural and reflexive complexity during a period when its fundamental economic position of exploitation and insecurity has been intensifying and diffusing throughout the social order and across the globe to the extent that it now also threatens the professional middle classes. Capital still needs some labour, but it can now seek it anywhere in the world where the price is low and insecure working people are grateful and acquiescent. As neoliberal economic restructuring diffuses across the globe, this insecurity can be manufactured where it did not previously exist by disrupting traditional agricultural communities, indebting pliable governments, levering up food prices and forcing or enticing new workers into areas of mineral extraction or industrialization where they become entirely dependent on wage labour.

The strong bargaining position that the old Western industrial proletariat enjoyed as a whole has fragmented and weakened. For some near the bottom end of the globalizing hierarchy of labour it has all but dissolved; all the King's reflexive modernity and all the King's identity politics couldn't put it together again. For instance, consider the recent economic fate of the US working class. Throughout the twentieth century the USA had developed a powerful socio-economic strand to its overall sentiment of exceptionalism (Wolff, 2011) because wage rises had kept up with corresponding rises in productivity, which, in the post-war period, had given most American workers an unprecedented degree of wealth and security. This ended abruptly in the 1980s, when the economic crisis that had begun in the early 1970s reached a tipping point. Competition from abroad, rising oil prices and the floating of the dollar had sent the US economy into a stagflationary recession, but the job losses and rapid descent of the average 'real wage' – the relative value of wages compared to living costs – were accelerated further by the introduction of new technology, most notably the personal computer, into the workplace. From 1980 Reagan's neoliberal government presided over a process of deindustrialization and destruction of working-class negotiating power, one half of the institutionalized conflict that in Wieviorka's (2009) perspective is essential to balanced and relatively civilized social relations in a capitalist economy. The USA was no longer the 'exception', and entered a new era of economic insecurity, which has been exacerbated by spiralling personal debt taken out to recover the customary living standards that had declined alongside the corresponding decline in the real wage. The era in which wages for the mass working class rose alongside productivity ended quite abruptly in the early 1980s (Wolff, ibid.).

During the same period a similar disjunction occurred in the course of British economic history, with similar results. The ratio of debt-generated money and fiat money in the British economy is now approximately nine to one, compared to an even fifty–fifty balance in the immediate post-war period, which indicates just how reliant the economy is on credit rather than the generation of real wealth and wages through manufacturing. The western European nations who based their economies on the social market model fared rather better, but when the jamboree of irresponsible lending exploded in 2008 in Britain, the USA and the other nations that had followed the neoliberal model with too much faith, their finance and credit-based economies teetered on the brink of collapse. They now face various permutations of taxpayer bailouts, austerity cuts, capital retraction and shrinking labour markets, all of which indicate proximity to an overall insolvency that renders the economic position of the general wage-earning working class even more precarious than it was during the initial period of deindustrialization in the 1980s. This time the difference is that the collapse from relative economic security to insecurity and the subsequent clash between high expectations and an abruptly experienced new reality will not, in terms of perception, be quite so severe. If we factor in the high prison populations, the advanced policing, risk management, surveillance and security systems, the demographic decline in the number of young adults, the virtualization of many illegally traded commodities and the apathy and anhedonic nihilism that we discussed earlier, a real and statistical 'crime explosion' of a similar magnitude is less likely. What we face instead is a less spectacular mutation of criminality alongside new markets and the 'virtualization' of sectors of the global consumer economy.

However, as sections of the 'precariat' (see Standing, 2011) become ever more disconnected from the mainstream economy, a real and statistical reversal of the crime decline is still possible, alongside a mutation in the practices of economic crime whose statistical significance might take years to research (see Treadwell, 2011). However, whichever way the trend goes, a further decline in the already precarious position of the wage-earning class is in little doubt. Alongside this we are also likely to see a deregulatory climate where harms done to workers by negligence and corner-cutting in the world of work (Tombs & Whyte, 2003) and harms done to consumers by the financial industry (Shaxson, 2011) will be increasingly difficult to control. The root of security, culture and identity in the economy tends to be somewhat marginalized in liberal sociology – dismissed as essentialist, reductionist, cynical and so on in the edicts of the watchful prefects we encountered earlier in the shape of Sibeon (2004) and Turner (2010) – along with the vital importance of some form of guaranteed economic participation as the platform for sociability and individual development. The problems caused by economic marginalization were seen largely in terms of relative deprivation, lack of equality and lack of social mobility rather than lack of security and identity. It's quite obvious that lack of finance blocks off most trajectories for social mobility, but the concept of social mobility as a 'good' is predicated on the notion that the working class is something to escape *from* rather than fight *for*. Middle-class analyses work with a narrow conception of the problems, and thus they underplay the experiential consequences of a former proletarian cultural form that, in specific economically marginalized social and geographical locations, is in deep trouble regarding socio-economic security and the ability to reproduce their multiple cultures and identities (Hall et al., 2005).

Representations of the reality of working-class experience in late modernity only rarely appear in the empirical literature. On the rare occasions when they do, we see a mass of casual workers in decaying physical and social infrastructures facing constant economic and cultural insecurity and the trashing of their identities by the symbolic violence of the middle and elite classes whilst occasionally being victimized by a minority of internal and external predators and irritated by a constant stream of minor incivilities. The current master narrative, however, is dominated by conservatives and liberals who are fixated on the notion of society-as-culture, the indomitability of the human spirit and the certainty of incremental progress if we hold the present course with a return to economic growth, a little more community cohesion and a few more opportunities for individual emancipation. In such analyses the 'precariat' simply cannot exist, except in the failure of the individuals within it to reconstitute their ethico-cultural vitality. The deleterious cultural and psychosocial effects of constant and grinding insecurity raise the ghost of the irruptive sense of lack

and helplessness that Lacan (2004) posited as the terrifying primal Real of
the human condition, whose escape is the first vital phase of building an
ego, learning to trust others and joining the social as a critical and reflexive
yet committed member of its symbolic community. Even the escape routes
celebrated by middle-class liberalism demand that to be human one must
immerse oneself in their favoured cultural institutions; after all, if Billy
Elliot found himself in ballet, if Jean Genet hauled himself out of misery by
his own bootstraps to find his authentic voice as a writer, and if a minority
of blacks, women and gays struggled out of oppression in the great
post-war civil rights era to climb the ladder of social mobility, why can't
everyone? Sometimes it becomes obvious that, at some points along the
river, it is only a few steps across a short bridge from left-liberalism to
neoliberalism.

Such a point is revealed in JoAnn Wypijewski's (2006) review of Louis
Uchitelle's (2006) book *The Disposable American*. Wypijewski rails at the
author's 'chastisement' of ordinary people as he accuses them of political
apathy and capitulation to the system:

> Uchitelle floats a theory that the acquiescence he describes has
> something to do with a breakdown of community – beginning in
> the fractural Sixties and worsening as distrust of government,
> economic contraction, oil shock, stagflation and the famous
> Carter-era 'malaise' drove people to topple Keynes and embrace a
> manic individualism, wallowing in Christopher Lasch's 'culture of
> narcissism'. This, he argues, prepared the way for … corporate
> chieftains who discarded workers for the sake of the quarterly
> earnings report and their personal pelf from stock options. Had
> Uchitelle specified an obsession with identity politics as among the
> people's failings, he would echo the clutch of liberal pundits who
> for at least ten years have chastized blacks, women and queers for
> insisting on their own pesky rights at the expense of a sentimentalized
> community and a notional progressive populist politics that could
> have addressed the real, as distinct from these allegedly inflated and
> distracting, sighs of the oppressed. (2006: 145)

There is, however, a sense in which Wypijewski's defence is more patronizing than Uchitelle's chastisement. The concrete manifestations of these
rights, once an escape from real historical oppression, are now expressed in
terms of mobility in the post-industrial class hierarchy, not in terms of being
able to exercise these rights politically in order to defend and repair what
working-class people themselves experience as their threatened identities

and their broken communities. Wypijewski's tirade reveals the weak, hollow core of the liberal-left argument, a refusal to engage with the real fate of community and subjectivity in late modernity, an assertion of the eternal goodness of individual and minority rights with no investigation whatsoever of how desire is being reformed in a world of constant disruption and insecurity. The question 'rights to what?' is never answered because it is never asked. Wypijewski gives a token nod to the 'human costs of disposability' and the 'structural rot' of American capitalism, but averts her eyes from the details of the actual consequences and the subjective experiences and reactions of the 'precariat', those who were consigned to the class-structured margins facing the grim prospect of total redundancy and insignificance. The sector of the liberal left that Wypijewski represents does something far worse than pathologize the shattered remnants of the Western working class; it places impossible expectations on their shoulders whilst neglecting the true gravity of their plight, which, in the wake of constant failure, will merely increase exasperation and turn them away from the liberal left as that which is capable of understanding and representing their interests. Conversely, all the liberal left can offer with their rights-as-social-mobility deal is an integrationist form of conditional respect; here are your formal rights, now take advantage of them and become like us.

Wypijewski's dismissal of memories of the solidarity project, imperfect though it might have been, as 'sentimentalized community' and 'populist politics', betrays the suspicion that the liberal left harbour about a lost world in whose destruction neoliberalism expended so much effort and risked so much unrest. Why was neoliberalism so intent on destroying something that was so hopelessly sentimentalist and populist – yet which provided the socio-political runway on which the civil rights movements gained so much momentum and actually got off the ground – and why did it encourage identity politics to flourish if they present any danger to its dominion? Wypijewski's tirade represents a defensive reaction to the failure of nerve and the discovery that identity politics were so divisive and politically destructive to the left, yet legitimizing to the neoliberal right on whose watch they flourished, which of course helped neoliberalism to destroy both palaeo-conservatism and palaeo-socialism and eulogize the benefits of competitive individualism and economic liberalism in one fell swoop. All that remained in the rubble were small groups of very grateful blacks, gays and women climbing up the socio-economic ladder whilst leaving their erstwhile identity-group comrades behind in the deteriorating circumstances of the 'precariat', even though, one assumes, they bore them no ill-will. The social-democratic project might have been an unsustainable compromise that needed to move towards a firmer political stance, but at least it was populist and sentimentalist enough to put solidarity, in the sense of mutual interests and universal and unconditional socio-economic security, on its agenda. All identity politics actually did was to declare equal rights for entry into the brutal interpersonal competition that organizes social mobility in the current neoliberal order, which of course neoliberalism was quite happy to accommodate because it increased recruitment to its ideology.

The dismissal of working class community and political solidarity as nostalgic sentimentalism – which, as we shall see later in Chapter 9, is precisely what it is not – has contributed to the erosion of the working-class perspective in social sciences. The impact of major economically grounded social disruption and the traumatic consequences of worklessness and marginalization for culture and subjectivity both warrant more serious investigation (Deranty, 2008). From Hegel and Marx through to Adorno, Honneth and Žižek, the pathological has been central to critical theory in sociology and philosophy (Dews, 2008). Without some awareness of it we are condemned to endless false dawns and compulsory celebrations of anything that looks like it is moving at a slightly different tangent in the worlds of identity and culture (Hall & Winlow, 2007). However, the pathological must never be used to condemn selected social groups but to understand currents that in one way or another are parts of human life in general. To this end the work of Deranty and Christophe Dejours is useful. The new work environment and the constant threat of worklessness have given rise to a sense of existential precariousness 'which manifests itself in new, sometimes dramatic, individual and collective pathologies' (Deranty, 2008: 444). For Dejours (2003), bonds created in work are socially constitutive. Deranty regards this as rather startling in today's intellectual climate, but Jacques Lacan (2001) wrote about it at length after visits to England during the Second World War, where he had observed that task-orientated togetherness in the absence of a symbolic authority figure reduces primal anxiety, fosters self-esteem and replaces delinquency with more sociable forms of subjectivity. Lacan had not encountered today's managerialist climate and the pressure it can bring to bear on the individual worker, but the principle still holds. The division of labour itself, often the *bête noire* of the left, has an integrative subjectifying effect and leads to a sustainably civilized form of life. Centralizing the 'fear of the future' that is the core of the unique and intense form of anxiety that characterizes the time-binding human as it is beset by incessant visions of future prosperity or demise, Adorno (1967) had also argued that we must ground our analyses of society in this core affect of the contemporary individual, and the feedback loop between the two.

Work in the real world assuages our fear of the future and also shows us the reality of our own limits as individuals, forcing us with no pretence of persuasion or alternative possibilities and choices to become aware of our dependency on others and the consequences we would all suffer without each other. It is the major social site of the vital reality principle, where whatever initial feelings of empathy force-grown inside us in the Oedipal phase develop as we approach adulthood. Biological anxiety, and possible narcissism and hostility felt towards others, are sublimated to make way for the direct affective link of erotic attachment in a situation where no other way is possible; this principle can be extended to make the quintessentially illiberal formulation that total freedom is bad for us. In the non-guaranteed act of collectively transforming reality, the fear generated by the prospect of failure represented by a universal understanding of suffering can be faced as a collective. This tells us why *collective economic participation* – which of course does not mean enforced and alienated wage labour but probably does mean some division of labour – is far more important than *personalized social outcomes* in terms of social mobility, identity projects, charitable gifts or rights-based welfare. Social relations and subjective identities must be anchored in reality, in the sense that relations and identifications mediated through objects and objective tasks open up a vital layer of mediation in which a more rational and empathetic form of subjectivity can be constituted and reproduced. Changes in the work environment, the flexibilization and fragmentation of work, the abstraction of tasks as performance indicators, untrustworthy and overcritical management, being forced to work badly – which negates Sennett's (2008) 'craftsman's moment' – and the absence of work altogether can all corrode this vital dimension of subjectification and socialization. The automated and isolationist 'leisure society' cannot effectively replace collective participaton in socio-economic reality.

The neoliberal economic model is pathogenic in the sense that its system of organizing and promoting fearful competition between individuals negates all these vital mechanisms for quelling fear and transforming it, via the collective recognition and transcendence of personal limits, into erotic social bonds by establishing functional and social human collectives (Deranty, 2008). We must add to this analysis the fragmentation of life outside the workplace and the increasing fear generated by the struggle for identity in consumer culture, precarious housing, financial debt, an unstable finance-based economy and ecological problems. The autonomous, rational individual sought by the liberal tradition is in reality a bundle of nerves forged in an economically-grounded 'politics of anxiety', hoping for the success of the self in the space created by the relative demise of the other, expressed by Rousseau (1990) and Žižek (2008) as the shift from the healthy ego-building condition of *amour de soi* to the narcissistic and suspicious condition of *amour propre*. The obvious sociological corollary is the structural proposition that self-identified classes will see their own survival in the destruction of a lumpen group that needs to be cleared out of the way (Dean, 2009). However, because the lumpen group sense this fear and hatred from other groups, and, as individuals, from their immediate competitors, there is no guarantee that relations and interactions will remain benign. There is far more to the issue of social antagonism than the relationship of the potentially reflexive individual to the state and the media, which, in the long shadow of the post-war liberal left, preoccupies current sociological and criminological theory

We have already seen that the explosion of street crime in the 1980s in Britain and the USA followed the severe disruption of working-class economic functionality and socio-political solidarity. The migration into criminality has occurred as the old proletariat split into three basic subclasses (George, 1999), and liberal criminology's failure to theorize this phenomenon, alongside liberal politics' inability to do anything about it beyond cheerleading personal reflexivity, managing risk and creating artificial credit-based booms to buy time, is to a large extent the product of the abandonment of dialectical thinking and politics. Intellectual labourers, the manual working class and outcast scavengers have emerged around the mutated functions of planning/marketing, casualized manual labour and marginal resource provision. Each has its own way of life and set of normalized post-political subjectivities:

> The enlightened hedonism and liberal multiculturalism of the intellectual class, the populist fundamentalism of the working class, and the more extreme, singular forms of the outcast fractions …The outcome of this process is the gradual disintegration of social life proper, of a public space in which all three fractions could meet – and 'identity politics' in all its forms is a supplement for this loss … postmodern identity politics in the intellectual class, regressive populist fundamentalism in the working class, half-illegal initiatic groups (criminal gangs, religious sects, etc.) among the outcasts … The proletariat is thus divided into three, each part played off against the others: intellectual labourers full of prejudices against the 'redneck' workers; workers who display a populist hatred of intellectuals and outcasts, outcasts who are antagonistic to society as such. The old call of 'Proletarians, unite!' is thus more pertinent than ever: in the new conditions of 'post-industrial' capitalism, the unity of the three fractions of the working class is already their victory. (Žižek, 2010: 226)

Here is the climate in which the undialectical antagonistic forces of a divided working class generate the threat – and occasionally the reality just to remind us that this is no joke – of the post-social, post-political barbarism of disorder and invite the extra-economic forces of the barbarism of order to flood in to the vacuum to 'manage the risk' of the return of the Real, about which liberalism never speaks. It is in the act of confronting this return that the theories and research programmes of liberal sociology and criminology show themselves to be the perfect institutionalized forms of fetishistic disavowal. To disavow capitalism's dialectical Real, its fundamental social exchange relation of pure exploitation and antagonism, whilst continuing to act as if it exists, and according to its logical commands, is the actual constitutive process that prolongs the conditions in which harmful crime is a manifestation of the antagonism felt by all classes – but especially by the outcasts and the elite undertakers, both of whom operate more effectively in their own variants of the 'state of exception' – to the social as such, towards its nerve-wracking disappearance, yet, also, paradoxically, towards the obligations upon which it would insist should it return. What Žižek's analysis misses is the fact that in some cases, such as Nigerian fraudsters, where the problems of surplus capital absorption and unemployment are so acute that it is often some among the outcasts who fare better in finding low-grade casual work, whilst the educated youth who experience the greater problem in finding work have little choice – apart from politics, of course, as we have seen recently in north Africa – but to utilize their skills in the more advanced forms of illegal enterprise (Onwudiwe, 2004).

As we saw in the previous chapter, the Foucauldian discourse is one amongst many left-liberal modes of thought that flatten and render passive in the epistemological realm what is in the ontological realm an active dialectical force (Bosteels, 2010). Communism and socialism became bureaucratic, totalitarian and criminal because of the failure to recognize the ethical polarity of the genuine class struggle, of the 'us' and 'them' dichotomy that the politics of solidarity tried to grapple with and transcend, the 'state of things' that it initially tried to abolish. This is not to say, alongside iconic liberals such as Havel (1989), that there is some precious 'human order' that predates and ethically transcends politics, because of course the exploitative class relation and the quest for special liberty were both products of the dark side of the historical 'human order' that has always tried to avoid political regulation or transformation. This ethical dichotomy is structured by a transhistorical relationship based on the material exploitation of a large proportion of all working-class lives, whose labour power produces a surplus of capital to be controlled, traded, reinvested, lent out, 'securitized' and creamed off by business and financial elites in a process that guides the continuous expansion of the system of debt and profit. The real difference today is the expansion and splintering away from the main body of wage-earners of the social group excluded from the exploitative relationship and dependent on welfare and/or scavenging. As we shall see shortly in Chapter 8, the transcendental materialist position suggests, in a stroke of unequivocal radicalism, that, for those who are willing and active as subjects of the ethos of unregulated winner-takes-all competition at the core of the system's justificatory ideology, no matter which location in the social hierarchy they inhabit and operate in, their attachment to sentiments of supremacism and practices of exploitation is 'in their bones' and not amenable to simple cognitive/linguistic/discursive closure and renewal.

The return to politicized ethico-social polarity and struggle is precisely what liberalism does not want. The shift from the dialectical contradiction between exploiting and exploited classes, with their attendant and oppositional cultural and political forms, to the undialectical relation between the masses and the state – which are both ontologically nebulous, fluid and interchangeable, especially in the era where the state is a major employer and the only institution capable of regulating the excesses of the financial and business oligarchs – ensured that no potent dialectical tension is possible. It is a process of self-alienation and political flight from reality, from the masses, and from the dialectical tension in which a true oppositional political movement could find itself. The masses can sense this evacuation of politics, representation and hope from the socio-economic reality they inhabit, which fuels resignation, cynicism, instrumentalism, anhedonic nihilism, withdrawal and – from those who identify more strongly with exploitative practices and seek their personal means of entry into the fray – criminality and violence.

Liberals have carefully and cleverly recast the former class struggle as the struggle between the mass of creative, atomized and freely associative individuals against the 'deadly repressive system' (Bosteels, 2010: 40). No amount of denial can negate the fact that, in this Manichean dichotomy, there is, if we descend to the level of fundamental principles, a powerful elective affinity and ethical homology between the liberal left and the liberal right. At this level the two virtually reveal themselves to be one when they express themselves in their extreme libertarian variants. The liberal left distinguishes itself solely by insisting that the individual subjugates itself to some forced empathy with others and an agreement to contribute through progressive taxation to some 'safety-net' of minimal redistributive welfare practices, which of course are impossible to ensure under capitalism's everyday economic logic. This undialectical tension between state authority and individual freedom misses the utopian element that exists in the third space beyond them (Jameson, 2010). This is the space in which creativity and radical indeterminacy can exist, but, crucially, it has no natural systemic existence as a constant antithesis to the state's imposed order, an assumption that is axiomatic in radical liberal thinking (see for instance Arrigo & Barrett, 2008); thus it must be brought into existence as the product of a fully engaged dialectical struggle.

The dual demonization of the state and the individual that we find across the spectrum of liberal–conservative (neoliberal) thought today is the demonization of previous catastrophes created by the *barbarism of order* and the *barbarism of disorder* as they were applied as rival projects in the overall attempt to combine two utopian visions of order and freedom as civilization. However, in the absence of dialectical movement, reflected in both the socio-political organization of needs and subjectivity, 'progress' can exist solely as an undialectical balance between the two opposing forces of individual freedom and state authority, a point on a linear scale between them. The illusion of radical indeterminacy is created precisely at this point of equilibrium, appropriately distanced from the catastrophic poles of total order and disorder but skewed in the direction away from collective oppression towards total freedom, which helps to give the impression of momentum towards a free space. If the individual looks back from this point the catastrophe of order, being more recent in time, assumes the shape of a horrific memory whilst the older memory of the catastrophe of disorder – as we saw in Chapter 2, a Dark Age criminal oligarchy in an enduring state of exception – is now almost forgotten as a horrific memory and exists only as sanitized romantic fable, eminently recyclable as something infinitely preferable to the more recent and easily remembered modernist catastrophes of order. We are far enough from the *barbarism of disorder* for it once more to appear attractive, and the feeling of radical indeterminacy, of 'anything can happen and we are free to make it so', wells up as a sentiment of false security and fatal attraction on the path to a renewed vision of total freedom. Meanwhile, the potential *Third Space* has splintered as it was held frozen at the point of equilibrium where the illusion of momentum on the path to freedom was at its strongest, but the illusion is despoiled as the public witnesses an ugly struggle for social mobility between the individuals and interest groups in the identity politics mêlée that has replaced class politics.

This illusion is sustained only if we are persuaded to imagine that the class struggle is over and its traditional exploitative bourgeois subjectivities are extinct; to this end all traces of its former existence must be 'disappeared', written over in academic and popular culture by the masses/state substitute. At the political level this undialectical disjunction between the masses and the state is ideologically maintained by the narrative of liberal democracy; a continuous noble struggle against the totalitarianism that would inevitably follow any serious seizure of power by the masses. Sometimes, from a coyly hidden perspective, it's difficult to tell the liberal position from Ortega y Gasset's (1985) quintessentially conservative jeremiad of the 'tyranny of the masses'. In this narrative, murderous military interventions can be justified on the ethical grounds of eliminating or preventing something far worse. This is the descent of politics into comedic melodrama, which portrays the likes of Bush, Blair, Sarkozy and Berlusconi primarily as the villains of the state, rather than what they are, individual representatives of the neoliberal elite class. The fact that for decades after the Second World War some states in western Europe had at least reached a compromise with capital and shifted partially in the direction of popular democracy, economic management, political education and redistribution, is absent from the popular narrative. The idea that although the state has machinery to at least partially protect the masses against the extremes of everyday personal harm, it is in its current configuration and major structural dealings the continuation of the unidimensional bourgeois state, designed and developed as a deep 'security state' to protect the power and property of an elite class, has been replaced by the idea of the state as intrinsically and inevitably totalitarian, to be held in check by the minimization of its spheres of operation whilst its latent power is retained. This, in turn, clears space for further bourgeois special liberty, which, in order to flourish, demands the further protection of the 'security state'. Under current political arrangements it is impossible to break into this loop.

The further idea that the state could become a popular democratic form, and could be reconfigured to act in a way entirely different to its current bourgeois form – in a non-state-like way (Žižek, 2010b) – is in liberal circles virtually forbidden, replaced by endless quasi-critical explorations of 'governmentality' that cast its motives and social technologies into doubt whilst never quite advocating its complete annexation and reconfiguration. The mass/state dichotomy must hold, and what Bosteels calls the 'the melodramatic purification and eventual depoliticization of antagonism' (2010: 46) must take centre stage, even though it is an absurd epistemological split of an ontologically and ethically unified whole; the bourgeois individual operating exploitatively in an environment politically neutralized and made safe by his bureaucratic protector. In the melodrama of individual versus state, of multitude versus Empire, of resistance versus totalitarian power, of slippery signified versus insistent signifier, of anarchic desire versus disciplinary technology and so on, the reality of the mass split by class interests is overwhelmed by the ideology of the multitude unified by an *a priori* orientation to unresolvable forms of resistance. The 'third party', the economically and culturally insecure, exploited, politically neutralized, badly educated and minimally protected class – itself divided into the three antagonistic sections outlined above – is airbrushed from its rightful position in the picture as the antagonistic pole in the currently inert but potentially active dialectical relation that still structures capitalism. This absence of dialectical thinking is part of the general negligence of historical processes and social-structural tensions by the liberal-postmodernist, culturalist and constitutionalist turns in sociology since the 1980s, to which criminological theory, as an importer discipline, has capitulated with barely a whimper of protest. The protests directed at these discourses have been powerful and erudite – Ricoeur (1984), for instance, attacked the symbolic interactionist and structuralist-based doctrines as overly synchronic, ignoring the diachronic movement over time, objectifying time in structural dynamics and removing from view the human ability to narrativize and understand a story – yet their pages have been systematically torn out of the official liberal-left hymnbook.

What is the dialectic, and, if it is as nonsensical and politically destructive as some liberals and even analytical Marxists say (see for instance Cohen, 2002), why should we wish its return? It's not something invented by Marxists in those heady days of the nineteenth century when revolution seemed imminent and inevitable. A very crude but quite useful basic metaphor is the warp drive engine in the Starship Enterprise; the contradictory opposites of matter and anti-matter collide to produce a synthetic energy that warps the normality of space–time in front of the ship, allowing it to proceed through this abnormality to its destination. Playful futuristic metaphors aside, however, the concept has a long and venerable history (Ollman, 2003), and it seems to have its origin and development in social thought, so it is not something inappropriately borrowed from outside, such as Foucault's importation of the automatic power-resistance reaction from Newtonian physics. In Aristotle's concept of *peripeteia* we see the mystery of the reorganization of the world into new dialectical opposites, which is accompanied by the *pathos* of the duality of cruelty and renewal, but it is his concept of *anagnorisis*, a metaphor that deals with the ebbing and flowing of recognition that occurs between parents and children during times of disruption and change, that speaks loudly of the disruption in social relations at the birth of capitalism. In fact the metaphor regains a literal basis in concrete reality, where the antagonist becomes a blood relation rather than an external enemy; the blind, narcissistic bonding of traditional communities and families hide potential enemies who emerge during periods of disruption. It is a sad and disturbing time, but also a point at which in the transformation of the structure of *anagnorisis* a substantial shot of energy is generated and reveals itself as some-thing that can be harnessed as a propellant in the line of flight to economic progress and the renewal of relations on a different plane. The pathos of dissolution can be overwhelmed by the heady potential of energetic socio-economic renewal powered by the dialectical tension of antagonism and freedom in a relation that 'is as divisive as it is associative, and can thus be said to embody Eros and Thanatos alike' (Jameson, 2010: 509).

As families and clans lose their politico-cultural reproductive grip on history and cease to be the building-blocks of society they lose their own dialectical opposition as the loci of security and destiny, as both structuring institutions and agents of change, but what replaces this is the dialectical tension between the nostalgia for guaranteed recognition and the threat of insignificance that befalls the lone individual swept up in the competition of market performance. It is important to remember this principle as one of the bases for the theory of the pseudo-pacification process and the expla-nation of the shape of modernist criminal subjectivity that will be explained in the penultimate chapter. In the meantime, we can note the introduction of a markedly powerful dialectical force, which is still a mainstay of capital-ist culture. Jameson reminds us that:

> Hegel still sensed this at the dawn of the bourgeois era when he wrote out several versions of the dialectic of the Master and the Slave, as the fundamental struggle that eventuates in the demand for the recognition of 'my' freedom. It is a demand which in a world of proliferating and indistinct identities involves a good deal more than the mere naming of a person; it includes the acknowledgement of the clan itself, something Hegel's language knows even if he does not. Anagnorisis thus designates an event – one around which is also a punctual contact or encounter, struggle or confrontation, from which hierarchy and a whole map of higher and lower social groups necessarily emerge; it is preeminently the place of the other, just as peripeteia is the place of time, and pathos is the fate of the body. (2010: 509/10)

It represents a renewed attempt by those looking up at the dissolving familial-social edifice above them to become 'free men' in an ancient, underlying and uninterrupted history where this freedom and status is achieved only on the back of the backbreaking labour of slave and serf classes (de Ste Croix, 1981). Nostalgia for the family and clan is part of the depoliticization process and the conservative organicization of working-class politics. In the same way today, in the wake of the abject failure of communism and the erosion of a social democracy that relies on the closed national political economy in the face of the irreversible process of an open global economy, all we have left are Gray's (1998) cultural-anthropological traditions, a return to the family, clan and Burkean organic tradition. In an important sense these traditions are ways of ironing out the contradictions that constitute the dialectic. This is usually done by making a decision between idealism and materialism. Jacques Barzun's *From Dawn to Decadence* (2001) lies alongside Daniel Bell's *Cultural Contradictions of Capitalism* (1978) as a classic conservative declinist work focused exclusively on the waning of the organic tradition's culturally constituted and reproduced ideals. However, as much as Barzun and Bell were wrong about the nobility of conservative ideals, the advocates of the counter-culture and identity politics, in their ill-considered and impetuous efforts to abolish everything, failed to distinguish between the ideals that were being reproduced – which were indeed divisive, exploitative and supremacist masquerading as unifying, stabilizing and just – and the institutional forms in their material contexts that are capable of cultural reproduction *per se*; families, work, unions, schools, communities and so on (Dean, 2009; Deranty, 2008); the liberal left did not shoot the messenger, but, in an act of even greater absurdity, shot the messenger's horse. If the dialectic is at root psychosocial, which its ancient origins suggest, the destruction of the social stalls the dialectic at the same time as it threatens the process of individuation itself, as the work of Stiegler (2010a) and Simondon (1964) demonstrates. For Adorno (1967), in this state of separation and frozen antagonism people cannot recognize society in themselves nor themselves in society. Capitalism is unique, as Jameson argues, insofar as it is 'a group organized by individuality and separation or atomization rather than any of the traditional modes of group unification' (2010: 55). It powers forward with the destructive energy of negative dialectics, ceaselessly negating all ethico-social positivities until all that is left is its immensely powerful destructive energy (Adorno, ibid.). All that atomized individuals can do is to carry on endlessly constructing and naming temporary, rootless, imagined collectives and identities in the midst of the destruction.

Before liberalism flattened and stalled the historical process, a cascade of positive dialectical oppositions could be listed; rich/poor, subject/object and so on. Luhmann (1986) posits foundational binaries as the incommensurable basal codes of various institutions; guilty/innocent in law, true/false in science, profit/loss in economics and so on, in a structure of multiple enclosed dialectics that are becalmed, static and uncommunicative in the social world but active and reproductive in their own institutional fields. In doing so he naturalizes these fragmented binary divisions and also becalms the foundational binary opposition of good/evil. Dialectical power can be generated by any opposition, but, humans being what they are, with their origin in the traumatic encounter with the Real, there is always a tendency to locate the oppositional forms on the good/evil axis, which affords them ethical positivity and weight. 'Opposition' seems to be thought of as the relation between essential and inessential, or greater and lesser, or lighter and darker terms, which reveals an original Manicheanism. Here 'law and crime' lies as a prime example, a direct institutionalized manifestation of the generative terms good and evil, which are primary proto-symbols in the indelible emotional bases of the psyche.

However, all possible axes are intersected by the principal social dialectic, the Hegelian Master–Slave opposition, the root of class societies and a dualism intrinsically connected to the primary sense of good and evil; that the freedom of the slave is good and the oppression of the master is evil, and that the slave is good because she seeks emancipation and the master evil because she wants to oppress, is an archetype that even the postmodernists could not escape as an ethical foundation for their thinking. It was Hegel who asked the most prescient question of the basic relation that constitutes the social dialectic. The oppositional and centrifugal forces generated by the distinction and tension between the two are obvious, but what is the attractor that generates the centripetal counter-force which retains the opposites as a pair? For Hegel, as we saw in Chapter 1, it was the fact that the Master needed the Slave's authorization of his power and was thus eternally dependent on the Slave's judgements, and, we could add, in the act of judging the Master the Slave embraces a power that is socially inert yet politically powerful. Despite this potential – or we might suspect because of it – the 'epistemological repression' (Jameson, 2010: 165) of advanced capitalism's intellectual paradigms and popular cultural forms has delinked the social and the cultural from political economy. Yet there can be no sense of individual or social reality and a stable, energetic dialectical relationship between the two unless there is some sort of exercise in politically organized collective production and distribution at the heart of the community. If the wealthy and powerful global elite can prevent such collective systems getting off the ground, simply by controlling financial investment and disrupting embryonic political systems with democratic potential, the position of social distinction and financial mega-rewards remains to be won by individual entrepreneurs. Despite the ostensibly sophisticated cosmopolitan identities and relations that configure late modernity:

What is paradoxical is that the crudest forms of ideology seem to have returned, and that in our own public life an older vulgar Marxism would have no need of the hypersubtleties of the Frankfurt School and of negative dialectics, let alone of deconstruction, to identify and unmask the simplest and most class-conscious motive at work, from Reaganism and Thatcherism down to our own politicians: to lower taxes so that rich people can keep more of their money, a simple principle about which what is surprising is that so few people find it surprising anymore, and what is scandalous, in the universality of market values, is the way it goes without saying and scarcely scandalizes anyone. (Jameson, 2010: 285)

The ideology of human beings as equivalences in the market system, able 'freely' to sell their labour-power or take up entrepreneurial opportunities as formally equal individuals, masks this class relation and the fundamental desire of incorporated individuals to transcend formal equality to achieve positions of economically derived and socio-culturally affirmed concrete domination and the special liberty it makes possible. Thus the concrete hierarchy appears meritocratic and just, almost coincidental to the system itself.

The hierarchy has also been ideologically naturalized to the extent that it seems unassailable. It does not take real poverty close to the absolute for people to be driven by the hard-wired memory of its past realities (Ehrenreich, 1997). Fearful, anxious populations vote on economic matters before all others. Today the ideology that capitalism is the only way to universal affluence is, despite the system's relative inequalities, stronger than ever. This is despite the fact that, as Robert Kurz (1991) and Giovanni Arrighi (1994) have argued, capitalism has lost its ability to produce and distribute new surplus value from standard processes of labour, production and consumption. Triumphant capitalism maintains its public image as the economic system *par excellence* by consigning huge swathes of the world's population to non-productivity and creating debt-generated paper money in a carousel of speculation, moneylending and financial trading. China and India are the anomalies, but – partially because, rather than investing in their own public infrastructure, their governments prefer to send capital over to the West to fund speculative financial trading and service-industry wages to buy their cheap goods – poverty still remains despite their emergence as economic powerhouses. It is doubtful that the bulk of their working populations will ever experience the affluence the Western proletariat did during the post-war settlement era. The extreme tension between the ideology of affluence, opportunity and freedom and the system's concrete inability to produce new surplus value at anything like the exponential rate of its heyday has created the new phenomenon of increasing illegality as the result of a frantic attempt to reproduce the ideological norm and the classic liberal identity of the successful, independent, free-trading entrepreneur. We must suspect that crime is tacitly if rather begrudgingly accepted, for its services rendered to the maintenance of the ideological norm and for providing the safe political option; when it gets down to the nitty-gritty, the system's political managers would rather contend with Pablo Escobar than with Lenin. The security and concrete rights offered by politico-economic collectivism – with the possible result of the deceleration of the economic dynamic and the loss of opportunities to invest, speculate and acquire – terrify liberal capitalism more than crime, war and permanent unrest. These are risks worth taking, the price of the classical-liberal first principle of individual economic freedom in free markets, which ethically opposes the collective freedom of whole populations to control their own destinies and change the economic, cultural and social coordinates of their existence.

Crime functions economically as a means of supplementing saturated markets, and, as long as it is kept in the public eye, ideologically in sustaining the cult of independent individualism and entrepreneurialism in opposition to all forms of collectivism. At the same time, it exists far too close to the underlying Real for comfort. We have known since Durkheim that crime marks out moral boundaries, even though his fatal mistake was to place the boundary at the marginal point beyond which we must not step rather than the point at which we enter the inner core of the obscene Real. The ideology of the human as an eternal sinner has served the system well, and demonstrable concrete examples can only help to sustain its legitimacy as the ultimate historical form of freedom, diversity and tolerance, and justify the authority it needs to contain its Real, the restless and destructive socio-economic dynamic forces within its functional multi-layered insulation, the vices that, as Mandeville (1970) recognized all those years ago, are cultivated to create the economic 'virtues' of competition and wealth and held in check by a thin insulating layer of morality and law. However, the Real is neither natural nor transhistorical, as Jameson reminds us:

> As for the conviction about the sinfulness of human nature, and although it might well seem to be a demonstrable empirical fact that human animals are naturally vicious and violent and that nothing good can come of them, it also might be well to remind ourselves that that is an ideology too (and a peculiarly moralizing and religious one at that). The fact that cooperation and the achievement of a collective ethos are at best fragile achievements,

at once subject to the lures of private consumption and greed and the destabilizations of cynical realpolitik, cannot strip them of the honor of having occasionally existed. (2010: 387)

Acquisitive criminality is a means of mimicking and practicing in unrefined ways this primary bourgeois ideology in paraspaces beyond the system's mainstream politico-legal and economic institutions. All this energy is now produced in the broadest of arenas as national/global tension is brought into play. The term 'glocalization' (Robertson, 1995) has been used by criminologists to describe the energetic effects of undialectical tensions operating in local markets that act as cultural and economic nodes in global economies (Hobbs, 1998), even though, in the post-war rush to erase Hegelian, Marxist and Freudian ideas from the intellectual canon (see Sumner, 1994), it has not been seriously analysed in dialectical terms. Actors in these markets energize the nodes of what could be a local/global dialectic with transformative potential beyond the innocuous cultural interchange of the 'cosmopolis', but in the social and political senses they feel part of neither. Yet, these criminals are not 'more alienated' than others, they simply practice the fundamental capitalist exchange relation – to acquire from the other a surplus, as large as possible, in relation to what one gives – in a state of unrelieved alienation in the raw rather than under the cover of contrived ethical symbolism. Like it or not, this cauldron of psychosocial and economic tension and energy, generated in the politically and historically stagnant space of the stalled dialectic, is capitalism's fundamental site of subjectification. The problem for social science in general, and criminology in particular, has been a feasible concept of subjectivity-in-alienation, one that does not have to make invidious positive choices between extremes of innate goodness or innate evil, determinism or freedom, essence or contingency and so on. As we shall see shortly, transcendental materialism seems to provide a way out of the impasse.

THE TRANSCENDENTAL MATERIALIST SUBJECT

Criminological theory can proceed no further until, using its own data gathered in empirical explorations of crime and harm, it ceases to be a pure importer discipline, a mere rendezvous for concepts produced in other disciplines, and begins to construct its own theoretical accounts of the relationships between the individual, the social, culture, politics and economy. Sociology sometimes presents itself as a productive exporter discipline, but the pre-existence of most of its ontological conceptions of human nature and human relations – and this includes the radically indeterminate anti-ontological ontology of radical liberalism and postmodernism – in disciplines such as anthropology, philosophy, political theory and psychology suggests that this judgement might be rather misleading. If this is true, then the theoretical wings of both criminology and sociology must join forces to construct new ontological syntheses and adjust their research programmes according to the need to use both inductive and deductive methods to gather evidence for new ideas. This does not simply mean rejecting everything from the internal and external intellectual traditions that have sustained the disciplines; on the contrary, as we have seen in previous chapters, it means recalling some rejected ideas and evaluating their possible contributions. This is the worst time to make such a suggestion; in Britain new government-led research management and funding programmes are attempting to force atheoretical pragmatism and abstracted empiricism on the social sciences in an effort to ensure that the squabbling cousins of neoliberalism and social liberalism continue to mark the oppositional boundaries. The scramble for the centre-ground that has characterized post-ideological politics since the 1980s now rules the social sciences. The end of history did not happen, but in a mass act of fetishistic disavowal we must continue to *act* as if it did happen, and persuading people to *think* that indeed it did end, and that progress is possible only by rearranging relations between the inhabitants of its flood plain, is the supporting role allocated to our intellectual institutions.

At the core of all intellectual inquiry in the humanities and social sciences is the ontology of the subject, and this is where we have experienced the greatest failure. Where can criminological theory, with a critical eye on sociological theory, begin its process of revision? In one short chapter there is space only for a few suggestions for what must be a collective effort, but the first encounter is with the thorny issue of biology. We cannot continue to reject this dimension of human existence as if it does not exist, as if it represents some form of universal soft determinism that obstructs our existential choices, dreams and ethico-cultural systems, and, as such, is just too horrific to contemplate. Many textbooks begin with grim warnings about the abuse of biological research and theory in racist, supremacist and imperialist discourses, especially the cold, mechanistic, amoral brutality at the heart of Darwin's theory of evolution. Liberal discourses take great pains to make us aware of the evils of the eugenics movements and the ethnic supremacism at the heart of Nazism, which led to the Holocaust, an act of barbarism so heinous that it still defies our understanding; no single discourse, from Arendt's (1963) banality of evil through Adorno's (1993) authoritarian personality and Stern's (1975) atavistic mystical rhetoric to Bauman's (1991) anti-modernism can capture the true horror of this event. Despite this, we cannot deny our existence as biological beings. Although it's foolish to portray human beings as 'clever automatons' who can do little more than respond in calculating utilitarian ways to unconscious evolutionary drives hard-wired into each individual, as Kanazawa (2008) attempts to do in a way that is almost comically mechanistic, nor can we deny the fact that biological impulses in their primal as well as their more sophisticated emotional forms influence the way we feel, think and act (Damasio, 2003). Whatever we do, and no matter how self-satisfied we become with our creative agency and cultural and social sophistication, we have to deal with the fact that our existence is rooted in biology, with the fact that we are first and foremost organic 'things' who had no say at all about our basic material construction and our primal drives.

However, this immutable fact is too easily used as an excuse for the continuation of conservative hegemony. Just as moral realism has been used to justify and reproduce hegemonic power and justify *realpolitik*, so has scientific realism. It's hard to swallow the claim made by those who openly admit to being conservatives that their scientific methods and propositions are neutral and objective, but, nevertheless, we have to admit that all human beings, including those who commit crime, are indeed 'flesh and blood … with brains, genes, hormones and an evolutionary history' (Walsh & Beaver, 2009: 8). We are indeed much more than free-floating ciphers in symbolic systems or entirely autonomous choice-makers in complete possession and control of our own desires and intentions. Walsh and Beaver eschew what biologists and biopsychologists call *preformationism* and readily admit that pre-existing evolutionary drives, behaviours and developmental trajectories interact in complex ways with environmental factors. The biology/environment relation has of course often been defined as a hopeless chicken and egg argument, but if we accept Lacan's (2001) principle of prematuration, which captures the epicentre of our existence as our innate helplessness at birth and our total reliance on others for recognition, security and sustenance, we have to err towards the probability that in our particular case this particular egg came first. The aftermath of natural disasters proves time and time again that, despite our tendency to degenerate into antagonism, and despite our existence as unique individuals with a tendency to narcissistic self-aggrandizement, we are at root social, communicative creatures who desperately need each other as an enduring response to both survival and any worthwhile existence beyond it in a hostile and amoral world of natural forces capable of destroying thousands of us with a flick of its tail.

The opposite radical liberal extreme is explored by Crewe and Lippens (2009), for whom existentialism is authenticity and freedom, and thus neither scientific nor moral inquiry can capture the essence of the human being, which is about choices made in the individual life project. Uniquely, we can inquire into our own being, about what it means to be, and as one searches for one's own ethical path there is no 'causation'. The existential injunction implores us to transcend other-driven inauthentic behaviour and, following Kierkegaard and Nietzsche, exhorts the free individual to transcend the limitations of biological drive and extant universal morality. This echoes Lacan's 'ethics of the Real' (Eagleton, 2009), except for the crucial prerequisite that for Lacan the entry of the primary narcissist into the Symbolic Order and a traumatic encounter with the Real as the congealed unspoken core of ideology are essential if the individual is to transcend primary narcissism and free choice is to produce civilized actions, which means that the existentialist position ignores the *prerequisites for freedom* outlined by Kant, Hegel and Lacan. Sartre's (1957) rejection of the 'thing' as the noumenon belies the whole thingness of being in the body, its neurological system and the external object world, both of which irrupt on the senses as the Real (see Hall et al., 2008). The existentialist claim that as a being becomes 'for itself' it can reject the self that has been constructed, or at least potentially influenced in its self-conception, by internal and external forces, the 'in-itself', is a powerful one. So is the accompanying injunction that we have no choice but to be free, and to achieve freedom we must engage politically with structures of oppression. It is perhaps an understatement to suggest that this represents most firmly the 'agency' side of the structure and agency debate in sociology.

However, this is itself a universal moral injunction produced and disseminated by a group of philosophers-as-political-activists. We are being told what is good for us, and tricked into thinking that it is a product of our own free choice. Advertising works on a similar principle, as does capitalist ideology in general, by placing the authentic sovereign being at the heart of politics and culture and positing what exists as the restrictive product of past choices. The idea that we can construct our own identities and life-projects within extant social structures is the perfect excuse to leave social structures as they are, to avoid challenging concentrations of wealth and power, and to avoid judging harshly those who oppress us on the principle that our judgements will have little effect on beings who will simply continue to construct their own life projects of their own free will. Politics is shifted onto the undialectical axis discussed in the previous chapter, and reduced to the prelectorial persuasion of potentially free individuals who believe they are free before they have organized social and politico-economic life in a way that allows them to reach their potential. Existentialism is a quintessential act of fetishistic disavowal driven by political catastrophism, the insertion of a dream of freedom found at the point just before a feasible measure of concrete freedom could be achieved by transforming the ideological, material and psychosocial coordinates of our existence, thus preventing the forcefulness and sacrifice that might be needed to actually change anything. In the social liberal realm its usefulness lies in preventing the demand for change going too far, a demand that, were it to be let back out of the box, would add weight to the shift from the undialectical relation to the dialectic itself.

We must avoid the habit of portraying all biologists as eugenicists and crypto-Nazis, but at the same time we must remember that when biology asserts itself into social matters it has form in degenerating into the type of pseudo-science that can grant authority to those in dominant cultural and political positions. Such scientific authority in the hands of racist-nationalists, military imperialists and other types of supremacist can produce catastrophic results, which, alongside the disasters that followed the Stalinists' attempt to impose egalitarianism on the masses whilst running a brutally inegalitarian bureaucratic state, is the kernel of truth in the political catastrophists' ideology. Genes do not determine but modulate our responses to and interactions with our environment, but of course environments are multi-dimensional and quite rapid shifts in mass behaviour have occurred without the slow process of genetic mutation having had time to take place. We might have to settle on the Freudian principle that genetic drives are very strong in some primary areas, such as sexual reproduction and physical survival, but quite weak and fragmented in the dimension of complex desires, personality traits and stimulus to action. The bridge between crude genetic drives and the symbolic seems to be the tree of emotions, the sophisticated part of our neurology which can deal with perceptions, responses and motivations that are far more complex than those which can be handled by the protein molecules that constitute genes (Damasio, 2003). Biocriminology's soft determinism is based on the principle that our early experiences are, when the brain is in its most impressionable developmental stages, engraved in neural networks that shape our behavioural trends and personality traits throughout the life-course. Once installed and operative they are not easily altered, yet, religious conversion, which involves the immersion of the self in a newly found symbolic order, can almost overnight both temper and sublimate these determining forces (Maruna, 2001), in effect 'changing' them in ways that eventually lead to reformed behavioural trends and personality traits. Crime and homicide rates move up and down according to shifts in political economy and culture (Reiner, 2007), which would suggest that radically altering hegemonic ideologies and establishing and reproducing stable and benign macro-environments are together conducive to beneficial child development because they provide the vital material and cultural support that primary caregivers need to perform their tasks. Primary caregivers who 'struggle against the odds' eventually to succeed must be admired, but in many ways social life is a percentage game, and we should not be too surprised that many buckle under the strain of living in unfavourable – and indeed sometimes brutalizing (see Stein, 2007) – material and cultural environments.

The problem is that biologists have a crude notion of the 'environment' as material. In the industrialized West the old environmental challenges and problems that might well have created basic genetic traits as responses have all but disappeared. This would suggest that such traits are redundant, yet they seem to persist; has evolution failed, or has it been suspended? Was cheating and exploiting once an adaptive genetic behavioural trait, once essential for survival, which is now turning on us and wreaking destruction? Perhaps; the Odyssean trickster was indeed a cultural hero in Dark Age Greece in the transition between the Mycenaean and Classical periods (Adorno & Horkheimer, 1992), but it was countered by the Platonic philosophy of moral realism and its injunction to strive for states of perfection as expressed by the realm of transcendental forms. But of course these 'traits' are always latent, not perpetually active. What stimulates our emotions, and what appear in our minds as possible choices in response to these provocations, are always mediated by culture and ideology, which is forgotten not only by genetic determinists but also by the behaviorists whose 'operant conditioning' is the mechanistic product of a balance of anticipated rewards and punishments. There is no way we can bypass the crucial role played by culture and ideology by recourse to genetic drives, behaviorist conditioning or pure autonomous rationality and choice.

In Walsh and Beaver's (2009) conservative terms, the 'cheats and exploiters' who refuse to comply with the social contract should be criminalized and receive the attention of criminology. On the other hand they also argue that positive and benign traits such as altruism, nurturance and empathy, also important to evolutionary survival because they demand the effective parenting and nurturing of future generations in preparation for the essential quality of sociability, must be encouraged by culture. However, biocriminologists, in their haste to portray our Western tradition as intrinsically good and crime and criminals as pathological aberrations produced by faulty socialization, belie the sophistication of the underlying capitalist economic system and its attendant cultural politics, which, as every economically literate thinker knows (see Akerloff & Shiller, 2009; Keynes, 1935), is based on the intrinsically volatile and risk-laden technique of stimulating vices and attempting to harness them, through the intermediary of anxiety- and envy-inducing socio-symbolic competition, to economic growth (Hall, 2007). The conservative biocriminologists make the fatal mistake of *naturalizing vices* and *culturalizing virtues*, whereas the liberal left make the equally fatal mistake of *naturalizing virtues* and *culturalizing vices*. In fact capitalism's co-evolutionary system constructs and reproduces in its multiple interactive dimensions (Harvey, 2010) both the vices and the virtues that are required to generate the constant undialectical tension that preserves the system yet drives it forward with immense force on a non-transformative trajectory. The systematic manifestation of crude latent drives provides the human energy for capitalism's dynamism, energy so immense that no alternative economic system can compete with capitalism in the art of generating it. Such energy requires stringent cultural and legal regulation, and such is the tension between the stimulated energy and the repression it requires to sublimate it into a socially acceptable and economically functional form that the system constantly teeters on a tightrope from which it can fall into either the *barbarism of order* or the *barbarism of disorder*. The specific types of fear that are provoked by these potentials underpin the two main 'catastrophist' liberal and conservative discourses in the allegedly rational-scientific discipline of criminology.

In a further publication Walsh (2009) ascribes strong biological determining factors to human behaviour one minute and the next argues that Nazism, although biological roots were 'tapped into', was the product of the politicized social and psychological 'mechanisms' that promoted nation-alistic sentiments and brutal genocidal actions. When it suits him, culture and politics become vices. Where the liberal left demonize biology, the conservative right demonize political and historical change, preferring to stick with the slow evolution of the organic cultural tradition. The notion that the liberal-capitalist West is innocent of brutality is risible (Seymour, 2008), and in its formative and imperialist decades its murderousness rivalled that of Nazism and Stalinism (Davis, 2002). However, Walsh's standard conception of mechanistic drives cathected to fixed objects is mis-leading because instincts and drives lack that sort of symbolic precision. Insecurity and fear can be attached to an infinite variety of objects and solutions – the individual can develop a 'phobia' about almost anything – and thus 'tribalism and xenophobia' do not have 'biological underpinnings' (Walsh, 2009: 291); these prejudices are culturally and politically mediated solutions to specific objects initially symbolized as threats in specific mate-rial and geopolitical circumstances, and culturally reproduced thereafter by the practice of commemoration. On its own and in its primary form, the basic neurological response to stimuli caused by combinations of experi-ence and symbolism is as nebulous as it is powerful, and it cannot connect to objects or conjure up solutions with such precision. Even Jung's arche-types lack the symbolic precision proposed by Walsh. The mediating and formalizing tasks are performed by culture and ideology. Where Walsh is correct, however, is in his claim that '[f]lesh and blood people commit crimes, not disembodied "social factors"' (2009: 292). However, he con-cludes that the bio-medical treatment of symptoms rather than root causes is appropriate because it is the medical model's tried and tested method. Here the conservative displays the same fear as the liberal, fear of the potentially catastrophic consequences of political intervention in what they regard as natural human inequality. What we need to do is move away from traditional ontological axioms; the conservatives' mechanistic notion of the hard-wired precision archetype, the classical liberal/neoliberal notion of the behaviorist individual conditioned by rewards and punishments, and the left-liberal notion of radical indeterminacy. Instead we must move forward to investigate the interface between experience, culture, ideology and the neurological system; the third human dimension where, in Hegel's term, *the spirit is a bone*.

Are we creatures out of time, trapped in obsolete and increasingly destructive genetic behavioural patterns? This seems unlikely because sym-bolism can create surrogate environments of complex stimuli that demand responses that are far too rapid and flexible for the cumbersome genetic mechanism. Most post-Socratic Greek philosophers were comfortable with the notion of primitive instincts, which was widespread in the literature and poetry, especially the Homeric legends and other epic tales of Dark-Age Greece. Socrates himself, when told by his physician that he had the face of a brutal, lascivious drunk, accepted this as his true nature, but was also proud that he had used his rational mind, foresight and sensibilities to overcome it and become what he was. Socrates presaged what we know now, that where genes are vehicles for crude drives and behaviours, it is the more sophisticated and flexible emotions or 'sensibilities' that can communicate with the more complex cultural world of symbolism. It is quite possible for symbolism to be used in ideological ways to deny the reality of 'environmental challenges' that would demand genetic and neurologically installed response patterns; in the comforting world of ideological symbolism we can sleepwalk to disaster. Conversely, in the grip of the politics of objectless anxiety where the function of ideological symbolism can instantaneously flip from the mode of comfort to the mode of extreme provocation and reaction, we can respond viscerally to things or 'environmental challenges' that are quite simply not there. Soft genetic and neural determinism, even where they take account of the complexity of neural pathways, cannot cope with symbolic systems and the flexibility of everyday emotional responses. Only in cases of extreme abuse and terror are neural pathways etched so firmly and deeply in young individuals that they cannot be overcome and reconfigured by a shift in symbolism and emotional experience (Stein, 2007). Thus biocriminologists tend to define the norm by its extremes, and the result is the overprediction of crime, the reduction of criminogenesis to early family experiences, the inability to explain crime committed throughout the social structure by individuals who function 'normally', and a reluctance to affirm the importance of cultural change and economic stability in the reduction of crime.

Jones (2008) argues that the division between psychology and sociology is untenable. Sixty per cent of prisoners are alleged to suffer from 'personality disorders', and the common motif here is that 'normal' modes of cognition and perception are accompanied by unpredictable and often hostile emotional responses to environmental stimuli. Most seem to have suffered 'negative life events' and childhoods deprived of love and security, often characterized by normalized violence. Moffitt (2003) distinguished between adolescent limited (AL) offenders and life-course persistent (LCP) offenders, the latter being those who have suffered emotional problems since early childhood. Many in this category suffer from mental health problems and they seem to have lost the sense of being autonomous individuals in relations with others and their environment. This echoes the theory of 'attachment disorder' and its claim that emotional attuning with parents or caregivers is essential (Bowlby, 1983). However, we do not have to disagree with these orthodox psychosocial theories to note that these 'chaotic' criminals represent the unsuccessful ones who keep getting caught, whose anti-social behaviour has not been insulated, ordered and harnessed in the most efficient way, and whose 'problems' become hidden, harnessed and potent drives. On the other hand, moderately and highly successful criminals, and corrupt operators throughout the social order, who have almost entirely escaped the clinical psychologists' radar, seem to function as social, cultural and economic beings at a higher level of dynamic intensity, where systematically incited anti-social energies are sublimated and harnessed into economically efficient operations at the minimal level of ethical and social acceptability. Their 'problems' of hostility and aggression have become hidden, harnessed and potent drives, producing competitive success rather than chaotic life-courses.

Jones (2008) goes on to argue that the individual's sense of autonomy can develop only in relations with others. We need, he argues, to integrate the individual personality with an understanding of how the 'provocation of shame' operates in its historical, cultural and socio-economic macro-contexts. Male violence is associated with shame and humiliation, and this can be linked to the super-ego variation and modern cultural forms of honour (see Winlow & Hall, 2009b). Men, because of the expectations placed upon them and internalized in the super-ego, are the least adept at coping with shame and the most vulnerable to sleights. What Jones describes as 'desperately bleak family lives' (2008: 252), often the product of being born to meet parents' own temporary needs and then rejected, is true enough, but we must ask the question that if, as Nightingale (1993) argued in his classic ethnography, many young males are receiving brutal treatment in these families to 'toughen them up', for what are they being toughened up? Is the harsh outside world simply a product of the parents' paranoid imaginations? Without a doubt, preparation for the harsh outside world is preparation for a socio-economic reality whose real harshness exists in different ways that correspond to different social spaces and economic sectors. Tying them all together is the fundamental capitalist-modernist form of competitive individualism, the primary economic energy source predicated on the systematic withdrawal of modes of security.

The messy, anxious human subject shot through with tense, conflictive emotions and desires has been ignored in favour of either the pure, rational, autonomous subject or the pure social construction. There can be no general theory of crime from either psychology or sociology, but it might be possible to construct a multi-layered theory of criminogenic conditions and experiences that at least offer explanations for many forms of harmful crime,

which is sorely needed in today's climate of intellectually rudderless pragmatism. Gadd and Jefferson (2007) are right that the human subject is
always internally complex and socially situated, but this does not diminish
the fact that some internal conflicts are more crucial than others, or that
some social situations, expressed as intersections between macro and micro
contexts, are more criminogenic than others. There are patterns and com-
monalities that can be discerned despite the complexity. They are also right
to suggest that we must bring back motives alongside the standard liberal
critique of control and criminalization, and we must 'convert voyeurism to
proper understanding' (2007: 2). Criminal tendencies are the products of
the same psychosocial processes that characterize all human beings; this is in
broad agreement with Stein's (2007) principle that harmful and violent
desires are matters of scale rather than qualitative difference, which also
concurs with the scalar conception of harm introduced earlier. For instance,
to use Gadd and Jefferson's example, if we all have neurotic tendencies we
are all susceptible to psychosis in specific psychosocial circumstances. Stein
would add that if we all possess latent aggressive drives we can, in the appropriate circumstances, all be violent too. Violence that is in specific circumstances normalized and psycho-emotionally internalized over long periods
of time – especially in the formative years of the life-course – can inscribe
itself in our neural pathways, influencing our ways of immediately perceiv-
ing, understanding and reacting to signs in the external world; in Hegelian
terms the 'spirit' as the perception and symbolic expression of Jones's
(2008) experiences with others becomes inscribed 'in the bone' and creates
a dialectical third being of 'spirit-bone', and the more extreme the experiences during the formative years the deeper the inscription. Criminal
actions are those of an individual who is both ideologically and neurologically motivated to *undertake* to go considerably further than the law-abiding
citizen. This rids us of the crude Manicheanism that bedevils the type of
criminological thought that divides and classifies human beings as either
normal or pathological. Neither is it adequate to think of the human being
as a 'mixture of both', because, in a more dialectical mode of thinking, these
categories construct and define each other in their constant interaction, and
dynamic force, the product of their eternal contradictions, operates in the
dialectical 'third space'. However, imbalances and aberrations exist, which
assume great importance when we consider the probability that the ontology and stability of both the subject and the social rely on a balance of forces.

When critical criminology took its place in opposition to the 'governmental project' that in Britain had been dominated by biology, psychology
and statistical studies of social phenomena, the subject virtually disappeared. The governmental project and its accompanying administrative

criminology still remained 'offender focused', but it was an offending subject in contexts strictly limited to family, community and state institutions
such as schools. Psychological and sociological attempts to theorize subjectivity in the context of capitalism – as we have seen, Veblen, Sombart,
Adorno, Althusser and many more – were dismissed by both the administrative and critical wings of British criminology, whilst American attempts
to connect the individual to the social were protected from becoming too
critical about the subject by American liberalism's hegemonic philosophical
principles of pragmatism, creativity and autonomy. Street criminality was
either pathologized by administrative criminologists or romanticized as a
way of coping with inequality and resisting dominance by critical criminologists; it was rarely seen as an *expression of that dominance*.

The exception was Freudian theory. There have been many Freudian
excursions into criminality; Smith, Glover, Bowlby, Lacan and Fromm to
mention but a few (see Gadd and Jefferson, 2007; Hall et al., 2008). Glover
(1960) emphasized the notion of scale, which locates the benign person
alongside the psychopath, both of which represent the extreme poles of a
complex spectrum of personalities; the norm, hopefully, is positioned
closer to the benign. Specific circumstances can cause short-term and long-
term shifts in sensibilities. According to these circumstances, all individuals –
as individuals, in small groups or *en masse* – are capable of movement along
the scale. Bowlby (1983) introduced the theory that the extended separation of young children from figures who represent maternal love is the
most crucial criminogenic context. In the large group of 'affectionless characters' he studied, he noticed that few had forged firm friendships or shown
tendencies to cheerfulness or sociability. Bowlby put it down to a failure
of super-ego development and the lack of guilt-inducing and super-ego-
building restraint provided by the social rules that govern the sublimatory
channelling of libidinal energy.

However, we must not see the super-ego, the unconscious and their
constitution as purely personal; we must key into their social, political and
historical reproductive forms (Jameson, 1981). Gadd and Jefferson (2007)
seek to move beyond internal drive-based psychoanalytical theories,
through the work of Melanie Klein (1975) to relational theories, but this is
a move, like that of Jones (2008), from the micro to the relational mid-
range, which, whilst bypassing the micro-world of drive, anxiety and narcissism, also does not account for the economic, socio-political and
hegemonic-cultural macro-contexts in which relations are forged. Where
parenting is not wholly negligent, we must see intimate familial relations as
at least in part ideological and neurological *preparation* for the social and
economic relations that the parents foresee the child experiencing in later

life. Even though those preparations take many different forms they also share vital purposes and contexts. The unconscious sense of weakness, inferiority and anxiety upon which Jefferson's (1994) Adlerian analysis relies is not generated and reproduced purely in intimate relations, but also in constant sensual proximity to the terrifying abyss of poverty and insignificance that capitalism quite systematically opened up in everyday social and economic life when it removed the traditional means of security (Hall and Winlow, 2005) for the specific purpose of forcing individuals to compete with others in order to avoid falling into it. On the edge of this abyss the potential suffering of the self as a failure can always be imagined as greater than the suffering of the other, who therefore must be out-competed in the circumstances in which both parties find themselves. In such ideologically naturalized competitive circumstances mistrust and potential trauma loom large in imaginary conceptions of the other.

For Stein (2007), who uses Sullivan's psychoanalytical concept of the 'dissociated self' or the 'not me', such mistrust and trauma are at the centre of her theoretical work. Many children badly traumatized by serious physical, sexual and psychological abuse in their early lives suffer from a splitting of the self which produces dissociated parts, variations of the 'not me', who are never explicitly known but are enacted in everyday life. Her research into violent criminals in prison revealed that all cases showed strong elements of dissociation. She admits that her 'horrid tales', as she puts it, represent the extreme, but hints that milder forms of abuse can produce milder forms of dissociation. This might sound unappealingly positivistic, even quite mechanically determinist, to today's interactionist, existentialist or postmodernist liberal of the linguistic turn, but her evidence and arguments are persuasive. Eighty per cent of the prison inmates she interviewed, whose crimes range from petty larceny to serial murder, reported physical assaults during childhood. Pathological levels of dissociation were evident amongst violent criminals.

In the midst of an assault or a threat, the brain goes into overdrive and disavows the reality of the incoming stimuli. In the Lacanian sense, the 'irruptions of the Real' that the incoming stimuli cause in the neurological system are simply too difficult to symbolize and understand. Unable to fend off their abusers, victims become predators and seek out victims weaker than themselves. Violence is enacted in an endless loop that is inaccessible to symbolism because the changes that occur are in the deep neurological system, beneath even the Freudian unconscious of repressed ideas and signs. Modern neuroscience is moving towards the theory that thought processes and the more sophisticated emotions we call 'feelings' are charged with energy from the more primitive areas of the brain (Damasio,

2003; Modell, 2003). This has echoes of the Freudian 'id', whose unconsid-ered 'evil' must not be entirely disregarded (Žižek, 2008), but the modern conception embraces the idea that early experience of the world can con-figure a far more sophisticated set of pre-linguistic emotional feelings. Early traumas can produce enduring hormonal and neurochemical changes in the deep autonomic system. Thus the way that emotional significance is placed on the brain's mental contents is compromised, fragmenting and isolating traumatic memories from other memories and, in extreme cases, remain-ing in an emotional form that is unavailable to language. In the motivational sense they simply announce their intention to act by acting; language and reflective thought are bypassed.

The moral sense is not compromised; in fact the basic sense of right and wrong is likely to be amplified as well as in some cases distorted or even inverted, feeding into dreams of threat, control and revenge that exceed the norm. The recourse to the 'not me' splits the self and allows the shift of values that is central to the pseudo-pacification process; values are replaced as drives by defence of an integrity that has already been lost and the 'good me' becomes the site of the operation of values as restraints on energetic, predetermined and pre-linguistic motivations to action. In a personalized 'state of exception' granted in an environment of threatening others by the self to the self in order to deal with an emergency, special liberty is pan-legitimized, and über-narcissistic feelings of omnipotence, immortality and righteous violence are given free reign; for Stein the individual can enter a condition where his self-reflective capacity is nullified. The brain is neuro-logically primed to overreact to subsequent stressors and to block off the neural pathways that associate words with feelings, often inducing the extreme impoverishment of linguistic ability. Behaviours 'in the realms of sensation, intuition and movement' (Stein, 2007: 31) become habitual, motivating and guiding embodied subsymbolic enterprises that can be aroused by a potential threat or pleasure of sufficient magnitude. The threat, in the form of memories of humiliation and the 'absence of what might have been' had more decisive action been taken to avoid the initial trauma, can also be carried internally and trigger violent reactions to others in order to launch the individual on a different historical path (Winlow & Hall, 2009b). The behavioural pattern will repeat itself over and over again unless its gen-esis is addressed at the autonomic neurological level where its motivational and reproductive capacity exists, and, because its enaction and reproduction are unconscious and pre-linguistic, there is no cognitive solution.

Elin (1995) argues that early physical, psychological and sexual abuse inhibits the development of linguistic competence, creating 'memory cap-sules' where 'words are suppressed and cut off from consciousness … [and]

… [s]ymbols are lost, embedded or dampened, and the world of objects remains less available for affective linkages' (in Stein, 2007: 32). Sensory awareness of events can become desymbolized and incoherent in what Weiss and Marmar (1997) call 'peritraumatic dissociations'. The subject attempts to impose a brutal order on what is essentially a vague threat that resists symbolization. It does not take a great leap of the imagination to see parallels here between the affectively reproduced 'vague threat' in the individual psyche and the culturally reproduced 'vague threat' of material impoverishment and social insignificance whose systematic purpose is to energize and incentivize the individual as a lone economic actor. They are not precisely the same thing or of the same scale, but they operate by the same principles and have similar psychosocial consequences of the attenuation of empathy and the intensification of aggression towards the other; the latter form is of course milder, domesticated and thus more controllable within a system of normative rules and strategies. Here we are looking at the psychological root of the broader political tactic of objectless anxiety.

This formulation supports many thinkers who operate across the spectrum of psychoanalytic subdisciplines, from orthodox object-relations theorists to radical Lacanians. There is not necessarily a lack of general cognitive and linguistic development, only that of the area that deals with trauma. There is a lack of context and syntax rather than symbols, and therefore a lack of vital connections. In fact trauma seems to create a non-linguistic shadow-world of perception and motivation that is etched into the brain and the neurological system. Compared to this, even the Bourdieusian (1990) *habitus* is relatively tractable and flexible; what we could be looking at is the neurological grounding for the *habitus*'s embodied subsymbolic dispositions, because the emotional arousal established by the trauma always seeks to desymbolize itself and its context in order to directly enact its urges as practice. For Stein there are therapeutic possibilities that rely on long-term living in non-threatening social environments. However, the neurological effects of trauma, unresponsive to appeals to choice and indeterminacy, are far from tractable and very difficult to shift; as such they constitute the polar opposite of the malleable linguistically-constituted subject of liberal-postmodernist thought, but we must also remember that they are not fixed, archetypal evolutionary drives responding mechanistically to traumatic stimuli.

Is there a cultural and political analogue to this extreme individualization process? Does a milder, tractable form of dissociation lie at the heart of the culture that we once unashamedly named 'bourgeois', a term that became pejorative during the era of dialectical class struggle? If the violent traumatized individual is driven by the urge to enact unsymbolized rage, is the

competitive-aggressive individual, normalized and lauded by capitalist culture although in principle subjectively grounded in the same basic anxiety,
driven by the cultural command to sublimate and symbolize the urge to
enact the milder traumatic form in a one-dimensional project of economic
expansion? Where the early familial relationships of violent criminals are
severely damaging, are the early general relationships and experiences of
the normalized competitive-aggressive liberal traumatizing in a more measured way, where rage is established and sustained in a less extreme form
that can be harnessed by normative systems? Social norms of dissociation
have not gone unnoticed by psychologists. Using the different feelings
aroused by killing puppies or flies as an illustration, as Stein suggests:

> The rest of us demonstrate similar contradictions and projections,
> in lesser forms during the daily exercise of moral relativism ...
> We socially approve some kinds of splitting because society
> cannot function without a certain level of aggression, and
> violence cannot be acted without a certain amount of dissociation.
> (2007: 58)

Stein is not clear about what she means by 'certain level' and 'certain
amount', or why non-aggression is 'dysfunctional' to 'society'? Even though
she expresses absolute disapproval of interpersonal and familial violence
throughout her study, when it comes to her brief social analysis she accepts
institutionalized violence as a functional necessity and shifts abruptly from
outright condemnation to a relativism of calculable degree; only be as violent as necessary when needs must. This could justify anything from police
brutality to the illegal invasion of Iraq. She acknowledges that a social
dimension exists:

> Such situational pathologizing has not gone unnoticed: Geoffrey
> White (2004) has suggested the inclusion in the *Diagnostic and
> Statistical Manual* of 'political apathy disorder', defined as the lack
> of a social conscience. Like psychopaths, sufferers of the disorder
> have no subjective distress. Their actions are characterized by a
> pervasive pattern of failing to help those in need (e.g., the poor,
> the oppressed, the underprivileged) combined with the
> overconsumption of the world's limited resources. Not
> surprisingly, White studies corporate power, trauma survival in
> the Third World, and the inaction of American Jews during World
> War II. (2007: 58)

Stein mentions this only briefly before turning back to her argument about the abuse of children, which she posits as a historical constant. Be aggressive, but don't take it too far and stop roughly at point X, which is not specified. Are Stein and White unconsciously defending US culture, which is pervaded by subliminal, symbolic and physical acts of aggression? Their thinking is influenced by Sullivan (1953), who proposed a gradient that goes from the 'good me' through the 'bad me' to the 'not me', from the normal through the vaguely immoral to the pathological. The 'good me' thrives in conditions of unconditional love and warmth, the 'bad me' is formed in the climate of anxiety that is generated by neglect and harsh punishment whilst the 'not me' is formed under conditions of extreme threat that engenders a total system shutdown because the threat cannot be incorporated by the psyche without risking its total eradication. The latter must be 'ignored' and the part of the psyche that experiences it dissociated. Victims can be conveniently 'derealized' by regarding them as flat, two-dimensional objects.

The problem with the psychological literature in general is the tendency to see aggression in the context of late-modern capitalist culture as a *disorder* that contrasts with an irenic norm, rather than a systematically stimulated drive held in check by a normative order; in its extreme forms this drive can leak through the insulation, especially where the insulation is relatively underdeveloped and weak (Hall et al., 2008). Capitalist culture does not want a mass of disordered psychopathic killers, but, in central and nodal positions in its political infrastructure and markets, it does require functionally ruthless individual undertakers in crucial positions who are willing to take the lead in disregarding others in order to 'get things done'. The shift of values from drivers to restraints when the dissociated self rears up to demand action occurs in the psychodynamic processes of the individual. However, there is no simple linear analogue or mirror-image between the psychic split self and the individual-social relationship. A Lacanian analysis allows us to extend our understanding of this process and see how it operates in culture and society. When this transition is made we can see that the specific narcissistic motivations that fuel the quest for self-aggrandizement, social distinction and subsequent economic expansion are generated and operated at the socio-cultural level. Each individual who operates as an energy-source need not suffer from the extreme dissociation that Stein posits. Upon entry to the Symbolic Order that currently represents the practico-logical demands of what the Marxists saw as the 'reified' market-driven economic system, the self becomes the potential 'good me' who must summon up the strength to resist the systematized 'not me' that issues commands to implement and defend the system's logical imperatives.

At specific points when the system demands the sort of excess of exploitation and destruction that it periodically requires, the conformist individual, whose occupational positions in the system can range from the corporate apparatchik to the fraudulent or violent economic criminal, must momentarily show unflinching allegiance to whatever practical manifestation of these logical demands presents itself as necessary. When morally offended onlookers respond with the rhetorical question "is this really necessary?" the active conformist has already decided that it is.

This is not simply embarking on a moral holiday, as Matza (1964) argued, but temporarily shifting one's allegiance from the practical morality of everyday interpersonal relations to the Real of domination and exploitation, which, after the extraction and reinvestment of surplus value, is reputed to be able to secure functional integrity and the 'general happiness' in the long-term, where happiness is expressed in terms of the ongoing expansion of opportunities for individual freedom and economic prosperity. This is not a moral holiday but a profound shift from everyday ethics to the anti-ethics of the obscene Real that, in a deliberate and assiduously maintained act of concealment, lie beneath the ability of the current Symbolic Order to express or deal with it in intellectual and political terms. In moments of required activity, the potentially 'good me' slips quietly along the gradient to become the 'bad me' who operates on behalf of the ethics of the systematized 'not me', and who in extreme cases of momentary agency can approach the psychological condition of the true dissociated self, the psychotic 'not me', the threatened individual who in his own micro-field wishes to (re)impose capitalism's robust moral order on those who jeopardize the group's functional position in the overall system that provides expanding 'general happiness'. Cultural and socio-economic splitting is similar to psychic splitting but not directly analogous. The former pairing does not produce a permanent psychotic dissociated self – although it is possible that in some hopefully rare cases such selves are *recruited* by the system in particularly unstable and brutal fields, which of course sets a reproducible precedent – but a morally flexible self whose brutal double can be brought into play at will when needs must.

At the extreme end of this process, the threatened individual projects the sadistic 'not me' onto the victim, who must be annihilated if the idealized self is to be reconstituted by returning it from shame to pride (Winlow & Hall, 2009b). The everyday competitive individualism that drives capitalism is a sublimated variant of this process, symbolized and restrained by an attenuated and modified symbolic order that, after it had proven its worth as an economic driver, was eventually to take its place as a cultural institution in the Protestant Reformation and, later, as a political institution in the classical liberal era when the economically and socially competitive individual was given partially free reign, a measure of special liberty, under the rule of law and its supporting socialization mechanisms. As we shall see in the following chapter, after the initial dissociation of the economic self in Late Mediaeval England, the development of ethics, politics and culture in seventeenth- and eighteenth-century Europe and the USA was an experimental period in which the competitive behaviour of the individual was stimulated and unleashed to generate economic energy and inform developing control mechanisms. The objective was not simply the discipline of the body, as Foucault (1991) claimed, but the knowledge of the maximal length to which the libidinal leash could be extended before the aggregate behaviour – in the sense of enacted desires – of free competitive individuals becomes socially toxic.

'Besting a competitor' exists in the same order of being as violent crime; it is a sublimated variant of the violence committed in the service of the split self's urge to attain psychic cohesion. Dissociation facilitates the aggressive action required, and the aggression itself exists on a scale that ranges from extreme physical violence to the everyday slights of symbolic violence. The dissociated self is the other in the process of *doubling* that has such a ubiquitous presence in most cultures (Vardoulakis, 2006), and which, when circumstances demand, can excuse all aggression on a scale from insults to killing. In politics, in business and in crime the toxic part of the split-self exists further down the gradient between the 'bad me' and the 'not me', seeking and justifying the special liberty that grants the freedom to do things every day that will inflict harm on others, and engaging in various degrees of denial, and therefore oscillating between the 'bad me' and the 'not me', depending on the extent of the harm that will be done to others as a consequence of decisions and actions. The perennial excuse is always the utilitarian calculation of the 'greater good' that will occur in the future, and which often does when calculated in terms such as economic growth and expansion of hedonistic opportunities. However, the agents of this uni-dimensional 'greater good', as Walter Benjamin (1968) noticed, have no choice but to gaze backwards at the wreckage constituted by the accumulation of harms done to others and to the vital physical, social and ethical environments on whose functional health our survival depends. The denial of such wreckage as accumulated harms is inscribed in mainstream liberal culture, and eventually in historical memory and record as a general synecdoche that restricts the narrative to the good part; denial in the present is simply a functional precursor to permanent erasure from historical memory. Denial in the service of the command to carry on regardless is the most potent product of a functioning ideology. In Lacanian terms harmful crime is the point on the scale where the denial as fetishistic disavowal is itself denied and the individual operates transparently, blowing the cover of those whose operations are more clandestine and exposing the Real:

> Many students of crime have concentrated in the hypothesized line that divides conformity from deviance, but I have been impressed by the continuum of behaviours that straddle that reified boundary. Law breaking seems to me part of a spectrum that includes completely legal forms of manipulation, corruption, and risk taking, as well as specifically outlawed acts like drunk driving or date rape ... Aggressive acts differ in magnitude and not essence; the same security operations that adaptively titrate survival processes in one person or situation may become disproportionately active in another. (Stein, 2007: 114)

Competitive individualist culture seeks to socialize the 'lite' version of the aggressive 'not me'. Empathetic relations between children and caregivers can certainly help the latter to facilitate a tolerable entry into the prohibitive Symbolic Order and restrain the expression of perceived fears and needs, but neoliberal culture does not want prohibitions emanating from any source other than itself. There is therefore a competition between capitalist culture and traditional parents for the right to reproduce specific cultural norms that restrain and shape desire; we must assume that in many cases in today's mass mediated culture neoliberalism has won, and in some cases its influence is combined with abusive parenting to push aggression into a different dimension. The 'lite' version functions in the highest tiers of the business world. Dodge's (2007) research, as we have seen, despite showing that men dominate the high-power corporate scene, comes to an interesting conclusion when she claims the smaller but growing number of women also tend to demonstrate the same motivations and ambitions, which casts doubt on Connell and Wood's (2005) pro-feminist idea that corporate aggression is simply an expression of a hegemonic 'transnational business masculinity'. The corollary is that encouraging women to move into top managerial positions would not affect much change in what is essentially a set of systemic imperatives for aggressive management and business dealing, which both attracts and reinforces a specific type of ruthless subject that can be recruited from any gender form.

There appears to be a complex and potent psychosocial form underneath what Murphy and Robinson (2008) describe as the 'maximizer', not simply culturally adaptive or reproductive but a foundational generative force in the capitalist project; these individuals are at the forefront of systematically constructing what they have to adapt to. In his research on corporate crime Punch also found that 'certain personality types make it into corporate leadership where their dominating style – related to power, control and egoism – can lead to rule-breaking by themselves, or by subordinates on their behalf' (1996: 233). Neil Shover (2007) also noticed middle-class competition at the heart of corporate crime. Brought up to believe that they are innovators and leaders – Sombart's undertakers – their inflated sense of the contribution they make to society in terms of progress and prosperity engenders them to think they have a right to cut corners and question all authority, for which they should receive not disapproval but perks and benefits. They are also expert in techniques of neutralization (see Matza, 1964), which shows that they are believers in their own moral probity. We can also agree with Glasbeek (2002) that the legal norms placed on corporations are designed to be flexible and easily transgressed, and with Punch (ibid.) that the pressure to simply 'get things done' defines the organizational context.

Many individuals seem to have internalized the principles of ruthless undertaking. In the criminal realm such individuals now tend to operate in loose networks (Morselli, 2009), unable to hold together for any significant length of time traditional criminal communities and organizations of the sort that McIntosh (1975) noted in the eighteenth and nineteenth centuries, and which persisted to some extent in the post-war period (Hobbs, 1995). We cannot avoid engaging with the *bête noir* of liberal social sciences, a 'types of people' question. However, we do not need to fall back into decontextualized, naturalistic, individualistic and deterministic arguments; the 'type' is not a form defined by qualitative difference to others but a point on a common linear scale. We can begin to approach this question when we acknowledge the intrinsically competitive nature of fragmented and divisive capitalist societies alongside the fact that although there's very little room in the lucrative hub of the market-capitalist machine there is gargantuan opportunity, and also the nodal points in its reticulation, where, in deregulated spaces/times, money and power are there for the taking. Whether crime is individual, networked or traditional-communal, 'ruthless undertaking' sits at the top of the cultural hierarchy. Gambetta's research revealed that:

> [C]riminals can also ask a potential partner or recruit to engage in a *display* crime – an act that a noncriminal would never do – and to commit the crime under their eyes or in such a way as to leave an unmistakable sign of authorship. (2009: 16, original in italics)

The criminal undertakers who will 'get things done' regardless of the harm inflicted on others put each other through tests and develop a set of complex cultural signals, what Bourdieu (1990) would call cultural and symbolic capital in this particular field. It filters out the untrustworthy and the reluctant, and the ultimate test is the willingness to harm others for the sake of the group's instrumental cause, a form of cultural and symbolic capital that crops up in Pitts' (2008) analysis of gang hierarchies. In an interview with the Italian criminologist Amedeo Cottino, 'Nino', a former member of a Catanian crime clan and responsible for multiple murders, extortion and other serious crimes, revealed the extent to which compulsory functional undertaking had established itself in his psyche as the kernel of the disavowed 'not me':

> 'A person like me has two personalities: one tough and one tender. Once you go into your house you forget what you left outside … I'd do a job and then talk about it with my friends, my buddies. And then I'd go home and for me it was as if it simply didn't exist … When you're in your own home you sort of lose your memory of what you've done … At home I could be like a puppy or a child; my wife called the shots, she'd slap me around … and then outside the house I changed, I was tough, I gave the orders … How was this possible? Well, as I see it, I've got a split personality. It becomes a single one when there's a job to do because, after all, it's just a job. Even though it's work that isn't nice, it's work I can live with … I'm emotional … like when I see a film, I cry. Yes, I cry, but that's my private life; the other is work. There's no place for emotions at work! I was a tough guy in the organization because I had to show a lot of other guys that I had no weaknesses. But, maybe with my friends, and for sure with my family, it was completely different.' (Cottino, 1998)

Further up the scale, ruthless leaders can commandeer whole regions and states, as in the case of post-conflict warlords in some regions of Africa, 'leaders of predatory armed groups that seek power for their personal enrichment without regard for the broader interests of any significant community' (Reno, 2009: 313). Illicit commerce is often used by criminal warlords and their private armies, who survive the ends of wars and become major forces in state-building, a repeat of what Tilly (1985) saw in Early-Modern Europe. Wiegratz (2010), informed by voices from the developing world, reports a renewed sense of moral decay in the wake of triumphant neoliberalism. This is not simply an ideology or politics as a discursive forum, but a purified economic ideology applied by ruthless, corrupt politics to the physical and social realities that frame individuals' lives. In Uganda it is not just the elite institutions but 'undertakings' in everyday economic transactions that are now permeated by various forms of malpractice; in the realm of 'undertaking' the distinction between the individual and the state is scalar rather than qualitative, and in many cases coordinated. Neoliberalism's *Zeitgeist* is not about 'freeing' but energizing subjects with asocial and ruthless forms of ambition:

> Many respondents noted a significant shift since the late 1980s regarding the way in which more and more Ugandans are made to think, feel and act. They also stated that the moral authority, integrity, and credibility of many people and institutions of power (both state and non-state) have significantly diminished due to the dynamics of the reform process. In sum then, notwithstanding the official rhetoric and statistics of reform success, many people actually experienced the day-to-day manifestations of neoliberal *pseudo-development* and *fake capitalism* in several realms of their lives. Many of these trends can be seen in the light of restructuring of Ugandan society towards a fully capitalist trajectory and the (cultural) 'turbulence' that this brings. (Wiegratz, 2010: 134; original italics)

The gamble taken by advanced capitalism is that its combination of flimsy normative codes and legal repression can cope with the extension of the limits of libidinal enjoyment (Fromm, 1993), which seems to provoke fears of regressing back to a subjectivity and social world driven by the libidinal economy of proto-symbolic affects, drives and desires, conceived in historical terms as a return to a visceral, violent past. However, the missing layer is the internalization of experience and ideology in a specific way that transforms the libidinal economy in the neurological system, which, as Damasio (2003) has shown, is capable of emotional desire formation and guidance only just short of the sophistication of language and culture. It takes only one step – albeit a rather large one that requires a lengthy trip through its complications – to understand that capitalist culture, dependent on sublimated aggression and social competition, has prevented the development of the type of experience and ideology that would transform the neurological system as the initial formative filter, which can orient the libido to civilization and sociability and normalize this transformation

across the social body. This is the great conundrum; to achieve true civilization we must become civilized, and the spirit must dwell in our bones
before it can structure our social lives, but for it to dwell in our bones we
must first live in its nurturing experiential and ideological climate.

To help criminological theorists think through this conundrum, the
philosophical position of *transcendental materialism* (Johnston, 2008) brings
the body, as a true neurological and subsymbolic 'thing', back into the
debate, and as such it has the potential, always present in psychoanalysis, to
perform two important tasks; to bring transcendental idealism back down
to earth and break the intellectual stranglehold that positivist-empiricist
science has on the West's cultural and political life. Since the rejection of
Cartesian ontology the question of how more-than-material subjectivity
arises immanently out of its material ground in the biological world has
been neatly avoided. This simply hands over to scientific positivism and
biological determinism their most valuable hostage. Psychoanalysis, especially that of Lacan, showed how the very material ground of the biological
body is shot through with multiple antagonisms, conflicts and tensions as
part of its basic constitution. Transcendental materialism's fundamental
insight, drawn from recent developments in neuroscience, is that the
human body is a hard-wired mechanism, but it is hard-wired specifically for
dysfunctionality and plasticity, a vital prerequisite for the adaptability of the
weakly evolved and equipped human being in multiple environments, a
plasticity that over time became manifest in the immense diversity of emotions, sensibilities, intuitions, linguistic concepts and physical capabilities
that constitute the earth's most complex industrious, philosophical and
communicative animal (Johnston, ibid.). Our abject and terrifying state of
prematurational helplessness means that the act of denaturalizing our
physical selves into dematerialized forms of subjectivity is natural; the sole,
primary ontogenetic determinism we have to deal with. Amongst the most
unruly forces of corporeal nature that we have to control are those that
exist within ourselves; the terror of the Real is internally and externally
sourced. Once dematerialized, the cogito-like forms of subjectivity resist
being re-assimilated back into the corporeal realm. The whole concept of
'embodiment' – along with its variants such as biopower, discipline, discursive constitution, subjectification, normalization, habitus and so on – is
problematic and in need of reformulation.

Throughout his voluminous works Žižek has approached the Lacanian
concept of the subject divided against itself and constitutive of a third realm
of being beyond the material and ideal by creatively combining German
idealism and psychoanalysis. He enjoins us to look for connections between
the insights of evolutionary biology, psychology, philosophy and politics

before we formulate an adequate conception of subjectivity. Until then, the sociological disciplines should be put on hold, and for criminology that means a lengthy detour; quite possibly more than any other discipline, criminology has been caught up in a struggle between crude biological determinism and equally crude social constructionism. The hand of potential collegiality has been offered by the hard sciences themselves, which in their most enlightened forms have rejected hard determinism. Richard Dawkins' (1989) concept of the *meme* connects the biological being – conceptualized as far more than a crude, robotic functionalist-survivalist machine – with the sociocultural and symbolic-linguistic worlds. Although they are replicators just like genes, memes are immaterial and flexible, and therefore capable of replicating both functional and dysfunctional – and all combinations between and beyond – units of information. Memes are produced as functional social glue in the act of survival, but their ability to replicate themselves as a supra-material system means that they can persist even when their original conditions of existence have vanished. Paradoxically, their inherent flexibility and reproductive independence can produce a rigid inertia when they become detached from their precipitative conditions of generation and mutation; in a profound counter-intuitive reversal, it would appear that it is the body and its neurological system that is reflexive and our symbolic life – even in forms such as liberalism or postmodernism that pride themselves on their reflexivity – that is rigid. In Johnston's (2008) notion of 'deaptation' it is perfectly possible for an initially functional and adaptive memetic strategy to become actively counter-productive in a new environment (Blackmore, 1999). This reproductive independence is of course the condition in which ideology can flourish and overwhelm reality and its more direct perceptions and conceptions; hegemonic ideology has the remarkable capability of being able by its very nature to insulate itself from the major shifts in material conditions and their immediate sensory-ethical aftershocks that, before ideology and its reproductive institutions became so sophisticated and fortified, would precipitate a shift in society's primary memes.

For Kant, subjectivity exists in a realm that transcends the material and is condemned to disinterested reflection; the ideal can only think and speak of itself, so any attempt to grapple intellectually with real nature will merely produce falsifying distortions. When Hegel (1979) claimed that 'the spirit is a bone' he meant that the subject is not separate from substance, and its reflections are inscribed and functionally operative in the ontological structure of real nature. By combining German idealism and Lacanian theory, read off against the physicists' most current and sophisticated conceptions of matter and energy, for Žižek (2006) the subject is brought into being by a burst of dialectical energy; the indeterminate material subject is cast out into a determining set of symbolic coordinates in the external world, the key images and words of identification in the ideologically constituted symbolic order. The virtual possibilities of the indeterminate reality of being become the reality constituted by a symbolic order constantly confirmed by the gridlocked social and economic practices of experiential reality. The being that has been through this identification process returns inwards to reconstitute and consolidate its identity in the neurological circuits of its material body. This identity is not entirely fixed, but it cannot be unfixed unless it passes yet again through a similarly traumatic process in an alternative symbolic order that governs an alternative practical reality, but to create these alternatives, dialectical being must court its own negativity to invoke the repressed Hegelian 'night of the world', the radically indeterminate being immanent within its material reality at the deepest level, to burst out yet again to disturb the status quo of the existing order and create space for its own subjective freedom. This would explain the strange success of religious conversion in prisons and the failure of more rationalist and existentialist approaches to desistance. The free subject is not to be found in language, image and discourse, which, despite the intellectual gymnastics of the post-structuralists, are not intrinsically flexible but the mechanisms of determinacy and entrapment. The subject can never be entirely free, but can eventually find itself in an unfree symbolic socio-cultural system of its own making (Johnston, 2008).

Material being is not a stable, integrated whole of ontological closure; in fact it is quite the opposite, and no change can be made in the subject or its external milieu without a return to material being's immanent indeterminacy. To do that it must struggle free from its symbolic fixings, so the first step is an ideological battle of thought against all the provisional yet durable determining symbolic systems and forces that intersect to constitute the integrated whole of the inert post-political 'end of history' in advanced capitalism. The true dialectical dynamism is not generated between different aspects of the material or the ideal, but between the material and the ideal; the tumultuous physical contours of the brain shape experience and symbolism, which then feed back to shape the contours of the brain itself. Real and Ideal combine in dialectical tension to create a third realm of structural dynamism that we call 'subjectivity'. Established politico-economic and socio-cultural systems get the types of subjectivity they need, which in turn willingly and actively participate as powerful actors in the reproduction of the system. Those who seem to fit the system's needs and perform well in its institutions will achieve power and influence authorized by the majority. The circle is difficult to break; in the dialectical model the endurance of the system and its active assimilated subjects is indeterminate.

The very material malleability immanent in the brain and its associated neurological circuits renders the argument between partisan materialists and idealists sterile and redundant. Reality is not socially constructed, but social constructions are themselves the constructs of a symbolic reality energized and in the first instance determined by the immanent indeterminacy at the heart of the material human being. As subjects, human beings are, as Sartre (1957) said, condemned to be free, determined only by their innate, immutable radical indeterminacy. This is not a paradox, as Dennett (2003) argues, because material plasticity and subjective indeterminacy are entirely functional for a weak animal forced to deal in groups with unexpected events in multiple changing environments; this staunch philosophical defender of Anglo-American cognitive science is, on this fundamental issue, agreeing with the high priests of European Critical Idealism. In fact the field of neuroscience is rapidly converging with psychoanalysis by positing the subject as the product of the natural ability of the neuronal network to transcend its functional-mechanical materiality and create a transcendental reflexive dimension of existence from which it can receive messages to modify itself (Ansermet, 2002). The neuronal network is not a rigid field saturated with a tight web of determinative causes; it is ready-built to accommodate and communicate with the phenomenological and structural subject, because the realm of signifiers creates a structural dynamic that is not directly controlled by the neuronal network. The neuronal network is emotionally sophisticated enough to respond sensually to a sophisticated web of signifiers, but only if the signifiers have been allowed over time to cultivate the complex branch-and-twig panoply of receptive emotional sensibilities (Damasio, 2003). The transcendental subject is of course connected to the external world of experience and socially constituted and reproduced symbols, the world of irruptive and imaginary/symbolic reality. In the strict materialist sense subjectivity might well be an illusion, but it is an illusion that shapes the individual's cognition, comportment and sensibilities down to the tumultuous neurology of the material being itself. Even though the self is something that exists only by the force of its own belief, it finds its way down to the material dimension as a formative and reproductive influence. The transcendental self must believe itself into a real existence as it appears to itself (Žižek, 2006; Zupančič, 2000), and here there is even a partial agreement with existentialism, apart from the vital caveat that experience and ideology shape the neurological system in ways that form drives and construct desires and fears that influence and restrict choice until that experience and ideology can be transcended and replaced. If we are indeed condemned and driven by our material nature to be free, as much as we have been oppressed by the institutions of state and religion we have been led astray by liberalism's specific ideological construct of freedom.

For Kant as for Dennett, if the human being ever revealed the noumenal world in the sense of coming to know the sum total of internal and external causes and effects that shape the self, its spirit would collapse and resign itself to its true condition of a lifeless puppet devoid of autonomy. Underneath the unbearable lightness of being lies the unbearable weight of a whole matrix of determinative causes. For Hegel and Žižek, however, it is just as important that we should not imagine beyond the superficial façade of empirical reality to this unknowable totality as a harmonious, functional order of causes constantly manufacturing a fixed and predictable unity of being. Unpredictability and contingency are even built into evolution, which has been imagined by some as the very quintessence of a uniformly ordered process. All dualistic theories based on a strict dichotomy that posits the material as determinative or the ideal as totally free and independent are redundant. Not only that, but to the criminological theorist they are both potentially dangerous, the former as the progenitor of pathologization and its fascist solutions and the latter as the prefect of catastrophism, the anxious annihilator of the vital cultural and political forms that can transform subjectivity at the material, experiential and ideological levels. Throughout late modernity we have fled the evil of eugenics only to becalm ourselves in the still waters of liberal inertia.

Liberal theory, predicated on the myth of innate and fully-functioning autonomy, rationality and creativity, is bedevilled by its underestimation of the formative subjectifying power of ideology, currently dominated by the advertising and mass media industries, which acts to impose an ideal order on the flexible yet anxious material substance of the proto-subject; like all past ideologies, it takes advantage of the inescapable ontological fact that the proto-subject is universally characterized by both flexibility and anxiety in its material substance. For Lacan the two alternative paths away from the terror of the infant's original condition of helplessness are the stupid solipsistic comfort of primary narcissism or the risky identification of the split ego with alienating external signs. Merging the two and producing political and subjective inertia alongside an economically powerful illusion of freedom and proliferating enjoyment has been consumer capitalism's most stunning triumph in the twentieth century (Hall et al., 2008). With such a direct correspondence between the internal *ideal ego* of the self mirrored in the primary other and the *ego ideal* of the self mirrored in the social other, the selfish, solipsistic narcissist and the other-directed sociable self, and all variations in between, are equally incorporable, as evidenced by current cultural forms that seem to have achieved an impossible fusion between solipsism and tribal affectivity. This apparent impossibility is explained by Lacan's (2004) concept of *le trait unaire*, the 'unary trait', the internalized ideal as a compilation of the important signs that represent the hegemony of the symbolic order. The compilation is flexible under a sign that operates at a high level of abstraction and can thus encapsulate and fuse a number of different and conflicting concrete qualities and practices.

For Lacan the unary trait of the Symbolic is primary, whereas the gestalt and therefore more flexible *imago* of the Imaginary is secondary, allowing the Symbolic Order, which always pre-exists the enunciative *cogito*, to dominate the imagination, except in the case of psychosis, where the imagination is invaded by stimuli that cannot be symbolized in a controlled manner. As Johnston puts it, 'there is no a priori void of non-empirical subjectivity timelessly preceding identificatory investments in operators of subjectification (features, insignias, marks, traits, etc.) presented by the individual's socio-symbolic milieu' (2008: 219). The unary trait is impressed upon the individual by early significant others, and it underpins the development of the ego, and later super-ego if there is an ideological correspondence between the early significant other and the social other that represents the figure of the broader ego ideal. Put simply, it helps the process if in early intimate life parents or carers reinforce the characters, the symbols and the general unary trait that are represented by the figures that predominate in advertising, mass media, business and politics, between which there is an increasing convergence around a far more crystallized unary image. Johnston continues:

> In Žižek's terms, Lacan's unary traits, Kripke's rigid designators, and Benveniste's linguistic shifters all would be examples of operators of subjectification, namely, master signifiers of identification hegemonically articulating the substance of human being (i.e., imposing order onto the destructive anarchy of the primordial Kantian-Hegelian night of the world, the chaos introduced into being by the de-synthesizing and re-synthesizing imagination at war with itself, an imagination fighting the imbalance that it itself introduces into the world). By contrast, the subject ($-as-for-itself) names the very gap between these stabilizing operators of subjectification and the unstable flux of lived experience, a flux that these operators never fully succeed in stabilizing. (2008: 220)

From symbolic interactionism to Derridean deconstruction and Foucauldian discursivity, all contemporary idealist theories fail because they have set up a 'straw-man Hegel' in their efforts to supersede him, one in which they posit his notion of the subject as 'one in which self-consciousness is capable of achieving a perfect transparency to itself, of reflexively transubstantiating itself from the opacity of finite immanence into the clarity of infinite transcendence' (Johnston, 2008: 221). For Žižek (2000), Hegel was well aware that there is no clear reflection and that the free subject is the stain on the Lacanian mirror, the spot where the symbolic order cannot reflect back its controlled images and operators of subjectification. The crucial shift into subjectivity is from death-driven negativity, seeking and welcoming an imposed order of operators of subjectification to a self-relating negativity that can transcend creatively both its natural and cultural surroundings. Liberal theories, whether subjectivist or discursive/constructivist, that posit either a hollow malleable immaterial subject or a natural autonomous subject upon which a subjectifying and normalizing order is imposed by an external power without authorization or solicitation, are missing the point; initially the distressed subject-in-itself, the victim of a natural and foundational vortex of conflicting drives, can do nothing but crave unary order, authority and identification, which it must later transcend by moving through the gaps in which subjectivity is possible. The fundamental problem for criminologists, who have, along with many other social scientists, accepted rationalist, transcendental idealist or discursive notions of subjectivity, is that they have denied the individual's initial need and solicitation for the imposition of a subjectifying symbolic order on the chaotic self-in-itself. This is what experienced parents and social workers mean when they say that children seem to seek boundaries and certainties. In the time-honoured trajectory of deaptation, it is these symbolic, identificatory certainties that people, if they sense themselves to be in a condition of anxiety, seek to retain and even intensify as they sense danger.

Nothing is more successful than botched left-liberalism – with its obsessive drive to create calm and cool rationalism in situations where only an idiot would feel entirely composed – at defeating its own aim as it disintegrates the symbolic efficiency that everyone craves and dissolves the symbolic objects of politics, thus opening the doors to the anxiety fomented by neoliberalism's real economic conditions and its prevailing ideology of social Darwinism. Thus left-liberalism's sheer ambiguity and vacillation (self-promoted as subtlety and nuance) deflects those in culturally and economically precarious situations from the path to politics and into the hands of apathy and nihilism, or, at the extremities, criminality, violence or nationalist politics. Criminality, tribalism and plutocratic power grow in the stagnant pond of neoliberal post-politics, which, at the end of the solidarity project's historical existence, occupies what should be a dynamic third space where new subjectivities and politics could thrive. In their absence, and amidst liberalism's cumulative failures to objectify and regulate deep structural processes, it's difficult to blame the many anxious and impotent onlookers who fall back on traditional conservatism, which at least admits the existence of the political object, turning pernicious anxiety into objective fear and offering to guarantee order by reintroducing traditional modes of discipline and punishment. The alternative is for individuals to 'undertake' to arrange their own prosperity, dominance and special liberty, where necessary at the expense of others. The current global flows of capital prevent any fixed forms of solidarity, and in them we face a 'nihilistic potency' (Badiou, 1999: 56) of which we are the inventors as well as the prey.

ON THE STIMULATION AND PACIFICATION OF POPULATIONS

9

It will probably not have escaped the attention of readers that this book has been highly critical of all factions of conservatism and liberalism, and their contributions to criminological theory. The critique of conservatism is one of the essential foundation stones of the liberal canon, but to criticize liberalism itself risks the 'Monty Python defence': in their film *The Life of Brian*, the writers lampooned factionalized Judaean socialists by having them pose the question 'what have the Romans done for us?' Immediately, the socialists found themselves answering it by effortlessly reeling off a list of the tangible benefits of Roman occupation: sanitation, medicine, education, wine, public order, fresh water, irrigation, roads and so on. Roman imperialism might seem like a rather odd metaphor for these quintessentially liberal comedy writers to use; perhaps a Freudian slip when considers the platform of imperialism – now known euphemistically as 'humanitarian intervention' – on which liberal capitalism continues to be built. Nevertheless, all who criticize liberalism are obliged to acknowledge its benefits; formal rights, freedoms, phases of economic prosperity and so on. The same obligation exists in the criminological realm. Despite the military violence, economic exploitation, social disruption and subjugation that have aided liberal-capitalist nations' efforts to impose the market economy across the world and quell internal dissent (Seymour, 2008), and despite the recent explosions of crime and incarceration in Britain and the USA (Reiner, 2007), it cannot be denied that Western nations have also been characterized by notable improvements in formal rights and freedoms (Valier, 2002) and long-term processes of internal pacification, indicated by the constant decline of brutal punishment and homicide rates from the early stages of the capitalist-modernist project until the mid-1970s (Eisner, 2001; Rodger, 2008). As we saw earlier, Elias (1994) argued that during this period these nations underwent a civilizing process, enabled by the state's monopolization of violence, the expansion of social interdependencies and the diffusion of behavioural codes throughout populations. In the cultural environment that evolved on these three institutional platforms the majority of Western individuals began to develop embodied sensibilities that inclined them to react with revulsion towards cruel physical punishments and eschew violence as a means of resolving interpersonal disputes (Fletcher, 1997). If indeed the 'spirit is a bone' then the liberal-capitalist *Zeitgeist* seemed to have cultivated neurologically inscribed sensibilities and relatively pacified subjectivities amongst the majority of individuals, perhaps similar to those which can be found amongst the more stable and pacified traditional communities (see Gilmore, 1990).

The majority of criminals also began to avoid the use of violence in the course of their acquisitive crimes, not simply because they were deterred by developing policing and security technology (see Matthews, 2002) and an increasingly efficient criminal justice system (see Reiner, 2010), but also because the sensibilities of the majority of individual criminals had developed beyond the normalized brutality of the Mediaeval era. Although Elias's explanation for the decline of physical cruelty is on balance more convincing than Foucault's notion of the historically interruptive statist conspiracy of panopticism and biopower, the criticisms that Elias's tripartite causal structure described above – the diffusion of social interdependencies, the state's monopolization of violence and the inculcation of behavioural codes in the psyche – is too simplistic, and that he underplayed the important role played by the logical demands of the developing economy, both hold water. In the light shed by previous critiques, Mucchielli (2010) argues that Elias's civilizing process should be called a pacifying process, and to Elias's three preconditions for the decline of violence must be added bureaucratization, socio-economic integration into Fordist manufacturing processes, the spread of literacy and education and the increase in social security enabled by welfarism. According to Mucchielli, Elias also neglects the fact that:

> French society has gradually experienced economic-socio-spatial segregation processes sparking stress, depression, anxiety, frustration, resentment, aggressiveness and anger in a portion of the population. Associated with the constant expansion of consumerism, this state of affairs represents the main factor contradicting the overall process of pacification that seems to have every reason to continue or even quicken the pace of the expansion started at the end of the Middle Ages and pursued through the beginning of the modern era. (Mucchielli, 2010: 825–6)

In contrast to Elias's standard Whiggish view of Western history as linear incremental progress threatened only by the possibility of temporary regressive glitches – 'decivilizing processes' in periods where founding principles fall into practical disrepair (see Fletcher, 1997) – Mucchielli returns disintegrative forces to the analysis as structural rather than sequential forms. In other words integrative and potentially disintegrative processes are contiguous rather than consecutive, which of course puts into question the fundamental ideological assumption that permeates main-stream criminological thought; that liberal capitalism produces constant linear social progress whose forms constantly transcend and supersede those of the past. It also compels us to reconsider more favourably the dual-istic and dialectical positions we encountered in earlier chapters. In what follows we will take this analysis one step further by suggesting the possibil-ity that modernity's pacification process has evolved to manage a 'dark heart' (Reiner, 2012) – which we have already posited in economic terms as the more visceral aspects of 'animal spirits' and in psychosocial terms as the dissociated and disavowed 'obscene Real' – that, despite being *poten-tially* disintegrative, is neither atavistic, chaotic nor external but fully inte-grated, concomitant and functional.

Mucchielli's analysis of the corrosive role of consumer culture is straightforwardly Mertonian: it promotes the competitive urge to acquire goods – aggressively and criminally if deemed necessary – and display them as signs of identity and status, which is criminogenic in areas where socio-structural disadvantage, relative poverty and the threat of social insignifi-cance weigh heavily on individuals (see also Hallsworth, 2006; J. Young, 1999). However, he does not explain why this 'stress, depression, anxiety, frustration, resentment, aggressiveness and anger' precipitates violence or criminality rather than a return to solidarity and political struggle in the French ghettoes, an omission that is perhaps partly answered by Wieviorka's (2009) notion of the deinstitutionalization of social conflict and Reiner's (2007) notion of the decline of Garland's (2001) 'solidarity project'. In association with neoliberalism's ideological assault on solidarity as a princi-ple and a politico-cultural practice, we have also encountered in previous chapters Sombart's (1998) cult of the undertaker, the egocentric pragma-tist who simply seeks to 'get things done' on behalf of the interests of the self, and according to the logic of the market's 'dark heart', in the midst of inherited circumstances, no matter how brutally competitive and unforgiv-ing they might be. There is of course resistance to neoliberalism in some quarters, but a politically significant majority in the West practice their socio-economic lives according to the silent injunctions of neoliberalism's fetishistically disavowed Real. More importantly, however, there is a hard core of undertakers who operate relatively successfully in capitalism's socio-economic nodes and arteries as the influential and committed reproductive agents of the project itself. Is this basic transcendental materialist subject – operating in situations that range from favelas and sink estates to corporate boardrooms and the corridors of power – the criminogenic role-model at the heart of the acquisitive and narcissistic types of crime that have flourished over the course of capitalism? Is the spirit of capitalism, including its dark, disavowed dimension, 'in the bones' of its influential undertakers, creating and reproducing a 'third space' of dominant functional subjectivity? What we have seen so far suggests that this might well be the case, and an investigation of capitalism's specific mode of pacification can add a little more substance to it.

The concepts of the 'civilizing process' (Elias, 1994) and the 'pacification process' (Mucchielli, 2010) do not take into account the development of the capitalist economy and its psychosocial dynamics as the principal context in which pacification took place. The development of the proto-capitalist market economy required the protection of transitory commercial property, including precious metals and money, and, therefore, the evacuation of violence from its market towns and arterial trade routes. It is no coincidence that the second and most effective stage of the development of the market economy in England at the end of the fourteenth century – after the early and sporadic stages of its development between the twelfth and early fourteenth century in the midst of lax politico-economic management by Norman warlords had ran aground as the Plague halved the population – coincides with the beginning of the decline of high rates of homicide. This second-stage development also required that the social and politico-economic competition that was often physically violent should be sublimated into pacified social competition, not just to protect property and allow risky business deals to take place without the threat of physical retribution but also to harness a vigorously stimulated yet pacified form of libidinal energy via competitive social struggle and consumption to the market in order to increase demand for production.

The prominent role that economic functionality played in the specific type of pacification that characterizes the dominant form of subjectivity in the capitalist project belies Elias's claim that modernity was driven by some inherent teleological urge to a pacified form of social order. That is not to say that a significant majority of individuals cannot become accustomed to it and develop transcendental material sensibilities orientated and committed to its continuation, but this also means that an influential minority or even a significant majority could become accustomed to the precise opposite. Because capitalism's cultural trajectory was not driven by an urge to civilization for its own sake, or even pacification for its own sake, and it has evolved as an economically functional dualistic form characterized by the dynamic tension between overstimulated libidinal energy and tenuously internalized sublimating and pacifying codes backed up by external systems of control, a more precise term would be a pseudo-pacification process (Hall, 2000; 2007). The end product of this process is, as Bernard Stiegler (2010b) has recently argued, a 'pharmacological' subjectivity that is both toxic and curative. The point is this; if the capitalist variant of economic functionality is prominent, in spaces where the violent libidinal part of this process once again regains its economic functionality with an attenuated need for the restraining measures of sublimation and pacification, a new elite cultural norm based on the conjunction between minimally restrained libidinal action and economic success will establish itself. The position in which minimally restrained libidinal action lies on an axis ranging from the violent to the unashamedly exploitative and corrupt will be influenced by the extent to which locally specific sublimating and pacifying restraints remain in place, or, to be more precise, are perceived to need to remain in place. For instance, in a way that echoes Simmel's (1955) formalism, both behaviour and pseudo-pacifying norms in sink estates, corporate board-rooms or paraspaces in failed states will be markedly different, but the central disavowed principle of linking libidinal action as the instantly effective implementation of the Real with social status and economic efficiency will remain the same. Whether it's pressurizing, sacking, exploiting, cheating or murdering people, sometimes, according to the logic of the capitalist market economy's dark heart, when it comes to the crunch, these things just have to be done. In a culture whose majority abstain from doing such awful things themselves – yet remain ideologically committed to the idea that they produce long-term benefits for all – high status, rewards and enduring power await those who are willing to do them. The bleeding heart and the work of art that together constitute liberalism's ideal subjectivity shudder at the undertakers violence, exploitation and vulgarity. Yet, whilst the undertakers benefit from performing functions in the system reproduced by their under-takings, the onlooking liberal subject – in a classic Hegelian relation of sub-servience and dependency tinged with mimetic admiration – reluctantly affords them their status and reward whilst hesitating to restore them to their structural position of the symbolic object of ethico-political opposition in the class struggle. The undertakers perform the role of the *pharmakon*, threatening to poison the community at the same time as increasing its security and material prosperity and thus saving it from decline.

We need to examine this proposition in a little more detail across capitalism's historical continuum. In the Middle Ages the internal violence that pervaded social relations in Europe was perpetrated largely in the defence of honour, land and property (Maddern, 1992; Mucchielli, 2010). There is little doubt that throughout the modernist-capitalist period the upper classes quite significantly reduced their use of interpersonal violence, preferring legal means of defence. On the other hand, the organized external violence that was deployed and ideologically legitimized to defend the nation and the power of its ruling elite increased its destructive capabilities to reach a peak in the 'short twentieth century' (Hobsbawm, 1994). The measures of violence that were used and also ideologically legitimized in the service of internal social control, in punishment and policing, were also reduced. For Mucchielli, the French example suggests that interpersonal violence in advanced capitalism today is closely tied to individuals' actual living conditions, their social integration through employment and the hostile relationships between these social groups and the state agencies which manage the 'problem', and in doing so often overstep the boundary of legitimate violence. This suggests that Elias has paid far too little attention to socioeconomic factors in Western societies that have become more divided and fragmented since neoliberalism tore up the post-war settlement.

Despite the so-called 'crime-drop', violence remains at high levels in specific impoverished geographical locales (Dorling, 2004; Parker, 2008). The pseudo-pacification process continues in mainstream societies, gradually enervating formerly visceral subjects whilst intensifying pacified socioeconomic competition, reducing interpersonal violence and eroding institutionalized conflict and political dissent. Mucchielli's standard prescription, that of the democratic redistribution of wealth, which 'shapes living conditions' (2010: 19), indeed promises to diffuse the economically-grounded pacification process more evenly across the social body. However, if we accept Durkheim's claim that there is no economic solution to anomic cultural currents – and here we must remember that, although the malady of infinite inspirations is not really natural, the spirit of the 'perfectionist' consumer culture that is 'in the bones' of so many individuals effectively reproduces it as such – we must also accept the probability that, in an unaltered ideological, political and economic climate, socio-economic equality and the diffusion of pacification are nothing more than fragile short-term solutions. Both Elias and Mucchielli neglect the problem at the root of criminology's 'aetiological' crisis (Young, 1987), that crime and violence rose in the post-war era despite increases in wealth and freedom, and also neglect periodic historical upswings in violence that are related to political economy, 'periods in which economic processes undermine social mobility and during which institutions of coercion emerge, [and] levels of homicide appear to surge' (Mares, 2009: 420). In an advanced capitalist culture whose potent mass media and marketing institutions inculcate personal ambition and dreams of elitist perfection and supremacy 'in the bones' of so many individuals, would the return of mere decent living conditions provide the solution? For many, quite probably yes, but for others the question becomes more complex, and much of this complexity is founded upon the principle that the presence of successful and influential 'ruthless undertakers' throughout the nodal structure of the capitalist economy, who display an entirely different 'winner takes all' moral outlook, makes it appear that social justice and economic stability are neither possible, desirable nor necessary.

We can trace the roots of this mentality, which is behind capitalism's modern forms of adaptive and tenuously pacified criminality, back to abrupt social change in the Late Middle Ages in England. A neglected aspect of Harvey's (2010) co-evolutionary capitalist process is that the trajectory, structures, ideologies and subjectivities set in motion at that juncture have continued, mutated and evolved to the present. The trajectory was set by changes in the mode of stimulation and pacification of key economic players in the English population, the transfer of the principal object of desire and repository of value from land to money, and the transfer of the principal source of status from the violent acquisition and defence of land, property and family honour to the pseudo-pacified struggle for social distinction and domination calibrated mainly by the degree of personal economic success achieved in the competitive market economy. The landscape of harmful crime is formally complex and diverse, but, roughly speaking, as we saw in Chapter 2, the overall criminological metamorphosis was from a premodern period in which physical violence was deployed liberally in the perpetration of acquisitive crime and the contested imposition of order to a modern period in which the use of physical violence diminished to be displaced by a diverse range of alternative means of material acquisition and social domination. Other Western nations followed a similar pattern over different periods of time; in the USA, for instance, the shift was uniquely condensed in its urbanization period from the mid-nineteenth century to the mid-twentieth century (Monkkonen, 1988). As the West entered the twentieth century, violence had largely become a last resort in the perpetration of acquisitive crime, the maintenance of modes of domination and the maintenance of public order, although the threat of violence from both criminals and the forces of law and order continues to loom in the background to be released in specific situations. It is important to note that the capitalist state's monopolization of organized political violence remains in place, supported by the ideology of democracy and popular authorization, whilst it has been outlawed amongst the population at large and, apart from occasional terrorist acts and skirmishes at demonstrations, continues to exist only in sporadic, privatized and depoliticized forms. The mode of domination and resistance has been transformed; an impermeable social class division maintained by the elite's violent subjugation of the population, which was always in danger of provoking collective revolt, has metamorphosed into a relatively permeable social class relation reproduced hegemonically and authorized by an atomized, depoliticized and rather enraptured majority.

However, where there have been gains there have also been losses. There is little doubt that in Late Mediaeval England, despite the prevalence of superstition, violence and political tyranny during the aftermath of the excessively disruptive Norman invasion, down in the nooks and crannies of everyday society and economy life was anti-capitalist in practice and reproductive of an anti-capitalist ideology and subjectivity. Throughout Europe, usury – the practice of charging excessive interest on loans – was severely restricted and the authorities insisted on the establishment of a 'just and fixed price' for goods. It was a market price, but everyone agreed to stick to it. Hoarding, undercutting and overcharging were forbidden, which contributed to the slow but sure restoration of the production centres and distributive nodes and arteries disrupted during the violent Dark Age towards the condition of economic functionality and relatively peaceful and stable social interdependency they had enjoyed during the Roman occupation (Ward-Perkins, 2005). Before the advent of the exploitative 'putting-out system' in the seventeenth century, which took the organization of production and trade and the profits out of the hands of producers, production was organized around the guilds system rather than the current mode of the labour market and limited companies owned by small groups of capitalists trading their shares and bonds on the stock exchange. Effectively, the workers owned the means of production and '[t]he principle of Mediaeval trade was admittedly comradeship and justice, while the principle of modern trade is avowedly competition and greed' (Chesterton, 2001: 60). It seems that there had been an attempt to diffuse the ideals of the family and community into the external productive and trading systems in the interests of social justice and civility. Just how successful this diffusion was in concrete practice is a matter of conjecture and further historical research, but, in principle and in the sense of its hierarchal structure of authority, it was the *precise opposite* of the current invasion of all social institutions by the competitive logic of the deregulated market now recognized by some contemporary criminologists (see Currie, 2010; Messner & Rosenfeld, 1997) as the primary criminogenic aspect of advanced capitalist culture.

However, significant change was to follow. Marxist and Weberian historians were wrong to posit English society between the Norman invasion and the end of the fifteenth century as 'peasant'. It was to some extent in its means of production, but not in its culture or trading economy; the market, accounting, the profit motive, mobility of labour and private ownership of land were well established by the thirteenth century (Macfarlane, 1978). Neither was Mediaeval society wholly rigid and restrictive (Dyer, 2000). In the fourteenth-century demesne system, Norman warlords, who were too concerned with war, prayer and their courts to bother with estate management, left peasants to manage important aspects of the economy. There was a move away from grain production to pasture and meat for a post-Plague population enjoying higher wages and increased opportunities for wealth and status. Peasants were migrating to towns, seeking opportunities, in possession of land and equipment, running clandestine markets in towns without market charters, bypassing legal institutions and trying to escape from rents and enforced services. They were also rejecting the communal village life, and 20 per cent were living in towns, mainly as proto-entrepreneurs and consumers, already developing 'sumptuary' tastes for food and clothes as status symbols.

As some became richer they began to emulate and compete with the aristocracy; we must accept that in this period 'resistance' drove a struggle for social distinction and increased economic opportunities, not a struggle on behalf of the collective and social justice. The transition to capitalism was not all about acquisitive gentry, explorers, inventors and so forth, it was largely about 'modestly wealthy countrymen responding to economic and social circumstances' (Dyer, 2000: xiv). In the severe disruption that was the aftermath of the Norman invasion many village communities were disharmonious places with high murder rates (Hanawalt, 1979); it's not too far-fetched to suspect that such a contrast existed between disrupted everyday socio-economic life and the life of the aristocracy that some collective form of *Stockholm Syndrome* might have existed amongst the subjugated, who admired as much as hated their conquerors. Not all Mediaeval criminalization was honour-related but often about trespass, theft and other economic issues in a rapidly commercializing economy with a heightened and diffusing sense of territory and property. The lower orders aped the gentry wherever possible, preferring fresh meat, fresh fish, white bread and strong ale; Chaucer satirized the social climbing of the Franklin with his pond well-stocked with freshwater fish, 'many a bream and many a luce in stuwe' (*Prologue to the Canterbury Tales*, in Dyer, 2000: 111).

In the first wave of market development the Late Mediaeval economy was highly reliant on domestic and international trade. By the late thirteenth century a complex network of commerce had evolved, weighing in at over 25 per cent of GNP. A large informal market developed alongside the formal market, and transactions were often made outside of towns and licensed markets, in fields, inns and other secret meeting places. Some Priories obtained less than 5 per cent of goods from official markets; hidden trade outside official market venues and institutions avoided rents, tolls and taxes. The relative decline of smaller village markets provided opportunities for broader travel between larger towns in a small country with a developing road system, which required more efficient means of protecting property. In the burgeoning market system more sophisticated consumption tastes developed alongside expanded opportunities for trade, for rural and town dwellers alike. Social ambition and emulation became associated with the avoidance of governance and taxes, and we can see the beginnings of a powerful proto-bourgeois cultural current that drew together entrepreneurialism, social climbing, aristophiliac consumption tastes, hatred of regulation and taxation, economic crime and the gradual erosion of the economy's ethical infrastructure. As early as the late fourteenth century successful English entrepreneurs began to abandon horticulture for international markets, leaving it to professionals and servants. The post-Plague years brought higher wages and job mobility, but, as richer workers acquired land holdings, set up craft workshops and abandoned work as they employed waged labour, there was also early evidence of de-skilling and regarding work as drudgery whilst developing the love of leisure, status, money and unregulated enterprise. As we have seen, the Peasant's Revolt was a protest aimed at the aristocracy's imposition of taxation and restriction of opportunities for self-improvement, more than it was a class revolt against the ruling elite; the politically-organized left did not invent itself until proletarianization in the nineteenth century gave workers a sense of mutual identity and interests.

The Whiggish view of the Middle Ages as gloomy limbo and drudgery is also wide of the mark (Dyer, 2000; Macfarlane, 1978). The English were becoming capitalist entrepreneurs, not simply by producing goods for expanding legal and illegal markets but also by developing the acquisitive, narcissistic mentality very early and loosening up communal structures and restrictions to allow the birth of virulent forms of opportunism, instrumentalism, competitive individualism and conspicuous consumption. Of course the cause for class conflict existed in the shape of the dispossession of the peasantry and the creation of landless wage labourers, but much of this was done by members of the socially and geographically mobile peasantry itself, who had merged with the merchant classes and adopted their opportunistic and exploitative tendencies. By the fifteenth century an upward spiral of production and consumption was evident (Sassatelli, 2008; Sombart, 1967). In the early years of the gentrification process merchants identified with the Lords, eventually intermarrying, and ambitious peasants keen to establish a life of trade also adopted that mentality and demeanour. Peasants were further liberated as the smaller post-Plague population found itself in a better bargaining position; wages rose, the market shrank, rents, tolls and taxes collapsed, demand for land diminished and aristocrats were forced to make political and economic concessions. The partially liberated peasantry could enter a 'free' market as wage-labourers or as producers and traders, accumulating capital, increasing consumption and seeking symbols of social distinction. However, many who could not raise funds for the purchase of land were still vulnerable to eviction as Enclosure gathered pace, which fuelled anxiety, social division and conflict. Many former peasants were proto-capitalists by the fifteenth century, but times were difficult and they were forced to arrange production and trade in what was effectively a long-term recession. Individualism, opportunism, anxiety and a rejection of the sentiments of communalism and common fate all combined to create a potent and volatile socio-economic dynamic.

The principle socio-economic dynamic in this period, in what looks like a process of diffusionary cell-division rather than simple vertical mobility, structuration and conflict, was supplied with psychosocial fuel by the earlier ejection of sons and daughters from the family and community, forcing them to leave and make a living elsewhere. Macfarlane (1978) traces the beginnings of bourgeois individualism to this separation of *homo economicus* from the ethico-political 'cell' of the traditional productive-defensive family unit, its land and its property. This thesis on the origins of English individualism was treated quite harshly by some critics, but, although we have to agree that it was reductionist and his rather partisan and teleological conception of the historical process as a road to egalitarian individualism was highly suspect, from another perspective it is still very useful. Basically, he argued that in twelfth-century England, a new anxious yet ambitious form of atomized individualism arose to undermine peasant communalism. The introduction of the laws of primogeniture and entail throughout the social order – in most regions of continental Europe this was restricted to the aristocracy – had the schismatic effect of breaking up the family as a social and geographical unit; the first-born would inherit the family estate whilst the other siblings lost their guarantee of inheritance. Relations of sociability and love that remained in the proto-bourgeois family were henceforth tainted by an underlying anxiety, mistrust and economic instrumentalism. This created a void in social relations and disrupted the security offered by the family, a cellular 'state of exception' where there was no longer a legal guarantee of inheritance and family loyalty was not strictly enforced by custom, in which the symbolic structure of the old order was cast aside and the vital ethical decision about inheritance was placed at the door of the individual. During the same period, the Norman warlords, who, as we saw earlier, were relatively disinterested in land management, allowed peasants to buy and sell land and property. A lot of land was sold outside of the family, a practice that exacerbated and diffused the sentiments of anxiety, mistrust and resentment that had already grown inside the family itself. The new custom of buying and selling land led to the beginnings of the Enclosure movement in the late fourteenth century, which proceeded to enclose land up to the nineteenth century when all but the less arable moorland fringes were under private ownership and many farmers who had worked the traditional 'open field' system were dispossessed and forced into the labour market.

The male individual was in the legal sense partially isolated and rendered significantly more vulnerable as he was ejected into a hinterland to secure his own wealth and social significance, whilst the disempowered female sought suitable marriage or battled against male domination to seek some sort of entry into business; only the wealthy could offer financial support to compensate for this weakening of the family bond. This occurred gradually in the Western capitalist nations, beginning in England. In other European lands, where the laws of primogeniture and entail were restricted to the aristocracy, peasant cultures did not separate economics from morality and politics or the individual from the fundamental reproductive units of land, family and community quite so early and quite so completely; in fact some in the Mediterranean regions still hang on to their traditional forms. Macfarlane did not deny the possibility of historical change, as some of his critics argued, but simply pointed out the very early emergence and continuity of a supporting cultural form through that change.

The process was accelerated by technology and production solely for the market, and eventually institutionalized by Protestantism, but the individualist dream was alive in English culture well before the Renaissance. It was based on the opportunistic economic actor more than anything else, the proto-entrepreneur, and the volatile ego-centred kinship system. Macfarlane, however, was wrong to see this as the beginning of a cultural continuum of egalitarian individualism; this mutated culture was at its cutting-edge ruthlessly competitive, egocentric and potentially narcissistic. This psychosocial aspect is the most interesting for criminology; the individual sees himself as more important than the group and its symbolic order, not primarily in the healthy form of a unique free individual with inalienable rights but as an outcast economic actor with the right and the pressing need to monopolize material and abstract socio-economic resources in unforgiving competition with others; to 'seek his fortune' in a condition of insecurity and adversity that was thrust upon him as a matter of course. The individual was struggling to free himself from the oppressive social order on behalf of himself and his immediate dependents, not on behalf of others or some political project to establish a new order; this sounds remarkably like the principle behind today's conservative and radical versions of liberal individualism, which structure the criminological debate, and it associates them both with the birth of bourgeois individualism.

This was the beginning of the paradoxical combination of ambitious, individualized social mobility and socio-economic class conflict that was to permeate capitalism's history, and it also paved the way for a market economy in which everything including labour became commodified. Status could be earned and effectively bought, and upon this principle emerged an economized meritocracy and a more permeable social structure based on market performance and the accumulation of money. As love and solidarity declined – albeit from a brutal form that required physical sacrifices – the more pacified yet simultaneously more competitive, opportunistic and unrestrained *homo economicus* was on the road to becoming the most successful socio-economic player. Alongside this a hyper-individualistic culture developed, and we can extrapolate that the source of anxiety in each proto-bourgeois individual shifted from the obligation to support and defend the family and community to the need to survive as a precariously and conditionally supported individual in the midst of the social competition and economic dynamism that were building up in the nascent proto-capitalist market economy.

From this point onwards 'the social' lacked any firm foundation in England. What families and communities could no longer offer in substantive economically-grounded love and security they made up in sentimentalism and preparation for a tough independent life in the competitive 'real world'. 'Tough love' evolved as a cultural norm, a sublimated and economized variant of the warrior code of child rearing. Dependency had to be disparaged and degraded, a precursor to the conservative/classical liberal detestation of any 'dependency culture' that might exist between a collective body and the individual; the 'dignity of dependency' was eroded along with the bonds it can constitute and reproduce. This created an undialectical but functional tension between new cultural values and economic necessities as networks of paradoxical 'competitive interdependency' evolved in the capitalist economy. Civilized life depended on the cultivation of a sensate and cognitive awareness of the importance of interdependency, one that was robust enough to prevent competitive individualism boiling over into an unmanageable hot vapour of duplicity, exploitation and violence; what replaced the traditional symbolic order was a high-pressure,

schizoid duality of stimulation and repression/sublimation whose important cultural task was to constitute and reproduce subjectivities morally
strong enough to repress and sublimate the chronic anxiety and obscene
libidinal energy that it was concurrently stimulating. At first glance this
bears a resemblance to the deterritorialization/reterritorialization thesis
offered by Deleuze (1984), where bourgeois forms still resemble their
traditional counterparts but have different functions and values on a different formal plane, but this misses their psychosocial pairing in a politically
and ethically undialectical yet socio-economically dynamic relationship that
resulted in 'the impoverishment of subjectivity and extinction of the older
subject itself ... [alongside] the immense power now granted to money
itself and the logic of finance' (Jameson, 2010: 189).

Law, culture and economics combined to create an upheaval in familial
relations where the death of the father became a wish of the one who was
forced out to imitate his success elsewhere, which invoked as a common
symbolic desire (although occasionally as a real drive or a real act) one of
the two most abhorrent primary Oedipal crimes, parricide (the other
being incest). Because the mother was the next in line for inheritance,
this misandry could easily be converted to misogyny. Siblings lower down
the pecking order were even more dependent on the parents' generosity
and sense of justice, so the love that was once possible in families, and
which carried the potential of being diffused amongst broader communities, was in the proto-bourgeois family always in danger of splitting and
reuniting as the far more volatile fusion of mistrust, anxiety, repressed
hatred and compulsory affected sentimentalism. In economic terms the
conversion of patrimony into capital set a long-term process in motion
that saw the replacement of the social by the economic, human life converted into wage-labour, the liquidation of organic society, the dominance of money as the universal unit of exchange in the general market,
the destruction of the commons and the absorption of energy into repay-
ing the constant debt that was necessary to expand business (Polanyi,
1957). We seem to be looking at a sort of socio-economic tumour, a rapid
cell-like growth with a simultaneous linear and diffusionary movement
starting in and spreading from locations where instances of overactive
binary fission take place in forms that were too intense and rapid for the
dissolving traditional social body and its institutions to restrain. The accumulation of these instances of precedence together built up powerful
pressure for coordinated change in the economic, social, cultural, legal
and political dimensions, but not necessarily of a progressive nature.
Speaking of the peasant breaking free of the order of the Middle Ages,
Georg Simmel wrote:

> It is true he gained freedom, but only freedom from something, not liberty to do something. Apparently, he gained freedom to do anything – because it was purely negative – but in fact he was without any directive, without any definite and determining content. Such freedom favours that emptiness and instability that allows one to give full rein to every accidental, whimsical and tempting impulse. Such freedom may be compared with the fate of the insecure person who has forsworn his Gods and whose newly acquired 'freedom' only provides the opportunity for making an idol out of any fleeting value. (1978: 402)

This is the negative freedom that Mill (2006) much later established as the principle of classical liberalism at a time when the shift from a culture of 'the public good' to a culture of 'individual rights' was at full throttle; all could be for one, but one could no longer be for all any more than she thought it prudent to be, and thus it generally panned out that the 'all' constantly struggled to be strong enough to 'be' for the 'one' in ways that were effective. In the burgeoning market economy of Late Mediaeval and Early Modern England, which was energized by the dissolution of the traditional social from specific schismatic points in its body, even witchcraft was individualized and commercialized; witches acted as lone businesswomen rather than in European-style covens and groups, targeting the lower orders rather than the *nouveaux riches* for commercial gain. Between the Norman invasion and the Industrial Revolution, England was not a standard 'peasant society'. English villeinage was highly individualistic (Bloch, 1967), and it's interesting that this term developed criminal connotations that expressed an 'untrustworthy character'. The process of individualization was aided by the concomitant centralization of justice and common law, the ease of transfer of property and impartible inheritance, which contributed to capitalism's tendency to prioritize exchange-value and degrade labour and the material world. In a similar vein Dumont followed Marx and Simmel in seeing the capitalist era characterized by a shift in direct relations between individuals to the mediation of private property, money and the market:

> [A]s Mauss and especially Karl Polanyi have ascertained – modern civilization differs radically from other civilizations and cultures. The truth is that our culture is permeated by nominalism, which grants real existence only to individuals and not to relations, to elements and not to sets of elements. Nominalism, in fact, is just another name for individualism, or rather one of its facets. (1986: 11)

Macfarlane's thesis chimes rather loudly with that of Philippe Ariès. His classic work *Centuries of Childhood* (1996) contained a number of controversial ideas, and, like Macfarlane, he received vitriolic critique. However, his assertion that before the eighteenth century parents were less sentimentally attached to their children because high infant and child mortality rates had accustomed them to loss, suggests that there was a cultural climate conducive to this socio-economic dynamic, which added to the psychological 'hardening' of individuals and the fragile conditionality of familial relations. For both authors, in the pre-industrial family, children did not 'matter' to parents in the same way as they came to matter as modernity gathered pace. The legal and economic position of the children became one in which the father's unconditional love, expressed in legal and material rights, bonding, support and gestures of affection – and the mother's in the case of the actual death of the father – became the primary lost object, the *objet petit a*, the unnameable *thing* behind the fundamental fantasy and the *death drive*; this lost object is the essential psychic energy source. Haunted by the spectral presence of the father's judgement that continues even after his death, rendering the symbolic figure of the father as 'undead', the sons and daughters are activated to reproduce the father's wishes yet also to keep on trying to kill the spectral image with myriad *sinthomes*, minute joys or stupid pleasures, expressed in great detail in the poetry of Sylvia Plath (Rose, 1991; Žižek, 2008). These harmless expressions are on their own little objects of *jouissance* symbolizing the guilt felt by the repressed knowledge that the subject is a blind follower of the coalesced obscene underside of bourgeois culture. Stimulated and systematized by advanced capitalism's consumer culture, however, they combine and expand exponentially into the immensely potent psychosocial force that continues to drive forward capitalism (Hall et al., 2008).

It looks like Macfarlane (1987), Wieviorka (2007) and Mucchielli (2010) are correct to question the existence of a 'civilizing process', because there is no evidence of a discernible cause. Very real violence and intimidation were simply reorganized and reformed; as well as their continued existence in street crime, they were privatized in the household and the workplace, monopolized as overt practices of social control and external military force by the state and its agents and adopted by the ruthless undertakers of organized crime. From Tudor times, when at least some reliable records were kept, petty property crimes and corruption in business burgeoned (Salgado, 1972). Honour was not being 'spiritualized', as Spierenburg (2008) suggested, but transferred from the body to commercial business and the money-form, which created a paradoxical split in honour itself. On one hand it was dishonourable to obtain money dishonestly and exploitatively, yet, on the other hand, dishonesty and exploitation were built into the system itself and embraced in everyday business because it was also dishonourable to fail in the attempt to make money as an independent individual, and one's justifications for failing were denounced as excuses. The poor 'failures' were 'rebadged' as lazy, ill-disciplined, incompetent and imprudent, whilst the enterprising, disciplined, hard-working and financially prudent were lionized (McFall et al., 2008). We must suspect that the fear of the dishonour that would follow failure, humiliation and poverty, which are unable to be concealed and disavowed, would have overwhelmed the risk of an alternative form of dishonour sourced in the practices of the obscene Real, active participation in which is eminently capable of being concealed and fetishistically disavowed as a standard bourgeois cultural expectation.

Some social crime, as an angry reaction to poverty or oppression, continued to exist, as customary economic practices of food gathering and hunting were criminalized during the various phases of the Enclosure Movement. The most oft-quoted example of the criminalization process was the Waltham Black Acts, which, beginning in 1723, placed over 50 new offences on the statute book, mostly concerned with customary means of obtaining food (Thompson, 1975). However, for many criminals who were not on the brink of starvation economic crime became a way out of the difficult double-bind that had appeared in mutating codes of honour, where the fear of the social and legal repercussions that might befall the individual who took illegal short-cuts to wealth and status was outweighed by the fear of failing altogether by sinking down a reconfiguring social order that was becoming more permeable and therefore carried more expectations of success and upward mobility. Yes, crime was about choice, but not in the first instance conscious, rational choice; these were acts of choosing, infused with and driven by the powerful emotions of saving face in an atomized post-collective world and preventing the anxious individual's slide into dishonour and social insignificance, of losing one's vital place in social systems of symbolic exchange whose symbols were becoming inextricably connected to the individual's successful performance in a market economy. It is an almost universal anthropological principle that if one cannot exchange socially recognized symbols, one ceases to exist in the eyes of all those who value them (Baudrillard, 1993; Bourdieu, 1990).

Hirschman (1977) grounds Elias's 'civilizing process' and Spierenburg's 'spiritualization of honour' into the economic context that is glaringly absent from both these theories. Present throughout the set of Renaissance pamphlets and treatises on the development of civility and cosmopolitanism was the grounded causal concept of *la doceur du commerce*, the domesticating of the 'rude' peoples of Europe for the purpose of expanding non-violent commercial activity. Dark Age Europe had been notably violent since the demise of the Roman Empire, a vast ungoverned paraspace in which warlords struggled for land and power, setting the cultural tone for their subjects (Ward-Perkins, 2005). By the later Middle Ages the intimidation/violence nexus had become a principal structuring force in politics and social relations (Maddern, 1992), normalized as it was practiced by aristocrats and to a large extent emulated by those amongst the subjugated who sought localized power and authority inside developing but still sparse legal and cultural codes. Whether we like it or not, the original impetus for civility was a quest for economic prosperity by reviving and expanding the production and trading systems that had functioned as imperial arteries during the Roman occupation of Europe. The introduction and early development of the pseudo-pacification process was celebrated throughout a growing body of Renaissance literature. In the West, the 'libidinization of the market' (Jameson, 2010: 448) proceeded rapidly in a relatively authoritarian politico-cultural context; the two poles of the constricted and economically harnessed pseudo-pacification process created immense undialectical generative tension, stimulating and sublimating desire in equally intense measures, which increased the degree of voluntarism in workers even though they had little choice but to dedicate their energies to the exploitative production process.

By the fifteenth century the large English manorial estate had become a rational capitalist enterprise run for economic profit. Food was produced not for local consumption but for cash-cropping and wider distribution. The traditional small self-sufficient family units had disappeared and large landlords dominated. Selling off land for individual gain would have been unthinkable in Russia, but in Britain and the USA such traditional restraints came to be seen as fetters to individual freedom and enterprise. Ownership was individualized and legalized, for men and women, and where wives had rights to one third of the estate, children still had none at all. They had no jurisdiction over the estate and could not stop their father or mother selling it, and by the sixteenth century there was a very active market in land. Unlike Europe, where primogeniture was restricted to the upper classes, in England it was common amongst the lower orders. Younger and less 'talented' – or perhaps less ruthless and competitive, we might suspect – children were often disinherited and cast out. Social mobility was *expected*, which created social divisiveness from the cell of the family itself; there was a polarization of wealth and status as the favoured sons and daughters inherited and bought more land whilst others joined the ranks of the landless labourers. This was also a push-factor in emigration, and in purely economic terms there was no external structural force oppressing the peasant class, either capitalism or the aristocracy or the nascent bourgeoisie; the individualization process and the atomization of the peasantry into competitive, suspicious and potentially hostile monads was internally generated; the peasants *were* the nascent bourgeoisie. We can see an accelerated illustration of this process of dissolution and cell-like diffusion into loosely structured but alluringly permeable layers of competitive individuals as the introduction of English common law into the colonies also had a devastating effect on communal traditions. Eagleton (1970) sees in Shakespeare the cultural crisis of early modernity, the tension between the spontaneous individual and the dying social. The nineteenth century was full of philosophers and educators who sought to release, cultivate and preserve the life-energy of the individual, burning like Nietzsche's sun, without any critical reflection on the possibility that that life-energy had already been pre-formed and fixated onto its objects by a centuries-old culture of communal dissolution and individual entrepreneurialism.

The egocentric economic mentality diffused into all other dimensions of life as individuals were cut loose from their families and cast into the marketplace and urban industrial life. Romantic love and courtship leading to the sentimental bonds of the nuclear family was perhaps an attempt to recapture what had been lost in an increasingly atomized and instrumental culture, but private inner feelings did not restore but further displaced communal morals and sentiments and the wishes of the parents (Shorter, 1975). The type of privatized desire that could be manipulated by the external forces of consumer culture was emerging as the cultural norm. Macfarlane, as we have seen, argues that this can be found much earlier, so it takes its place as a driver rather than an effect. Goody (1983) traces it back even earlier, as far as Dark Age England, perhaps a reaction to the disruption of English communalism by the Roman invasion and the eventual withdrawal from Christianity, which was re-joined later as a ritualized ideal rather than a communal practice. It is the timing and the direction of causality between individualism and capitalism that is possibly wrong in most history and social theory; the presence of individualized irrationalism and sentiment combined with an acceptance of the cold rationality of law, bureaucracy, economy and social competition allowed the English individual to embrace the rise of capitalism with enthusiasm and fascination as well as fear and trepidation. Individualized romantic love, with all its fragile anxieties and yearnings, is a much more malleable and extractable source of energy than territorial, communal and familial sentiments bolstered by the defensive self-respect of traditional honour.

Thus, in 1497, according to Sombart (1998), an Italian visitor's impression of the English proto-bourgeois individual was of a self-confident, arrogant and suspicious character, out for himself and with no sincere and solid friendships. He displayed a lack of trust, was uncommunicative and would not reveal private affairs. Our visitor was horrified by the lack of affection in families and the willingness to put young children out to apprenticeships, most of whom did not return to the family because of the widespread adoption of primogeniture, which meant they had little hope of parental inheritance. These individuals were suited to a harsh economic meritocracy of compulsory 'undertaking' that leads to greed, anxiety, competitiveness and the tendency of either sex to marry for money. Most saw nobility and status in transcending manual work and becoming a 'master' of others, so the chance to dominate and wield authority over others seemed to trump even the allure of Veblen's (1994) leisure class. England was more prosperous than its continental neighbours, but English commentators tended to see value only in prosperity and social mobility and judged Europe accordingly. The good points of autonomous and spontaneous individualism, prosperity and social mobility were outweighed by a notable lack of public-spiritedness and sympathy for others; the early rise and self-affirmed triumph of *homo economicus*.

By the seventeenth century production for exchange was the norm, the extended family was breaking up and the exclusive private ownership of land was replacing the joint corporate ownership of a genuine peasant society; the land belonged to the individual who held the deeds. Sons lived under the constant threat of disinheritance and children were no longer economic assets. On a legal and economic platform where there was no inalienable right to land and property, the tradition, ethos and taste for collective ownership and collective power had dissipated. The period from the seventeenth to the nineteenth centuries was, after the Civil War, characterized by further declines in violence and homicide and a rise in property crimes, further evidence of the sublimation process and the conversion of anxiety, honour and physical hostility into social and economic competition. Theft has been the most prosecuted crime in England since the fourteenth century, fraud and counterfeiting were common, and burglaries and highway robberies were often planned in order to steal goods to exchange for money. Most of this was not social crime because there was no evidence of redistribution or ethico-political motives, but crime perpetrated to comply with the compulsion of private enterprise fuelled by the subjective drives of cynicism, instrumentalism and bitterness.

There was no real social battle between the classes, which explains why, before conscious proletarian political organization from the mid nineteenth century, English socialism tended to be the dream of guilty bourgeois philanthropists; for the anxious, internally exiled English individual money, market performance and social mobility were paramount. Many individuals admired their betters and wanted to emulate them, especially after the repeal of the sumptuary laws. There was a distinct absence of inter-family feuding, evidence of the dissolution of family loyalties. Thieves did not steal from the upper classes, but from their relatives, neighbours and weaker members of the locale; most petty acquisitive crime was cowardly, bullying, cynical, instrumental and nothing to do with politics or honour. There was also very little organized vagabondage or banditry; wandering beggars were individualists too, and there were no pitched battles between bandits and the forces of law and order as in France, Sicily, China and other countries.

Trade and commerce were vitally important, and their revival fuelled production for exchange, but Sombart (1967) argued that localized luxury urban consumption was even more vital, creating cities as consumer nodes in trade arteries. As we saw earlier, the enrichment of the elite urban courtiers was proving to be essential to the expansion of consumption, which in turn was required to attract investment and kick-start new productive industries. At the same time land enclosure, dispossession and the severance of individuals from protective families and communities produced anxiety and resentment, which injected a degree of bitterness into the admiration and envy generated by the consumer-cultural relation. Commerce attracted serfs into towns in a long process of Enclosure and urbanization, but the drive was not towards political opposition but the maximization of individual opportunities as the technically and financially adept worker became accustomed to developing at least some degree of personal initiative and financial sense in the putting-out system. This was different to independent cottage production in that it maintained links with major commercial arteries and merchants, who supplied materials, requested designs attuned to consumer tastes and guaranteed sales. Immersed in the developing system, it was becoming increasingly easy for the worker to learn the skills and knowledge necessary to enter the world of commerce and enterprise. However, we must stress that from the beginning this process of self-improvement and social mobility was individually competitive, ethically and culturally corrosive and socially divisive, and it was happening in an environment increasingly bereft of traditional forms of security. There was no organic, evolutionary means by which the working class could ever become a class in-itself or for-itself, and its failure to recognize its own identity and social position was not simply a product of 'false consciousness' but also the opposite; a very clear, ambitious and cynical conscious awareness, exhibited by the majority, of the socio-economic reality they had inherited, a personalized *realpolitik*.

The Protestant Ethic was more than simply the ideological expression of a class relation, it was also the vital moral insulation that was needed to prevent a system in the early stages of diffusing personal ambition and trading/consumption rights from collapsing rapidly back into the condition of political violence and social chaos that had characterized English history between the eleventh and fourteenth centuries. We could say that Protestantism had to promote 'new values' in the seventeenth century as the capitalist process picked up pace, but if we apply the Lacanian triptych to the analysis we can see that what was being promoted were externalized value-ideals in tension with real forces as the Symbolic promoted work, frugality, profit and investment, the Imaginary promoted progress, freedom, individual sovereignty, hedonism, and the ideological Real promoted and simultaneously disavowed socio-economic disruption, exploitation, conspicuous consumption, envy, greed, corruption, atomism, fractious competition and so on; what was in the air was necessarily different from what was in the bones, and this captures the dynamic tension of the pseudo-pacification process. Weber's (2002) and Sombart's (1998) 'unethical adventurers' and speculators were simply the capitalists who eschewed the concealing capacity of the Symbolic and the Imaginary to allow their unrefined commitments to the Real to bubble up too close to the surface.

What we can see clearly, though, in the work of Sombart (1967) and others (see Campbell, 1987; Sassatelli, 2008), is the existence of a desire for luxury and conspicuous consumption in the early stages of its diffusion outwards throughout the social body at the same time as the Protestant ethic was supposed to be restricting it. The narcissistic, brash and guilt-free adventurer/speculator was described by Weber (ibid.) as not a real Protestant, but this argument about whether businessmen were rational, honest, trustworthy and thrifty wealth creators or disreputable speculators, exploiters and conspicuous consumers is rather pointless. These categories represent the two poles of the pseudo-pacification process, active to varying degrees in each individual; apart from saints or devils, of course, which we might assume were rather few in number. He was also wrong to see tax-farming, money-lending, colonial expansion and adventurism as aristocratic traits that were displaced by the honesty, prudence and modesty of the 'genuine' bourgeoisie. The greatest fortunes amongst the bourgeoisie were made not in the honest manufacture and distribution of useful objects but in finance, especially state finance during wars (Marshall, 1982), and the import of exotic goods at the expense of domestic producers was also very lucrative (Sombart, 1967), as it still is to this day. We could argue that bourgeois economic activity and its supporting culture, policy and law were regressive when compared to Mediaeval practices regarding usury, fair wages, honest conduct and the reluctance to encroach on the territory and threaten the livelihoods of others. There is no doubt that liberalism's

record on individual freedoms and rights is superior, but we must understand modernist progress as a combination of gains and losses polarized
across the material/abstract nexus, an understanding that, as we have seen,
does not shine too brightly in the standard Whiggish criminological literature. These local and regional customs were broken down by the expansion
of the export trade (Power, 1941), whose distancing of economic actors,
which demanded only weak social and political relations beyond the basic
economic transaction, helped to break down the relations of trust, respect
and civility that had developed in local trade (Wilson, 1967). These anti-
social and apolitical relational traits are also to be found amongst criminal
groups; notions of mutual trust, respect and reliability in social relations
and economic transactions amongst criminal groups and networks tend to
be grossly overestimated (Gambetta, 2009). That these traits were hidden
and disavowed would make them more attractive to criminals, who could
import and adapt ready-made techniques of subterfuge, concealment and
denial to aid the ethically uninterrupted continuation of business practice.

Did any force *really* oppose the rise of bourgeois instrumentalism, individualism and pseudo-pacification? By the eighteenth century, in the run-up
to full-blown industrial capitalism, Western culture was moving into an age
of sentiment as well as reason, fostered and reproduced by a middle-class
movement concerned with refined sensibilities such as pity and benevolence (Eagleton, 2009). If capitalism was driven forward by the
psychosocial forces of hostile interpersonal competition and exploitation,
the cultural elite, apprehensive in the midst of all this ambitious energy
crackling amongst the masses, were concerned with the construction of a
counter-force. The lust for power, wealth and narcissistic social distinction
was to be sublimated by what Frances Hutcheson named the 'calm desire
for wealth' (ibid. :15). The means to commercial ends, no matter how
unethical and provocative some might have been, had to be civilized in their
manner of practice to make life less turbulent and hostile, and therefore less
likely to erupt into the sort of violence and unrest that would jeopardize
the whole project of property and money accumulation. Calm in the social
and political realms was not simply a pleasurable consequence of burgeoning prosperity but a vital functional necessity. As Eagleton puts it, drawing
from Pocock (1989), the eighteenth century was characterized by 'the ideology of so-called commercial humanism, for which the proliferation of
trade and the spawning of human sympathies are mutually enriching'
(2008:18).

Throughout their works, eighteenth-century benevolentist and sentimentalist philosophers such as Hutcheson and Goldsmith seemed to be
busy in an attempt to construct an intermediary realm, a middle deck that

housed a social club where a fragile artificial bonhomie could be orchestrated between the boiler-room of reptilian economic predation and the bridge of dutiful obedience to restrictive norms and laws cobbled together from the detritus of deracinated and relocated values. We should *feel* for each other, extend sympathy to each other, listen to each other's problems and share each other's dreams, have fun and romance, but only in the clubhouse dedicated to such contrived sentimental activities; to extend our fellow-feeling elsewhere – especially in economic transactions – was personally naive and socio-economically destructive. Despite their critiques of ultra-cynics such as Mandeville, for whom instrumentalism pervaded all social activities, benevolentists were also subtle ideologues for the status quo. The 'warre of all against all' in the obscene underbelly beneath the social contract and the benevolentist pseudo-civility that tried to construct and advertise itself as the attractive supplement to the dreary utilitarian normative/legal order were both constructs of capitalism's co-evolutionary process, the two opposing forces that fuelled the dynamic socio-economic impetus that the pseudo-pacification process had evolved to generate and maintain. The liberal-utilitarian maxim that, as Eagleton (2009:38) puts it, 'the truly vicious are as much the enemies of utility as the angels', reveals the perceived functional need for the subjects of the pseudo-pacification process to reside in the field of dynamic tension between its two poles. Moving too close towards good or evil risks dysfunction and danger, and Nietzsche's injunction to move 'beyond good and evil' in the sublimated realm of art is of course the ultimate form of functional and political domestication.

In Lacanian terms pseudo-pacification was a dream of the Imaginary, an undialectical and apolitical third category produced in the tension between the drive of the Real and the law of the Symbolic; *if only* we could spread benevolence, sentimentalism and fellow-feeling throughout the social body whilst retaining the obscene supplement of the Real that pumps its predatory energy into the economy to be restrained and sublimated by the Symbolic Law. Blake and the other early critical Romantics, who were at the beginning of a current that would run through the Frankfurt School to the vestige of Romantic critical theory that exists today, were wonderfully sensitive and literate reporters of the Real and the underlying infrastructural reality it was constructing – just as Winter, Scorsese and the other writers and directors of *Boardwalk Empire* are today – but in the unstable 'age of revolution' (Hobsbawm, 1996) they were considered far too radical, and indeed pessimistic, for the faithful of liberal capitalism's New Order. Romantic critical theory is still the principal enemy of the optimistic Imaginary of the 'late capitalist 'things can only get better' managerialism that now pervades the intellectual life and policymaking of the liberal left and neoliberal right in criminology and its associated disciplines.

For instance, William Blake was the quintessential Romantic visionary who saw the problems created by this shift, and pointed his finger at the 'mind-forged manacles' of the new liberal ideology of individualism, rationalism and scientism, which presaged the 'death of love' posited by Nietzsche. Needless to say, this searing social critique was largely ignored by early social and criminological thinkers, and continues to be by today's left-liberal social commentators. In his poem *London*, Blake averred that:

> In every cry of every Man,
> In every Infant's cry of fear,
> In every voice, in every ban,
> The mind-forg'd manacles I hear.

The poem was written in 1792, a time of great oppression, social disruption and political turbulence wedded to economic opportunity, but the important yet consistently neglected message was that even the poor were infused 'in the bones' with economic liberalism's destructive ideology and sentiments. In the early period of industrial capitalism alliances of merchants, finance capitalists and proto-industrialists were disrupting the socio-economic fabric of the nation, which for many resulted in rapid urbanization and a descent into poverty, insecurity and misery. Occupational and cultural identities were being crushed and forced to reconstitute themselves. In the period 1780–1830 there was a 540 per cent rise in recorded crime in London (Rusche & Kirchheimer, 1939). Blake's poem connected the economic oppression, social disruption and its deleterious effects of poverty, misery and confusion with the ideological oppression of the 'intellectual cuffs' placed *on all minds* by the prevalent hegemonic ideology, which justified this destructive change as the 'tough medicine' required to establish the capitalist system and guarantee future wealth for all. To maintain the pseudo-pacification process a truncated, apolitical 'moral sense' must be built into the constitution of its subjects. We must be thoroughly decent people in our cultural lives whilst in our socio-economic lives seek to outcompete and humiliate others as we try to disparage their social positions, exploit their labour, siphon off their disposable income, encroach on their market share and, if push comes to shove, destroy their livelihoods.

So much classical theory suggested that modernity was disruptive and that socio-legal rules and cultural norms cannot be permanent and binding; in other words formal rationality co-exists with underlying 'chaos' (Turner & Rojek, 2001). This formulation is certainly an improvement on the crude teleological linearity of Weber's (1978) conception of historical progress from formal irrationality through substantive irrationality and substantive rationality to the final 'disenchanted' mode of bureaucratic formal rationality. It capture's capitalism's underlying dualism, but it is problematic insofar as the naming of the underlying form is premature; chaos is only a *potential* and hitherto temporary result of periodic breakdowns of the fragile dynamic relation that exists between the two manufactured poles of atomized rebellion and social conformity (Hall et al., 2008), an unintended consequence that occurs periodically in various forms – economic crashes, crime-waves, outbreaks of violence and so on. However, it appears that this 'ferment of energy' (Turner & Rojek, 2001) was unleashed in the aftermath of familial/communal dissolution and anxious individuation *before* and not *by* Protestantism and industrial capitalism, which were both means of harnessing it. In a dualistic continuum idealistic expectations of trust, honesty and public-spiritedness ran alongside cynical realist expectations of the exploitation, profiteering, deception, miserliness and aggressive monopolistic practices that were experienced yet fetishistically disavowed in everyday ideological life. In a process of ethical inversion the latter became drivers necessitated by business logic and internalized 'in the bones' of bourgeois individuals by constant immersion in business practices, whilst the former, once the beating heart of the ethico-social collective, became irksome restraints that stabilized and civilized the volatile economic transactions that had become the bedrock of the social. The extent to which the former were also inculcated 'in the bone' as durable sensibilities depended on the individual's upbringing and willingness to risk a relative loss of competitive edge.

Social peace was thus largely dependent on the constant expansion of opportunities for enrichment and social significance in the new commercial order. The murderous wars and eruptions of violence and repression that have characterized the liberal-capitalist epoch occurred in periods when the expansion of these opportunities was placed under threat, and as such they are not products of a regressive 'decivilizing' phase but eruptions of the Real that is built into the contingent reward logic at the heart of the process. Capitalist-modernist culture is a dynamic yet fragile contingent reward system, and it bears no resemblance to solidarity in any sense of the term; when the majority get the rewards promised by the system they are reasonably happy – even if the minority do not – but the minute the rewards become difficult to come by most individuals respond not with solidarity but with increased efforts to seize dwindling opportunities and positions of advantage at the expense of 'lazy and feckless' others.

The new 'social' and 'associational' networks trumpeted by liberal-postmodernist social theorists (see Lash, 1990; Latour, 2005) are simply banal descriptions of the latest substitutes for the 'lost object' of social solidarity. The constant expansion of the limits of hedonistic-solipsistic individualism facilitated by technological development and the need to produce and consume a constant stream of superficial novelties – the joint critique of Marxists, Freudians and traditional conservatives alike, who can be brought together in unholy yet productive intellectual alliances such as Eliot and Adorno (Shusterman, 1993) – are now the main coordinates of the contingent rewards, which must be provided for individual gratification, the great historical promise of capitalist modernity. Is this what really happened to the 'evil' of Dark Age violence, whose barbarity is still the stuff of our nightmares; was it bought off, sublimated and harnessed as a source of energy in capitalism's contingent reward system? If so, the deal is not without precedent. For instance, when the Legalists began to displace the Confucians in Chinese history, the idea that 'evil' was a product of disobeying traditional codes and should be stifled by re-imposing these codes on the population was replaced by the idea that evil could be accepted for what it is and harnessed to state power with a political theory and practice that was 'beyond good and evil'. The 'right theory' saw evil as a challenge that justified the institutionalization and enforcement of strict laws by the state apparatus. In other words, this ancient variation of the pseudo-pacification process was located in the state's authoritative institutions rather than the psychosocial structure of the nexus between the individual and the economy. It is only one small step from this to the modernist-capitalist variant of encouraging 'evil' in specific individualized forms that can be harnessed by the economy with classical liberalism's 'night-watchman state' as the backstop. As Žižek explains:

> [T]he Chinese Legalists, these proto-totalitarians, already formulated a vision later propounded by liberalism, namely a vision of state power that, instead of relying on people's mores, submits them to a mechanism which makes their vices work for the common Good. (2010:16)

The 'evil' of privatism was established before the Protestant Reformation by an Aquinian doctrine based on the acceptance of human imperfection; the perfect form of shared collective property was too Godly for imperfect sinners on earth, whose demand for egalitarianism was deemed as sinful. Liberalism took up the theme with the Kantian notion that the liberal utopia must be of such a form and strength that it can cope with a 'race of devils'. Thus, according to Kant (2003: 36) the 'cunning of reason' should work in the service of 'perpetual peace', pacifying and harnessing the egocentric energies of 'intelligent devils'. Kant often fulminated against the 'serpent windings' of the British utilitarians, but at the ontological root there was less difference between them than he liked to think. The utilitarians adopted the 'realistic' stance of Bernard Mandeville (1970), the notion that natural private vices work for the public good, which was also adopted by Adam Smith (1984), although the latter's position was tempered by his recognition of the importance of moral codes and the removal of superfluous temptation as essential insulation. However, it is only one small step from this to say that we should quite deliberately *stimulate*, *proliferate* and *diffuse* private vices *because* they work for the public good, which, to the classical liberal, means economic growth. Thus, capitulating to one's private obscene egoism and envy is the most effective way to ensure the common Good. The tension between individual freedom and the eternal apparatus that regulates collective behaviour is accepted by liberalism, but we must accept that liberalism was a latecomer in a process that was already well under way in the constitution 'in the bone' of the desires the individual wishes to be free to gratify.

Today's liberal social management system focuses on the defence of the individual's negative human rights, which do not act as a symbolic guide to the Good but only as a loose boundary placed at the estimated point at which Evil might be encountered, and as compensation for loss. The fundamental, undialectical but economically powerful dynamic force that exists between stimulated and atomized 'little evils' and repressive state authority remains intact. A pure liberal-postmodern society operating in the free space between these poles and freed from all moral prejudices would not just be a society that, as Jean-Claude Michéa (2007) puts it, 'sees crimes everywhere', but one which, oscillating between acceptance and condemnation, *sees crimes everywhere and nowhere* and begins to dissolve in its own irredeemable symbolic inefficiency. Many liberal theorists celebrate symbolically inefficient life in this hollowed space, whilst ignoring the poles of drives and repression that create it as a space in time, a space that exists only if the undialectical pressure can continue to drive forward the technological and sensate novelties – "the iPod changed my life" waxed the fawning eulogists upon the recent death of "visionary genius" Steve Jobs, a successful corporate computer salesman – that are now the only attractors remaining in the liberal-capitalist project. For Lash (1990), for instance, in a quintessential postmodernist statement, subjectivity is permanently hollowed out, dedifferentiated, externalized, fragmented and collapsed into global flows of information and media that suggest emergent structures at the micro and macro levels. He suggests that we mourn the collective identities and efficient symbolic orders of the past, and, because the post-human will always retain the trace of the old human, that we accept a certain melancholic current in the New World. However, we can mourn only what is already dead, and with Lash and others it always seems that, at any moment now, their barely repressed excitement of witnessing the brave new world will leap out to overwhelm the dutiful but perhaps rather brief and affected melancholy of which they speak. There are times when their breathless intellectual enthusiasm sounds almost child-like, in the sense of a desperate recourse to some magical spacecraft that can follow Deleuze and Guattari's (1987) 'lines of flight' to reach escape velocity and spirit away the young from their dying communities to some place 'out of this world' (Hallward, 2006).

All of this enthusiasm for new life is predicated on the assumption that at some recent point in modernity's history we left behind our predatory pre-humanity. We cannot go backwards, avers Lash (see Gane, 2004: 100), but for Badiou (2007 and *passim*), Harvey (2007) and Žižek (2010a and *passim*), in the neoliberal era that began in the 1980s *we have already gone backwards* in a spectacular Restoration of classical liberalism in its technologically enhanced form, a move that, because of the system's destructive capabilities, also required the associated regression to conservatism, in its revised culturo-political form of neoconservatism, to try to put some moral brakes on economic neoliberalism's amoral runaway train. Lash talks about brief and intense relationships in the networks of communication technology, but we have to question whether these disembodied, competitive and obligation-free leisure relationships are *bona fide* relationships at all (Winlow & Hall, 2009). He claims that the true vitality is to be found in flows of information; for him it is the information that is 'alive', but in the material sense we can see clearly that his move is to *devitalize* life, to dissolve its passion for the real and its political bodies and posit it as pure spirit on the transcendental-phenomenological plane. Lash attributes this move to Wittgenstein, but we could argue that his later philosophy of the subject-in-language presupposed a drive and a will to perform a physical or political action before engagement with the linguistic and social rules that guide the expression of such wishes (Nodenstam, 1978). Given Lash's failure to deal with the punctuated evolution and splitting of the meaning of *élan vital*, he cannot deal with its ambivalence. He is not clear whether his meaning coincides with any point in the continuum from Bergson's evolutionary force through Schopenhauer's 'will-to-live' to Deleuze's failure to decide between the organic and inorganic roots of the force, and thus his attempt to establish 'vitalism' in the new flows and networks of information is arbitrary to say the least. It is more useful to posit the source of this vitalism, as Lippens (2012) does, as the grounded, visceral desire for control over emergence, if indeed it has evaded consumer culture's snare to continue to exist in such an authentic generative form.

Whether the seeds of Lash's 'new life' are present in information society's new networks and flows or not, criminological research tells us that some of the uglier embodied forms of predatory 'old life' are certainly active there; fraudsters, paedophiles, pornographers and so on (Dean, 2009; Yar, 2006), not simply products of opportunities that proliferate in new forms of communicative interaction but also of the abandonment of the project of establishing a grounded, nurturing social life. In order that a basic functional efficiency can be achieved, every overt legal system or set of social rules needs an underlying, unwritten and disavowed set of shared rules. These rules structure social relations, behaviours and the sense of ethics that make them possible and liveable. The new media enable individuals to enter into transactions with each other without entering into proper relationships; all that is required is that the value of the disembodied self's cultural and symbolic capital – created and ratified by the mass media and marketing industries – is, like money, universally recognized, and that the transactions are carried out with a certain level of trust and confidence. This social death and rebirth in an atomized, disembodied and politically impotent form is not simply an unwanted result of liberal capitalism, it has always been its basic presupposition and functional requirement (Žižek, 2010a). The state's constant failed attempts to create artificial grounded sociality amongst reluctant individuals contrasts with the media and the marketing industry's remarkable success at creating the conditions in which the ephemeral identities that proliferate in post-social and post-political cyber networks can constantly construct, destroy and reconstruct themselves around the symbols of consumer culture. Underneath the fake communities and disembedded identities dwell ruthless egoism and competitive individualism, and Žižek asks whether they enact:

> the silent pathological presupposition of Kantian ethics – that the Kantian ethical edifice can only maintain itself by silently presupposing the 'pathological' image of man as a ruthless utilitarian egotist? In exactly the same way, the Kantian political structure, with his notion of ideal legal power, can maintain itself only by silently presupposing the 'pathological' image of the subjects of this power as a 'race of devils'. (2010a: 42)

What liberal theorists see today as a constitutive space of freedom is in the reality of everyday desires and relations more like a gladiatorial arena where a great deal of psychic blood is spilt, not an escape from but a more intensive continuation and proliferation of liberal capitalism's competitive social life. New communications networks are not transformative, apart from the 'usual activists', they simply provide a space for the efficient and politically safe constitution and reproduction of liberal-capitalist subjectivities according to the logic of neoliberal economics. We now find ourselves in a situation where the obscene Real of an 800-year-old experientially and culturally reinforced ideology is entering the new world of global communications technology to breathe further life into the ultimate passive-aggressive forms that populate the later stages of the pseudo-pacification process, allowing the Real and its undertakings to be practiced in disembodied transactions and relations that avoid physical violence and other forms of direct confrontation. The capitalist Real's time has been extended, but simultaneously, now that the financial credit and the social time borrowed from the past are running out, the corrosion of reality – the physical and social infrastructure on which at the most basic level we all depend – has been accelerated.

CONCLUSION 10

The root of criminological theory's aetiological crisis is its palpable failure to explain why liberal-capitalist life constitutes and reproduces throughout its social structure conspicuous and influential subjectivities that reject solidarity for a form of competitive individualism, one which is willing to risk harm to others as it furthers its own interests. The time has come to consider the possibility that this failure has been self-imposed. The liberal-left thinking that dominates the discipline as the sole official opposition to conservatism honed its thinking in the shadow of the Gulag and the Holocaust. Whilst these unsurpassed historic crimes taught us of the evils of hatred, pathologization and demonization, the revulsion and guilt we felt in the aftermath constituted an inverted 'politics of anxiety'. The imagined object giving fearful shape to this anxiety is the possible return of the Promethean solution to the revolutionary transformation of unstable and unjust societies, and the inevitability of the horrors that will follow. So profound and institutionalized has this inverted object of fear become over the past 65 years, it now overshadows all other intellectual concerns and inquiries. It now continues to exist in intellectual life as an overextended and pervasive negation, a monitoring system that produces nothing of its own as it presides over degenerate research programmes, inducing intellectual sclerosis as it outlaws or at least strictly limits the investigation of reality and the production of ideas and explanations.

Criminological theory has been monitored more closely than most disciplines because it operates at the cutting edge of ethical condemnation; before approval, every analysis of crime and its underlying conditions must first pass through a filter, which insists that the first consideration must be that the objects of enquiry are the products of yet another 'moral panic'. This negating fear also made a weighty contribution to the left's political failure of nerve, weakening class-based opposition in the 1980s and ushering in neoliberalism to crush the ideas behind conservatism, communism, socialism and social democracy alike. Social philosophy and science have almost entirely lost their ability to recognize, understand and condemn capitalism's obscene underlying psychosocial drives, preferring to turn its critical eye on the corporate state, the institutional symptom of these drives. The relentless condemnation of universal ethics and symbolic efficiency, and the glorification of the endless theatre of politically aimless transgression and marginality, have helped to reproduce the perfect climate for the growth of the dark side of liberal individualism; the self-imposed isolation, the escape from ethical and social responsibility and the unforgiving competition and social exfoliation of the undertakers' quest for special liberty.

Returns to universalism in the wake of liberal-postmodernism's descent into farce, such as risk theory, have produced little more than administrative solutions to compensate the political failure of the 'third way'. Recent politico-economic events such as the financial crisis, the austerity cuts and liberal capitalism's serial military interventionism have joined the expansion of the global shadow-economy and the seamless integration of criminality into everyday life as potent reminders of need for intellectual life to return to universal ethics, political economy, class and subjectivity. Revived universalism in criminological theory now looks towards the concept of harm, and the removal of obstructive liberal filtering and class bias in the definition of harm in the political and legal systems and their attendant hegemonic culture. If criminalization is to be based on the universal ethical naming of harm, talk should be about the decriminalization of social crimes driven by desperation and the recriminalization of harmful crime, not decriminalization alone. Liberal ethics based on the deontological command that the individual empathize with others are not enough in an unforgivingly competitive capitalist world, where the ethical has become a safe substitute for the political. If critical theory, as the nexus of universal ethics, subjectivity and politics, is to return as the backbone of criminological theory, the discipline needs a clear definition of harm. The idea of grounding the concept of social harm in theories that draw on the Hegelian philosophy of social recognition is promising, but the problem is that advanced capitalism's severed socio-economic relation disempowers the judgement of the slave and sets the master free to seek the realm of special liberty. Aspiring others follow, and thus, in the climate set by the master's total transgression of the social and capture of the power of judgement, there can be no opposition or transgression that registers politically in acts of communication. Once more, the question of how to oppose – and indeed who and what to oppose – is thrown open.

An inquiry into the shape of crime and harm across history might help to at least begin to answer that question. We have seen the roots of European crime in early forms of brigandage, which was concerned with the monopolization of important nodes in markets and the acquisition of land and precious metals; it was a form of purified primitive accumulation and mini-governance by violence and intimidation with no responsibility to the social body. In the shift to the proto-capitalist market economy after the Plague, sovereignty, discipline and control acted in concert and in tension with increasing economic opportunities, individualism, seduction and aspiration. Criminology needs a more continuous view of capitalist/modernist history, and a dualistic view of subjectivity, the social and their complex intersections. During the capitalist-modernist period the decline in homicide and serious violence was accompanied by rises in property crimes, fraud, counterfeiting and so on, which indicates neither a 'civilizing process' nor a 'disciplinary society' but a shift in the way that exploitation and harm can be exercised and special liberty sought; basically, a process of dematerialization of the Real, a move from the pursuit of honour, land and treasure to the pursuit of money, and honour signified by success displayed in the diffused sociosymbolic economy of consumption. As the violent acquisition of objects and domination of others was sublimated to the realm of symbolic objects and provisionally pacified socio-economic competition, possibilities for the stimulation of vice became greater precisely because of the sublimation of its practices; this functional stimulation and control of the libidinal Real constitutes a pseudo-pacification process.

The rise in property crime was not simply the product of the rise in oppression, dispossession and social crime; a large proportion of property crime was individualistic and entrepreneurial, an illegal shadow of bourgeois subjectivity and economics. However, despite the growing dependency on markets, trade, money and wages in the industrial capitalist West and the rise in property crimes, all crime fell during the solidarity project that launched itself in the nineteenth century, which engendered amongst the working class an imperfect yet potent political culture that fostered the recognition of mutual interests and alternative ideologies. During the early stages of this project dualistic theories emerged amongst the left, based on the principle that those who rejected solidarity had allowed themselves to be driven by unrefined variants of bourgeois culture's obscene Real. However, they were on the whole rejected by the emerging liberal establishment, a fatal move that allowed the conservative establishment to naturalize the subjective 'dark side' that had been stimulated by capitalist culture and offer more convincing populist explanations of crime and the need for draconian forms of control. The development of permanent psychosocial restlessness and the anxiety-driven fetish for consumer symbolism in the construction of identity and the achievement of status fuelled the growth of a pervasive faith in money as a storehouse of accumulated value, and obsessive money-hoarding became a substitute for the lost objects of security and faith in others.

Liberal theorists, suspicious of collectivism and all notions of animal spirits, drives, desires and so on, were fixated on choice and individualism and willing only to give concessions to the concept of social needs. Many liberals from both the classical and social wings saw this enforced compensation of consumer choice and free identity-construction as progressive. The declining crime during Europe's solidarity project, quite probably based on a genuine reduction in motivations alongside improved policing, contrasts quite starkly with the rise in violent acquisitive crime in the USA as its liberal and conservative power-blocs rejected the solidarity project and its socialist politics in the period between 1900 and 1933. The economic management programmes of the New Deal from 1937 did help to reduce violent crime in the USA, but in the 1980s, when the programmes and the spirit introduced by the USA's New Deal and the British solidarity project both fell apart as the result of the systematic restoration of classical liberal political economy in the guise of neoliberalism, both nations experienced explosions of social and entrepreneurial crime. The significant statistical decline in crime since the 1990s must be seen in the light of increased surveillance and mass imprisonment in the USA and Britain, and the 'disappearance' of some crime and criminal markets into cyberspace. The current age of global neoliberal restructuring has brought with it urbanization, mass unemployment, the decline of economic stability and communal solidarity and the inexorable rise of 'glocal' criminal markets in a global shadow-economy. Mounting structural unemployment, especially amongst young people, has increased the drift into marginality and crime and the versatility and intensity of acquisitive crime in a cultural climate of depoliticization, anhedonic nihilism and resignation that grows amidst the hegemonic ideological narrative that history has ended and no feasible alternative to neoliberalism exists. Criminological research has demonstrated how reluctant recruits are drawn into criminality by active undertakers, operating mainly in huge global drug markets connected to corrupt corporations, states and a banking industry that offers money-laundering operations in a network of tax havens. Overall, the historical development of capitalism from England and Europe to be exported across the globe as a dominant form of political economy has been a diffusionary process, from *somewhere*, the violent acquisition and defence of land and treasure, to *nowhere*, the legal and illegal accumulation of non-taxable money laundered through tax havens and stored in the orbital economy. The solidarity project was little more than a brief period of respite, in danger of fading from memory through lack of commemoration.

A subtle but resolute liberal narrative dominates criminological thought as the official opposition to conservatism. Subjective dualism and class struggle have been replaced by ethical individualism and the undialectical individual–state relation, represented by the anodyne and sterile agency–structure debate in sociology. The liberal narrative is largely uninterested in the motivations behind individual selfishness, positing instead a benign, creative human nature that will flourish if the oppressive authority of the state can be minimized and converted to a supportive rather than a punitive power. The idea that capitalism and its prominent subjects who achieve success in legal and illegal markets are driven by potentially harmful drives was roundly dismissed, yet the promise of freedom in a civilized environment is still reliant on the continued presence of the repressive institutions from whose grip it fought to free the individual. Žižek has coined the term 'liberal conservatism' to denote this unholy alliance. It seems quite obvious that criminology needs a reconstructed critical view of liberal capitalism's unique form of dualistic subjectivity, but the fear that 'depth theory' will resurrect the ghosts of pathologization, cynicism or class politics means that it enjoys only an attenuated presence in theory and research programmes. Liberal sociology's edicts continue to distract attention from big political and economic issues, ensuring that it makes its own small contribution to the decline of our ability to exercise at least some control over our own destiny. The systematic avoidance of depth-thinking and ideology critique with an advanced conception of ideology helps to cover over the obscene Real; the envy, cynicism and exploitation that drive forward the capitalist system and its leading undertakers.

The history of criminological theory is a linear process of selection and deselection governed by liberal principles that shore up the overall liberal narrative. Both wings of liberalism share the same ambition; the end of class struggle and its associated politics. We can see this clearly in the rejection of not just the stringent Marxist, socialist and neo-Freudian critiques of capitalism and its dominant subjectivities but even the relatively innocuous Durkheimian critical theory of anomie and social disorganization, and the subsequent shift to appreciative studies in the Chicago School. The risk that the criminal undertakers should roam free under the cover of social crime has been taken on behalf of everyone by liberalism; far more important than continuing economic instability, broken working-class communities and the harm inflicted on victims was the destruction of communist and socialist tendencies in western Europe and the USA and the establishment of social liberalism as the sole official opposition. Criminological theory's contribution to this political manoeuvre was the rejection of all dualism and all depth-thinking, and the adoption of the sort of interpretivism that denies all unconscious and systemic desires and drives. This reached its peak in labelling theory, moral panic theory and liberal-postmodernism, where the dialectical class struggle was diluted to an undialectical symbolic struggle between the individual and the state. Criminological theory is in need of a revised concept of ideology and subjectivity, based on the congealment and disavowal of the Real and its energizing of desire rather than the distortion of truth. It's time to ditch traditional ideology critique, but more importantly symbolic interactionism, post-structuralism, postmodernism and risk theory, the current functional ideologies of advanced capitalism. The popularity of such thought in the shadow of the failure of collective politics has contributed to a complete failure of nerve and the downfall of politics itself. All the liberal left had to offer was the denial of the Real, the naturalization of ethical agency and resistance and the 'inclusion' of selected forms of functional marginality in a post-political human rights lobby that could do nothing to prevent neoliberalism achieving almost complete success in the destruction of the politics, culture and economic bargaining position of the working class.

The broken worlds of post-industrialism, the decline of politically centred solidarity and the further cultural diffusion of competitive bourgeois subjectivity – which some feminists and profeminists posited as an expression of masculinity – were ignored by all but a handful of left realists and Critical Criminologists. For the left-liberal mainstream, who opposed the positivist explanations of faulty socialization into an otherwise harmonious and just society, the problem was not capitalism's dominant subjective drives but a bureaucratic system of control whose discursive practices created its own criminalized objects and subjects. The intellectual assault on the control system reached its peak with liberal-postmodernism and its endless deconstruction of all stable meaning and political authority. However, there are movements in late-modern criminological theory seeking to bring the whole idealist edifice down to earth and force it to deal with the existence of harmful core crimes committed by individuals and organizations throughout the social structure. It seems that the political catastrophism that dominates post-war liberal thought has generated a fear of the *barbarism of order* that is so strong and pervasive that the *barbarism of disorder* is offered up as that which is to be tolerated as the least-worst option. Here a potentially fatal mistake has been made; the continuation of vague, objectless anxiety is far more likely than objective fear of the real forces of harm to risk the return of fascist or totalitarian solutions. When an accumulation of 'little evils' is allowed to build up, people become accustomed to it, and gradually accruing cultural decay and political apathy the results are, which of course create the ideal conditions for an eventual Promethean explosion. The Foucauldian project, with its obsolete notion of power and its collapse of ontology and subjectivity into epistemology as it relocated the 'positive unconscious' on the dark side of external discursive objects, has distracted attention from the current 'disappearance' of politics, subjectivity and identity into simulacra, anhedonic nihilism and consumer narcissism. Biopower is undialectical because it has no opposite, and we must be suspicious of the idea of automatic resistance – which mistakes transgression for the stupid pleasures of the depoliticized prosumer – and move back to ontology, universal ethics and politics.

The liberal left shifted the critical focus from capitalism and its dominant predatory subjectivity to bureaucracy; it must now be shifted back, whilst retaining a critical stance against the bureaucratic abuse of human rights. Criminological theory can produce little of value when it has no convincing conception of evil, only the impoverished notions of a natural hard-wired survival instinct, a failure of the will, the lust for domination and power or a reaction to oppression. Nor does criminological theory currently work with a conception of drive, and an understanding of why freedom is possible only in its denial, and therefore it cannot understand how capitalism's dominant subjective drive – a pseudo-pacified variant of the barbarism of *death drive* that preceded it – seeks the realm of special liberty, and it mistakes the drive's constant striving to break through its restraints as a leap for freedom. For Adorno, the drive orientated by the need to fend off threats by means of violence and domination is inherited from the past and inculcated in our neurological systems; will, cognition and social communication are not the formative ontological roots of our existence. Liberal capitalism failed to establish a cultural opposition to this force of *death drive* at the root of subjectivity, preferring to appease, sublimate and control it as an economic driver. Thus left-wing thought can no longer approach real problems, the current effects of the enacted Real, and remains stuck with the problems of the past. As new forms of dominant undertaking emerge in the spaces abandoned by the fragmented liberal left and dislocated by neoliberalism, criminological theory continues its theatrical circumnavigation around the Real with its eyes turned outwards so it does not remind itself of its failure of political nerve.

As the liberal left celebrate the absence of symbolic efficiency at the core of values, politics and social relations it has no choice but to place its faith in the ability of a flimsy and fragmented normative order to contain the libidinal energy generated by the disavowed Real. The subject of the Real is now inconsolable as it is overstimulated and disorientated by the profusion and diversification of points of *jouissance* symbolized by the 'stupid pleasures' of consumerism. In the shadow-economy harmful criminality is diversifying alongside its less harmful forms, as versatile but potentially violent criminal undertakers carve out short-cuts to these points of *jouissance* and pursue the dream of special liberty, thus attracting the hatred and envy of the victims. Prohibitions allow secret desires for obscene enjoyment to be symbolized as commodities, which are sought by versatile combinations of legal acquisition, street crimes and suite crimes, but crimes of hate and domination punctuate the norm where the dissociated subject temporarily seeks the core of the obscenity in an uninhibited outburst of special liberty.

Contemporary criminological theory has marginalized the experience, the voice and the political agenda of the working class, the main victims of neoliberalism and its criminal subjectivity. All experience is filtered through a middle-class liberal lens, using the functional ideologies issued from its official warehouse. Liberal sociology has disrupted the idea of the working class as a potential ideological, political and economic unit, preferring identity politics and multiculturalism. Amidst the destruction of unifying history, mythology and bargaining power, labour is now severed from its relationship of interdependency and the global bourgeoisie see special liberty within their grasp. Neoliberalism is proceeding to a Randian outcome, the glorification of the entrepreneurial plutocrat, and the crudity of her thinking is matched by the crudity of the current socio-economic reality as it is constructed by her special undertakers operating in legal and illegal markets. Liberal identity politics fails to understand that the security of work and community is essential to the individuation process, to the social recognition essential for the constitution of sociable subjectivities. Imagining ourselves being together is no substitute for actually working and living together, of recognizing our own individual limits and knowing that we can face the future together and trust each other for recognition and support. Guaranteed participation is far superior to vague retractable offers of personal liberties, rights, opportunities and outcomes. Pathogenic and fearful competitiveness thrives in this atomized neoliberal environment – more so than it ever did in the traditional conservative environment – where the 'precariat', lagging behind the intellectual workers and manual workers as the truly marginalized part of a three-way split in the working class, are unable to find unity.

The liberal left's abandonment of the dialectical class struggle in favour of the undialectical individual–state relation is itself part of the criminogenic process, helping to reproduce cynicism, exasperation and mistrust. At root the liberal left and the liberal right are as one insofar as they are relieved by the current dialectical paralysis and remain equally fearful of the rise of working-class power in a democratic state, which invokes memories of catastrophe. The historical root of the social dialectic lay between recognition and insignificance, but now that the threat of insignificance has been fully individualized and made into a permanent structural feature it is able to generate tremendous economic energy, but ultimately the ceaseless power of its negative dialectics is socially destructive. The liberal left disavow this reality, so they avoid the former working-class's broken worlds and report instances of the indomitability of the human spirit as the norm. Now that most markets are saturated, acquisitive crime functions to allow surplus capital absorption; crime's proceeds constitute at least one-third of the trillions of dollars floating in the tax-free orbital shadow-economy and thus it is more functional and less threatening than the return of politics and the social dialectic.

To move forward, criminological theory must revive some previously deselected ideas. Firstly, we are biological beings; neither clever automatons nor existential or post-structural free-floaters able to transcend our biology. These positions and the personal politics they affirm leave existing structures intact; we find freedom and *jouissance* in the joyful playing out of predetermined drives or in their theatrical transgression. Transcendental materialism presents the discipline with another way forward. If genetics are weak in the areas of the complex emotional desires that connect drives with symbolism and external reality in a two-way formative process, experience and ideology can be engraved in neuronal networks. With our flexible neurology, human beings are geared for deaptation and malleability; as Hegel said, 'the spirit is a bone', and if the spirit is to move forward it must take the bone with it into the 'third space' beyond both. Both conservatism and liberalism misunderstand the undialectical tension that drives forward capitalism; where conservative biocriminologists naturalize vices and culturalize virtues, left-liberal immaterialists culturalize vices and naturalize virtues. In reality both are cultural and psychosocial but capable of being temporarily engraved in the neurological system, the inscription of the mentality that developed in relation to the capitalist economic system, part of its co-evolutionary constitution.

We must be careful with this. Where conservative biocriminology defines the norm by its extremes, rationalism allows us to ignore our emotional responses and sleepwalk to disaster. However, it's possible for extreme experiences to be etched in neural pathways, from which they are very difficult to erase. Capitalist 'undertaking', in the pure sense of 'getting things done' to serve the interests of the self whilst risking harm to others, is, to different degrees on a scale, both ideologically and neurologically inscribed in leading individuals in various social and occupational spaces. Early trauma produces the dissociated self, the 'not me', with its parallels to the disavowed obscene Real, the constitution of a personality magnetically attracted to the unspoken kernel of the competitive individualist ideology at the heart of capitalist culture. Extreme trauma and mistrust produce neurologically inscribed tendencies to violence, whilst further down the scale more controllable forms of aggression can be cultivated. The disassociated self does not compromise the moral or rational sense, it simply acts, and in the emergency in which it constantly locates itself the undertaker's entitlement to special liberty is ideologically justified. There is no reflective or cognitive solution to this 'doubling' process, and nor indeed is there an economic solution; the extreme undertaker is perfectly anomic, a fact that crops up often in criminological research but consistently fails to be integrated into mainstream theory.

Perhaps a way forward for criminological theory could be carved out by importing a new philosophical basis in the shape of transcendental materialism, the theory that the body is hard-wired for dysfunction and adaptable down to the neurological level, but therefore prone to terror and allegiance to rigid ideologies that outlive their functionality. In this formulation we can see that the disavowed Real is a means of protecting this allegiance from critique and displacement. Memetic persistence leads to 'deaptation', where the 'bone' resists the 'spirit' and lags behind in its comfort zone. The human being must pass through an alternative symbolic order to be reconstituted, a politically established practical order that can change both ideology and experience, a major shift in belief and practice that will send messages to the neuronal system to reconstitute itself. The principle here is that *only the material is truly transcendent and capable of freedom* after a traumatic encounter with the Real it harbours, and thus all transcendental idealist philosophies are destined for permanent political failure and the road to nihilism. Social democracy, with its relative socio-economic stability, was partially successful in bringing the bone closer to the spirit, but it lost its nerve in the neoliberal restoration, allowing the triumphant return of the extreme undertakers. The sort of primal ideological and simultaneously spiritual and material conversion, witnessed occasionally in prison, is perhaps the only way out of the grip of criminal subjectivity; it must begin with an admission of what we are, or, more precisely, what we have become.

Liberalism must be given its due in the realm of rights, but can what it arranged be called a 'civilizing process' that released the agentic powers of the benign creative individual against the forces of tyranny? Perhaps it is time to admit that the process that triggered the decline of violence and the proliferation of acquisitive crime evolved to cultivate and control a manageable and economically functional form of the dissociated and disavowed obscene Real. This is not a civilizing process but a pseudo-pacification process, the sublimation and conversion of physical violence and visceral aggression to an economically energizing form of competitive individualism fuelled by a struggle for social distinction; the energizing of destructive,

competitive drives and desires and the concomitant expansion and sophistication of external and internal control measures in a relation of mutual
amplification. This is why the return of dualistic thinkers to the criminological fold is of vital importance, alongside the reinvestigation through a
criminological lens of the birth of bourgeois individualism and the constitution of communal love and recognition as the lost object in the individuation process, the beginnings of which were laid out earlier in the book.

The construction of a new theory must also be resolute in its empirical
research of the reality of current life in the neoliberal era, where the inhabitants of the 'planet of slums' (Davis, 2006), the broken communities that
are either being deserted in the countryside or expanded in the conurba-
tions by neoliberalism's economic restructuring programme, encounter
each day the possibility of taking up with the system's disavowed criminal
violence, the ruthless application of a market logic that must continue
onwards whether the results are progressive or chaotic and destructive. The
current global expulsion of labour from agriculture, rural villages and traditional religious and family forms continues the process that began in
England and Europe, but this time the recruitment of labour by capital and
the expansion of legal markets to satisfy the ambitions of entrepreneurs
cannot possibly occur at anything like the required rate. The scale is gargantuan: the 3 billion plus currently congregated in urban areas will grow to
around 10 billion in the next few decades. Cities of over 20 million inhabitants will grow in the global south where the transition is at its most acute.
However, the phenomena of jobless growth and casualization of labour will
not lead to the pacified 'settlement' that occurred in the original Western
industrialized nations; stable tenured labour, rising wages, the improvement of the urban habitat and the growing political solidarity of proletarian
communities will be denied to neoliberalism's 'precariat'. The phenomenon of 'circular labour', where casual workers on temporary contracts
move back and forth from rural villages and urban industrial areas, ensures
constant disorientation and the weakening of the individual's socio-
economic and political participation in either the urban or rural community.
The overall process is leading to slums, socio-cultural dissolution, social
unrest and atomized entrepreneurialism in a burgeoning criminal shadow-
economy (Nordstrom, 2007).

This global regime generates forms of poverty that are neither residual,
nor cyclical or transitional, but inscribed in the future of contemporary
societies insofar as they are fed by the ongoing fragmentation of the wage
labour relationship, the functional disconnection of dispossessed neighbourhoods from the national and global economies, and the reconfiguration
of the welfare state in the polarizing city. Some argue that this 'precariat'

forms its subjectivity from its objectification by others (Wacquant, 2007: 66), but this constructionist formulation oversocializes a psycho-social process and ignores the internalization of everyday practice and ideology 'in the bones' of the successful undertakers who are leading initially reluctant others into new forms of socio-economic shadow-activity. Without respite biographical experiences are somatically and mentally framed by everyday encounters with neoliberal ideology's Real and its reality as they permeate the new urban economies and their socio-economic relations. Will disembedded 'new communities' eventually construct an oppositional force? This is doubtful, because in their imaginary forms they cannot restore the lost objects of communal love, participation and recognition, and the obligations and sacrifices such primal forms demand. In such a climate, some degree of social harm is almost the default outcome of socio-economic transactions. At the moment the pseudo-pacification process walks a tightrope between the *barbarism of order* and the *barbarism of disorder* as the relentless overstimulation of the libido demands new forms of consumerist sublimation and technological and organizational control. In the absence of an alternative ideology and an oppositional politics of solidarity, in the neoliberal age led by the new global plutocrats, the realm of special liberty beckons all as its visceral yearning becomes the 'spirit and the bone' of an increasing number of individuals. For these individuals, who seek ever more inventive ways of separating the self from the social, the risk of inflicting some degree of harm on others is always worth taking.

REFERENCES

Aas, K. (2007). *Globalisation and Crime*. London: Sage.

Academy of Social Sciences. (2010). *Making the Case for the Social Sciences, No. 1: Well-being*. Swindon: ESRC.

Adler, A. (1999). *The Neurotic Constitution*. London: Routledge.

Adorno, T. (1967). 'Sociology and Psychology, I and II'. *New Left Review*, 46, 47.

Adorno, T. (1973). *Negative Dialectics*, trans. E. B. Ashton. London: Routledge & Kegan Paul.

Adorno, T. (2000). *Metaphysics: Concept and Problems*. Cambridge: Polity Press.

Adorno, T., Frenkel-Brunswik, E., Levinson, D., & Sanford, N. (1993). *The Authoritarian Personality, Studies in Prejudice Series*, vol. 1. New York: W. W. Norton.

Adorno, T., & Horkheimer, M. (1992). *Dialectic of Enlightenment*. London: Verso.

Agamben, G. (2005). *The State of Exception*, trans. Kevin Attell. Chicago: University of Chicago Press.

Aichhorn, A. (1931). *Wayward Youth*. New York: Viking Press.

Akerlof, G., & Shiller, R. (2009). *Animal Spirits: How Human Psychology Drives the Economy, and Why It Matters for Global Capitalism*. Princeton: Princeton University Press.

Aldridge, J., Medina, J., & Ralphs, R. (2010). 'Collateral Damage: Territoriality and Violence in an English City'. In B. Goldson (ed.), *Youth in Crisis? 'Gangs', Territoriality and Violence*. Cullompton: Willan.

Althusser, L. (1969). *For Marx*, trans. B. Brewster. London: Verso.

Anderson, P. (2011, March). 'Lula's Brazil'. *London Review of Books*, pp. 3–11.

Ansermet, F. (2002). 'Des neurosciences aux logosciences'. In N. Georges, J.-A. Miller, & N. Marchaison (eds), *Qui sont vos psychoanalystes?* Paris: Seuil.

Antonopoulos, G. (2008). 'The Greek Connection(s): The Social Organisation of the Cigarette Smuggling Business in Greece'. *European Journal of Criminology*, 5(3), 263–88.

Arendt, H. (1963). *Eichmann in Jerusalem: A Report on the Banality of Evil*. New York: Viking Press.

Ariès, P. (1996). *Centuries of Childhood: A Social History of Family Life*, trans. R. Baldick. London: Pimlico.

Arrighi, G. (1994). *The Long Twentieth Century*. London: Verso.

Arrigo, B., & Barrett, L. (2008). 'Philosophical Criminology and Complex Systems Science: Towards a critical theory of justice'. *Critical Criminology*, 16, 165–84.

Badiou, A. (1999). *Manifesto for Philosophy*, trans. N. Madarasz. Albany: State University of New York Press.

Badiou, A. (2002). *Ethics: An Essay on the Understanding of Evil.* London: Verso.

Badiou, A. (2006). *Being and Event.* London: Continuum.

Badiou, A. (2007). *The Century.* London: Polity.

Barzun, J. (2001). *From Dawn to Decadence.* New York: Perennial.

Baudrillard, J. (1993). *Symbolic Exchange and Death.* London: Sage.

Baudrillard, J. (1994). *Simulacra and Simulation*, trans. S. F. Glaser. Ann Arbor: University of Michigan Press.

Baudrillard, J. (2005). *The Intelligence of Evil.* Oxford: Berg.

Baudrillard, J. (2007). *Forget Foucault.* Los Angeles: Semiotext(e).

Bauman, Z. (1991). *Modernity and the Holocaust.* Cambridge: Polity.

Bauman, Z. (1997). *Postmodernity and its Discontents.* Cambridge: Polity.

Beattie, J. (1986). *Crime and the Courts in England 1660–1800.* Oxford: Oxford University Press.

Beck, U. (1992). *Risk Society: Towards a New Modernity.* London: Sage.

Bell, D. (1978). *The Cultural Contradictions of Capitalism.* New York: Basic Books.

Benjamin, W. (1968). 'Theses on the Philosophy of History'. In *Illuminations*, trans. H. Zohn. London: Fontana.

Benn, C. (1992). *Keir Hardie.* London: Hutchinson.

Bentham, J. (1996). *An Introduction to the Principles of Morals and Legislation*, eds J.H. Burns and H.L.A. Hart. Oxford: Oxford University Press.

Berger, P., & Luckmann, T. (1966). *The Social Construction of Reality: A Treatise in the Sociology of Knowledge.* New York: Anchor Books.

Berlin, I. (1969). 'Two Concepts of Liberty'. In I. Berlin, *Four Essays on Liberty.* Oxford: Oxford University Press.

Bhaskar, R. (1997). *A Realist Theory of Science.* London: Verso.

Blackmore, S. (1999). *The Meme Machine.* Oxford: Oxford University Press.

Bloch, M. (1967). *Land and Work in Mediaeval Europe.* London: Routledge and Kegan Paul.

Blumer, H. (1969). *Symbolic Interactionism.* Berkeley: University of California Press.

Bonger, W. (1916). *Crime and Economic Conditions.* London: Little Brown.

Bosteels, B. (2010). 'The Leftist Hypothesis: Communism in the Age of Terror'. In C. Douzinas & S. Žižek (eds), *The Idea of Communism.* London: Verso.

Bottoms, A. (2002). 'Morality, Crime, Compliance and Public Policy'. In A. B. Tonry (ed.), *Ideology, Crime and Criminal Justice.* Cullompton: Willan.

Bourdieu, P. (1986). *Distinction: A Social Critique of the Judgement of Taste.* London: Routledge.

Bourdieu, P. (1987). 'The Force of Law: Towards a Sociology of the Juridical Field'. *Hastings Law Review*, 38, 814–53.

Bourdieu, P. (1990). *The Logic of Practice.* Cambridge: Polity.

Bourdieu, P., & Wacquant, L. (1992). *An Invitation to Reflexive Sociology.* Chicago: University of Chicago Press.

Bourgois, P. (2003). *In Search of Respect: Selling Crack in El Barrio.* Cambridge: Cambridge University Press.

Bowlby, J. (1983). *Attachment*, 2nd edn. New York: Basic Books.

Boyne, R. (2001). 'Cosmopolis and Risk: A Conversation with Ulrich Beck'. *Theory, Culture & Society*, 18(4), 47–64.

Braudel, F. (1995). *The Mediterranean and the Mediterranean World in the Age of Phillip II.* Berkeley: University of California Press.

Brink, D. (2003). *Perfectionism and the Common Good: Themes in the Philosophy of T.H. Green.* Oxford: Clarendon Press.

Brown, R., Clarke, R., Shepticki, J., & Rix, B. (2004). *Tackling Organised Vehicle Crime: The role of NCIS.* London: Home Office.

Burdis, K., & Tombs, S. (2012). 'After the Crisis: New Directions in Theorising Corporate and White-Collar Crime'. In S. Hall & S. Winlow (eds), *New Directions in Criminological Theory.* London: Willan/Routledge.

Bushaway, R. (2003). *Managing Research.* Buckingham: Open University Press.

Cain, M., & Birju, A. (1992). 'Crime and Structural Adjustment in Trinidad and Tobago'. *Caribbean Affairs*, 141–53.

Callewaert, S. (2006). 'Bourdieu, Critic of Foucault: The Case of Empirical Social Science Against Double-game Philosophy'. *Theory, Culture and Society*, 23(6), 73–98.

Callinicos, A. (1989). *Against Postmodernism: A Marxist Critique.* Cambridge: Polity.

Campbell, C. (1987). *The Romantic Ethic and the Spirit of Modern Consumerism.* Oxford: Blackwell.

Carlen, P. (1988). *Women, Crime and Poverty.* Milton Keynes: Open University Press.

Carrington, K., & Hogg, R. (eds) (2002). *Critical Criminology: Issues, Debates & Challenges.* Cullompton: Willan.

Centre for Retail Research (2009, Nov. 10). 'Report for Checkpoint Systems'. *Times Online*.

Chesterton, G. (2001 [1926]). *William Cobbett.* Kelly Bray: House of Stratus.

Chevalier, L. (1973). *Labouring Classes and Dangerous Classes in Paris During the First Half of the Nineteenth Century.* London: Routledge & Kegan Paul.

Chomsky, N. (2003). *Hegemony or Survival.* London: Hamish Hamilton.

Christie, N. (1994). *Crime Control as Industry: Towards Gulags Western Style.* London: Routledge.

Clayre, A. (1977). *Nature and Industrialization: An Anthology.* Oxford: Oxford University Press.

Cohen, A. (1955). *Delinquent Boys: The Culture of the Gang.* New York: Free Press.

Cohen, G. A. (2002). 'Deeper into Bullshit'. In S. Buss & L. Overton (eds), *Contours of Agency: Essays on Themes from Harry Frankfurt.* Cambridge, MA: MIT Press.

Cohen, P. (1972). 'Sub-cultural Conflict and Working Class Community'. In *Working Papers in Cultural Studies, No. 2.* Birmingham: University of Birmingham.

Cohen, S. (1972). *Folk Devils and Moral Panics.* London: MacGibbon and Kee.

Cohen, S. (1985). *Visions of Social Control.* Oxford: Blackwell.

Cohen, S. (1988). *Against Criminology.* New Brunswick, NJ: Transaction Books.

Cohen, S. (2000). *States of Denial: Knowing About Atrocities and Suffering.* Cambridge: Polity.

Cohen, S. (2009). 'Carry on Panicking'. *British Society of Criminology Newsletter*, 64(Autumn), 5–10.

Cole, D. (2001). '"An Unqualified Human Good": E.P. Thompson and the Rule of Law'. *Journal of Law and Society*, 28(2), available at SSRN: http://ssrn.com/abstract=268952.

Collini, S. (2010, Nov. 4). 'Browne's Gamble'. *London Review of Books*, 32(21).

Connell, R. (1995). *Masculinities.* Cambridge: Polity.

Connell, R., & Wood, J. (2005). 'Globalisation and Business Masculinities'. *Men and Masculinities*, 7(4), 347–64.

Coser, L. (1964). *The Functions of Social Conflict*. New York: Free Press.

Cottino, A. (1998). 'Nino: Journey into the Heart of Darkness'. http://www.crimetalk. org.uk/frontpage-articles/nino-journey-into-the-heart-of-darkness.

Cowling, M. (2008). *Marxism and Criminological Theory: A Critique and a Tool Kit*. London: Palgrave-Macmillan.

Crewe, D., & Lippens, R. (eds) (2009). *Existentialist Criminology*. Abingdon: GlassHouse/Routledge-Cavendish.

Crogan, P. (2010). 'Knowledge, Care and Transindividuation: An Interview with Bernard Stiegler'. *Cultural Politics*, 6(2), 157–70.

Curran, J., & Seaton, J. (2003). *Power Without Responsibility: The Press, Broadcasting, and New Media in Britain*. London: Routledge.

Currie, E. (2010). 'Plain Left Realism: An Appreciation and Some Thoughts for the Future'. *Crime, Law and Social Change*, 54, 111–24.

D'Amico, R. (1989). *Historicism and Knowledge*. London: Routledge.

Damasio, A. (2003). *Looking for Spinoza: Joy, Sorrow, and the Feeling Brain*. Orlando, FL: Harcourt.

Davies, P. (2003). 'Is Economic Crime a Man's Game?'. *Feminist Theory*, 4(3), 283–303.

Davis, M. (2002). *Late Victorian Holocausts: El Niño Famines and the Making of the Third World*. London: Verso.

Davis, M. (2006). *Planet of Slums*. London: Verso.

Dawkins, R. (1989). *The Selfish Gene*, 2nd edn. Oxford: Oxford University Press.

de Grazia, V. (1996). *The Sex of Things: Gender and Consumption in Historical Perspective*. Berkeley: University of California Press.

de Saussure, F. (2006). *Writings in General Linguistics*. Oxford: Oxford University Press.

de Ste Croix, G. (1981). *The Class Struggle in the Ancient Greek World*. London: Duckworth.

Dean, J. (2009). *Democracy and Other Neoliberal Fantasies: Communicative Capitalism and Left Politics*. Durham, NC: Duke University Press.

Dejours, C. (2003). *L'Evaluation du travail à l'épreuve du réel*. Paris: INRA Editions.

Deleuze, G. (1988). *Foucault*, ed. and trans. S. Hand. London: Athlone Press.

Deleuze, G., & Guattari, F. (1984). *Anti-Oedipus: Capitalism and Schizophrenia*. London: Athlone.

Deleuze, G., & Guattari, F. (1987). *A Thousand Plateaus: Capitalism and Schizophrenia*. Minneapolis: University of Minnesota Press.

Dennett, D. (2003). *Freedom Evolves*. New York: Viking.

Deranty, J.-P. (2008). 'Work and the Precarisation of Existence'. *European Journal of Social Theory*, 11(4), 443–63.

Derrida, J. (1967). *Of Grammatology*, trans. Gayatri Chakravorty Spivak. London: Johns Hopkins University Press.

Dewey, J. (1998). *The Essential Dewey*, vol. 1, eds L. A. Hickman and T. M. Alexander. Bloomington: Indiana University Press.

Dews, B., & Law, C. (eds) (1995). *This Fine Place So Far From Home: Voices of Academics from the Working Class*. Philadelphia: Temple University Press.

Dews, P. (2008). *The Idea of Evil*. Oxford: Blackwell.

Ditton, J. (1979). *Contrology: Beyond the New Criminology*. London: Macmillan.

Ditton, J., & Innes, M. (2005). 'The Role of Perceptual Intervention in the Management of Crime Fear'. In N. Tilly (ed.), *Handbook of Crime Prevention and Community Safety*. Cullompton: Willan.

Dodge, M. (2007). 'From Pink to White with Various Shades of Embezzlement: Women who Commit White-collar Crimes'. In H. Pontell & G. Geis (eds), *International Handbook of White-collar and Corporate Crime*. New York: Springer.

Dorling, D. (2004). 'Prime Suspect: Homicide in Britain'. In P. Hillyard, C. Pantazis, S. Tombs, & D. Gordon (eds), *Beyond Criminology: Taking Harm Seriously*. London: Pluto.

Douzinas, C., & Žižek, S. (2010). *The Idea of Communism*. London: Verso.

Downes, D. (1966). *The Delinquent Solution: A Study in Subcultural Theory*. London: Routledge & Kegan Paul.

Downes, D., & Rock, P. (2007). *Understanding Deviance*, 5th edn. Oxford: Oxford University Press.

Dumont, L. (1986). *Essays on Individualism: Modern Ideology in Anthropological Perspective*. Chicago: University of Chicago Press.

Durkheim, E. (1970). *Suicide: A Study in Sociology*. London: Routledge and Kegan Paul.

Durkheim, E. (1982). 'The Normal and the Pathological'. In *The Rules of Sociological Method*, ed. G. E. G. Catlin. New York: Free Press.

Durkheim, E. (2001). *The Elementary Forms of Religious Life*, trans. Carol Cosman. Oxford: Oxford University Press.

Dyer, C. (2000). *Everyday Life in Mediaeval England*. London: Hambledon and London.

Eagleton, T. (1970). *Shakespeare and Society*. London: Chatto and Windus.

Eagleton, T. (1995). 'Where do Postmodernists Come From?'. *Monthly Review*, 47(3), 59–70.

Eagleton, T. (2009). *Trouble with Strangers: A Study of Ethics*. Chichester: Wiley-Blackwell.

Eagleton, T. (2010, 1 April). 'Of Men and Monsters'. *New Statesman*.

Eckberg, D. (1995). 'Estimates of Early Twentieth-century US Homicide Rates: An Econometric Forecasting Approach'. *Demography*, 32(1), 1–16.

Ehrenreich, B. (1997). *Blood Rites: Origins and History of the Passions of War*. London: Virago.

Eisner, M. (2001). 'Modernization, Self-control and Lethal Violence: The Long-term Dynamics of European Homicide Rates in Theoretical Perspective'. *British Journal of Criminology*, 41, 618–38.

Elias, N. (1994). *The Civilizing Process*. Oxford: Blackwell.

Elin, M. (1995). 'A Developmental Model for Trauma'. In L. Cohen, J. Berzoff, & M. Elin (eds), *Dissociative Identity Disorder*. Northvale, NJ: Aronson.

Emsley, C. (2010). *Crime and Society in England 1750–1900*. London: Longman.

Engels, F. (1987). *The Condition of the Working Class in England*. London: Penguin.

Ericson, R. (2006). *Crime in an Insecure World*. Cambridge: Polity.

Farrington, D. (1996). *Understanding and Preventing Youth Crime*. York: Joseph Rowntree Foundation.

Feeley, M., & Little, D. (1991). 'The Vanishing Female: The Decline of Women in the Criminal Justice Process, 1687–1912'. *Law and Society Review*, 25(4), 719.

Ferrell, J. (2007). 'For a Ruthless Cultural Criticism of Everything Existing'. *Crime, Media, Culture*, 3(1), 91–100.

Ferrell, J., Hayward, K., & Young, K. (2008). *Cultural Criminology: An Invitation*. London: Sage.

Ferri, E. (2009). The Positive School of Criminology. In T. Newburn (ed.), *Key Readings in Criminology*. Cullompton: Willan.

Fish, S. (2010). *The Fugitive in Flight: Faith, Liberalism and Law in a Classic TV Show*. Pennsylvania: University of Pennsylvania Press.

Fisher, M. (2009). *Capitalist Realism: Is There No Alternative?* Alresford: 0 Books.

Fletcher, J. (1997). *Violence and Civilization*. Cambridge: Polity.

Foucault, M. (1970). *The Order of Things: An Archaeology of the Human Sciences*. London: Tavistock.

Foucault, M. (1988). 'Technologies of the Self'. In L. Martin, H. Gutman, & P. Hutton (eds), *Technologies of the Self*. Amherst: University of Massachusetts Press.

Foucault, M. (1991). *Discipline and Punish: The Birth of the Prison*. London: Penguin.

Foucault, M. (1998). *The History of Sexuality, Vol. 1: The Will to Knowledge*. London: Penguin.

Frank, T. (1997). *The Conquest of Cool: Business Culture, Counterculture and the Rise of Hip Consumerism*. Chicago: University of Chicago Press.

Freud, S. (1979). *Civilization and its Discontents*, trans. Joan Riviere. London: Hogarth Press.

Freud, S. (1979). *On Psychopathology; Inhibitions, Symptoms and Anxiety and Other Works*, ed. and trans. J. Strachey. Harmondsworth: Penguin.

Friedman, M. (2002). *Capitalism and Freedom*. Chicago: University of Chicago Press.

Fromm, E. (1974). *The Anatomy of Human Destructiveness*. London: Jonathan Cape.

Fromm, E. (1993). 'Infantilization and Despair Masquerading as Radicalism'. *Theory, Culture & Society*, 10, 197–206.

Fromm, E. (2000). 'On the Psychology of the Criminal and the Punitive Society'. In K. Anderson & R. Quinney, *Erich Fromm and Critical Criminology: Beyond the Punitive Society*. Urbana, IL: University of Illinois Press.

Gadd, D. (2002). 'Masculinities and Violence against Female Partners'. *Social and Legal Studies*, 11, 61–80.

Gadd, D., & Jefferson, T. (2007). *Psychosocial Criminology: An Introduction*. London: Sage.

Gambetta, D. (2009). *Codes of the Underworld*. Princeton, NJ: Princeton University Press.

Gane, N. (2004). *The Future of Social Theory*. London: Continuum.

Garfinkel, H. (1967). *Studies in Ethnomethodology*. Englewood Cliffs, NJ: Prentice-Hall.

Garland, D. (1985). 'The Criminal and His Science: A Critical Account of the Formation of Criminology at the End of the Nineteenth Century'. *British Journal of Criminology*, 25(2), 109–37.

Garland, D. (1990). *Punishment and Modern Society*. Oxford: Clarendon.

Garland, D. (2001). *The Culture of Control*. Oxford: Oxford University Press.

George, S. (1999, November). *The Corporate Utopian Dream*. Retrieved from Transnational Institute: http://www.tni.org/es/archives/act/1519.

Ghodse, H. (2009). *International Drug Control into the 21st Century.* Aldershot, UK: Ashgate.

Giddens, A. (1984). *The Constitution of Society: Outline of the Theory of Structuration.* Berkeley: University of California Press.

Giddens, A. (1998). *The Third Way: The Renewal of Social Democracy.* Cambridge: Polity Press.

Gilligan, C. (1982). *In a Different Voice: Psychological Theory and Women's Development.* Cambridge, MA: Harvard University Press.

Gilmore, D. (1990). *Manhood in the Making: Cultural Concepts of Masculinity.* New Haven, CT: Yale University Press.

Gilroy, P. (1987). *There Ain't No Black in the Union Jack: The Cultural Politics of Race and Nation.* London: Routledge.

Girard, R. (1977). *Violence and the Sacred*, trans. P. Gregory. Baltimore: Johns Hopkins University Press.

Glasbeek, H. (2002). *Wealth by Stealth: Corporate Crime, Corporate Law and the Perversion of Democracy.* Toronto: Between the Lines.

Glover, E. (1960). *The Roots of Crime: Selected Papers on Psychoanalysis*, vol. 11. London: Imago.

Goffman, E. (1959). *The Presentation of Self in Everyday Life.* New York: Doubleday.

Goode, E., & Ben-Yehuda, N. (2009). *Moral Panics: The Social Construction of Deviance*, 2nd edn. Chichester: Wiley/Blackwell.

Goodey, J. (2004). *Victims and Victimology: Research, Policy and Practice.* London: Longman.

Goody, J. (1983). *The Development of the Family and Marriage in Europe.* Cambridge: Cambridge University Press.

Gottfredson, M., & Hirschi, T. (1990). *A General Theory of Crime.* Palo Alto, CA: Stanford University Press.

Gouldner, A. (1973). *For Sociology: Renewal and Critique in Sociology Today.* London: Allen Lane.

Gray, J. (1998). *False Dawn: The Delusions of Global Capitalism.* London: Routledge.

Gray, J. (2002). *False Dawn: The Delusions of Global Capitalism.* London: Granta.

Green, P., & Ward, T. (2004). *State Crime: Governments, Violence and Corruption.* London: Pluto.

Gurr, T. (1981). 'Historical Trends in Violent Crime: A Critical Review of the Evidence'. *Crime and Justice*, 3, 295–353.

Hall, S. (1988). *The Hard Road to Renewal.* London: Verso.

Hall, S. (2000). 'Paths to Anelpis: Dimorphic Violence and the Pseudo-pacification Process'. *Parallax*, 6(2), 36–53.

Hall, S. (2007). 'The Emergence and Breakdown of the Pseudo-pacification Process'. In K. Watson (ed.), *Assaulting the Past.* Cambridge: Cambridge Scholars Press.

Hall, S., Critcher, C., Jefferson, T., & Clarke, J. (1978). *Policing the Crisis: Mugging, the State and Law and Order.* London: Macmillan.

Hall, S., & Jefferson, T. (eds) (1976). *Resistance through Rituals: Youth Subcultures in Post-war Britain.* London: Hutchinson.

Hall, S., & McLean, C. (2009). 'A Tale of Two Capitalisms: Pleminary Spatial and Historical Comparisons of Homicide Rates in Western Europe and the USA'. *Theoretical Criminology*, 13, 313–39.

Hall, S., & Winlow, S. (2003). 'Rehabilitating Leviathan: Reflections on the State, Economic Regulation and Violence Reduction'. *Theoretical Criminology*, 7(2), 139–62.

Hall, S., & Winlow, S. (2005). 'Anti-nirvana: Crime, Culture and Instrumentalism in the Age of Insecurity'. *Crime, Media, Culture*, 1(1), 31–48.

Hall, S., & Winlow, S. (2007). 'Cultural Criminology and Primitive Accumulation: A Formal Introduction for Two Strangers Who Should Really Become More Intimate'. *Crime, Media, Culture*, 3(1), 82–90.

Hall, S., Winlow, S., & Ancrum, C. (2005). 'Radgies, Gangstas and Mugs: Imaginary Criminal Identities in the Twilight of the Pseudo-pacification Process'. *Social Justice*, 32(1), 100–12.

Hall, S., Winlow, S., & Ancrum, C. (2008). *Criminal Identities and Consumer Culture: Crime, Exclusion and the New Culture of Narcissism*. Cullompton: Willan.

Hallsworth, S. (2006). *Street Crime*. Cullompton: Willan.

Hallward, P. (2006). *Out of this World: Deleuze and the Philosophy of Creation*. London: Verso.

Hanawalt, B. (1979). *Crime and Conflict in English Communities: 1300–1348*. Cambridge, MA: Harvard University Press.

Harding, C. (2007). *Criminal Enterprise: Individuals, Organisations and Criminal Responsibility*. Cullompton: Willan.

Hardt, M., & Negri, A. (2001). *Empire*. Cambridge, MA: Harvard University Press.

Harvey, D. (1991). *The Condition of Postmodernity: An Enquiry into the Conditions of Social Change*. Oxford: Wiley-Blackwell.

Harvey, D. (2007). *A Brief History of Neoliberalism*. Oxford: Oxford University Press.

Harvey, D. (2010). *The Enigma of Capital: And the Crises of Capitalism*. London: Profile.

Harvey, D. (2011). *A Companion to Marx's Capital*. London: Verso.

Havel, V. (1989). *Living in Truth*. London: Faber and Faber.

Hay, D. (1975). 'Property, Authority and the Criminal Law'. In D. Hay, P. Linebaugh, J. Rule, E. P. Thompson, & C. Winslow (eds), *Albion's Fatal Tree: Crime and Society in Eighteenth Century England*. London: Allen Lane.

Hayek, F. (1948). *Individualism and Economic Order*. Chicago: University of Chicago Press.

Heath, J., & Potter, A. (2006). *The Rebel Sell: How Counterculture Became Consumer Culture*. London: Capstone.

Hegel, G. W. (1979). *Phenomenology of Spirit*, trans. A. V. Miller. Oxford: Oxford University Press.

Henry, S., & Milovanovic, D. (1996). *Constitutive Criminology: Beyond postmodernism*. London: Sage.

Herrnstein, R., & Murray, C. (1994). *The Bell Curve: Intelligence and Class Structure in American Life*. New York: Free Press.

Hibbert, C. (2003). *The Roots of Evil*. Stroud: Sutton.

Hier, S. (2008). 'Thinking Beyond Moral Panic: Risk, Responsibility, and the Politics of Moralization'. *Theoretical Criminology*, 12(2), 173–90.

Hil, R. (2000). 'A Gloomy Vista? "Globalisation", Juvenile Crime and Social Order'. *Crime, Law & Social Change*, 33, 369–84.

Hillyard, P., Pantazis, C., Tombs, S., & Gordon, D. (2004). *Beyond Criminology: Taking Harm Seriously.* London: Pluto.

Hirschman, A. (1977). *The Passions and the Interests.* Princeton: Princeton University Press.

Hobbes, T. (1996). *Leviathan*, 2nd edn, ed. R. Tuck. Cambridge: Cambridge University Press.

Hobbs, D. (1989). *Doing the Business: Entrepreneurship, the Working Class, and Detectives in the East End of London.* Oxford: Oxford University Press.

Hobbs, D. (1995). *Bad Business.* Oxford: Oxford University Press.

Hobbs, D. (1998). 'Going Down the Glocal: The Local Context of Organised Crime'. *The Howard Journal*, 37(4), 407–22.

Hobsbawm, E. (1972). 'Social Criminality: Distinctions Between Socio-political and Other Forms of Crime'. *Bulletin of the Society for the Study of Labour History*, (25), 5–6.

Hobsbawm, E. (1994). *The Age of Extremes: The Short Twentieth Century 1914–1991.* London: Penguin.

Hobsbawm, E. (1996). *The Age of Revolution: 1789–1848.* London: Vintage.

Hoggart, R. (1957). *The Uses of Literacy.* London: Chatto and Windus.

Honneth, A. (1996). *The Struggle for Recognition: The Moral Grammar of Social Conflicts.* Cambridge: Polity Press.

Horkheimer, M. (1982). *Critical Theory.* New York: Seabury Press.

Horne, R., & Hall, S. (1995). 'Anelpis: A Preliminary Expedition into a World without Hope or Potential'. *Parallax*, 1, 81–92.

Horney, K. (1937). *The Neurotic Personality of our Time.* New York: W.W. Norton.

Horney, K. (1950). *Neurosis and Human Growth.* New York: W. W. Norton.

Hume, D. (1967 [1740]). *A Treatise of Human Nature.* Oxford: Oxford University Press.

Hunt, A. (2003). 'Risk and Moralization in Everyday Life'. In R. Ericson & A. Doyle (eds), *Risk and Morality.* Toronto: University of Toronto Press.

International Labour Office. (2010). *Global Employment Trends for Youth.* Geneva: ILO Publications.

Jackson, J., & Gray, E. (2010). 'Functional Fear and Public Insecurities About Crime'. *British Journal of Criminology*, 50, 1–22.

James, W. (1981). *Pragmatism: A New Name for Some Old Ways of Thinking.* Indianapolis: Hackett.

Jameson, F. (1981). *The Political Unconscious: Narrative as a Socially Symbolic Act.* London: Methuen.

Jameson, F. (1991). *Postmodernism, Or, The Cultural Logic of Late Capitalism.* London: Verso.

Jameson, F. (2010). *Valences of the Dialectic.* London: Verso.

Jefferson, T. (1994). 'Theorising Masculine Subjectivity'. In T. Newburn & E. Stanko, *Just Boys Doing Business: Men, Masculinities and Crime.* London: Routledge.

Jefferson, T. (2002). 'Subordinating Hegemonic Masculinity'. *Theoretical Criminology*, 6(1), 63–89.

Jewkes, Y. (2004). *Media and Crime.* London: Sage.

Joas, H. (1998). 'The Autonomy of the Self: The Meadian Heritage and its Postmodern Challenge'. *European Journal of Social Theory*, 1(1), 7–18.

Johnston, A. (2008). *Žižek's Ontology: A Transcendental Materialist Theory of Subjectivity.* Evanston, IL: Northwestern University Press.

Jones, D. (2008). *Understanding Criminal Behaviour: Psychosocial Approaches to Criminality.* Cullompton: Willan.

Kanazawa, S. (2008). 'Evolutionary Psychology and Crime'. In A. Walsh & K. M. Beaver (eds), *Biosocial Criminology: New Directions in Theory and Research.* London: Routledge.

Kant, I. (1998). *Groundwork of the Metaphysics of Morals*, trans. M. J. Gregor. Cambridge: Cambridge University Press.

Kant, I. (1999). *Critique of Pure Reason*, trans. P. Guyer & A. Wood. Cambridge: Cambridge University Press.

Kant, I. (2003). *Perpetual Peace: A Philosophical Sketch.* Indianapolis, IN: Hackett.

Katz, J. (1988). *The Seductions of Crime.* New York: Basic Books.

Kent, A. (2007). *Key Domestic Burglary Crime Statistics.* London: Home Office CREC.

Keynes, M. (1935). *The General Theory of Employment, Interest and Money.* New York: Harcourt, Brace and Co.

Kidd-Hewitt, D., & Osborne, R. (eds) (1995). *Crime and the Media; The Post-modern Spectacle.* London: Pluto.

Klein, M. (1975). *The Writings of Melanie Klein, Vol. 1: Love, Guilt and Reparation and Other Works.* New York: Free Press.

Kojève, A. (1969). *Introduction to the Reading of Hegel*, ed. A. Bloom, trans. J. H. Nichols Jr. New York: Basic Books.

Kuhn, T. (1962). *The Structure of Scientific Revolutions.* Chicago: University of Chicago Press.

Kurz, R. (1991). *Der Kollaps der Modernisierung.* Frankfurt am Main: Eichborn.

Lacan, J. (1992). *The Seminar of Jacques Lacan, Book VII, The Ethics of Psychoanalysis*, ed. J.-A. Miller, trans. D. Porter. London: Routledge.

Lacan, J. (2001). 'British Psychiatry and the War', trans. P. Dravers and V. Voruz. In *Psychoanalytical Notebooks of the London Circle*, Spring 2000. In *Autres écrits.* Paris: Seuil.

Lacan, J. (2001). *Le Séminaire de Jacques Lacan, Livre VIII: Le transfert, 1960–1961*, ed. J.-A. Miller. Paris: Seuil.

Lacan, J. (2004). *The Seminar, Book 10: Anxiety, 1962–3*, ed. J. A. Miller. Paris: Seuil.

Lacan, J. (2006). 'A Theoretical Introduction to the Functions of Psychoanalysis in Criminology'. In J. Lacan, *Ecrits*, trans. B. Fink. London: W. W. Norton.

Lakatos, I. (1978). *The Methodology of Scientific Research Programmes: Philosophical Papers*, vol. 1. Cambridge: Cambridge University Press.

Langley, P. (2006). 'Securitising Suburbia: The Transformation of Anglo-American Mortgage Finance'. *Competition and Change*, 10(3), 283–99.

Lasch, C. (1991). *The Culture of Narcissism: American Life in an Age of Diminishing Expectations.* London: W. W. Norton.

Lash, S. (1990). *Sociology of Postmodernism.* London: Routledge.

Latour, B. (2005). *Reassembling the Social: An Introduction to Actor-Network-Theory.* Oxford: Oxford University Press.

Lea, J. (2002). *Crime and Modernity.* London: Sage.

Lea, J. (2006). *Criminology and History*. Retrieved 11 May 2011, from John Lea's Criminology Website: http://www.bunker8.pwp.blueyonder.co.uk/history/36801.htm.

Lea, J., & Young, J. (1993). *What Is To Be Done About Law and Order?* London: Pluto Press.

Lechner, F. (2009). *Globalization: The Making of World Society*. Chichester: Wiley-Blackwell.

Lemert, E. (1967). *Human Deviance, Social Problems and Social Control*. Englewood Cliffs, NJ: Prentice-Hall.

Lemert, E. (1974). 'Beyond Mead: The Social Reaction to Deviance'. *Social Problems*, 21, 457–68.

Levi, M. (1987). *Regulating Fraud: White Collar Crime and the Criminal Process*. London: Tavistock.

Levi, M. (2005). 'International Fraud'. In M. Natarajan (ed.), *Introduction to International Criminal Justice*. New York: McGraw-Hill.

Levi, M. (2008). *The Phantom Capitalists: The Organisation and Control of Long-firm Fraud*, 2nd edn. Aldershot, UK: Ashgate.

Levinas, E. (1999). *Otherwise than Being*. Pittsburgh: Duquesne University Press.

Lévi-Strauss, C. (1970). *The Raw and the Cooked*, trans. J. Weightman & D. Weightman. London: Jonathan Cape.

Linebaugh, P. (1991). *The London Hanged: Crime and Civil Society in Eighteenth Century England*. London: Allen Lane.

Lippens, R. (forthcoming 2012). 'Radical Sovereignty and Control Society: Images of late Modern Sovereignty in Rebeyrolle's Le Cyclope'. *Crime, Media, Culture*, 8(1).

Lippens, R., & Crewe, D. (eds) (2009). *Existentialist Criminology*. London: Routledge/Cavendish.

Loader, I., & Sparks, R. (2010). *Public Criminology?: Criminological Politics in the Twenty-first Century*. London: Routledge.

Locke, J. (1997). *An Essay Concerning Human Understanding*, ed. R. Woolhouse. London: Penguin Books.

Luhmann, N. (1986). 'The Autopoiesis of Social Systems'. In F. Geyer & J. van der Zouwen (eds), *Sociocybernetic Paradoxes*. London: Sage.

Lyng, S. (2005). *Edgework*. London: Routledge.

MacCoun, R., & Reuter, P. (2001). *Drug War Heresies: Learning from Other Vices, Times and Places*. Cambridge: Cambridge University Press.

MacDonald, R., & Marsh, J. (2005). *Disconnected Youth? Growing Up In Britain's Poor Neighbourhoods*. Basingstoke: Palgrave.

Macfarlane, A. (1978). *The Origins of English Individualism: The Family, Property and Social Transition*. Oxford: Blackwell.

Macfarlane, A. (1981). *The Justice and the Mare's Ale: Law and Disorder in Seventeenth Century England*. Oxford: Wiley-Blackwell.

Macfarlane, A. (1986). 'English Violence'. *London Review of Books*, 8(13), 8–9.

Macfarlane, A. (1987). *The Culture of Capitalism*. Oxford: Blackwell.

Machiavelli, N. (1961). *The Prince*, trans. G. Bull. London: Penguin.

Machiavelli, N. (2003). *The Discourses*, trans. L. J. Walker & B. Richardson. London: Penguin.

Maddern, P. (1992). *Violence and Social Order: East Anglia 1422–1442*. Oxford: Oxford University Press.

Mandeville, B. (1970). *Fable of the Bees: Or Private Vices, Publick Benefits*. London: Penguin.

Marazzi, C. (2010). *The Violence of Financial Capitalism*, trans. K. Lebedeva. New York: Semiotext(e).

Mares, D. (2009). 'Civilization, Economic Change, and Trends in Interpersonal Violence in Western Societies'. *Theoretical Criminology*, 13(4), 419–49.

Marks, H. (1997). *Mr Nice*. London: Vintage.

Marshall, G. (1982). *In Search of the Spirit of Capitalism: An Essay on Max Weber's Protestant Ethic Thesis*. New York: Columbia University Press.

Martin, H., & Schumann, H. (1997). *The Global Trap: Globalisation and the Assault on Democracy and Prosperity*. London: Pluto.

Martuccelli, D. (2001). *Dominations ordinaires: Explorations de la condition moderne*. Paris: Balland.

Maruna, S. (2001). *Making Good: How Ex-Convicts Reform and Rebuild their Lives*. Washington, DC: American Psychological Association.

Marx, K. (1954). *Capital*, vol. 1. London: Lawrence and Wishart.

Marx, K. (1963). *The Eighteenth Brumaire of Louis Bonaparte*. New York: International Publishers.

Marx, K. (1973). *The Gundrisse: Foundations of the Critique of Political Economy*, trans. M. Nicolaus. Harmondsworth: Pelican.

Marx, K., & Engels, F. (1972). *The Communist Manifesto*. London: Penguin.

Matthewman, S., & Hoey, D. (2006). 'What Happened to Postmodernism?'. *Sociology*, 40(3), 529–47.

Matthews, R. (2002). *Armed Robbery*. Cullompton: Willan.

Matthews, R. (2005). 'The Myth of Punitiveness'. *Theoretical Criminology*, 9(2), 175–201.

Matthews, R., & Young, J. (eds) (1992). *Rethinking Criminology: The Realist Debate*. London: Sage.

Matza, D. (1964). *Delinquency and Drift*. New York: Wiley.

McAuley, R. (2007). *Out of Sight: Crime, Youth and Exclusion in Modern Britain*. Cullompton: Willan.

McFall, L., Du Gay, P., & Carter, S. (2008). *Conduct: Sociology and Social World*. Manchester: Manchester University Press.

McIntosh, M. (1975). *The Organisation of Crime*. London: Macmillan.

McSweeney, T., Turnbull, P., & Hough, M. (2008). *Tackling Drug Markets and Distribution Networks in the UK*. London: Institute for Criminal Policy Research, King's College.

McVicar, J. (1974). *McVicar by Himself*. London: Hutchinson.

Mead, G. (1934). *Mind, Self, and Society*, ed. C.W. Morris. Chicago: University of Chicago Press.

Mellor, M. (2010). *The Future of Money: From Financial Crisis to Public Resource*. London: Pluto.

Melossi, D. (2008). *Controlling Crime, Controlling Society*. Cambridge: Polity.

Merton, R.K. (1938). 'Social Structure and Anomie'. *American Sociological Review*, 3(5), 672–82.

Messerschmidt, J. (1993). *Masculinities and Crime*. Lanham: Rowman & Littlefield.

Messner, S., & Rosenfeld, R. (1997). *Crime and the American Dream*. Belmont, CA: Wadsworth.

Mestrovic, S. (1993). *The Barbarian Temperament: Towards a Postmodern Critical Theory*. London: Routledge.

Mestrovic, S. (2003). *Thorstein Veblen on Culture and Society*. London: Sage.

Michéa, J.-C. (2007). *L'Empire du moindre mal: Essai sur la civilisation libérale*. Paris: Climats.

Mill, J. S. (2006). *On Liberty*. London: Penguin.

Miller, W. (1958). 'Lower Class Culture as a Generating Milieu of Gang Delinquency'. *Journal of Social Issues*, 14(3), 5–19.

Mills, C. (1956). *The Power Elite*. New York: Oxford University Press.

Mills, C. (1959). *The Sociological Imagination*. Oxford: Oxford University Press.

Minkes, J., & Minkes, L. (eds) (2008). *Corporate and White Collar Crime*. London: Sage.

Modell, A. (2003). *Imagination and the Meaningful Brain*. Cambridge, MA: MIT Press.

Moffitt, T. (2003). 'Life-course Persistent and Adolescence-limited Antisocial Behaviour: A 10-year Research Review and a Research Agenda'. In T. M. B. Lahey (ed.), *The Causes of Conduct Disorder and Serious Juvenile Delinquency*. New York: Guilford.

Monbiot, G. (2011, 8 Feb.). 'A Corporate Coup d'état'. *The Guardian*.

Monkkonen, E. (1988). *America Becomes Urban: The Development of US Cities and Towns 1780–1980*. Berkeley: University of California Press.

Morselli, C. (2009). *Inside Criminal Networks*. New York: Springer-Verlag.

Mouzelis, N. (1995). *Sociological Theory: What Went Wrong? – Diagnosis and Remedies*. London: Routledge.

Mucchielli, L. (2010). 'Are We Living in a More Violent Society? A Socio-historical Analysis of Interpersonal Violence in France, 1970s–Present'. *British Journal of Criminology*, 50(5), 808–29.

Mukerji, C. (1993). 'Reading and Writing with Nature: A Materialist Approach to French Formal Gardens'. In J. Brewer & R. Porter (eds), *Consumption and the World of Goods*. London: Routledge.

Muncie, J. (2001). 'The Construction and Deconstruction of Crime'. In J. Muncie & E. McLaughlin (eds), *The Problem of Crime*. London: Sage/Open University Press.

Murphy, D. S., & Robinson, M. B. (2008). 'The Maximizer: Clarifying Merton's Theories of Anomie and Strain', *Theoretical Criminology*, 12(4): 501–21.

Murray, C. (1994). *Underclass: The Crisis Deepens*. London: Institute of Economic Affairs.

Nabert, J. (1955). *Essai sur le mal*. Paris: PUF.

Naim, M. (2005). *Illicit: How Smugglers, Traffickers and Copycats are Hijacking the Global Economy*. New York: Doubleday.

Nightingale, C. (1993). *On the Edge: A History of Poor Black Kids and Their American Dreams*. New York: Basic Books.

Nodenstam, T. (1978). 'Explanation and Understanding in the History of Art'. In E. Leinfellner, W. Leinfellner, H. Berghel, & A. Hübner (eds), *Wittgenstein and his Impact on Contemporary Thought*. Vienna: HPT.

Nordstrom, C. (2007). *Global Outlaws: Crime, Money and Power in the Contemporary World*. Berkeley: University of California Press.

Nozick, R. (1974). *Anarchy, State and Utopia*. Oxford: Blackwell.

O'Malley, P. (2010). *Crime and Risk*. London: Sage.

Oakeshott, M. (1996). *The Politics of Faith and the Politics of Skepticism*. New Haven: Yale University Press.

OFT. (2006). *Research on Impact of Mass-marketed Scams, Report no. 883*. London: Office of Fair Trading.

Ollman, B. (2003). *Dance of the Dialectic: Steps in Marx's Method*. Chicago: University of Illinois Press.

Onwudiwe, I. (2004). 'Transnational Crimes: The Case of Advanced Fee Fraud in Nigeria'. In A. Kalunta-Crumpton & B. Agozino (eds), *Pan-African Issues in Crime and Justice*. Aldershot, UK: Ashgate.

Pahl, R. (1995). *After Success: Fin-de-Siècle Anxiety and Identity*. Cambridge: Polity.

Paoli, L., Greenfield, V., & Reuter, P. (2009). *The World Heroin Market*. Oxford: Oxford University Press.

Paoli, L., Spapens, T., & Fijnaut, C. (2010). 'Drug Trafficking'. In F. Brookeman, M. Maguire, H. Pierpoint, & T. Bennett (eds), *Handbook on Crime*. Cullompton: Willan.

Park, R., Burgess, E., & McKenzie, R. (1925). *The City*. Chicago: University of Chicago Press.

Parker, K. F. (2008). *Unequal Crime Decline: Theorizing Race, Urban Inequality and Criminal Violence*. New York: New York University Press.

Parkin, F. (1967). 'Working Class Conservatives: A theory of Political Deviance'. *British Journal of Sociology*, 18, 278–90.

Parsons, T. (1964). *Social Structure and Personality*. New York: Free Press.

Passas, N. (2005). 'Lawful but Awful: "Legal Corporate Crimes"'. *Journal of Socio-economics*, 34, 771–86.

Passavant, P. (2005). 'The Strong Neoliberal State: Crime, Consumption, Governance'. *Theory and Event*, 8(3) http://muse.jhu.edu/login?uri=/journals/theory_and_event/v008/8.3passavant.html.

Pearson, G. (1992). *Hooligan: A History of Respectable Fears*. Basingstoke: Palgrave Macmillan.

Pierce, C. (1887–8). 'Illustrations of the Logic of Science'. *Popular Science Monthly*, 12–13 (series).

Pitts, J. (2008). *Reluctant Gangsters: The Changing Face of Youth Crime*. Cullompton: Willan.

Pocock, J. (1989). 'Civic Humanism and Its Role in Anglo-American Political Thought'. In J. Pocock, *Politics, Language and Time: Essays on Political Thought and History*. Chicago: University of Chicago Press.

Polanyi, K. (1957 [1944]). *The Great Transformation: The Political and Economic Origins of Our Time*. Boston: Beacon Press.

Popper, K. (2006). *The Open Society and Its Enemies*, vol. 1. London: Routledge.

Postman, N. (1982). *The Disappearance of Childhood*. New York: Delacorte.

Power, E. (1941). *The Wool Trade in English Mediaeval History*. Oxford: Oxford University Press.

Presdee, M. (2000). *Cultural Criminology and the Carnival of Crime*. London: Routledge.

Punch, M. (1996). *Dirty Business: Exploring Corporate Misconduct*. London: Sage.

Punch, M. (2008). 'The Organization Did It: Individuals, Corporations and Crime'. In J. Minkes & L. Minkes (eds), *Corporate and White-collar Crime*. London: Sage.

Raftis, J. (1966). 'The Concentration of Responsibility in Five Villages'. *Mediaeval Studies*, 28, 92–118.

Rawlings, P. (1999). *Crime and Power: A History of Criminal Justice 1688–1998*. London: Longman.

Ray, L. (2011). *Violence and Society*. London: Sage.

Reiman, J. (1979). *The Rich Get Richer and the Poor Get Prison*. New York: Wiley.

Reiner, R. (2007). *Law and Order: An Honest Citizen's Guide to Crime and Control.* Cambridge: Polity.

Reiner, R. (2010). *The Politics of the Police*, 4th edn. Oxford: Oxford University Press.

Reiner, R. (2012). 'Political Economy and Criminology: The Return of the Repressed'. In S. Hall & S. Winlow (eds), *New Directions in Criminological Theory.* London: Willan/Routledge.

Reno, W. (2009). 'Illicit Markets, Violence, Warlords, and Governance: West African Cases'. *Crime, Law and Social Change*, 52, 313–22.

Renzetti, C. (2007). *Feminist Criminology.* London: Routledge.

Reuter, P., & Stevens, A. (2007). *An Analysis of UK Drug Policy: A Monograph Prepared for the UK Drug Policy Commission.* London: UK Drug Policy Commission.

Ricoeur, P. (1984). *Time and Narrative*, trans. K. Blamey and D. Pellaver. Chicago: University of Chicago Press.

Ritzer, G. (1993). *The McDonaldization of Society.* Thousand Oaks, CA: Pine Forge Press.

Roberts, M. (2003). *Drugs and Crime: From Warfare to Welfare.* London: NACRO.

Robertson, R. (1995). 'Glocalization: Time–Space and Homogeneity–Heterogeneity'. In M. Featherstone, S. Lash, & R. Robertson (eds), *Global Modernities.* London: Sage.

Rock, P. (1979). *The Making of Symbolic Interactionism.* London: Macmillan.

Rodger, J. (2008). *Criminalising Social Policy: Antisocial Behaviour and Welfare in a De-civilised Society.* Cullompton: Willan.

Rojek, C. (1995). *Decentring Leisure: Rethinking Leisure Theory.* London: Sage.

Rojek, C. (2010). *The Labour of Leisure.* London: Sage.

Rojek, C., & Turner, B. (2000). 'Decorative Sociology: Towards a Critique of the Cultural Turn'. *Sociological Review*, 48(4), 629–48.

Rose, J. (1991). *The Haunting of Sylvia Plath.* London: Virago.

Rousseau, J.-J. (1990). *Rousseau, Judge of Jean-Jacques.* Hanover, NH: Dartmouth College Press.

Rowbotham, M. (1998). *The Grip of Death: A Study of Modern Money, Debt Slavery and Destructive Economics.* London: Jon Carpenter.

Rusche, G., & Kirchheimer, O. (1939). *Punishment and Social Structure.* New York: Columbia University Press.

Ryan, J., & Sackey, C. (eds) (1984). *Strangers in Paradise – Academics from the Working Class.* Boston: South End Press.

Salgado, S. (1972). *Cony-Catchers and Bawdy Baskets: An Anthology of Elizabethan Low Life.* Harmondsworth: Penguin.

Sartre, J. P. (1957). *Being and Nothingness.* London: Methuen.

Sassatelli, R. (2008). *Consumer Culture: History, Theory and Politics.* London: Sage.

Schopenhauer, A. (2008). *The World as Will and Representation*, trans. R. E. Aquila and D. Carus. Harlow: Longman.

Schutz, A. (1967). *The Phenomenology of the Social World.* Evanston, IL: Northwestern University Press.

Selke, W., Cosaro, N., & Selke, H. (2002). 'A Working Class Critique of Criminological Theory'. *Critical Criminology*, 11, 93–112.

Sennett, R. (1998). *The Corrosion of Character: The Personal Consequences of Work in the New Capitalism.* London: Norton.

Sennett, R. (2008). *The Craftsman.* New Haven: Yale University Press.

Seymour, R. (2008). *The Liberal Defence of Murder.* London: Verso.

Sharpe, J. (1996). *Crime in Early Modern England 1550–1750*. Harlow: Longman.

Shaxson, N. (2011). *Treasure Islands: Tax Havens and the Men Who Stole the World*. London: The Bodley Head.

Shorter, E. (1975). *The Making of the Modern Family*. New York: Basic Books.

Shover, N. (2007). 'Generative Worlds of White-collar Crime'. In H. Pontell & G. Geis (eds), *International Handbook of White-collar and Corporate Crime*. New York: Springer.

Shusterman, R. (1993). 'Eliot and Adorno on the Critique of Culture'. *Theory, Culture and Society*, 10, 25–52.

Sibeon, R. (2004). *Rethinking Social Theory*. London: Sage.

Silverstone, R. (1994). *Television and Everyday Life*. London: Routledge.

Simmel, G. (1955). *Conflict and the Web of Group Affiliations*. New York: Free Press.

Simmel, G. (1978). *The Philosophy of Money*, trans. T. Bottomore and D. Frisby. London: Routledge and Kegan Paul.

Simondon, G. (1964). *L'Individu et sa genèse physico-biologique*. Paris: PUF.

Skeggs, B. (2004). *Class, Self, Culture*. London and New York: Routledge.

Sloterdijk, P. (1987). *The Critique of Cynical Reason*. London: Verso.

Smart, B. (2010). *Consumer Society*. London: Sage.

Smart, C. (1976). *Women, Crime and Criminology: A Feminist Critique*. London: Routledge and Kegan Paul.

Smith, A. (1984). *The Theory of the Moral Sentiments*. Indianapolis: Liberty Fund.

Snider, L. (1993). *Bad Business: Corporate Crime in Canada*. Scarborough, Ont.: Nelson.

Sokal, A., & Bricmont, J. (1998). *Fashionable Nonsense: Postmodern Intellectuals' Abuse of Science*. London: Picador.

Sombart, W. (1967). *Luxury and Capitalism*. Ann Arbor: University of Michigan Press.

Sombart, W. (1998). *The Quintessence of Capitalism*. London: Routledge.

Soothill, K., Francis, B., Ackerley, E., & Humphreys, L. (2008). 'Changing Patterns of Offending Behaviour among Young Adults'. *British Journal of Criminology*, 48, 75–95.

Sorel, G. (1972). *Reflections on Violence*. New York: Collier.

Spalek, B. (2008). *Communities, Identities and Crime*. Bristol: Policy Press.

Sparks, R. (1992). *Television and the Drama of Crime*. Buckingham: Open University Press.

Spierenburg, P. (2008). *A History of Murder*. Cambridge: Polity.

Spinoza, B. (1996). *Ethics*, trans. E. Curley. London: Penguin.

Standing, G. (2011). *The Precariat: The New Dangerous Class*. London: Bloomsbury Academic.

Stiegler, B. (2010a). 'Telecracy Against Democracy'. *Cultural Politics: An International Journal*, 6(2), 171–80.

Stiegler, B. (2010b). *For a New Critique of Political Economy*. Cambridge: Polity.

Stein, A. (2007). *Prologue to Violence: Child Abuse, Dissociation and Crime*. Mahwah, NJ: The Analytic Press.

Stern, J. (1975). *Hitler: The Führer and the People*. London: Fontana.

Sullivan, H. (1953). *Conceptions of Modern Psychiatry*. New York: W. W. Norton.

Sumner, C. (1994). *The Sociology of Deviance: An Obituary*. Milton Keynes: Open University Press.

Sutherland, E. (1937). *The Professional Thief: By a Professional Thief, Chic Conwell. Annotated and Interpreted by E.H. Sutherland*. Chicago: University of Chicago Press.

Sutherland, E. (1947). *Principles of Criminology*, 4th edn. Philadelphia: J.B. Lippincott.

Sutton, M. (2009). *Stolen Goods Markets: Tackling the Roots of Theft*. Retrieved from Problem Oriented Guides for Police: http://www.popcenter.org.

Tannenbaum, F. (1938). *Crime and Community*. New York: Ginn.

Taylor, I. (1999). *Crime in Context: A Critical Criminology of Market Societies*. Cambridge: Polity.

Taylor, I., Walton, P., & Young, J. (1973). *The New Criminology: For a Social Theory of Deviance*. London: Routledge.

Thomas, K. (2009). *The Ends of Life: Roads to Fulfilment in Early Modern England*. Oxford: Oxford University Press.

Thompson, E. (1975). *Whigs and Hunters: The Origin of the Black Act*. London: Allen Lane.

Tillich, P. (1980). *The Courage to Be*. Glasgow: Collins.

Tilly, C. (1985). 'War Making and State Making as Organized Crime'. In P. Evans, D. Rueschemeyer, & T. Skocpol (eds), *Bringing the State Back In*. Cambridge: Cambridge University Press.

Todorov, T., & Brown, A. (2010). *The Fear of Barbarians*. Cambridge: Polity.

Tombs, S., & Whyte, D. (eds) (2003). *Unmasking the Crimes of the Powerful: Scrutinizing States and Corporations*. New York: Peter Lang.

Tonry, M. (2004). *Punishment and Politics: Evidence and Emulation in the Making of English Crime Control Policy*. Cullompton: Willan.

Touraine, A. (1995). *Critique of Modernity*, trans. D. Macey. Oxford: Blackwell.

Treadwell, J. (2011). 'From the car boot to booting it up? eBay, online counterfeit crime and the transformation of the criminal marketplace', *Criminology and Criminal Justice* DIOI: 10.1177/1748895811428173

Turner, B. (2006). 'British Sociology and Public Intellectuals: Consumer Society and Imperial Decline'. *The British Journal of Sociology*, 57(2), 169–88.

Turner, B., & Rojek, C. (2001). *Society and Culture: Scarcity and Solidarity*. London: Sage.

Turner, C. (2010). *Investigating Social Theory*. London: Sage.

Uchitelle, L. (2006). *The Disposable American: Layoffs and Their Consequences*. New York: Alfred A. Knopf.

Ungar, S. (2001). 'Moral Panic versus the Risk Society: The Implications of the Changing Sites of Social Anxiety'. *British Journal of Sociology*, 52(2), 271–92.

Unger, R. (1987). *Social Theory: It's Situation and Task*. Cambridge: Cambridge University Press.

Valier, C. (2002). *Theories of Crime and Punishment*. London: Longman.

van Creveld, M. (1999). *The Rise and Decline of the State*. Cambridge: Cambridge University Press.

Vardoulakis, D. (2006). 'The Return of Negation: The Doppelgänger in Freud's "The Uncanny"'. *SubStance*, 35, 100–16.

Veblen, T. (1994). *The Theory of the Leisure Class*. London: Penguin.

Vighi, F., & Feldner, H. (2007). 'Ideology Critique or Discourse Analysis; Žižek against Foucault'. *European Journal of Political Theory*, 6(2), 141–59.

Von Lampe, K., & Johansen, P. (2004). 'Organized Crime and Trust: On the Conceptualization and Empirical Relevance of Trust in the Context of Criminal Networks'. *Global Crime*, 6(2), 159–84.

Wacquant, L. (2007). 'Territorial Stigmatization in the Age of Advanced Marginality'. *Thesis Eleven*, 91, 66–77.

Walker, A., Flatley, J., & Kershaw, C. (2009). *Crime in England and Wales, Vol. 1, Findings from the British Crime Survey and Police Recorded Crime.* London: HMSO.

Walsh, A. (2009). *Biology and Criminology: The Biosocial Synthesis.* London: Routledge.

Walsh, A., & Beaver, K. (eds) (2009). *Biosocial Criminology: New Directions in Theory and Research.* Aldershot, UK: Ashgate.

Ward-Perkins, B. (2005). *The Fall of Rome and the End of Civilization.* Oxford: Oxford University Press.

Warr, M. (2000). 'Fear of Crime in the United States: Avenues for Research and Policy'. *Criminal Justice*, 4, 451–89.

Weber, M. (1949). *The Methodology of the Social Sciences.* New York: Free Press.

Weber, M. (1978). *Economy and Society: An Outline of Interpretive Sociology*, eds G. Roth and C. Wittich. Berkeley: University of California Press.

Weber, M. (1978). 'Politics as a Vocation'. In H. Gerth & C. Mills (eds), *From Max Weber*. London: Routledge.

Weber, M. (2002). *The Protestant Ethic and the Spirit of Capitalism*, trans. S. Kalberg. Oxford: Blackwell.

Weber, M. (2007). 'Science as a Vocation'. In H. Gerth & C. Mills (eds), *From Max Weber*. London: Routledge.

Webster, C. (2002). 'Race, Space and Fear: Imagined Geographies of Racism, Crime, Violence and Disorder in Northern England'. *Capital & Class*, 80, 95–122.

Weiss, D., & Marmar, C. (1997). 'The Impact of Scale – Revised'. In J. Wilson & T. Keane (eds), *Assessing Psychological Trauma and PTSD: A Practitioner's Handbook.* New York: Guilford.

White, G. (2004). 'Political Apathy Disorder: Proposal for a New DSM Diagnostic Category'. *Journal of Humanistic Psychology*, 44, 47–57.

Wiegratz, J. (2010). 'Fake Capitalism? The Dynamics of Neoliberal Moral Restructuring and Pseudo-development: The Case of Uganda'. *Review of African Political Economy*, 37(124), 123–37.

Wieviorka, M. (2009). *Violence: A New Approach*, trans. David Macey. London: Sage.

Wilkinson, I. (1999). 'Where is the Novelty in our Current "Age of Anxiety?"'. *European Journal of Social Theory*, 2(4), 455–67.

Wilkinson, R., & Pickett, K. (2009). *The Spirit Level: Why More Equal Societies Almost Always Do Better.* London: Allen Lane.

Williams, R. (1971). *Culture and Society, 1780–1950.* Harmondsworth: Penguin.

Willis, P. (1977). *Learning to Labour: How Working-class Kids Get Working-class Jobs.* Farnborough: Saxon House.

Wilson, C. (1967). 'Trade, Society and the State'. In E. Rich & C. Wilson (eds), *The Economy of Expanding Europe in the Sixteenth and Seventeenth Centuries.* Cambridge: Cambridge University Press.

Wilson, E., & Lindsey, F. (eds) (2009). *Government of the Shadows: Parapolitics and Criminal Sovereignty.* London: Pluto.

Wilson, J. (1975). *Thinking About Crime.* New York: Basic Books.

Wilson, J. (2002). 'Blue Ring Around a White Collar: An Application of Marginality'. *A Review of General Semantics*, 59, 25–32.

Wilson, J., & Herrnstein, R. (1985). *Crime and Human Nature.* New York: Simon and Schuster.

Winlow, S. (2001). *Badfellas.* Oxford: Berg.

Winlow, S., & Hall, S. (2006). *Violent Night: Urban Leisure and Contemporary Culture.* Oxford: Berg.

Winlow, S., & Hall, S. (2009a). 'Living for the Weekend: Youth Identities in North-east England'. *Ethnography*, 10(1), 91–113.

Winlow, S., & Hall, S. (2009b). 'Retaliate First: Memory, Humiliation and Male Violence'. *Crime, Media, Culture*, 5(3), 285–304.

Wolff, R. (2011, 18 Jan.). 'The Myth of American Exceptionalism Implodes'. *The Guardian*.

Wolfgang, M., & Ferracuti, F. (1967). *The Sub-culture of Violence.* London: Tavistock.

Wood, E. (2002). *The Origin of Capitalism: A Longer View.* London: Verso.

Wypijewski, J. (2006). 'Workless Blues'. *New Left Review*, 42, 141–9.

y Gasset, J. (1985). *The Revolt of the Masses*, trans. A. Kerrigan, ed. K. Moore. New York: Notre Dame / W.W. Norton.

Yar, M. (2006). *Cybercrime and Society.* London: Sage.

Yar, M. (2012). 'Critical Criminology, Critical Theory and Social Harm'. In S. Hall & S. Winlow (eds), *New Directions in Criminological Theory.* London: Willan / Routledge.

Young, J. (1971). 'The Role of the Police as Amplifiers of Deviancy, Negotiators of Reality and Translators of Fantasy'. In S. Cohen (ed.), *Images of Deviance.* Harmondsworth: Penguin.

Young, J. (1987). 'The Tasks Facing a Realist Criminology'. *Crime, Law and Social Change*, 11(4), 337–56.

Young, J. (1990). 'Thinking Seriously About Crime'. In M. Fitzgerald, G. McLennan, & J. Pawson (eds), *Crime and Society: Readings in History and Theory.* London: Routledge / Open University Press.

Young, J. (1999). *The Exclusive Society.* London: Sage.

Young, J. (2004). 'Voodoo Criminology and the Numbers Game'. In J. Ferrell, K. Hayward, W. Morrison, & M. Presdee (eds), *Cultural Criminology Unleashed.* London: Glasshouse Press.

Young, J. (2007). *The Vertigo of Late Modernity.* London: Sage.

Young, T. (1999). 'A Constitutive Theory of Justice: The Architecture of Affirmative Postmodern Legal Systems'. In S. Henry & D. Milovanovic (eds), *Constitutive Criminology at Work: Applications to Crime and Justice.* New York: State University of New York Press.

Zimring, F., & Hawkins, G. (1997). *Crime Is Not the Problem: Lethal Violence in America.* Oxford: Oxford University Press.

Zinn, H. (1980). *A People's History of the United States.* London: Longman.

Žižek, S. (1989). *The Sublime Object of Ideology.* London: Verso.

Žižek, S. (2000). *The Ticklish Subject: The Absent Centre of Political Ontology.* London: Verso.

Žižek, S. (2003). *Organs Without Bodies: On Deleuze and Consequences.* London: Routledge.

Žižek, S. (2006). *The Parallax View.* Cambridge, MA: MIT Press.

Žižek, S. (2008a). *Violence: Six Sideways Reflections.* London: Profile.

Žižek, S. (2008b). *In Defence of Lost Causes.* London: Verso.

Žižek, S. (2010a). *Living in the End Times.* London: Verso.

Žižek, S. (2010b). 'How to Begin from the Beginning'. In C. Douzinas & S. Žižek (eds), *The Idea of Communism.* London: Verso.

Zola, M. (2007). *Money.* Stockport: Mondiale.

Zupančič, A. (2000). *Ethics of the Real: Kant, Lacan.* London: Verso.

INDEX